An Introduction to Programming

An object-oriented approach with C++

C. THOMAS WU

THEODORE A. NORMAN

WCB
McGraw-Hill

Boston, Massachusetts   Burr Ridge, Illinois   Dubuque, Iowa
Madison, Wisconsin   New York, New York   San Francisco, California   St Louis, Missouri

To Mari and Iris
  –C.T.W
To Tove
  –T.A.N

WCB/McGraw-Hill

A Division of the McGraw-Hill Companies

AN INTRODUCTION TO PROGRAMMING: AN OBJECT-ORIENTED APPROACH WITH C++

1 2 3 4 5 6 7 8 9 0 DOC/DOC 9 0 9 8 7

ISBN 0-256-19390-8

Editorial director: *Tom Casson*
Executive editor: *Elizabeth A. Jones*
Developmental editor: *Bradley Kosirog*
Marketing manager: *John Wannemacher*
Project manager: *Beth Cigler*
Production supervisor: *Melonie Salvati*
Design and composition: *Manning Publications*
Typeface: *11/14 Garamond*
Printer: *R. R. Donnelley & Sons Company*

Library of Congress Cataloging-in-Publication Data

Wu, C. Thomas
      An introduction to programming : an object-oriented approach with C++
  /   by C. Thomas Wu and Theodore A. Norman
          p.   cm.
      Includes index.
      Romanized record.
      ISBN 0-256-19390-8
      1. Object-oriented programming (Computer science) 2. C++
  (Computer program language)   I. Norman, Theodore A. II. Title.
  QA76.64.W8   1997
  005.13'3—dc20   96-33477

http://www.mhhe.com

acknowledgments

from C. Thomas Wu

This is the first textbook I have written. It seems like ancient history when my department chairman Ted Lewis first brought me an idea of writing an introductory programming textbook using C++ based on the draft written by my coauthor Tad Norman. At that time, I did not realize what I was getting into. I looked at Tad's draft, liked what I saw, and decided to participate. Tad used Object Pascal in his draft. I figured it wouldn't take too long to convert Tad's sample Object Pascal programs to C++, modify or expand his chapters, and add my chapters to complete the book. Well, I was wrong. It took many more months than I anticipated. But it was also a great learning experience. Thank you, Ted and Tad. I thank many students who have gone through my early drafts: Chris Eagle for single-handedly implementing the UNIX version of object libraries and debugging and improving the Windows version; Bernadette Brooks for finding errors in my early draft chapters; and Erhan Akyuz for taking the screenshots used in the final manuscript. Lastly, I thank my wife, Mari, and my daughter, Iris, for being my reason and inspiration to work harder and do a good job.

from Theodore A. Norman

I want to thank my colleagues at Brigham Young University, especially Gordon Stokes, for using early drafts of this text in their courses and for many helpful suggestions. I am also grateful to over 1000 students who studied from the drafts and provided invaluable feedback.

from both of us

We thank our reviewers for their diligence in finding errors and making numerous suggestions for improvement. We thank our editors Betsy Jones at Irwin/McGraw-Hill and Marjan Bace at Manning Publications for their infinite patience while the work was in progress. And we thank the editorial staff at Irwin/McGraw-Hill and Manning Publications for their patience.

contents

preface   *ix*

1   Algorithms and computers   1
    1.1   A chalkboard algorithm 1
    1.2   A look inside the computer 6
    1.3   The binary number system (optional) 7
    1.4   Representation of data in RAM (optional) 9
    1.5   Machine language and assembly language 13
    1.6   High level languages and compilers 14
    1.7   Executing computer programs 16
    1.8   Exercises 18

2   Starting to program   20
    2.1   The first program 21
    2.2   Object diagrams 26
    2.3   Sequential execution 27
    2.4   C++ syntax 29
    2.5   The `Turtle` object 33
    2.6   Sample programs using `turtle` objects 39
    2.7   Object behavior 41
    2.8   Exercises 43

3   Numerical data   46
    3.1   Constants and variables 47
    3.2   Integers 52

3.3   Sample programs using integers   60

3.4   Real numbers   65

3.5   A sample program using real numbers   68

3.6   Exercises   70

4   *Character-based input and output*   *73*

4.1   Character-based output   75

4.2   Formatted output   81

4.3   Character-based input   83

4.4   Sample program   87

4.5   Exercises   88

5   *Repetition control flow*   *92*

5.1   Repetition control flow—`for` loops   92

5.2   Repetition control flow—`while` loops   100

5.3   Logical expressions   106

5.4   Sample program: computing the sum and average   110

5.5   Repetition control flow—`do-while` loops   111

5.6   Nested loops   113

5.7   Sample program: ManySquares   115

5.8   Sample program: drawing a circle and round-off error   117

5.9   Exercises   125

6   *Selection control flow*   *130*

6.1   Selection control flow—`if` statement   130

6.2   Multiple selections   140

6.3   Sample program: drawing many squares   145

6.4   Sample program: computing statistical values   149

6.5   Selection control flow—`switch` statement   151

6.6   Making programs more general   160

6.7   Exercises   163

7 *Nonnumerical data*   167

7.1   The `char` data type 167

7.2   Standard character functions 175

7.3   String data 180

7.4   Standard string functions 184

7.5   Sample program: detecting palindromes 190

7.6   Exercises 195

8 *Functions*   199

8.1   Function basics 200

8.2   Multifile program organization 207

8.3   Decomposing a program with functions 209

8.4   Local and global variables 217

8.5   Sample program 222

8.6   Exercises 227

9 *Passing pointers and references to functions*   231

9.1   Pointers 232

9.2   Pass-by-pointer passing 238

9.3   Pass-by-reference passing 242

9.4   Sample program: solving quadratic equations 242

9.5   Exercises 246

10 *Defining objects*   249

10.1   Defining a `Volume` object 250

10.2   Defining a `Person` object 260

10.3   Interface and implementation files 265

10.4   Defining a `Fraction` object 267

10.5   Exercises 279

11 *Defining objects using inheritance*   283

11.1   Creating a `SmartTurtle` by inheritance 284

11.2   Sample program: two-dimensional graph 292

11.3   Objects and code reuse 297

11.4 Exercises 302

12 Event-driven programming 308

12.1 Event loops 308

12.2 Editor windows 310

12.3 Event processing 317

12.4 Grading program 320

12.5 `Menu`, `MenuHandler`, and `MessageHandler` objects 326

12.6 Grading program with menus 331

12.7 Handling events with SmartTurtle 338

12.8 Exercises 339

13 One-dimensional arrays 344

13.1 Numerical arrays 345

13.2 Passing array arguments to functions 348

13.3 Arrays of objects 352

13.4 Array of pointers to objects and dynamic allocation 354

13.5 Grading program 358

13.6 Enumerated types 369

13.7 Exercises 372

14 Multidimensional arrays 379

14.1 Two-dimensional arrays 379

14.2 `for` loops and arrays 384

14.3 Sample program: temperature 385

14.4 Three-dimensional arrays 393

14.5 Passing multidimensional arrays to functions 397

14.6 Sample program: Crypt-Tester 398

14.7 Exercises 402

15 Object-oriented program construction 407

15.1 Sample program: Encryption 408

15.2 Forward reference and include files 414

15.3 Object reusability and program extensibility 421

15.4 Exercises 424

16 *Files* 426

16.1 Writing data to text files 427

16.2 Reading data from text files 433

16.3 The `FileBox` object 438

16.4 Sample program: Encryption2 439

16.5 Exercises 450

17 *Object-oriented software development* 454

17.1 Software life cycle 455

17.2 Developing an address book program 457
Address book requirements analysis 457, Address book specification 458, Design 458, Coding 474, Testing 478, Operation 479

17.3 Program listing for the address book 479

17.4 Exercises 491

18 *Fundamental algorithms—searching and sorting* 494

18.1 Searching 495
Linear search 496, Binary search 497, Hashing 501

18.2 Sorting 505
Selection sort 506, Bubble sort 510

18.3 Recursive algorithms 514
A sample recursive function 515, Recursive search algorithms 517, Recursive mergesort 519

18.4 Sample program: completing the address book 522

18.5 Exercises 528

appendix A: GUI objects 531

appendix B: Turtle 542

appendix C: Utility 546

appendix D: Syntax rules 548

index 556

preface

Overview

As the notion of object-orientation becomes pervasive in the computer science community, it is becoming increasingly important to teach object-oriented thinking to students from the very beginning of the curriculum. This book is our attempt to teach introductory programming to beginners with object-orientation as its central theme. We teach traditional introductory computer programming concepts such as control structures, recursion, and file processing, in addition to newer topics such as event-driven programming and graphical user interfaces in a unified object-oriented framework. Thus, our goal is not only to teach object-oriented concepts, but to use object-oriented thinking as a unifying tool in teaching traditional and contemporary fundamental concepts in computer science.

Why C++?

Although our main objective is to teach the concepts of computer programming from the object-oriented perspective and not to teach a specific language, the choice of a programming language is critical. One important consideration in choosing a language is how easily the language will allow us to illustrate concepts. A second important issue is the extent to which the chosen language is used in practice. Our book would have less appeal if we had chosen an obscure language used by few, no matter how attractive the language might be from other points of view.

C++ has become the language of choice for the majority of professional programmers. Students who plan to take other computer science courses will have a very good chance of using C++, so they will benefit from learning and using C++ as their first programming language. Since C++ compilers are available on all platforms (UNIX, DOS, Windows, and Macintosh), students and instructors are not restricted to any particular platform to adopt this book. Considering all the alternatives, we decided to use C++.

Since our goal is to teach programming concepts, advanced C++ features like inline functions and friends are not covered. Also, we minimize the use of the C/C++ style of coding. For example, instead of writing

```
str[j++] = 0;
```

we write

```
str[j] = 0;
j = j + 1;
```

Even though we exclude many C++ features, students will become proficient enough to write practical object-oriented programs using C++. We describe in sidebars features of C++ that are not required for understanding the main text, but that are useful in writing a C++ style program.

C++   A sidebar with this heading describes additional features of C++ not mentioned in the main text, or shows an alternative style of writing code that exploits the language characteristics of C++.

Major features of the book

Full object orientation   To teach object orientation, we start by using objects from the very first sample program. We use objects such as graphical user interface (GUI) and `Turtle` objects throughout the book to illustrate different concepts. By using these objects, students will gradually, but surely, become proficient in object-oriented program development. From the object-oriented perspective, this book is divided into two parts. In the first part, we teach students how to use objects in their programs. In the second part, we teach students how to define their own user-defined objects, and we explain the power of inheritance, and the importance of design methodology.

Predefined reusable objects   We believe that object-oriented programming (OOP) can be taught effectively only by providing highly reusable predefined objects. Many books start teaching OOP by showing how to define an object. This is not the best approach because students lack any understanding or motivation for defining a new object, unless they first learn the power of using existing objects. Therefore, we start by explaining how to use an object. This information puts students into the mind frame to fully master object-oriented concepts. We have a collection of predefined objects that are useful and reusable to show the benefits of OOP.

Windows programming Two topics that other introductory books do not cover are windows programming and event-driven programming. As the windows environment is becoming a standard, it is important to teach windows programming early on. However, no other introductory programming books teach windows programming. Ironically, students use a windows environment for their own work (e.g., using a compiler, editor, or word processor), but the programs they learn to write use decade-old, character-based input and output. Teaching windows programming is considered to be difficult, especially at the introductory level. We do not think it difficult to teach windows programming to beginners, because we use GUI objects such as dialog boxes and menus. Our predefined GUI objects allow beginners to write true windows-based programs. Since our predefined objects are available for all three windows environments (MS Windows, Macintosh, and X Windows/Motif), the students' programs will run on all three platforms by using the corresponding GUI objects. Our predefined GUI objects that encapsulate the platform-specific lower level details make cross-platform development possible. Support of encapsulation is one of the benefits of OOP, and we demonstrate it with our predefined GUI objects.

Event-driven programming This introductory book is unique in that it teaches event-driven programming. Teaching event-driven programming with traditional process-oriented programming languages such as C and Pascal is difficult. The object orientation in this book makes the teaching of event-driven programming easier. We use predefined objects such as `Menu`, `MenuHandler`, and `MessageHandler` to illustrate event-driven programming.

Object-oriented design methodology So that the students can make steady progress in learning object-oriented design methodology, we incorporate object diagrams similar to those used by object-oriented design books such as *Object-Oriented Design with Applications* (Booch, 2nd Ed., 1993) and *Object-Oriented Modeling and Design* (Rambaugh et. al., 1991). We use object diagrams throughout the book to document the sample programs, and we also devote one chapter to object-oriented design and program construction.

Book organization

Chapter 1: Algorithms and computers   This chapter introduces the basic concepts of algorithms and computers. We describe a chalkboard algorithm that illustrates variables and the necessity of detailed instructions. We also explain a simplified hardware architecture of a computer in this chapter.

Chapter 2: Starting to program   We start with a very short program that uses an object. Students will get acquainted with object-oriented thinking from the very beginning. The objects we introduce in this chapter are GUI objects such as dialog boxes and `Turtle` objects (as in Papert's turtle graphics). We use these objects throughout the book to provide coherent and unified sample programs. In addition to the introduction to object-oriented thinking, we describe basic C++ syntax.

Chapter 3: Numerical data   We provide a simple description of variables, constants, types, and objects, and explain arithmetic expressions. We provide sample programs that improve upon earlier programs, using the concepts learned in this chapter.

Chapter 4: Character-based input and output   Not all programs require a windows interface. In this chapter we discuss nonwindows, character-based input and output procedures using the predefined objects `cin` and `cout`.

Chapter 5: Repetition control flow   We explain the language syntax and semantics of repetition control flow. We cover the `for`, `while`, and `do-while` statements, and we give ample programs that use repetition control flow.

Chapter 6: Selection control flow   The second control flow necessary in writing nontrivial programs is selection control flow. We explain the language syntax and semantics of selection control flow in this chapter. We cover the `if` and `switch` control flow statements, and we give sample programs that use selection control flow.

Chapter 7: Nonnumerical data   In chapter 3, we used very simple numerical data. In this chapter we describe nonnumerical data—characters and strings (arrays of characters). We also show how to use the C++ standard functions for manipulating strings. As always, we provide sample programs to illustrate the use of nonnumerical data.

Chapter 8: Functions   In addition to the two nonsequential control flows studied earlier—selection and repetition—we have function control flow. In this chapter we describe the use of functions in decomposing programs. We also explain how to write reusable functions, that is, functions that may be used in many different programs.

Chapter 9: Passing pointers and references to functions   We explain pointers and references and show how these concepts are used in passing values to functions. The full understanding of a pointer is indispensable in designing computer programs, especially C++ programs, and therefore we dedicate a chapter to these concepts.

Chapter 10: Defining objects   Up to this point, students will have used only existing objects. In this chapter, they learn how to define their own objects. We define three objects to illustrate object definition and progress from a very simple object definition to a more complex one.

Chapter 11: Defining objects using inheritance   In this second chapter on object definition, we explain how to define new objects by using the feature called *inheritance.* Inheritance is a powerful (and often misused) feature of OOP. In this chapter we explain inheritance and how it helps one make code reusable, for faster program development and easier program modification.

Chapter 12: Event-driven programming   We first explain the basic concepts of event-driven programming, and then illustrate the concept using our GUI objects—EditWin, Menu, MenuHandler, and MessageHandler. From this chapter on, all major sample programs are windows-based, event-driven programs.

Chapter 13: One-dimensional arrays   In this chapter we describe one-dimensional arrays and explain arrays of numbers (e.g., int and float) and arrays of objects. We also explain the use of pointers and arrays for better allocation of memory space. A sample event-driven grading program is given in which we define our own objects and use a one-dimensional array.

Chapter 14: Multidimensional arrays   Two- and three-dimensional arrays are described in this chapter. We define a new object, Crypter, to illustrate the use of a three-dimensional array for simple encryption and decryption of text.

Chapter 15: Object-oriented program construction   Our sample programs so far will have used only a small number of objects. For more practical real-world programs, students will be required to use a large number of different types of objects. In this chapter we introduce guidelines for designing objects and composing programs from them, and we describe object-oriented program composition.

Chapter 16: Files   In this chapter we introduce the topic of file processing. We explain how to read data from and write data to external files, and we discuss `fstream` objects for storing and reading data. The Encryption sample program of chapter 15 is modified so the text can be saved to and read from external files.

Chapter 17: Object-oriented software development   We introduce object-oriented design methodology and the software life cyle in this chapter. We describe the activities of the software development process, and we illustrate some of those activities in the context of designing the Address Book program.

Chapter 18: Fundamental algorithms—searching and sorting   We describe basic sorting and searching algorithms in this chapter, and introduce recursive algorithms. We use a search algorithm to complete some of the operations for the Address Book program of chapter 17.

chapter 1

Algorithms and computers

Let us begin our study of computer science with two of its major ingredients: algorithms and computers. Instead of trying to define these terms formally, we will begin with examples that illustrate both concepts.

1.1 A chalkboard algorithm

Suppose we have a pile of six canceled checks that we have used to pay for groceries during the past month. We are interested in knowing our total grocery expenses for the month. We want to give instructions to Hal, our younger brother, so that he can find this total for us. Hal may be smart enough so that we only need to say, "Hal, add up the amounts on these checks and write the total on this sheet of paper." However, let's suppose that Hal has only learned to add two numbers at a time. Since he does not yet know how to add an entire column of numbers at once, our instructions to him must be very detailed and should not include individual steps more complex than the addition of two numbers.

1

Suppose further that Hal has a small chalkboard to use in his calculations. One possible sequence of instructions which we might give him is the following:

1 Copy the amount from the first check onto the chalkboard.

2 Copy the amount from the next check onto the chalkboard.

3 Add the two numbers together.

4 Copy the amount from the next check onto the chalkboard.

5 Add this new amount to the result of step 3.

6 Copy the amount from the next check onto the chalkboard.

7 Add this new amount to the result of step 5.

8 Copy the amount from the next check onto the chalkboard.

9 Add this new amount to the result of step 7.

10 Copy the amount from the next check onto the chalkboard.

11 Add this new amount to the result of step 9.

12 Write the result of step 11 on the answer sheet.

13 Stop.

The above sequence of instructions is an example of an algorithm. An *algorithm* is a step-by-step procedure which a person or machine can follow to solve a problem.

This algorithm has a number of drawbacks. First of all, though it may seem to be overly detailed, in some respects it may not be detailed enough. For example, we have not made it clear to Hal how to determine which check is the next check in the even-numbered steps. Of course, Hal would, most likely, simply take the checks in the order in which they are stacked in the pile—the top one first, then the next one, and so on. But if he fails to remove a check from the pile as he copies its amount, then he may copy that same amount again and thereby get an incorrect total. In an effort to avoid this possibility, we could modify the instructions that refer to the next check to read

> Take the top check from the pile, copy its amount onto the chalkboard and set the check aside.

Another error that Hal could easily make is losing track of which results on the chalkboard go with which instruction steps. For example, when he gets to step 9, his chalkboard may look like figure 1.1.

Hal has just copied the amount 14.83 from a check, and he is supposed to add it to the result of step 7. But suppose he can't remember which of the three results on the chalkboard came from step 7. Of course, we realize that the largest result must be the

```
14.52
13.90
─────
28.32           15.65
       10.90    39.22    14.83
       28.32    ─────
       ─────    54.87
       39.22
```

Figure 1.1 Hal's chalkboard diagram

Figure 1.2 Hal's chalkboard boxes

right one, since the total increases with each step, but maybe Hal doesn't realize this relationship. Or he may realize it and yet inadvertently pick the wrong result to add to the 14.83. Hal can avoid this problem if he uses the space on his chalkboard systematically, copying each new amount directly below the most recent result. However, we can't require this kind of insight from someone as young and inexperienced as Hal. We had better amend our instructions so that, even without such insight, he can compute the correct total. We decide to draw boxes on the chalkboard and give them names. Our instructions can then refer to the boxes by name so that Hal never has to remember the location of a previous result. Taking this approach, we set up the chalkboard as in figure 1.2.

We amend our algorithm as follows:

1 Take the top check from the pile, copy its amount into the box named AMT, and set the check aside.

2 Take the top check from the pile, copy its amount into the box named TOT, and set the check aside.

3 Add the number in the box name AMT to the number in the box named TOT and write the answer in the box named TOT after erasing what was there before.

4 Take the top check from the pile, copy its amount into the box named AMT after erasing what was there before and then set the check aside.

5 Add the number in the box named AMT to the number in the box named TOT and write the answer in the box named TOT after erasing what was there before.

6 Take the top check from the pile, copy its amount into the box named AMT after erasing what was there before, and then set the check aside.

7 Add the number in the box named AMT to the number in the box named TOT and write the answer in the box named TOT after erasing what was there before.

8 Take the top check from the pile, copy its amount into the box named AMT after erasing what was there before, and set the check aside.

9 Add the number in the box named AMT to the number in the box named TOT and write the answer in the box named TOT after erasing what was there before.

10   Take the top check from the pile, copy its amount into the box named AMT after erasing what was there before, and then set the check aside.

11   Add the number in the box named AMT to the number in the box named TOT and write the answer in the box named TOT after erasing what was there before.

12   Write the number in the box named TOT on the answer sheet.

13   Stop.

We now have an algorithm so detailed it is hard to imagine that Hal will be unable to follow it and compute our month's grocery expenses. You may want to set up a sheet of paper like Hal's chalkboard, prepare six slips of paper to represent checks, and follow this last algorithm through yourself.

We are still not completely satisfied with our algorithm. Notice that we wrote the same instructions for each of the checks except the first one. If, instead of the checks for one month, we had the checks for an entire year, say 75 checks, then this approach would require 151 instructions rather than the 13 we have now. But since the instructions repeat themselves in pairs, we should be able to write an algorithm that instructs Hal to repeat the same two instructions for each check. Consider, for example, the following algorithm:

1   Take the top check from the pile, copy its amount into the box named TOT, and set the check aside.

2   For each check still in the pile repeat steps 3 and 4. When the pile is empty, continue at step 5.

3   Take the top check from the pile, copy its amount into the box named AMT after erasing what was there before, and then set the check aside.

4   Add the number in the box named AMT to the number in the box name TOT and write the answer in the box named TOT after erasing what was there before.

5   Write the number in the box named TOT on the answer sheet.

6   Stop.

This algorithm instructs Hal to repeat steps 3 and 4 for each successive check in the pile. Such repetition of a sequence of instructions is called *looping*. If you are unsure of the implications of this condensed version of the algorithm, you should step through it using a piece of paper set up like Hal's chalkboard with the boxes AMT and TOT.

This algorithm has two nice features. First, notice that no matter how many checks are in the pile, unless of course the pile is empty to begin with, this algorithm will work. That is, if Hal follows it, he will get the correct total. The other nice feature is that the algorithm is short. It didn't take long to write down. But more important than the

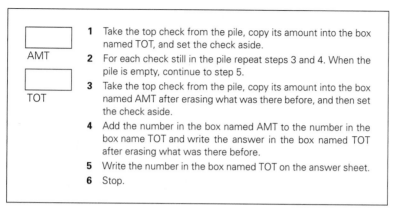

Figure 1.3 Hal's chalkboard with algorithm

length of time we need to write it down is the fact that the algorithm requires very little space. If it were an algorithm for a computer rather than for Hal, we would have to place the algorithm in the computer. This situation is analogous to placing the algorithm on Hal's chalkboard. If it were necessary to write our algorithm on Hal's chalkboard, then this last version would probably fit. The others would not fit unless we wrote so small that Hal would get eyestrain trying to read the instructions. Figure 1.3 shows Hal's chalkboard with our algorithm written on it as we might present it to him for execution. By *execution* we mean "carrying out the instructions of the algorithm," or "following the algorithm to accomplish its purpose."

We will now relate Hal, his chalkboard, and our check-totaling algorithm to some important aspects of computers. Notice that it makes no sense to talk about an algorithm without the notion of some agent that will or can execute it. Hal was to be the agent executing our chalkboard algorithm. A computer is a machine for executing algorithms.

Recall the effort we made to make sure Hal would understand our algorithm. We tried to use a precise and detailed language so that he would not be required to use any real intelligence, but could just follow our instructions by rote. For a computer to understand and execute an algorithm, that algorithm must be expressed in terms even more precise than the instructions we wrote for Hal, because computers are infinitely less intelligent. For this reason, algorithms for computers are not written in English or other natural languages. Rather, we use special programming languages for writing computer algorithms, and the algorithms written in these languages are called *programs*. C++, the language adopted in this book, is a very popular and powerful programming language.

1.2 A look inside the computer

A computer is made up of the basic components shown in figure 1.4.

RAM (random access memory) is composed of cells or locations called *bytes* in which small units of information, such as a single character, can be stored. Each byte has an address, a number that we use to refer to its content. RAM is like the chalkboard, where the rectangles we drew on Hal's chalkboard are composed of several bytes. Just as we named the rectangles on Hal's chalkboard, we can assign names such as AMT and TOT to a sequence of bytes, so we will be able to refer to the quantities stored in those bytes with meaningful and easy-to-remember names instead of nonmeaningful numbers. Both the program and the data that it manipulates are stored in the RAM while the computer is executing a program.

The *CPU* (central processing unit, or processor for short) is the part of the computer that executes the program. Thus, the CPU is something like Hal himself. Hal (we hope) reads each instruction inside the program in turn, executing an instruction before reading the next one. This procedure is exactly what a CPU does. It fetches (reads from RAM) an instruction, executes it, fetches the next instruction, executes it, and so on, until it encounters a stop instruction. The CPU also maintains a small number of *registers*. A register, composed of 4 to 8 bytes, is a high-speed device for storing a data item or an instruction temporarily. We frequently refer to the CPU as the brain of a computer, and as such, a computer is normally described by the type of CPU it contains. For example, 486 DX2/66 means that the computer contains an Intel 80486 DX2 CPU, whose speed is 66 megahertz. A *hertz* is a unit of frequency equal to 1 cycle per second. All CPU operations are synchronized by the CPU's clock pulse, which repeats on and off states in a cyclic manner (see figure 1.5). A *cycle* is a period of time between two on states or off states. *Mega* means $1,000,000 = 10^6$, so 66 megahertz means the CPU is capable of going through 66,000,000 cycles per second. And that's a lot of cycles. On

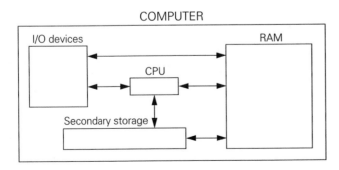

Figure 1.4 A computer's basic components

the other hand, you need millions and millions of cycles to perform a straightforward task, such as alphabetically sorting names in a mailing list.

I/O devices (input/output devices) include such things as keyboards, printers, and screens. Input devices such as keyboards are used to get data (information) from the outside world and to transfer that data into RAM. Output devices such as screens are used to display information for people to read. In our example with Hal, we could say that the pile of checks is like an input device and that the sheet of paper on which he writes the total is like an output device.

Secondary storage refers to disks and tapes on which data and programs can be stored indefinitely. Secondary storage devices are called *nonvolatile memory,* while RAM is called *volatile memory. Volatile* means the data stored in a device will be lost when the power to the device is turned off. Being nonvolatile and much cheaper than RAM, secondary storage is an ideal medium for permanent storage of large volumes of data. A secondary storage device cannot replace the RAM, though, because it is far slower in data access speed (getting data out and writing data in) compared to RAM. A counterpart for secondary storage in our chalkboard example would be a filing folder or an envelope which we can use to store cancelled checks indefinitely.

1.3 *The binary number system (optional)*

Maybe because people have 10 fingers, the decimal number system is and has been widely used. Let's recall some facts about the decimal number system.

First, we know that in the decimal system, we use 10 different symbols or digits— 0, 1, 2, 3, 4, 5, 6, 7, 8, and 9. To represent any number, we use a sequence of one or more of these digits. In a sequence of decimal digits, the positions of the digits have a value that is an integral power of 10. The position values can be determined by counting from the decimal point. The powers increase by one for each position as we proceed to the left, and decrease by one as we proceed to the right. Figure 1.6 illustrates these facts.

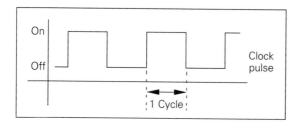

Figure 1.5 CPU clock pulse and cycle

The actual value of a digit in a sequence of decimal digits is found by multiplying the digit by its position value (see below).

$$
\begin{array}{llllll}
892.35 & = 8{\times}10^2 & + 9{\times}10^1 & + 2{\times}10^0 & + 3{\times}10^{-1} & + 5{\times}10^{-2} \\
 & = 8{\times}100 & + 9{\times}10 & + 2{\times}1 & + 3{\times}1/10 & + 5{\times}1/100 \\
 & = 800 & + 90 & + 2 & + 3/10 & + 5/100 \\
 & = 800 & + 90 & + 2 & + .3 & + .05 \\
 & = 892.35
\end{array}
$$

Notice the significance of the number 10 in the decimal system. There are 10 symbols in the system, and position values are integral powers of 10. We say that 10 is the *base* or *radix* of the decimal number system.

As mentioned before, our use of 10 as the base of our number system is probably related to our anatomy. There is nothing sacred about the number. In fact, maybe if early people had found it convenient to count on their ears rather than their fingers, we might now be using the binary number system.

The binary number system uses 2 as its base. The binary number system has two symbols (we use 0 and 1), and its position values are integral powers of 2 (see figure 1.7). To avoid confusion as to the base of a number, we sometimes include the base as a subscript to the number. Thus 101_2 is a binary number and 101_{10} is a decimal number. In the binary system, just as in the decimal system, the actual value of a digit in a sequence of binary digits is found by multiplying the digit by its position value:

$$
\begin{array}{llllll}
1101.01_2 & = 1{\times}2^3 & + 1{\times}2^2 & + 0{\times}2^1 & + 1{\times}2^0 & + 0{\times}2^{-1} & + 1{\times}2^{-2} \\
 & = 1{\times}8 & + 1{\times}4 & + 0{\times}2 & + 1{\times}1 & + 0{\times}1/2 & + 1{\times}1/4 \\
 & = 8 & + 4 & + 0 & + 1 & + 0 & + .25 \\
 & = 13.25_{10}
\end{array}
$$

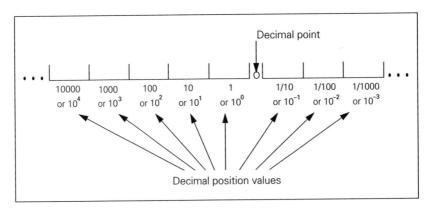

Figure 1.6 Decimal number system

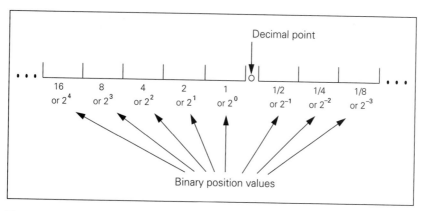

Figure 1.7 Binary number system

This example shows that the binary number 1101.01 is numerically equivalent to the decimal number 13.25. It also suggests how to convert from the binary representation of a number to its decimal representation.

1.4 Representation of data in RAM (optional)

The checks, or more precisely the amounts on the checks, are the data used in our chalkboard algorithm. These amounts are numbers, and the operations our algorithm directs Hal to perform on them are numeric operations. Numeric data is only one kind of data. Another kind, *text data*, or just *text* for short, is like the words in this book. Pictures or diagrams are also data that can be used by computers. Ultimately, of course, all of these kinds of data are represented by bit sequences.

Numeric data falls into two general categories—integer and real. An integer number has no fractional part, while a real number may have a fractional part. Integers may occupy 1, 2, or 4 bytes, depending on the range of possible values needed. For example, if we only need integers in the range 1 to 100, then a single byte is enough. The 8 bits in a byte have 256 different configurations that can be used to represent the integers 0 thru 255. We would interpret the bit patterns as binary integers, that is, with an assumed binary point just to the right of the rightmost bit, as shown in table 1.1.

In this case we are interpreting the byte as an unsigned 8-bit number. If we need negative as well as positive integers, we could use one bit, maybe the leftmost bit, as a sign. We could interpret 0 as positive and 1 as negative, giving us the possible values shown in table 1.2.

Table 1.1 8-bit binary integers

8-bit binary integer	Decimal equivalent
00000000	0
00000001	1
00000010	2
00000011	3
00000100	4
...	
11111100	252
11111101	253
11111110	254
11111111	255

Table 1.2 Negative and positive binary integers

8-bit binary integer	Decimal equivalent
00000000	+0
00000001	+1
00000010	+2
...	
01111111	+127
10000000	-0
10000001	-1
...	
11111101	−125
11111110	−126
11111111	−127

Some computers in the past have used the above representation for signed integers, but today's computers use *twos-complement* representation. Twos-complement representation avoids the problem of having two different representations for zero (+0 = 00000000 and −0 = 10000000), and facilitates a simpler circuitry for numeric operations. In twos-complement notation, all the positive numbers have zero as their leftmost bit. The negative of a number is found by inverting all the bits (changing 1s to 0s and 0s to 1s) and adding 1. For example, the representation of −9 is found by taking the representation of 9, which is 00001001, inverting all the bits to get 11110110, and then adding 1 to get 11110110+1 = 11110111 = −9. Table 1.3 shows the 8-bit signed integers using twos-complement representation.

If a wider range of integers is required, we can use 2 bytes, which is sometimes called a 16-bit word, or 4 bytes, which is sometimes called a 32-bit word. Twos-complement notation would be used for signed numbers in either case. Table 1.4 shows the 32-bit binary integers and their decimal equivalents.

To represent real numbers in, for example, a 32-bit word, we could arbitrarily choose a position for an assumed binary point, perhaps right in the middle, allowing 16 bits to the left and 16 bits to the right of the binary point, as shown below.

0001010111001101.1101000100011011

Using twos-complement notation for the integer part (the 16 bits to the left of the binary point) would allow the integer part of a real number to range from −32768 to +32767. If we interpret only the fractional part as a binary fraction, we can represent the fractions as shown in table 1.5.

Table 1.3 8-bit binary integers using twos-complement representation

8-bit binary integer	Decimal equivalent
00000000	+0
00000001	+1
00000010	+2
...	
01111110	+126
01111111	+127
10000000	−128
10000001	−127
...	
11111101	−3
11111110	−2
11111111	−1

However, this approach is not a good way to represent real numbers because the range of possible values is too small. In scientific calculations we often need to use numbers whose magnitude (absolute value) is much smaller than 0.0000152587890625, the smallest nonzero number we can represent with the above scheme. Large numbers are also common in science (and in other areas too, e.g., the national debt), but the largest number we can represent in our scheme is 32767.999984741210938. For these reasons, real numbers are represented in the computer using *scientific notation*. In decimal scientific notation, a number's representation includes the significant digits of the number and a power of 10, to avoid writing long strings of zeros. For example, the mass of the hydrogen atom in grams is 0.00000000000000000000000167339. In scientific notation this number is 1.67339×10^{-24}. In scientific notation we call the significant digits the *mantissa* and the exponent of 10 the *characteristic*. Thus in the number 1.67339×10^{-24}, 1.67339 is the mantissa and −24 is the characteristic. The characteristic is a signed integer representing a power of 10 by which the mantissa must be multiplied to get the actual number.

Table 1.4 32-bit binary integers using twos-complement representation

32-bit binary integer (4 bytes)	Decimal equivalent
00000000 00000000 00000000 00000000	+0
00000000 00000000 00000000 00000001	+1
00000000 00000000 00000000 00000010	+2
...	
01111111 11111111 11111111 11111111	+2147483647
10000000 00000000 00000000 00000000	−2147483648
10000000 00000000 00000000 00000001	−2147483647
...	
11111111 11111111 11111111 11111101	−3
11111111 11111111 11111111 11111110	−2
11111111 11111111 11111111 11111111	−1

Table 1.5 Binary fraction representation

16-bit binary fraction	Conversion to decimal	Equivalent decimal fraction
0.00000000 00000000	0	0.0
0.00000000 00000001	2^{-16}	0.000015258789062
0.00000000 00000010	2^{-15}	0.000030517578125
0.00000000 00000011	$2^{-15} + 2^{-16}$	0.000045776367187
...	...	...
0.11111111 11111101	$1/2 + 1/4 + ... + 2^{-14} + 2^{-16}$	0.999954223632813
0.11111111 11111110	$1/2 + 1/4 + ... + 2^{-14} + 2^{-15}$	0.999969482421875
0.11111111 11111111	$1/2 + 1/4 + ... + 2^{-14} + 2^{-15} + 2^{-16}$	0.999984741210938

In RAM, real numbers are represented using binary scientific notation. The mantissa is a binary fraction, and the characteristic is a signed binary integer representing a power of 2. One scheme uses a 32-bit word in which 24 of the bits are the mantissa and the other 8 bits are the characteristic. Figure 1.8 is an example of the representation of a real number in a 32-bit word.

The above real number represented with binary mantissa and characteristic is

$$0.001000101010000000000000 \times 2^{00100110}$$

Represented with decimal mantissa and characteristic, the number is

$$0.13525390625 \times 10^{38}$$

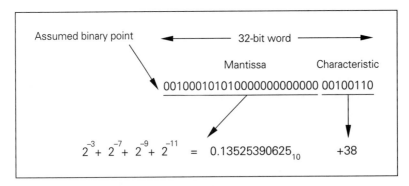

Figure 1.8 Representation of a real number in a 32-bit word

1.5 Machine language and assembly language

The check-totaling algorithm we wrote for Hal was written on his chalkboard. Similarly, a computer CPU cannot execute a program unless it is placed in RAM. In addition, the program needs to be expressed in machine language. *Machine language* is a set of binary-coded instructions that the CPU can recognize and execute. These instructions are very low level, which means that, individually, they don't do very much. A single machine language instruction might do nothing more than transfer the contents of one byte of RAM into another, add the number in one word of RAM into a register in the CPU, or set a bit to zero or 1 depending on whether one byte is equal to another. Thus, it takes many machine language instructions to accomplish even a simple task like totaling up a set of check amounts. Hal's check-totaling algorithm, expressed in machine language, might include hundreds of instructions.

Each machine language instruction consists of an operation code, which uniquely identifies the instruction, and from zero to two operands. The operation code tells what to do (like a verb), and the operands tell what to do it to (like the objects of a verb). An operand may be the address of a byte or word in RAM or a reference to a CPU register or actual data. In any case, the operands, like the operation code, are just sequences of bits 1, 2, 3, or 4 bytes long.

You can imagine how tedious and error prone it would be to write a program in machine language. First, you would have to learn a set of low-level machine language instructions for the computer. You would have to master the binary operation codes, and learn how to reference the CPU registers, and how the RAM addresses are represented in instructions. Then you would have to figure out what sequence of machine instructions would accomplish the objectives of your program. You would probably organize your program one instruction per line, maybe with comments in the margins to help you remember what each instruction is supposed to do. Your machine-language program might look like this:

```
10110111 00011001              Read first amount
01001010 1101000110110000      Move amount into a register
10110111 00011001              Read next amount
00101100 1101000110110000      Add to the register
11011011 1101000110110010      Store in total
       etc.
```

Then you would have to input the program, as a long sequence of bits, into RAM for your program to be executed. The opportunity for error is enormous. But that is exactly how the first computers were programmed back in the early 1950s. The programs were input one instruction at a time by toggling switches to represent the bits and then pushing a button to store the instruction in the next RAM location. It is no wonder that some of the first programs were programs to help programmers program.

Loaders were written to read instructions from punched cards or tape, which made it easy to get a program into RAM for execution. Assembly languages were invented to allow higher level symbolic programming. Assembly language is one big step up from machine language. It allows the programmer to write programs using mnemonic operation codes and symbolic operands. Mnemonic means "aiding the memory." A mnemonic operation code is one or two letters chosen to abbreviate the operation description, for example, RD for "read" or MV for "move." Symbolic operands are short names for registers or names invented by the programmer to represent RAM addresses. An assembly language program might look something like this:

```
RD   AMT       Read first amount
MV   AMT,AC    Move amount into the register AC
RD   AMT       Read next amount
ADD  AMT,AC    Add to AC
STO  TOT,AC    Store in total
     etc.
```

An *assembly program* (*assembler* for short) translates programs written in assembly language into machine language instructions. Assembly language frees programmers from dealing with computer details so they can concentrate on solving a problem. But assembly language is still at the same level as machine language in the sense that a single assembly language instruction doesn't do any more than the corresponding machine language instruction. However, the assembly language instruction is easier for humans to read and understand.

1.6 High level languages and compilers

Soon after the development of assembly languages, computer scientists began developing higher level languages. These languages were designed to help programmers write programs for a certain class of problems. They looked much less like machine language and much more like the language or notation used in the problem area. For example, FORTRAN (FORmula TRANslator) was developed for scientific problems in which mathematical formulas were important. COBOL (COmmon Business Oriented Language) was developed for business data processing applications. FORTRAN and COBOL were developed in the late 1950s and early 1960s. Pascal was developed by Nicklaus Wirth of Switzerland in the early 1970s. It was not designed for any particular problem area, but rather as an academic language that would foster the good program-

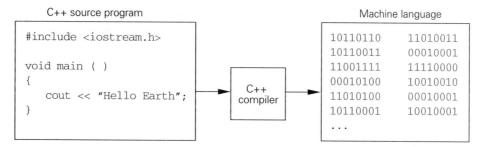

C++ source program

```
#include <iostream.h>

void main ( )
{
    cout << "Hello Earth";
}
```

C++ compiler

Machine language

```
10110110    11010011
10110011    00010001
11001111    11110000
00010100    10010010
11010100    00010001
10110001    10010001
. . .
```

Figure 1.9 Translation of C++ source program into machine language

ming techniques that had been discovered in the first 20 years of the computer age. These programming languages have been modified and improved over the years and are still used today.

The programming language C was developed in the early 1970s by Dennis Ritchie of AT&T Bell Labs. It is a general-purpose programming language that has become the language of choice for many professional programmers. The C++ programming language was developed as a successor of C in the early 1980s by another AT&T Bell Labs researcher Bjarne Stroustrup. By far the most important extension of C, C++ supports object-oriented programming. Object-oriented programming (OOP) was one of the most important programming developments in the 1980s, and its significance will increase as we progress through the 1990s. The concept of object-oriented programming is in fact quite old (the first object-oriented programming language, Simula, was developed in the late 1960s), but its significance wasn't realized until the early 1980s. We are not going to try to explain OOP here. Rather, we will use this whole book to immerse you into the philosophy of object-oriented programming. By the time you finish studying this book, you will be able to design and write programs in an object-oriented manner.

Programs written in a high-level language like C++ must still be translated into machine language for execution. Since high-level languages are much more different from machine language than are assembly languages, the translation process is more complex. For high level languages the translation process is called *compiling*, and the translator program is call a *compiler*. For example, a C++ compiler translates a C++ *source program* (a program written in C++) into the machine language of a computer, as shown in figure 1.9.

We will write our very first C++ program in the next chapter.

1.7 Executing computer programs

Writing a C++ program is only a part of the story. Before we can actually execute the program, we must carry out additional tasks. To actually execute a program, we must do the following:

1 Write a C++ program using an editor or a word processor and save it in a file. The file that contains the source program, or source code, is called the *source file*. Depending on the compiler, you either must or should name the source file with a suffix *.cpp*. For example, we will name our first C++ program *ProgOne.cpp*. Notice that the period in front of *cpp* is required. We pronounce the period "dot." We pronounce the source file "ProgOne dot cpp."

2 Compile the source file by using the compiler. The output of compiling is the machine language equivalent of the source file, as explained above. You can direct the compiler to save the output in a file of your choice. The file that contains the compiling output is called the *object file*. Notice that the term *object* in *object file* is not related to the term *object* in *object-oriented programming*. When the compiler does not give you this option, or you choose not to specify the name for a file, the compiler will name the object file by replacing the .cpp of the source file with .obj. For example, the compiled version of ProgOne.cpp becomes ProgOne.obj if you don't specify the name. We highly recommend using the same name for the source and object files, even if the compiler lets you use different names.

3 Almost all nontrivial C++ programs cannot be executed by themselves, because they require the use of functions defined in other object files. For example, a program may require the use of trigonometric functions sine and cosine. Instead of writing these functions ourselves, we say in our program, "We want to make all functions defined in the object file `trig.obj` available to my program. We call functions defined outside of our program *external functions*. If such *inclusion* of external functions is declared in a program, then for this program to be executable, we must link all the included object files. This process is called *linking*. After all the necessary files are linked, the object file becomes an *executable file*. The executable file frequently has a suffix .exe.

4 Finally, the program is ready for execution. To execute the program, we may either type in the name of an executable file or double-click on its icon, depending on the operating system. [*]

---

[*] As stated in the Preface, we assume the readers are familiar with the basic operations of either UNIX, Windows, or Mac OS.

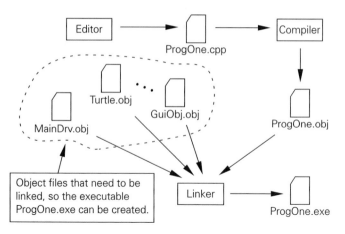

Figure 1.10 Edit-compile-link-execute cycle

Figure 1.10 summarizes these steps.

At each step of the edit-compile-link-execute cycle,[*] errors can occur. Errors not detected at one stage of the cycle will be detected in the subsequent stages. At the editing stage, typographical errors occur frequently. Some of the obvious ones are easily detected and corrected. An error that occurs during the compilation stage is called a *compiler error.* A compiler error occurs when a given program does not follow the grammatical rules of a C++ program. For example, you may have typed the word `main` erroneously as `maim`. Most of the typographical errors that are not corrected at the editing stage will be detected during the compilation. When a compiler error occurs, no object file is generated. An error that occurs during the linking stage is called a *linker error.* A linker error typically occurs when the linker cannot locate the file to be linked. Finally, an error that occurs during the execution of a program is called an *execution error.* These are the most troublesome errors to correct. Execution errors are also called *logical errors* because the logic of the program as written is different from our intention. In other words, what we have expressed in a C++ program is not logically equivalent to what we have in mind. For example, we may have erroneously stated that two numbers be multiplied when in fact we wanted to divide the first number by the second number. Logical errors materialize in two ways: either a program terminates prematurely or it produces erroneous results.

Although we call products such as Borland C++ or Visual C++ compilers, they are really *integrated development environments* (IDEs) that include an editor, a compiler, a

---

[*] It is a cycle because when a program does not work exactly as planned, we must go back to the beginning and repeat the whole process.

linker, and other program development tools. Instead of dealing separately with three different pieces of software (namely, the editor, compiler, and linker) to develop computer programs, an integrated development environment allows us to specify all three processes at once. Assuming a program is correct, all we have to do to execute it is to click a button or select a menu choice. The IDE will compile, link, and execute the program without any further intervention from us.

1.8 Exercises

Note: Questions marked with an asterisk require the knowledge of topics covered in the optional sections.

1 Write an algorithm to find the average of five numbers. Can you generalize your algorithm for ten numbers? Twenty numbers?

2 Write an algorithm to find the largest of three given numbers.

3 Write an algorithm to find the difference between the largest and the smallest of five given numbers.

4 Write an algorithm to compute the perimeter and area of a triangle given the lengths of its three sides.

5 Write an algorithm to count the occurrence of negative numbers in ten numbers.

6 Write an algorithm to compute the sum of an arbitrary number of integers. Since you do not know how many integers will be given to the algorithm, you need to incorporate some kind of instruction into the algorithm to stop the execution when it has no more integers to process.

7* Convert the following binary numbers to decimal numbers:

a. 1000   d. 1010101
b. 10011   e. 110011
c. 110.01   f. 1011.001

8* Hexadecimal numbers (base 16) use 16 digits 0, 1, ..., 9, A, B, C, D, E, and F. For example, $1F_{16} = 31_{10}$. Convert the following hexadecimal numbers to decimal numbers:

a. 2A9   d. FFFF
b. 115   e. A09
c. 23.0F   f. 44.00C

9* Convert the following decimal numbers to binary and hexadecimal numbers:

a. 29   d. 2345
b. 115   e. 999
c. 123.015   f. 44.008

10* The following numbers have a 5-bit mantissa and a 3-bit characteristic. The characteristic is in a signed binary integer format representing a power of 2. Convert the following numbers to decimal mantissa and characteristics:

a. 00111 001   d. 10101 111
b. 10111 011   e. 10000 101

chapter 2

Starting to program

Since we learn best by doing, and programming is no exception, we will immediately start with a complete C++ program. You are encouraged to spend as much time as you can at your computer trying out the example programs and modifying them in ways suggested by this book, or better still, suggested by your own imagination. Working through the exercises will also be very instructive. Actually running the programs should give you good practice with the programming environment you will be using. It is always a great feeling to see your program run and produce some output, no matter how trivial the program may be. In no time, you will be writing fairly sophisticated programs.

In this chapter you will write your first C++ programs. You will see an OKBox, a GUI (graphical user interface) object for displaying messages, and a Turtle object for drawing lines. You will be introduced to the object-oriented view of a program, in which it is viewed as a collection of objects that perform tasks in response to messages, or commands, sent from other objects. This object-oriented view of a program is a new way of thinking about programs. In this book we teach the fundamentals of computer programming from this new object-oriented approach.

The object-oriented view of programs is one way to interpret the semantics, or meanings, of programs. The view provides a way to look at a program and understand the tasks it is performing and how it is accomplishing them. It is much like understanding the plot and theme of a novel. In addition to the program semantics, programmers must be concerned with the program syntax rules, which define the grammatical rules for writing programs. In this chapter you will learn how to read the syntax rules of C++. Given the syntax rules and a small program, you should be able to tell whether the program is grammatically correct. Unlike novels, every C++ program (actually any computer program) must be 100 percent correct syntactically, so understanding the syntax rules of C++ is very important.

2.1 The first program

Our first C++ program doesn't do very much, but it illustrates a few key aspects of C++ programming.

```
// Program One: A simple program using an OKBox.

#include "GUIObj.h"

void main ( )
{
    OKBoxmyBox;
    myBox.Display("Hello, World!");
}
```

Running this program will display the window in figure 2.1 on your computer screen. We'll discuss each line of the program.

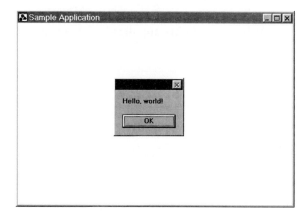

Figure 2.1 Program One screen capture

Line 1 →

```
// Program One: A simple program using an OKBox.

#include "GUIObj.h"

void main ( )
{
    OKBox   myBox;
    myBox.Display("Hello, World!");
}
```

Figure 2.2 Line 1 of program

Line 1 (figure 2.2) is a comment. Comments do not affect the way the program works, but they can make it easier for others to understand what your program does and how it does it. More important, comments can help you to understand your own program weeks (or even hours) after you write it. When you have more than one line of comments, each line must be preceded by double slashes (//). Another way to put a comment in the program is to precede it with /* and terminate it with */. A comment can extend beyond one line if you surround it with /* and */.

```
/*  This is a multiline
    comment. Your comment can go beyond
    one line. */
```

Line 2 (figure 2.3) informs the compiler that the program uses things defined in a *header file*, or more simply a *header*, named GUIObj.h. This header file contains predefined program components, one of which is an object. As a convention, we use the suffix .h for a header file name. In this sample program, we use an OKBox object defined in this header file. You should notice that because objects are already defined in the

Line 2 →

```
// Program One: A simple program using an OKBox.

#include "GUIObj.h"

void main ( )
{
    OKBox   myBox;
    myBox.Display("Hello, World!");
}
```

Figure 2.3 Line 2 of program

```
// Program One: A simple program using an OKBox.

#include "GUIObj.h"
```

Line 3 ——▶
```
void main ( )
{
    OKBox   myBox;
    myBox.Display("Hello, World!");
}
```

Figure 2.4 Line 3 of program

GUIObj.h header, we are able to write this "simple" program. If there were no GUIObj.h, then we would have to write a tremendous amount of code for this program. The objects in GUIObj.h take care of all the low level details of opening a window and displaying a message in it. You can use the predefined objects without worrying about details. Moreover, once an object is created for performing a specific task, you can simply reuse the object over and over again in many different programs.

In this book we will use several headers supplied by the C++ compiler as well as GUIObj.h and Turtle.h, the headers we have written specifically for this book. For the earlier part of this book, you will use only the predefined objects, but later, you will be able to define your own objects.

Every C++ program must have one function named main (see figure 2.4). We call this function the *main function*. It serves as the main controller of a program and is also called the *main program*. The programming language C++ is derived from the programming language C, in which a program is viewed as a collection of functions consisting of one main function and many subfunctions. C++ inherits this view, but with C++ you can use objects along with functions. A function can use objects just as the main function in our first program uses a GUI object. Objects, in turn, can contain functions. For example, a GUI object contains the function Display. Functions attached to an object define the object's behavior. We will discuss object behavior in section 2.7.

We list input values to a function inside parentheses ( ). Since there is no input to this main function, there is nothing inside the parentheses. Normally, we do not provide any input to the main function. In writing a C++ function, we must specify what kind of output the function produces. For example, a function may compute a sum of two input integer values. The result of the function is then an integer. The output, or result of a C++ function, is called the *return value*. A function in mathematics must return a value, but a C++ function does not have to return a value. A C++ function that does not return a value is called a *void function* and is designated as such by the word void in

```
// Program One: A simple program using an OKBox.

#include "GUIObj.h"

void main ( )
{
    OKBox   myBox;
    myBox.Display("Hello, World!");
}
```

Line 4 ⟶

Figure 2.5 Line 4 of program

front of the function name. The main function of this sample program is a void function, as are the main functions of all other sample programs in this book.

Other than this main function, which must be named main, we can name functions
any way we want, as long as the names don't violate the rule given below in section 2.4.
We call these names *identifiers*. Beside naming functions, we use identifiers to name
other components of a program, such as objects.

Line 4 (figure 2.5) signals the beginning of the function body. Since this is the main
function, it signals the beginning of the program. A function body consists of two major
types of statements—declarations and commands. In this program we have only one declaration statement (line 5) and one command statement (line 6). Statements correspond
to instructions in the algorithm. We will learn about C++ statements throughout the
remainder of this book. The function body is terminated by a right brace } (line 7).

Line 5 (figure 2.6) is a declaration statement that declares the identifier myBox as the
name of an OKBox object. We normally say, "myBox is an OKBox object," although strictly
speaking, we must say, "myBox is an identifier for an OKBox object." If you need to use

```
// Program One: A simple program using an OKBox.

#include "GUIObj.h"

void main ( )
{
    OKBox   myBox;
    myBox.Display("Hello, World!");
}
```

Line 5 ⟶

Figure 2.6 Line 5 of program

```
// Program One: A simple program using an OKBox.

#include "GUIObj.h"

void main ( )
{
    OKBox   myBox;
    myBox.Display("Hello, World!");
}
```

Line 6 ──────▶ (points to `myBox.Display("Hello, World!");`)

Figure 2.7 Line 6 of program

more than one object—say three—then you need a unique identifier for each, declared as follows:

```
OKBox myBox, yourBox, herBox;
```

Every statement in C++ must be terminated with a semicolon.

Line 6 (figure 2.7) is a command statement that commands the OKBox object myBox to display the message "Hello, World!". We can think of this command as sending a message Display to the myBox object. Receiving this message, the myBox object carries out the requested task. For an object to be able to respond to a message, a corresponding function must be defined for the object. This function tells the object exactly what to do to carry out the task. Many functions are normally defined for an object, and this collection of functions defines the behavior of an object. If no corresponding function is available to the received message, an error will result. Viewing a command statement as the sending of a message, a program is then a collection of cooperating objects sending messages to each other to carry out tasks.

```
// Program One: A simple program using an OKBox.

#include "GUIObj.h"

void main ( )
{
    OKBox   myBox;
    myBox.Display("Hello, World!");
}
```

Line 7 ──────▶ (points to `}`)

Figure 2.8 Line 7 of program

With C++, we view line 6 as calling, or invoking, the function `Display` defined for an `OKBox` object. The text `"Hello, World!"` is an input value we provide to the function. The text must be surrounded by double quotes, so that the compiler can distinguish it from the identifiers. An input value to a function is called an *argument*. If a function has two or more arguments, they are separated by commas. The general format for calling an object's function is

```
object_identifier.function_name ( argument_list ) ;
```

The left and right parentheses must be present even if there is no argument. Because of the period between the object identifier and its function name, this style of calling an object's function is called *dot notation*.

Line 7 (figure 2.8) signals the end of the function body of the main program.

2.2 *Object diagrams*

It is easier to understand a program when we can see a graphical representation of its objects and their interactions. Figure 2.9 depicts an object diagram for our first program.

This object diagram is comprised of the following components (see figure 2.10).

1 In an object diagram, objects are depicted by an object icon, which is a rectangle with rounded corners.

2 The program itself is represented as an object. The program's name is written inside the rectangle, because this name is not used by any other object. It is mainly for our own reference.

3 An object's function is listed on its edge. (`Display` is a function of `myBox`.) The name of the object is written outside the box to signify that the name is visible to other objects and is used by them.

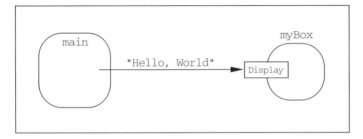

Figure 2.9 Program object diagram

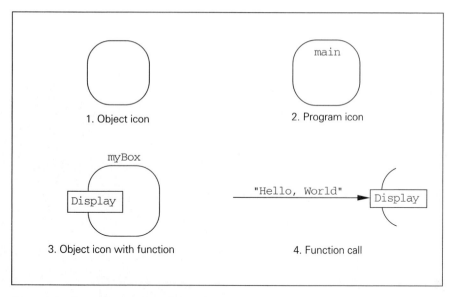

Figure 2.10 Components of an object diagram

4   An arrow from one object to a function in another object represents a function call. Arguments in a function call are written along the arrow.

Object diagrams aren't really necessary for small programs, such as our first program, because we can easily understand them without any visual aids. However, to encourage the use of object diagrams in the development of larger programs, when they can be very helpful, we will provide object diagrams for many of our sample programs.

2.3 Sequential execution

Statements in a program are executed in the order in which they appear, from top to bottom. We can expand our first program to illustrate this sequential order of execution.

```
//Program Two: Another simple program using an OKBox.

#include "GUIObj.h"

void main ( )
{
    OKBox    myBox;

    myBox.Display("Hello, World!");
```

```
        myBox.Display("Welcome to Object Land");
        myBox.Display("May you have fun and learn a lot!");
        myBox.Display("Goodbye");
    }
```

We have four command statements, for a total of four function calls. When this program is executed, it initially displays the same message box as the first program (by the execution of the first statement `myBox.Display("Hello, World!")`). (See figure 2.11.)

Figure 2.11 First message box

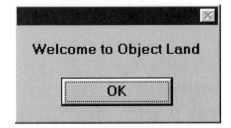

Figure 2.12 Second message box

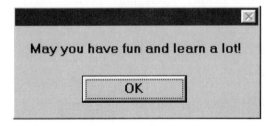

Figure 2.13 Third message box

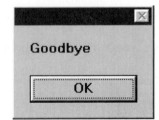

Figure 2.14 Fourth message box

When the user clicks the OK button, another message box appears, because clicking the button completes the execution of the first statement and allows the second one to be executed. The execution of the second statement causes `myBox` to display the second message (see figure 2.12).

Clicking the OK button on this box causes the third message to appear (see figure 2.13). Clicking the OK button on this box causes the fourth statement to be executed and produces message as shown in figure 2.14. Clicking OK on this last message box terminates the program because it completes the execution of the final statement in the program.

This expanded program illustrates how the statements of a program are executed one at a time. It also shows more about what an `OKBox`'s `Display` function actually does.

Notice that when an OKBox displays text, it adjusts the size of the box to accommodate the length of the text. Also notice that the execution of a Display function isn't completed until you click the OK button.

2.4 C++ syntax

While explaining the first C++ sample program, we stated that a C++ program must have at least one function and one of the functions must be named main. We also stated that a function must adhere to a precise format: it must start with an identifier followed by an argument list surrounded by parentheses, and must have a function body of zero or more statements, all surrounded by the curly braces { and }. This rule defines the form, or structure, of a program. In addition to the rule for functions, we have rules for the various kinds of statements and all other components of the C++ language, much like we have complete grammatical rules for the English language.

Just as the grammatical rules of the English language impose a strict structural requirement for English sentences, the grammatical rules of the C++ language dictate the structural validity of C++ programs. Strictly speaking, a program is not a C++ program if it violates any one of the many C++ grammatical rules. These grammatical rules are called *syntax rules*, and they collectively enforce the valid syntax for C++ programs.

Syntax rules can be stated in a narrative form, as we have done for the function syntax above. Although this form may be acceptable for a small portion of the language, it is too cumbersome and awkward, and more importantly, too imprecise for the complete language. Stating syntax rules in a narrative form opens them to misinterpretation. To be precise and concise, we usually show syntax rules for programming languages as diagrams or in some stylized form. C++ syntax rules are normally stated in a stylized form called a *Backus Naur Form*, or BNF for short, which we shall use in this book. Let's look at the BNF rules for the C++ identifiers.

(1) *identifier*
    letter character-list$_{opt}$

(2) *character-list*
    character
    character character-list

③ *character*
　　digit
　　letter

　　_

④ *digit*
　　　0　| 1 |...| 9

⑤ *letter*
　　　a | b | ... | z | A | B | ... | Z

Each of the five rules are listed above defines a *syntax category* of the C++ language. A syntax category is like one of the parts of speech in English. If we were to construct similar syntax rules for English, we would have rules for the syntax categories *noun, verb, subject, prepositional phrase, sentence*, etc. A syntax category with the subscript $_{opt}$ denotes an optional element.

Rule 1　　An identifier is a letter followed by an optional character-list.

Rule 2　　A character-list is a character or a character followed by a character-list. The alternatives are listed on separate lines. For example, a *character-list* is either a *character* (the first alternative) or a *character* followed by another *character-list* (the second alternative). The recursive nature of this rule—that a *character-list* is defined in terms of another *character-list*—in effect designates that the *character-list* is a sequence of characters.

Rule 3　　A character is either a digit, a letter, or a special underscore symbol _.

Rule 4　　A digit is either 0, 1, 2, 3, 4, 5, 6, 7, 8, or 9. The vertical bar | is another way of showing alternatives. For example, we can use the vertical bars to state Rule 3 as

character
　　digit | *letter* | _

A three-dot symbol ... is used to denote a sequence of values without explicitly listing them.

Rule 5　　A letter is any one of the alphabetic characters.

These five rules collectively state that an identifier is a sequence of letters, digits, or underscore characters with the first character being a letter. Here are some valid identifiers according to the above syntax rules:

```
MyBox   Box2   sam   x   Address   temperature   Bill_Clinton
```

Here are some that are not valid. (Can you tell what's wrong with each one?)

```
2Box    First.Name    ?okay?    Bill-Clinton    Sam*Spade
```

In some programming languages (e.g., Pascal and Ada), lowercase and uppercase letters are not distinguished. These languages consider the identifiers HELLO, hello, and Hello to be the same, for example. C++, however, does distinguish between cases. Languages that distinguish between lowercase and uppercase letters are called *case-sensitive languages*, and those do not are called *case-insensitive languages*. This type of information is not stated with the syntax rules. Another type of information that is not explicitly stated is the length of identifiers. The syntax rules place no limit on the number of characters we use for the identifiers. This freedom, of course, is not acceptable in practice. A compiler puts some limit on the number of characters that can be used for an identifier. One compiler, for example, puts the limit at 63 characters. Actually, you can define an identifier that has more than 63 characters, but the compiler will read only the first 63 characters. So, for example, the following two identifiers would be considered to be identical.

```
this_is_a_very_long_identifier_probably_longer_than_you_or_I_would_ever_useAAAAA
this_is_a_very_long_identifier_probably_longer_than_you_or_I_would_ever_useBBBBB
```

The third piece of information that is not stated with the production rules for an identifier is the exclusion of certain words called reserved words. *Reserved words* have special meanings and purposes in C++, and they cannot be used as identifiers. Table 2.1 lists the C++ reserved words

Although you are not going to learn all of the reserved words (you will use about half of them in this book), you should be aware of them. Suppose, for example, you attempt to use continue as an identifier in your program. Since it is a reserved word, the compiler will generate an error message. The problem is that the compiler is not intelligent enough to provide a meaningful error message, such as "Reserved word 'continue' cannot be used as an identifier." More likely, it will say something like "Unterminated declaration statement" or "Continue statement missing" or some other cryptic message. You can avoid this problem by being aware of the reserved words. Since

Table 2.1 C++ reserved words

asm	continue	float	new	short	try
auto	default	for	operator	signed	typedef
break	delete	friend	overload	sizeof	union
case	do	goto	private	static	unsigned
catch	double	if	protected	struct	virtual
char	else	inline	public	switch	void
class	enum	int	register	this	volatile
const	extern	long	return	template	while

C++ is case sensitive, you can use `Continue` as an identifier, but it is not prudent to do so. Using identifiers that differ in case only, for example, `total` and `Total`, is very confusing and should be avoided.

One last point about identifiers has to do with the names you select. Actually, naming identifiers has nothing to do with their syntax, but we might as well add an important guideline. We mentioned that it is a good idea to comment your program clearly. Another good idea is to choose meaningful names for identifiers. If a name tells how and why something is used in a program, then that name functions as an explanatory comment. If you use meaningful names, some comments may not be necessary. For example, the identifier `StudentAddress` is much more meaningful than `zxyqs`, `a`, or even `addr` as an identifer for a student's address.

The BNF rules listed above are also known as *production rules* because they are rules for "producing" additional syntax categories from a given syntax category. In other words, a production rule explains how to expand a syntax category into other syntax categories. We say that a C++ program is syntactically correct if we can produce it by applying the production rules, starting from the top-most syntax category *program*. A syntax category is also called *nonterminal,* because we can expand it further (i.e., we can produce more syntax categories from a given syntax category by applying some production rule to it). Reserved words, identifiers, and some other characters that we have not yet learned, are called *terminals* because we cannot expand them any further (i.e., there are no further production rules that can be applied to them). Different font styles are used in the syntax rules. Syntax categories, or nonterminals, are shown in italic font with all lowercase letters. Reserved words, characters, and special symbols, such as parentheses and braces, are shown in bold font.

Let's look at a sample production. Keep in mind that we do not use these production rules to actually write a C++ program. These rules are for a compiler to verify whether a given program is syntactically correct. We start productions from a single nonterminal *identifier.*

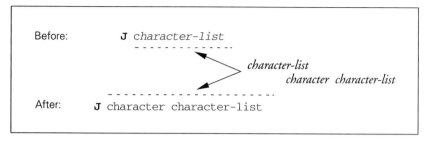

Figure 2.15 New production rule sequence

```
identifier

    ===>  letter character-list

    ===>  J character-list

    ===>  J character character-list

    ===>  J letter character-list

    ===>  J o character-list

    ===>  J o character

    ===>  J o letter

    ===>  J o e
```

(*Note:* the actual identifier generated here is Joe. The spaces between the letters have been added to make the identifier more readable.)

Figure 2.15 illustrates how the production rule is applied to `J character-list` to derive `J character character-list`. The new sequence is derived by applying the production rule to the nonterminal character-list in the old sequence.

We will provide syntax rules for each new type of C++ statement we introduce in this book.

2.5 *The* Turtle *object*

In the early 1970s Seymour Papert at MIT built a programmable, mechanical "turtle" that could move around a drawing board, pushing a pen to draw all sorts of shapes. He used it to study the ability of young children to learn about programming and to write meaningful programs on their own. His experiments showed that children as young as five years old can write sophisticated programs to draw interesting shapes.

We will use turtle objects to illustrate many new concepts in this book. In this and the following sections, we explain the basics of using turtle objects. The `Turtles.h` header file defines a `Turtle` object that behaves very much like Papert's mechanical turtle. Here is a simple program that uses a `Turtle` object to draw a square.

```
// Program Square: A program that draws a square.

#include "Turtles.h"

void main ( )
{
    Turtle myTurtle;

    myTurtle.Init(260,180); //Start from location (260,180).

    myTurtle.Move(50); // Draw the bottom of the square.
    myTurtle.Turn(90); // Turn to draw the right side.

    myTurtle.Move(50); // Draw the right side.
    myTurtle.Turn(90); // Turn to draw the top.

    myTurtle.Move(50); // Draw the top.
    myTurtle.Turn(90); // Turn to draw the left side.

    myTurtle.Move(50); // Draw the left side.

    myTurtle.Done();
}
```

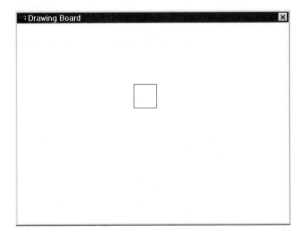

Figure 2.16 Program Square screen capture

```
1   #include "Turtles.h"

2   void main ( )
3   {
4       Turtle myTurtle;

5       myTurtle.Init(260,180);

6       myTurtle.Move(50);
7       myTurtle.Turn(90);

8       myTurtle.Move(50);
9       myTurtle.Turn(90);

10      myTurtle.Move(50);
11      myTurtle.Turn(90);

12      myTurtle.Move(50);

13      myTurtle.Done();
14  }
```

Figure 2.17 Numbered program example

When it is executed, the program draws the screen as shown in figure 2.16.

(*Note:* when you execute this program, the square shows up immediately after the drawing board appears on the screen. If you wish to see how the square is drawn, you can make the Turtle move slowly. See exercise 6 on page 44.)

Let's analyze the program. We will first assign line numbers to it for easy reference, as shown in figure 2.17. Please note that program comments are removed from this program example.

Now let's go through the program line by line.

Line 1   informs the compiler that the program uses the header file Turtles.h.

Line 2   declares the main function main.

Line 3   signals the beginning of the function body.

Line 4   declares a Turtle object called myTurtle.

Line 5   calls the Init function of myTurtle. The function opens the turtle's drawing board window, and the arguments 260 and 180 provide the initial position of myTurtle on the drawing board. We will describe the drawing board and explain each of the `Turtle` object's functions later in this section.

Line 6   calls the `Move` function of `myTurtle`, which causes the bottom line of the square to be drawn. After the execution of this statement, we see the line at right on the drawing board.

Line 7   calls the `Turn` function of `myTurtle`, which makes `myTurtle` point up (its initial heading is to the right) in preparation for drawing the right side of the square.

Line 8   draws the right side of the square. After the execution of this statement, we see the figure at right on the drawing board.

Line 9   turns `myTurtle` to the left.

Line 10 draws the top of the square. After the execution of this statement, we see the nearly completed square on the drawing board.

Line 11 turns `myTurtle` down.

Line 12 draws the left side. After the execution of this statement, we see the completed square on the drawing board.

Line 13 calls the `Done` function of `myTurtle` to terminate the drawing. All programs that use a `Turtle` object must include a call to the `Done` function at the end of drawing. If a program does not include a call to the `Done` function, the drawing board window will appear only for a moment and an execution error will occur. Also, no additional drawing will take place once a call to the `Done` function is made, which means that any turtle command you include after the `Done` statement will have no effect. A more detailed explanation of the `Done` function is given in chapter 12. For now, remember include a call to the `Done` function at the end of any program that uses a `Turtle` object.

Line 14 signals the end of the main function, which is also the end of program.

This program makes nine calls to the functions of `myTurtle`. We can represent the program as an object diagram, but the diagram is somewhat cluttered (see figure 2.18).

For all but the smallest programs, the number of function calls is too many to be usefully depicted in an object diagram. For this reason, individual function calls are not

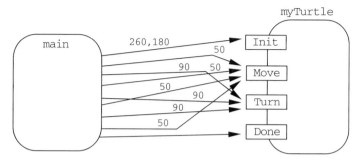

Figure 2.18 Cluttered object diagram

normally included as arrows in object diagrams. Instead of drawing an arrow for each function call, we draw only a single arrow from object A to B if object A makes any calls to object B, regardless of the number of calls made. With this convention, the previous object diagram now looks like the diagram in figure 2.19

For the remainder of the book we will use this simplified style for object diagrams. The remaining programs in this chapter all use a single Turtle object, and thus the diagram above will be the object diagram for all of the remaining sample programs in this chapter. We won't repeat this diagram for each program.

The turtle's drawing board is a window with a drawing space consisting of 612 × 433 dots, or *pixels* (picture elements), as shown in figure 2.20.

The pixels are arranged in 433 rows and 612 columns so that each pixel has a column number (x coordinate) and a row number (y coordinate). The coordinates of the upper-left pixel are (0,0) and the coordinates of the lower-right pixel are (611,432). The turtle draws on the drawing board by setting pixels to different colors. Initially all the pixels are white. When the turtle moves and its pen is down, it will set each pixel it moves across to the color of the pen. The pen is initially down, and its color is initially black. If we wish to start with a different color, then we have to set the pen's color by using the ChangePenColor function. Here are the descriptions of the primary functions of the Turtle. (A complete listing is provided in the Appendix.)

Figure 2.19 Uncluttered object diagram

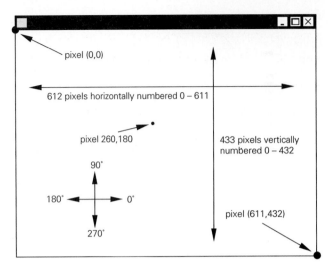

Figure 2.20 The turtle's drawing board

Init(x,y)	Opens the drawing board window and initializes the turtle by facing it to the right (i.e., 0 degrees) at pixel (x,y) with its pen down and pen color BLACK.
Move(distance)	Moves the turtle distance pixels in the direction it is currently facing. If the pen is down, the pixels it moves across are set to the current pen color. If the pen is up, then nothing is drawn.
Turn(angle)	Turns the turtle angle degrees counterclockwise.
TurnTo(angle)	Turns the turtle so that its heading becomes angle.
GoToPos(x,y)	Moves the turtle from its current position to pixel (x,y). Its heading does not change. If the pen is down, any pixels the turtle moves across changes to the current pen color.
PenUp()	Sets the turtle object's pen position up. If it is already up, then this function does nothing.
PenDown( )	Sets the turtle object's pen position down. If it is already down, then this function does nothing.
ChangePenColor(clr)	Changes the turtle object's pen color to clr. Possible values for clr are BLACK, BLUE, GREEN, CYAN, RED, MAGENTA, LIGHTGRAY, DARKGRAY, YELLOW, WHITE, DARKRED, DARKGREEN, DARKBLUE, DUSTYBLUE, PURPLE.

`Done()`	This statement is required at the end of the program to make the drawing board window remain on screen.
`GetXY(x,y)`	Returns the current coordinates of the turtle in x and y.

2.6 Sample programs using `turtle` objects

Here are some sample programs that use a `Turtle`. The first program draws a square much like the one drawn by the program `Square` except that it has `myTurtle` back up all the way. You can make a `Turtle` move backwards by using a negative distance in a call to `Move`. Moving backwards does not change the direction the turtle is heading.

```
// Program Square2: A program that draws the square backward.

#include "Turtles.h"

void main ( )
{
    Turtle myTurtle;

    myTurtle.Init(260,180);

    myTurtle.Move(-50);
    myTurtle.Turn(-90);

    myTurtle.Move(-50);
    myTurtle.Turn(-90);

    myTurtle.Move(-50);
    myTurtle.Turn(-90);

    myTurtle.Move(-50);

    myTurtle.Done();
}
```

Do you notice the difference between the square drawn by the first square program and the one above? (They are in different positions on the drawing board.)

The next program also draws the same square but at a different position. The program uses the `GoToPos` function four times (the `myTurtle` object's heading does not change).

```
//Program Square3:  A program that draws the square with
//                  the GoToPos functions.

#include "Turtles.h"

void main ( )
```

```
{
    Turtle myTurtle;

    myTurtle.Init(260,180);

    myTurtle.GoToPos(310,180);
    myTurtle.GoToPos(310,230);
    myTurtle.GoToPos(260,230);
    myTurtle.GoToPos(260,180);

    myTurtle.Done();
}
```

The final program uses the PenUp, Pen-Down, TurnTo, and Turn functions to draw a house (see figure 2.21). After drawing the bottom square, the Turtle draws a roof by moving into a position without drawing. The numbered arrows show the order in which the Turtle draws the lines of the house.

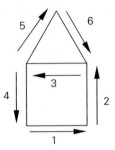

Figure 2.21 House with roof

```
//Program House: A program that draws a simple house.

#include "Turtles.h"

void main ( )
{
    Turtle t;

    t.Init(260,180);

    // Draw the bottom square
    t.Move(50); t.Turn(90);
    t.Move(50); t.Turn(90);
    t.Move(50); t.Turn(90);
    t.Move(50);

    //Reposition t for the roof
    t.PenUp(); //don't draw while repositioning
    t.GoToPos(260,130);
    t.TurnTo(60);
    t.PenDown();

    //Now draw the roof
    t.Move(50); t.Turn(-120);
    t.Move(50);

    t.Done();
}
```

CHAPTER 2 STARTING TO PROGRAM

The house program illustrates several new concepts. First, we have not used a descriptive identifier such as `myTurtle` to name a `Turtle` object. In this program we used a simple nondescriptive `t`. Because it is very short, the use of a single-letter identifier does not make the program any less readable. The key objective is to make a program readable and understandable, and using descriptive names is just a means for achieving that objective. As long as the use of nondescriptive identifiers does not make a program any harder to read, the practice is acceptable. In some cases, nondescriptive identifier may be preferable, for example, using `x`, `y`, and `z` to store the length of the three sides of a triangle rather than using the more "descriptive" identifiers `side1length`, `side2length`, and `side3length`. You have to use your good judgment in determining which approach will make a program more readable and understandable.

Second, we put two statements on a single line.

```
t.Move(50); t.Turn(-120);
```

C++ doesn't require statements be on separate lines. The semicolon signals the end of a statement. However, if statements are jammed together, several to a line, a program can be very hard to read. We nearly always put just one statement on each line for readability, but sometimes the program is more readable if we place logically related statements in one line. Here again, the key objective is to make a program more readable, so you should use your good judgment to determine which way is better.

The roof of the house is drawn by using the geometric rule for an equilateral triangle—a triangle with all three sides having the same length and all angles having 60 degrees. You can try different geometric figures for drawing more interesting houses in exercise 8 on page 45.

2.7 Object behavior

B. F. Skinner, a Harvard psychologist, was famous for his work in behaviorism. According to Skinner, humans are nothing but machines that exhibit well-defined responses to environmentally controlled stimuli. His work in operant conditioning showed that animals modify their behavior to adapt to new stimuli. We can easily imagine a live turtle being conditioned to move forward for five steps in response to a green light. Its behavior can be modified readily to move backward instead if a proper reward is associated to a new behavior.

Similar to a live turtle, our virtual turtle also exhibits well-defined behavior. Our virtual turtle, of course, is not capable of learning new behavior or adapting behavior on its own (at least not with our current state of computer science). In the case of virtual turtles and other computer objects, their behaviors are defined by the set of functions we attach to those objects. Remember that we have defined functions such as Move, Turn, TurnTo, PenUp, and so forth to tell the turtle objects what to do. If we view the the calling of functions as an external stimulus, then these functions dictate well-defined responses to the stimuli. Thus the attached functions collectively define the object's behavior. When we add new functions or modify the existing functions, we change the object's behavior.

In addition to the set of functions, another aspect of objects also affects their behavior. Consider an animal a little more intelligent than a turtle. For instance, a monkey may respond differently to the same stimulus depending on whether it is hungry. In other words, its state of being affects its behavior. As another example, consider a turtle with its legs tied. The turtle will not (cannot) respond to the stimuli in the same manner as when its legs are not tied. Just as live animals have different states, our computer objects also have different states. Our virtual turtle, for example, could be in the state of heading north with the pen down. Receiving a command in different states would result in a different response; for example, Move(40) draws a different line at a different location depending on the state of the turtle. A computer object has a set of attributes to keep track of its state. A turtle, for example, has attributes such as heading, pen color, pen status, and so forth. The set of values for these attributes determines the state of a turtle.

Some functions modify the attributes, thus affecting the state of an object. For a Turtle object, functions such as Turn and TurnTo change the direction, PenUp and Pen-Down change the pen status, and ChangePenColor changes the pen color. Other functions elicit a response from an object, but do not affect the object's state. An example is GetXY, which simply returns the values and makes no change to the state of a turtle.

For review, let's describe the GUI Object OKBox by giving its attributes and functions. An OKBox has three attributes that collectively make up its state. They are display status (whether it is displayed), the text it displays, and its size. All three attributes of an OKBox object's state may change when its only function, Display, is called. Its display

Note **Computer objects have no intelligence**

An object is described fully and completely by its associated functions and attributes. Given the state of an object and a function call, we can determine unambiguously the behavior of the object. A set of attributes describe the state of an object, and a set of attributes and a set of functions collectively define the behavior of an object. Unlike living objects, who are intelligent enough to adapt to the environment and modify their behavior on their own, programmers must define computer objects unambiguously and precisely for them to work correctly. Computer objects work exactly as they are programmed. They have no intelligence.

status changes from "not displayed" to "displayed," the text being displayed changes to whatever argument is passed in the `Display` call, and its size changes to a dimension big enough to display the whole text. A user can change the OKBox's display status by clicking its OK button. This changes the display status from "displayed" to "not displayed."

2.8 Exercises

1   Write a program that displays your name and address in an OKBox.

2   Is there any difference between the two programs listed below? Draw object diagrams for both. Execute both versions and verify your answer.

```
void main ()                      void main ()
{                                 {
    OKBox msg;                        OKBox msg1, msg2;

    msg.Display("one");               msg1.Display("one");
    msg.Display("two");               msg2.Display("two");
}                                 }
```

3   What are the coordinates of the corners of the squares drawn by the first three turtle programs?

4   Show what the following programs will draw when they are executed. Try to figure out the anwers without actually executing the programs.

```
//Exercise A                      //Exercise B
#include "Turtles.h"              #include "Turtles.h"
void main ( )                     void main ( )
{                                 {
    Turtle t;                         Turtle t;
    t.Init(260,180);                  t.Init(260,180);

    t.Move(40); t.Turn(90);           t.Move(25);
    t.Move(30); t.Turn(-90);          t.GoToPos(260,135);
    t.Move(30); t.Turn(90);           t.GoToPos(285,135);
    t.Move(20); t.Turn(-90);          t.GoToPos(260,135);
    t.Move(20); t.Turn(90);           t.Done( );
    t.Move(10); t.Turn(-90);      }
    t.Move(10);

    t.Done( );
}
```

```
//Exercise C
#include "Turtles.h"
void main ( )
{
    Turtle t;
    t.Init(260,180);

    t.Move(5);  t.Turn(90);
    t.Move(10);t.Turn(90);
    t.Move(15);t.Turn(90);
    t.Move(20);t.Turn(90);
    t.Move(25);t.Turn(90);
    t.Move(30);t.Turn(90);
    t.Move(35);t.Turn(90);
    t.Move(40);t.Turn(90);

    t.Done( );
}
```

5 For each of the programs in exercise 4, determine the state of the Turtle object at the time the Done function is called. Give the values for its heading, pen color, pen state (up or down), angle, and position.

6 When you executed Program Square in Section 2.5, you saw the result immediately. You can slow down the turtle to see how the shape is drawn by using the function SlowDown() as shown in the following code.

```
#include "Turtles.h"
void main ( )
{
    Turtle myTurtle;
    myTurtle.Init(260,180);

    myTurtle.SlowDown();

    // Do the drawing here.

    myTurtle.Done();
}
```

Modify the program to verify that the program in fact draws the square as explained in the text.

7 Write programs to draw each of the following shapes.

8 Write a program to draw houses of various shapes. Some of the possible shapes are

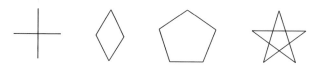

9 We can draw a tree by changing the shapes of the basic components of the house we drew in this chapter. By changing the square to a rectangle and the equilateral triangle to an isosceles triangle (two equal sides), we have a tree (a rather primitive one, but a tree nonetheless). Write a program to draw a tree.

10 After completing the program for drawing a tree in Exercise 9, it is time to write a program that draws a Chinese character for a tree.

11 A book consists of (printed) papers, and the papers are produced from trees. Write a program that draws a Chinese character for a book. (Is it our imagination that the horizontal bar symbolizes a saw cutting down a tree?)

chapter 3

Numerical data

In 1942, John P. Eckert, John W. Mauchly, and their associates at the Moore School of Electrical Engineering of the University of Pennsylvania built the first fully electronic digital computer (the earlier ones were electromechanical types based on mechanical switches) known as ENIAC, for Electrical Numerical Integrator And Calculator. At the height of World War II, new weapons were developed, but the trajectory tables and other data necessary to operate these weapons systems were lacking. ENIAC was built to create such trajectory tables. Once the power of the computer was realized, it did not take long for computers to be used in nonnumerical applications. Large corporations and government agencies started using computers for data processing. Data processing refers to what might be called clerical work—filing, posting, or record keeping.

In numerical or data processing applications, the notion of data is very important. Every computer program that does something meaningful will use some kind of data. Numerical applications manipulate numerical data such as integers and real numbers, while data processing applications manipulate other types of data such as employee and inventory records. In this chapter, you will learn how to use numerical data in C++ programs.

3.1 Constants and variables

Every computer program, even the simple ones given in Chapter 2, use data. (Of course, a program that does nothing may not use any data, but we're not interested in such a program.) The simplest kind of data is a constant, which as the name suggests, is a data value that remains unchanged. One kind of constant data we have seen in the sample programs is a *literal constant*. Let's look again at the sample program that draws a square.

```
// Program Square:  A program that draws a square.

#include "Turtles.h"

void main ( )
{
    Turtle myTurtle;

    myTurtle.Init(260,180); // Start from location 260,180.

    myTurtle.Move(50); // Draw the bottom of the square.
    myTurtle.Turn(90); // Turn to draw the right side.

    myTurtle.Move(50); // Draw the right side.
    myTurtle.Turn(90); // Turn to draw the top.

    myTurtle.Move(50); // Draw the top.
    myTurtle.Turn(90); // Turn to draw the left side.

    myTurtle.Move(50); // Draw the left side.

    myTurtle.Done();
}
```

The numeric arguments 260, 180, 50, and 90 are literal constants (to be precise, they are literal integer constants). They are constants because their values do not change, and they are literal because we "literally" specify their constant data values instead of using some kinds of identifiers.

The program above always draws a square 50 pixels in size. Suppose we wanted to draw squares of different sizes. We could certainly change the numbers in the calls to the Move function before running the program, but this method is inconvenient. We would end up changing values for all four calls to the Move function every time we wanted to draw a square with a different size. We could reduce the number of places to be modified by using a *named*, or *symbolic, constant*. Here's the modified program Square with a named constant.

```
// Program Square4:   A program that draws a square
//                     whose side has the length of size.

#include "Turtles.h"

void main ( )
{
    const int size = 50;// Use the named constant size.

    Turtle myTurtle;

    myTurtle.Init(260,180); // Start from location 260,180.

    myTurtle.Move(size);   // Draw the bottom of the square.
    myTurtle.Turn(90);     // Turn to draw the right side.

    myTurtle.Move(size);   // Draw the right side.
    myTurtle.Turn(90);     // Turn to draw the top.

    myTurtle.Move(size); // Draw the top.
    myTurtle.Turn(90);     // Turn to draw the left side.

    myTurtle.Move(size); // Draw the left side.

    myTurtle.Done();
}
```

The statement

```
const int size = 50;
```

declares that `size` is an integer constant whose value is 50. Notice the use of the reserved words `const` and `int` for declaring a constant data value of type integer. The named constant `size` is used in four different places in the program. By using this named constant, whenever we want to run the program again with another value for the size of a square, the only statement we have to modify is the constant declaration statement.

Although the use of a named constant improves the situation somewhat, drawing many squares of different sizes is still a chore. Imagine trying out squares of different sizes until you find the one you like. You may end up going through the edit-compile-run cycle 20 or 30 times. In fact, the real use of a named constant is mainly for good documentation. For example, using the named constant `PI` throughout the program is more meaningful than repeating the literal constant 3.14 over and over.

A program that requires us to edit and compile again for each new value is not very useful. To make the program more useful, we need an input statement that gets a value for the size of a square. This statement eliminates the need for editing and compiling the program for each new value of the square size. Here is an improved program that uses a new GUIobject called `IntTypeIn` for getting a value.

```
// Program AnySquare:   A program that draws a square of
//                      any size.

#include "Turtles.h"
#include "GUIObj.h"

void main ( )
{
    int size;
    IntTypeIn inputBox;// object for getting input
    Turtle myTurtle;

    myTurtle.Init(260,180); // Start from location 260,180.

    //Get the square size from the user.
    size = inputBox.GetInt("Square Size",
                           "Enter the square size");

    myTurtle.Move(size);  // Draw the bottom of the square.
    myTurtle.Turn(90);    // Turn to draw the right side.

    myTurtle.Move(size);  // Draw the right side.
    myTurtle.Turn(90);    // Turn to draw the top.

    myTurtle.Move(size);  // Draw the top.
    myTurtle.Turn(90);    // Turn to draw the left side.

    myTurtle.Move(size);  // Draw the left side.

    myTurtle.Done();

}
```

The object diagram for this program is shown in figure 3.1.

The identifier size is not a constant anymore; it is a *variable*. The declaration statement

```
int size;
```

declares that size is the name for a variable of type int (integer). Instead of saying "a size is the name for a variable of integer type," we say "a size is an integer variable."

A variable is very similar to a constant[*] in many ways (notice that the calls to the Move functions are the same in both programs) except for one big difference. Whereas a

---

[*] From now on, we will use the words *constant* for a named constant and *literal* for a literal constant.

value assigned to a constant remains fixed, a value assigned to a variable can change. In other words, the value assigned to a variable can vary—thus the name *variable*. A value assigned to a variable, however, cannot be of any value—it is restricted to a value of a declared type. In the program AnySquare, for example, the identifier `size` is declared to be an integer variable, so it can assume any integer value.

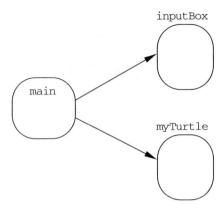

Figure 3.1 Program AnySquare object diagram

Let's get back to our sample program. Every time the program is executed, it gets a new value from the user via the `IntTypeIn` object `inputBox`. When the function `GetInt` of `inputBox` is invoked by the statement

```
inputBox.GetInt("Square Size", "Enter the square size");
```

the message box shown in figure 3.2 appears on the screen.

The `inputBox` object waits for the user to enter a value. When the value is entered and the OK button is clicked, `inputBox` disappears from the screen. The value entered is then assigned to the variable `size` by the assignment statement

```
size = inputBox.GetInt("Square Size","Enter the square size");
```

If the user enters 10, for example, the above statement is equivalent to stating

```
size = 10;
```

The diagram in figure 3.3 summarizes how the `GetInt` function works.

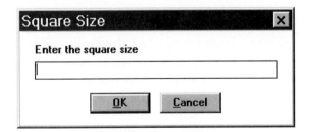

Figure 3.2 Square size message box

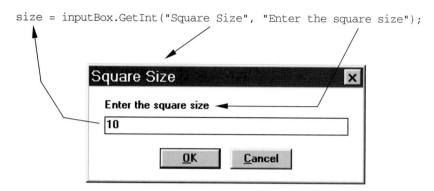

```
size = inputBox.GetInt("Square Size", "Enter the square size");
```

Figure 3.3 Screen result of GetInt function

When you click the Cancel button, the entered value is erased and `inputBox` remains on the screen. When you enter invalid data (a noninteger value or no value at all) and click the OK button, an error message is displayed. Again, `inputBox` remains on the screen. The only way to close an `IntTypeIn` object, that is, to make it disappear from the screen, is to enter an acceptable value and click the OK button.

A C++ function is very much like an ordinary mathematical function because it returns the result from a given number of arguments. However, a C++ function is not limited to returning numerical values—it can return any valid C++ data value, including objects. In addition, a C++ function does not even have to return a value. None of the functions we have seen so far, other than `GetInt`, in fact, returned a value. They were all void functions.

An integer value entered by the user is assigned to the variable `size`, and then this value is passed to the function `Move` in the statement

```
myTurtle.Move(size)
```

If the user enters 10 and clicks the OK button, the square would be as in figure 3.4. If the number 150 is entered instead, then the square would be as in figure 3.5.

By incorporating an input routine and using a variable, we have made a significant improvement to the program. With this improved program, we do not have to modify the program to draw squares of different sizes. Editing and compiling the program for each new value for the square's size is no longer necessary. We only must execute the program to draw a square of a different size.

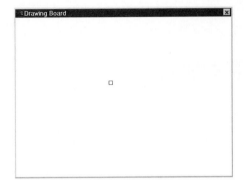

Figure 3.4 Square when user enters 10

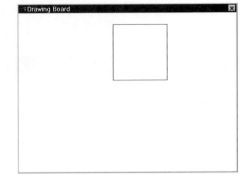

Figure 3.5 Square when user enters 150

3.2 Integers

The program AnySquare introduced the notions of integer values and data types. In this section, you will learn more about them. We will cover data types for real numbers in section 3.4, and other data types later in the book.

As explained earlier, we must declare each variable and constant we use in a C++ program. We declare a variable by designating its name (identifier) and type, and we declare a constant by designating its name, type, and value. In declaring a variable, we can also assign an initial value to it. Let's look at some examples.

```
int          x = 435;
const int    v = 123;
long         y = 25310, z, w;
```

The first declaration declares the identifier x as an integer variable with the initial value of 435. Since x is a variable, its value can change later in the program. The second declaration declares the identifier v as an integer constant whose value is 123. The last declaration declares three integer variables y, z, and w. The variable y is also initialized to the value 25310. The type long (or equivalently, long int) is used to represent a larger integer value. The following table describes the various data types for storing integers.

Simple operations such as addition, subtraction, multiplication, and division can be performed on integers. The following example illustrates an arithmetic computation involving integer values. Suppose we want to draw a square of a given size and position it at the center of a window. To do so, the program must first move the turtle to the correct position before drawing the square as shown in figure 3.6.

Table 3.1 Integer data type with varying range of values

Data Type	Explanation
`int`	An integer value ranging from –32,768 to 32,767. Uses 2 bytes.
`short`	Shorthand for `short int`. Normally equivalent to `int`, but could be different depending on the actual C++ compiler.
`long`	Shorthand for `long int`. An integer value ranging from –2,147,483,648 to 2,147,483,647. Uses 4 bytes.

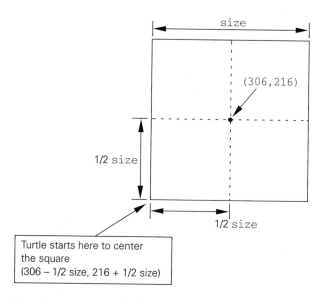

Figure 3.6 Positioning of turtle in program

The following program does the correct positioning by initializing the `turtle` one half the size of the square to the left of the window's center and one half the size of the square below the window's center. The coordinates for the center are 306 and 216. Here is the complete program:

```
// Program AnySquare2:  A program that draws a square of any size
//                      at the center of the window.

#include "Turtles.h"
#include "GUIObj.h"

void main ( )
{
    int size;      // size of a square
```

```
IntTypeIn inputBox;
Turtle myTurtle;

//Get the size from the user
size = inputBox.GetInt("Square Size",
                        "Enter the square size");

myTurtle.Init(306 - size/2, 216 + size/2);
// Initialize a turtle to correct
// starting point so the square is centered.

myTurtle.Move(size);   // Draw the bottom of the square.
myTurtle.Turn(90);     // Turn to draw the right side.

myTurtle.Move(size);   // Draw the right side.
myTurtle.Turn(90);     // Turn to draw the top.

myTurtle.Move(size); // Draw the top.
myTurtle.Turn(90);     // Turn to draw the left side.

myTurtle.Move(size); // Draw the left side.

myTurtle.Done();
}
```

Its diagram is shown in figure 3.7.

Can you see the differences between the modified program and the one given earlier in this chapter? First, the Turtle isn't initialized until after the call to GetInt. Second, the call to Init has arithmetic expressions as its arguments, as shown in figure 3.8.

These expressions represent the (x,y) coordinates to which the Turtle is initialized. C++ arithmetic expressions are made up of operators (like - and /) and operands

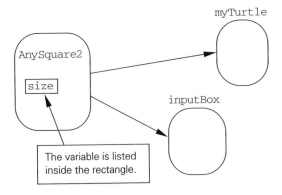

Figure 3.7 Program AnySquare2 diagram

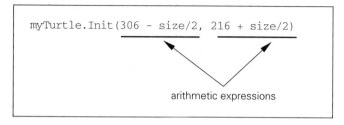

myTurtle.Init(306 - size/2, 216 + size/2)

arithmetic expressions

Figure 3.8 Init's arithmetic expressions

(like 306, size, 2, and 216). An operator tells what action to perform on operands. An arithmetic expression, when evaluated, results in a value. Evaluating a C++ arithmetic expression is just like evaluating an expression in ordinary mathematics. For example, if AnySquare2 is executed and a user enters 150 as the size of the square, the expression

        306 - size/2

will be evaluated as 231 (306 - 150/2 = 306 - 75 = 231). The division operator / will return the quotient portion only—no remainder or fractional value—if both operands are of type int. The division operation that involves only integers is called an *integer division.*

    The C++ arithmetic operators for integer operands are shown in table 3.2. The examples assume that x and y are integer variables having values 10 and 3, respectively. The following rules explain how to combine operators and operands to formulate valid C++ arithmetic expressions (limited to integer operands):

• Operands may be integer constants (e.g., 12, 77, or 1), integer variables (e.g., i, size, or n) or other arithmetic expressions possibly enclosed in parentheses (e.g., (size + 5) or (n - 2)).

Table 3.2 C++ arithmetic operators for integer data

Operator	Description	Example expression	Expression value (x=10; y=3)
+	addition	x + y	13
–	subtraction	x - y	7
*	multiplication	x * y	30
/	quotient division (integer)	x / y	3
%	modulo division — remainder after division	x % y	1
–	unary minus	- y	- 3
+	unary plus	+ y	3

- All binary operators (=, -, *, /, %) must have an operand on either side. They are called binary operators because they require two operands.

- A unary operator must have an operand to its right. Thus, -3 is a valid arithmetic expression but 3- is not.

- Parentheses must match—left parentheses must have matching right parentheses. For example, (3 + 5) is valid while (3 + (5 - 3)) is not.

Syntax rules for the C++ arithmetic expressions will be given in section 3.4, after the float data type is explained.

C++ uses an assignment operator for assigning a value to a variable. This operator is the equal symbol, and the general format is

```
variable = value
```

where value is any expression that results in a value when evaluated. Here are some examples:

```
x = 2;
y = x + 3;
z = x * y - 4;
```

When these three statements have been executed, the variables x, y, and z will have values 2, 5, and 6, respectively. Now consider the statement

```
x = x + 6;
```

The same variable x appears on both sides of the assignment. The execution of this statement results in adding the value 6 to the value of x and assigning the sum back to the same variable x. If the value of x was 3 before the execution, then after the execution the variable x will hold the value 9. The assignment statement in effect increments the value of x by 6 in this example—the old value of 3 is overwritten by the newly computed value of 9. In writing computer programs, we frequently encounter situations where we increment or decrement the value of a variable by a certain amount. We will be seeing more of this type of statement in chapter 5.

Another convenient usage of the assignment operator allows us to cascade the operators to assign a value to multiple variables. If we want to set the variables x, y, and z to 5, instead of stating

```
x = 5;
y = 5;
z = 5;
```

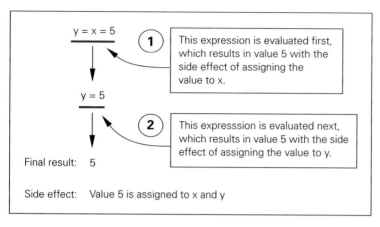

Figure 3.9 Cascaded assignment operator

we could state

    z = y = x = 5;

Some readers may note that the above does not seem to follow the general format

    variable = value

mentioned earlier. It seems like a violation, but it is not. How do the cascaded assignment operators follow the general format? An expression is a sequence of operands and operators, composed according to the prescribed syntax rules. Since assignment is an operator, the statement

    x = 5;

for example, is an expression. That is, it results in a value when evaluated.

It may not be obvious, but the expression containing the cascaded assignment operators is really the same as the preceding expression. The only difference is that the cascaded expression has the *side effect* of assigning a value to a variable. Figure 3.9 shows how we interpret cascaded assignment operators.

The body of a C++ function contains a sequence of statements, with each statement terminated by a semicolon. Every expression is a statement, so we can say something like:

    . . .
    int x;

```
OKBox msgBox;

x = 4 + 5;          ┌─────────────────────────────┐
msgBox.Display(x);  │ This line is an expression, and │
                    │ therefore, a valid statement.  │
  . . .             └─────────────────────────────┘
```

In fact, the following is a perfectly valid C++ program:

```
void main()
{
    4 + 5;
}
```

It won't do much, but it is still a valid C++ program because 4 + 5 is an expression, and therefore, a C++ statement. Although every expression is a statement, not every statement is an expression; that is, not every statement, when evaluated, will result in a value. Only certain types of statements will result in values when evaluated. You will learn more about different types of C++ statements in the remainder of this book.

When an arithmetic expression has more than one operator, the result depends on the order in which the operators are evaluated. For example, the expression

```
5 + 2 * 4
```

could be evaluated to 28 or to 13, depending on whether the addition or the multiplication is performed first. C++ defines an *operator precedence*, which determines the order of evaluating operations, so an expression is evaluated precisely in one way. C++ follows this operator precedence:

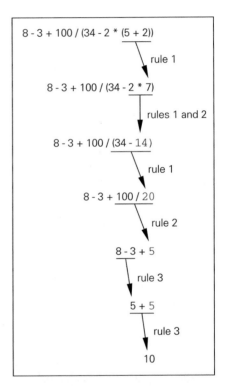

Figure 3.10 Example of how precedence rules are applied

- Subexpressions enclosed in parentheses are evaluated before operators outside the parentheses are evaluated.

- The operators are grouped into five categories. The highest category contains the unary operators. The second category has multiplicative operators (`*`, `/`, and `%`), the third category has additive operators (`+` and `-`), and the last category has assignment operators. Operators in the higher categories are applied before those in a lower category, unless parentheses dictate otherwise (see rule 1).

- In the absence of parentheses, if two operators are from the same category, then the operators are evaluated from left to right, except for the assignment and unary operators, which are evaluated from right to left.

Figure 3.10 illustrates the precedence rules.

We must know the precedence rules to read other programmers' code. However, when we write an arithmetic expression ourselves, we should use parentheses and not rely on the precedence rules. The use of parentheses makes the order of evaluation explicit, so it eliminates the need to remember the precedence rules in detail.

C++   **Unique C++ shorthand operators**

An expression such as

```
x = x + 6
```

can become quite tedious to write, especially when the identifier is long. The expression can be written more concisely in C++ as

```
x += 6
```

The following table lists other shorthand assignment operators

Normal expression	Shorthand expression
x = x + 5	x += 5
x = x - 5	x -= 5
x = x * 5	x *= 5
x = x / 5	x /= 5
x = x % 5	x %= 5

Two other shorthand operators are the increment/decrement operators. In computer programs, incrementing or decrementing a variable by 1 (`+1` or `-1`) happens very frequently. Using the ordinary expression, the increment and decrement operations are expressed as

```
y = y + 1
```

and

```
y = y - 1
```

In C++, you can use the shorthand

```
++y     or    y++
```

for incrementing and

```
--y     or    y--
```

for decrementing.

If you do not use the increment/decrement operator within another expression (including assignment), then the prefix (the operator before the variable) and postfix (the operator after the variable) versions are the same. If the increment/decrement operator is used within another expression, then you must be aware when the increment or decrement operations occur. The prefix version increments (or decrements) the variable and then its value is used. The postfix version, on the other hand, uses the value first and then increments (or decrements) the variable. For example, consider the following example. Executing the following two statements results in assigning the value 10 to x.

```
y = 10;
x = y++;
```

Executing the following two statements, on the other hand, results in assigning the value of 11 to x.

```
y = 10;
x = ++y;
```

The precedence of increment and decrement operators is between the unary (the first category) and multiplicative operators (the second category).

3.3 Sample programs using integers

With our newly acquired knowledge of integers, let's write a program that draws an equilateral parallelogram given values for the length of the sides and the angle between the base and the right side, as illustrated in figure 3.11.

```
// Program Parallelogram:  A program that draws a parallelogram
//                         of length and angle.

#include "Turtles.h"
#include "GUIObj.h"

void main ( )
{
    int length, angle;
    IntTypeIn inputBox;
```

```
        Turtle  myTurtle;

        myTurtle.Init(306,216); // Start from the center.

        //Input the data from the user
        length = inputBox.GetInt("Length", "Enter the length");
        angle  = inputBox.GetInt("Angle", "Enter the angle");

        myTurtle.Move(length);   // Draw the bottom.
        myTurtle.Turn(180 - angle); // Turn to draw the right side.

        myTurtle.Move(length);   // Draw the right side.
        myTurtle.Turn(angle);   // Turn to draw the top.

        myTurtle.Move(length); // Draw the top.
        myTurtle.Turn(180 - angle);   // Turn to draw the left side.

        myTurtle.Move(length); // Draw the left side.

        myTurtle.Done();
    }
```

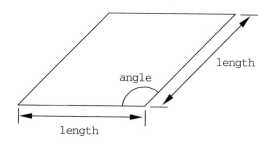

Figure 3.11 Equilateral parallelogram

The program diagram is shown in figure 3.12.

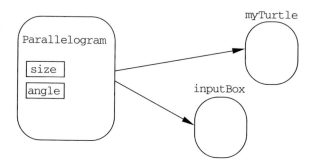

Figure 3.12 Diagram for parallelogram program

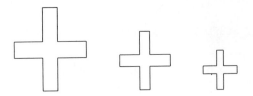

Figure 3.13 Plus signs

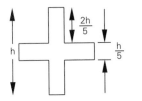

Figure 3.14 Plus sign dimensions

The next sample program will draw a plus sign like any of the ones in figure 3.13. We want our program to ask the user for the height of the plus sign, and then the program will calculate the lengths and widths of the legs. We'll assume that the width of each of the four legs of the plus sign should be one-fifth of the height. Therefore the length of each leg would be two-fifths of the height, as shown in figure 3.14.

The object diagram for the plus-sign program is shown in figure 3.15. The following is the program.

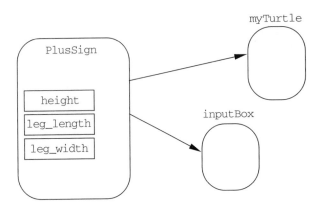

Figure 3.15 Plus sign program diagram

```
// Program PlusSign: A program that draws a plus sign.

#include "Turtles.h"
#include "GUIObj.h"

void main ( )
{
    int height, leg_length, leg_width;
    IntTypeIn inputBox;
    Turtle    myTurtle;

    myTurtle.Init(306,216); //starting point
```

```
//Get values from the user.
height = inputBox.GetInt("Length","Enter the height");

leg_width = height / 5;
leg_length = 2 * leg_width;

myTurtle.Move(leg_width);   // End of bottom leg
myTurtle.Turn(90);

myTurtle.Move(leg_length);   // Right side of bottom leg
myTurtle.Turn(-90);

myTurtle.Move(leg_length);   // Bottom of right leg
myTurtle.Turn(90);

myTurtle.Move(leg_width);    // End of right leg
myTurtle.Turn(90);

myTurtle.Move(leg_length);   //Top of right leg
myTurtle.Turn(-90);

myTurtle.Move(leg_length);   //Right side of top leg
myTurtle.Turn(90);

myTurtle.Move(leg_width);    //End of top leg
myTurtle.Turn(90);

myTurtle.Move(leg_length);   //Left side of top leg
myTurtle.Turn(-90);

myTurtle.Move(leg_length);   //Top of left leg
myTurtle.Turn(90);

myTurtle.Move(leg_width);    //End of left leg
myTurtle.Turn(90);

myTurtle.Move(leg_length);   //Bottom of left leg
myTurtle.Turn(-90);

myTurtle.Move(leg_length);   //Left side of bottom leg
myTurtle.Turn(90);

myTurtle.Done();
}
```

We could have written the program without using assignment operators. Instead of using the variables leg_width and leg_length, we could have used expressions as arguments in the Move calls. For example, each of the calls

```
myTurtle.Move(leg_width)
```

could have been written as

```
myTurtle.Move(height / 5)
```

and each of the calls

```
myTurtle.Move(leg_length)
```

could have been written as

```
myTurtle.Move(2 * height / 5)
```

We do not use this technique for at least three reasons. First, using the assignment operator means that we evaluate the expressions

```
height / 5 and 2 * leg_width
```

only once. The alternative approach evaluates the expression for the leg length

```
2 * height / 5
```

eight times and the one for the leg width

```
height / 5
```

four times. These redundant calculations may not be too significant in this little program but in some programs we can save considerable time if we calculate the values once, instead of recalculating them each time they are used.

Second, if we decide to change our program so that the legs of the plus sign are fatter or skinnier, then we need to modify the expressions for calculating the lengths and widths of the legs. In the program using assignment operators, the changes would have to be made only in the two assignment statements, but the alternative approach would require 12 changes in the 12 Move calls. It is always best to minimize the portions of a program that need to be modified.

Third, the assignment operators allow the use of meaningful identifiers, which will increase the program's readability. Even without the comment, we can tell that this statement

```
myTurtle.Move(leg_length)
```

draws the length of a leg. The meaning is not as obvious in a statement such as

```
myTurtle.Move(2 * height / 5)
```

As a general rule, when choosing names for variables, select descriptive names so the program can be as self-explanatory as possible. The only time we may not want to follow this general rule is when the use of nondescriptive names does not diminish the clarity of a program, as we did in the sample program House in Chapter 2. Remember that the key objective is to make programs readable and understandable, and although nondescriptive names are sometimes acceptable, descriptive names are in general better.

3.4 Real numbers

We have been using the int data type for dealing with integers. Let's now study additional data types for real numbers. Real numbers may include a fractional part, or decimal places, something that integers cannot. In C++, we have the data types float, double, and long double for representing real numbers. The word float is derived from the way the real numbers are stored in a computer, that is, in floating-point representation. The double and long double data types simply increase the number of bytes used for representing real numbers, thereby increasing the accuracy of the numbers represented. The actual number of bytes used for representing real numbers of different precision depends on the computer or compiler being used. It is typically 4 bytes for float, 8 bytes for double, and 10 bytes for long double. Table 3.3 describes the three data types for representing real numbers. Notice that the table lists the information most representative of all compilers; your compiler may have slightly different precisions. The way we declare real numbers is the same as for integers. Moreover, the syntax and semantics of arithmetic expressions involving real numbers are essentially identical to those of integers. As for the operators, applying the division operator / to real numbers will result in

Table 3.3 Data types for real numbers with varying range of values

Data type	Explanation
float	A real value with 7-digit precision ranging from 3.4×10^{-38} to 3.4×10^{38}. Uses 4 bytes.
double	A real value with 15-digit precision ranging from 1.7×10^{-308} to 1.7×10^{308}. Uses 8 bytes.
long double	A real value with 19-digit precision ranging from 3.4×10^{-4932} to 1.1×10^{4932}. Uses 10 bytes.

a real number. In addition, the modulo division operator %, that computes the remainder of a division, is not applicable to real numbers.

The result of division between two integers is an integer (with the fractional part truncated; e.g., 6 / 4 is 1), and the result of division between two real numbers is real (e.g., 6.0 / 4.0 is 1.5). What about the case when one of the operands is an integer and the other is a real? The result is a real. In other words, the integer is first converted to a real and then the operation is carried out. This is because the float has a higher precision than an int: converting an int to a float will not result in any loss of data, but converting a float to an int could cause data to be lost. The following statements cause the variable y to hold a float value of 1.5.

```
int i = 6;
float x = 4.0, y;

y = i / x;
```

An arithmetic expression that contains different data types is called a *mixed-mode expression*. A mixed-mode expression is evaluated by converting the data types of operands, so that the operations are carried out between the same data types. In the example above, the data type of the first operand i is converted to float and then the division operation is carried out between two float values. In mixed-mode expressions, a lower-precision data value is converted to the next higher precision data type. The ranking of data types, from high to low is long double, double, float, long int, int, and short. Figure 3.16 illustrates the evaluation of a mixed-mode arithmetic expression.

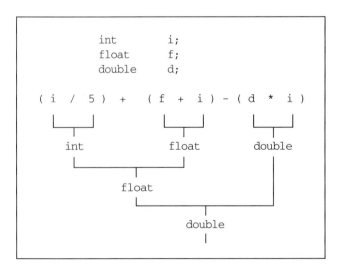

Figure 3.16 Evaluation of a mixed-mode arithmetic expression

To summarize the declarations and arithmetic expressions for integers and real numbers, we will list the syntax rules:

type-declaration-list
    type-declaration ;
    type-declaration   *type-declaration-list*

type-declaration
    type-specifier id-list
    `const` *type-specifier id-initializer-list*

type-specifier
    `int` | `short` | `long` | `short int` | `long int` |
    `float` | `double` | `double long`

id-list
    id-declarator
    id-declarator , *id-list*

id-declarator
    identifier initializer$_{opt}$
    id-initializer-list

    id-initializer
    id-initializer , *id-initializer-list*

id-initializer
    identifier initializer

initializer
    = *constant*

expression
    expression binary-operator expression
    identifier = *expression*
    term

term
> *factor*
> > − *expression*
> > + *expression*

factor
> (*expression*)
> *constant*

binary-operator
> + | − | * | / | %

The syntax category *constant* is any valid constant of data types for integers and real numbers (e.g., `short`, `int`, or `float`).

3.5 A sample program using real numbers

As an illustration of using real numbers, we will write a program to solve quadratic equations of the form

$$Ax^2 + Bx + C = 0$$

where the coefficients *A, B,* and *C* are real numbers. The two solutions are derived by the formula

$$x = \frac{-B \pm \sqrt{B^2 - 4AC}}{2A}$$

Depending on the values of the coefficients *A, B,* and *C,* we could have no real number solutions (i.e., the solutions are imaginary numbers), only one real number solution, or two real number solutions. We will worry about these situations when we learn about selection statements in Chapter 6. For now, we assume that

$$B^2 \geq 4AC$$

is true, so there will be either one or two real number solutions for x. Here is the program:

```
//Program Quad:      Find the two solutions for the quadratic
//                   equation Ax² + Bx + C = 0.

#include "GUIObj.h"
#include "math.h"

void main ()
{
    float A, B, C, x1, x2, sqrtOfDiscriminant;
    FloatTypeIn    floatInpBox;
    OKBox          msgBox;

    //get three inputs
    A = floatInpBox.GetFloat("INPUT","Type in value for A");
    B = floatInpBox.GetFloat("INPUT","Type in value for B");
    C = floatInpBox.GetFloat("INPUT","Type in value for C");

    //compute the sqrt of a discriminant and two solutions
    sqrtOfDiscriminant = sqrt( B*B - 4*A*C );
    x1 = (-B + sqrtOfDiscriminant) / (2 * A);
    x2 = (-B - sqrtOfDiscriminant) / (2 * A);

    //display the results
    msgBox.Display(x1);
    msgBox.Display(x2);
}
```

The program uses a new GUI object, FloatTypeIn, for inputting values of data type float. The function to accept an input value is GetFloat, whose functionality is analogous to the GetInt function. The only difference is whether an input value is an integer or a real number. For both functions the first argument is the title of the input box, and the second argument is the prompt inside the input box. The function sqrt, which is used to compute the discriminant, is a compiler-supplied function defined in the header file math.h.

Notice that we have used parentheses to dictate the order of computation in the program. We have not relied on the precedence rules for the arithmetic operators. We must be careful in writing the expressions, especially those involving the division operator. For instance, if we express the computation for x1 as

```
    x1 = (-B + sqrtOfDiscriminant) / 2 * A;
```

it may seem to be equivalent to the one used in the program, but it is not. The preceding statement computes

$$\frac{-B + \sqrt{B^2 - 4AC}}{2} \times A$$

If we write the expression mathematically, as shown here, we can see the difference very easily. However, in C++ and other programming languages, we write arithmetic expressions as a single line of text, which obscures differences. To avoid mistakes in stating arithmetic expressions, the order of evaluation should be made explicit by using parentheses.

A keen observer may have noticed that the program is somewhat inefficient when a given quadratic equation has only one solution, i.e., when $B^2 = 4AC$. In such cases, instead of computing both x1 and x2, which are equal, the program should compute only one of them. We will modify the program in chapter 6 so as to avoid the unnecessary computation.

3.6 Exercises

1 Modify each of the programs you wrote for exercise 7 on page 45 so the user can specify the size of the shape drawn by the program.

2 Write a program that accepts three integer values from the user. The first value will be the size of a square, and the other two will be the coordinates of the lower-left corner of the square. The program draws the square starting at the position indicated by the coordinates rather than at the center of the screen.

3 Tell whether each of the following variable declarations is syntactically correct. For those that aren't correct, tell why.

```
int x = y = 5;
Turtle int;
x,y,x int;
const long int y = 12345678;
int x = y + 5;
```

4 Write a program that draws an equilateral triangle centered in the window. The length of the side should be obtained from a user using an IntTypeIn object.

5 Suppose we have integer variables a, b, and c with values 3, 50, and 17, respectively. Tell whether each of the following 12 expressions is syntactically correct. For those that aren't correct, tell why. For those that are correct, give their values.

```
a + b - c            b / 6
2 * (b - c)          b % 6
2 (* b - c)          2 * b - c
a + b - c / 3        (a + b - c) / 3
a * / b c +          a b c
5 *   - a            7 *   + a
```

6 Assume that the integer variables a, b, and c have the values 3, 50, and 17, respectively. Tell whether each of the following 14 assignment statements is syntactically correct. If it is correct, state what values are assigned to the variables on the left of the assignment operator. The expressions with a special marker (†) use the operators discussed in the C++ sidebar on page 59. *Note:* statements are not executed in sequence; treat each statement individually.

```
a, b, c = 15;                    a = 25;

a = 2 * (b - c);                 a = a + 1;

int = a + b + c;                 25 = a + b;

a + b - c = a - c + b;           a = b = 4 / c;

b = a = c + 1 + 2;               b = (a = c + 1) + 2;

c = (b - a) * 2;                 a = 3 % b + --c;  (†)

c = b %= 6;  (†)                 b += 5;  (†)
```

7 Suppose we have the following declarations:

```
int        i = 15;
float      f = 4.56;
double     d = 8.99999;
```

Give the result and its data type for each of the following expressions.

```
i + f + d                  (i / 12) + 5

d / f * 15                 d / (f * 15)

i * d + f                  2 * f / d - i
```

8 Write a program that will accept a size from the user and then draw three squares centered in the drawing window. The sides of the first square will be size pixels long, the sides of the second will be three times longer, and the sides of the third will be five times longer, like this:

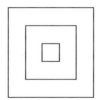

9 Modify the program PlusSign so that the plus sign is drawn at the center of the window. With the current program, the plus sign's left-bottom edge is at the center of the window. With the modified program, the center of the plus sign will be at the center of the window.

10 Modify the program PlusSign so that the width of each leg is one-ninth of the height.

11 Repeat exercise 8 on page 45, the program for drawing a house in various shapes. Use the techniques learned in this chapter to improve the program.

12 Write a program that draws a pine tree:

13 The area of a cylinder having radius r and height h can be computed by the following equation:

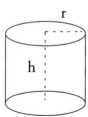

$$Area = \pi r^2 h$$

Write a program that computes the area of a cylinder given its radius and height as inputs. Use a FloatTypeIn object for getting two inputs and a float constant PI declared as

```
const float PI = 3.14159;
```

chapter 4

Character-based input and output

In chapters 2 and 3, we introduced three GUI objects—OKBox, IntTypeIn, and Float-TypeIn. We used these objects for rudimentary input and output operations. We will be seeing additional GUI objects for handling more elaborate user interfaces later in the book. We use GUI objects for managing the user interface of a window-based program that contains windows, menus, dialogs, buttons, and so forth. GUI objects, however, are not the only objects that can handle the user interface of a program. An alternative user interface to a program uses the predefined istream and ostream objects for input and output.

The predefined ostream object cout is for displaying the output of a program, and the predefined istream object cin is for getting input into a program. Both of these objects are already declared in a file that comes with the compiler, and therefore, we do not have to declare them explicitly in our program. We just have to include the header file iostream.h where these objects are declared. As we will see shortly, using cin and cout objects is very easy. The downside is that the program will not have a graphical interface like the one we expect from any window-based commercial program. The cin

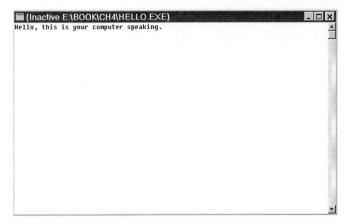

Figure 4.1 A cout window

and `cout` objects are for *character-based user interface* (CUI) in which output and input operations are done with characters only. For instance, with the `cout` object, we can output only characters (letters, digits, etc.), and with the `cin` object, we can input only characters. With the GUI objects, on the other hand, we are not limited to characters. We can, for example, write a program that outputs a bar chart graph (using a `Turtle` object). Similarly, with the `Menu` objects, we can write a program that accepts a user's command via the selection of menu choices. Notice that input is not necessarily restricted to entering data. A user's command to the program is considered to be an input to it. This type of command input (as opposed to data input) is done via characters with the CUI. Typing in the character *A* instructs the program to compute an average, and typing in *S* instructs the program to compute a sum, for example.

We must use some form of GUI objects if we wish to develop a program that supports a graphical user interface. Not all programs, however, require a GUI. For example, we may write a more computation-intensive program, such as inputting two or three values and performing an intensive numerical computation, which does not need a GUI. A CUI would suffice for this type of program. Another case for using a CUI is testing. Suppose we define an object that does some kind of numerical computation and wish to test it. A quick and easy way to do this is to use the CUI input and output routines, because they are much simpler to use than GUI objects. Setting an elaborate interface is not necessary if our purpose is only to test the object. In this chapter we will study a CUI input and output.

Because the CUI and GUI have completely different setup and programming models, they cannot coexist in the same program.[*] You cannot, for example, mix cout and IntTypeIn in the same program. Your program's interface supports either CUI (with cout and cin) or GUI (with our or somebody else's GUI objects), but never both.

4.1 Character-based output

Let's start our discussion with the predefined ostream object cout. The purpose of an ostream object is similar to the purpose of an OKBox object. Here is a sample program for displaying a simple message.

```
//Program Hello:  A simple program that displays a message
//                by using the standard ostream object cout.

#include <iostream.h>        ◄────   The brackets < and > are used to designate the
                                     header files that come with the compiler. All sys-
void main()                          tem header files are placed in the same directory.
{
    cout << "Hello, this is your computer speaking";
}
```

Executing the program will result in a window with the message displayed in it (see figure 4.1). We shall call this window a *cout window*.[†] You terminate the program by closing the cout window.

Let's analyze the program. The standard ostream and istream objects cout and cin are both defined in the header file iostream.h. Notice that we use brackets < and > to surround the header file name, instead of the double quotes we have been using so far. Instead of

```
#include "iostream.h"
```

---

[*] This restriction does not hold for the UNIX environment. The GUI objects for the UNIX version may be used in conjunction with cout and cin.

[†] The cout window that actually appears on the screen is bigger than the one shown in figure 4.1. It is resized so the image of the entire window fits the page smoothly. This comment holds for all other images of the cout window in this chapter.

we have

```
#include <iostream.h>
```

The only difference between the two is the directory where the compiler starts looking for the header file. If you surround a header file name with double quotes, then the compiler begins the search for the designated header file from the local directory where the file that contains this include statement is stored. If you surround a header file with brackets, then the compiler begins the search from the specific directory where all the system header files are stored. The *system header files*, such as iostream.h, come with the compiler. They are all placed in one directory, and most commonly this directory is named include. In either case, if the header file is not located in the first directory the compiler searches, it will look for the second directory. The search continues until the header file is found or no directory is left to be searched. The list of directories to be searched and the order in which they are searched depend on how we set the compiler option for searching the header files.

If only one header file has a given name, then format you use does not matter. The only difference is how quickly the compiler locates the designated header file. However, if two header files have the same name, then you have to make sure to include the right header file by using the correct format. For example, if you have two files with the name myHeader.h, one in the include directory and the other in the local directory, then you can specify which myHeader.h to include by stating #include "myHeader.h" or #include <myHeader.h>. Even if the programmer-defined header file does not have the

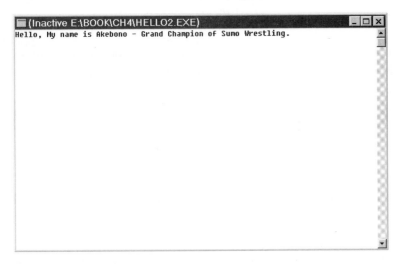

Figure 4.2 Hello2 cout window

same name as one of the system header files, the custom is to use the brackets for including the system header files, as we have done in the preceding sample program.

To output a value to cout, we use the output operator << (two less-than symbols put together). Whatever data we output to cout will be displayed on the cout window. One nice thing about cout is that the data we output remain on the cout window. Remember that when we use an OKBox for displaying a sequence of messages, the messages are displayed one at a time. In other words, an OKBox is capable of displaying a single piece of data value we pass to the Display function. When the next Display function is called with the next data value, only this new value is displayed. Also, you have to close the first window before the second window can appear on screen, as we saw in Chapter 2. An OKBox is intended solely for displaying a short message. With cout, however, a sequence of messages will stay on the window. (We will see a GUI object that has this capability later.)

Consider the following program, where we output four strings to cout in succession.

```
//Program Hello2: A program that displays messages using cout.

#include <iostream.h>

void main()
{
    cout << "Hello, ";
    cout << "My name is ";
    cout << "Akebono - ";
    cout << "Grand Champion of Sumo Wrestling.";
}
```

The cout window looks like figure 4.2. Notice how the four output values are placed together. The values sent to cout are simply appended to the previous output. So the following statements result in the same output.

```
cout << "Akebono ";
cout << "Taro";
```

and

```
cout << "Akebono Taro";
```

You may ask, "What if we desire to print the output values on separate lines?" In addition to sending an output of (printable) data, we can also send a nonprintable *control character* to the output. For example, if we want to print the four string values in the program Hello2 on four separate lines, we output the "new line" command endl (for *end line*) to cout as

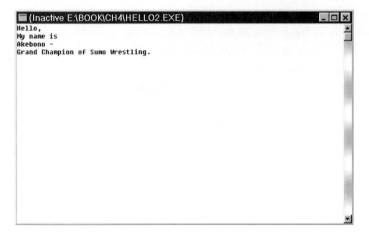

Figure 4.3 Printing output values on separate lines

```
cout << "Hello, " << endl;
cout << "My name is " << endl;
cout << "Akebono - " << endl;
cout << "Grand Champion of Sumo Wrestling.";
```

which results in the screen as shown in figure 4.3. The command endl is called a *manipulator* because it manipulates the appearance of output. We will learn more about other manipulators later in the section.

The output operator accepts any primitive data type, for example:

```
x = 5 + 7;
cout << x;
```

or more concisely

```
cout << 5 + 7;
```

Instead of using one output operator for each output value, such as

```
x = 145.67;
y = 3343.77
cout << x;
cout << y;
```

we can cascade the operators as

```
x = 145.67;
y = 3343.77;
cout << x << y;
```

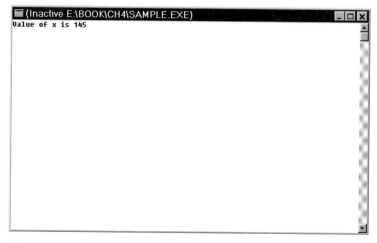

```
(Inactive E:\BOOK\CH4\SAMPLE.EXE)
Value of x is 145
```

Figure 4.4 Output of different types of data

Notice that both

```
cout << x;
cout << y;
```

and

```
cout << x << y;
```

produce the same result. Also, cascading of output operators is not limited to the same type of data. We can output different types of data. For example, we can say

```
cout << "Value of x is " << x
```

to get the result shown in figure 4.4.

To illustrate the use of cout, let's write a simple program that computes the volume of a triangular prism, shown in figure 4.5.

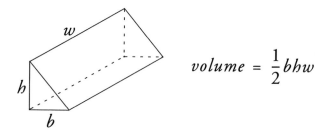

$$volume = \frac{1}{2}bhw$$

Figure 4.5 A triangular prism.

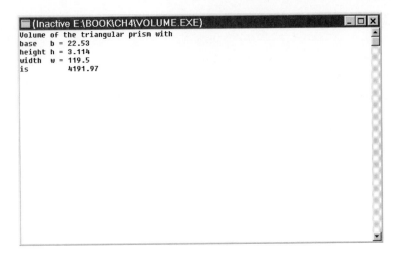

Figure 4.6 Result of triangular prism program

```
// Program Volume:   A program that computes the volume of
//                   a triangular prism using the formula
//                   (1/2) * b * h * w.

#include <iostream.h>

void main()
{
    float b = 22.53;
    float h = 3.114;
    float w = 119.5;
    float volume;

    volume = 0.5 * b * h * w;

    cout << "Volume of the triangular prism with" << endl;
    cout << "base   b = " << b << endl;
    cout << "height h = " << h << endl;
    cout << "width  w = " << w << endl;
    cout << "is         " << volume;
}
```

The spaces after the word is leave a wider margin before the value of volume is printed.

The output of the program is shown in figure 4.6.

4.2 Formatted output

Although the output of program Volume is correct, the numbers are not aligned neatly. We can use manipulators available in the header file `<iomanip.h>` to format the output so their decimal points are aligned. The following version of program Volume formats the output.

```
// Program Volume2:    A program that computes the volume of a
//                     triangular prism using the formula
//                     (1/2) * b * h * w and
//                     aligns the output values.

#include <iostream.h>
#include <iomanip.h>

void main()
{
    float b = 22.53;
    float h = 3.114;
    float w = 119.5;
    float volume;

    volume = 0.5 * b * h * w;

    cout <<  setiosflags(ios::fixed);
    cout <<  setprecision(3);

    cout << "Volume of the triangular prism with" << endl;

    cout << "base   b = " << setw(10) << b << endl;
    cout << "height h = " << setw(10) << h << endl;
    cout << "width  w = " << setw(10) << w << endl;
    cout << "is         " << setw(10) << volume;
}
```

Manipulators setprecision, setw, and others are defined in this header file.

The output of the program is shown in figure 4.7.

The manipulator `setw` (set width) determines the number of spaces occupied by the value that follows the `setw` manipulator. So, in the previous example, we are allocating ten positions for all four values. The function `setprecision` determines the number of decimal places for the values that follow the manipulator. In the above program, we are setting three decimal places. Since the whole width is 10, we have enough spaces to represent numbers up to 999999.999. There are six spaces for the whole part, three spaces for the fractional part, and one space for the decimal point. Notice that we have to specify `setw(10)` in front of all values because the `setw` command applies only to the

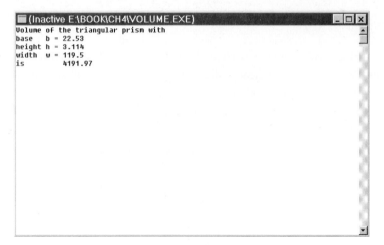

```
(Inactive E:\BOOK\CH4\VOLUME.EXE)
Volume of the triangular prism with
base    b = 22.53
height h = 3.114
width  w = 119.5
is        4191.97
```

Figure 4.7 Screen result with aligned decimal points

value that immediately follows it. The `setprecision` and all other manipulators apply to all of the values that come after the manipulators. Thus we have only one `setprecision` specified in the above program.

The manipulator `setiosflags` (set input and output stream flags) specifies various settings for the output values. There is one flag, or setting, specified in the program—`ios::fixed`. The flag `ios::fixed` forces all real numbers to be displayed with the fixed-point format; that is, all the numbers are displayed with the same number of decimal places. Let's discuss this and other flags with examples. Consider the statements

```
float x = 5.0, y = 21.5555;

cout << "[" << x << "]" << endl;
cout << "[" << y << "]" << endl;
```

Their output will be

```
[5]
[21.5555]
```

The decimal point did not appear for the x value, since the numbers are displayed in the floating-point format where the number of decimal places is not fixed. To display the decimal points, we set the `ios::fixed` flag as

```
cout << setiosflags(ios::fixed);
cout << "[" << x << "]" << endl;
cout << "[" << y << "]" << endl;
```

and now the output will be

```
[5.000000]
[21.555500]
```

All real numbers (`float`, `double`, `long double`) are displayed with six decimal places (six is the *default* value—a value preset by the compiler) after the `ios::fixed` flag is set. To change the default of six decimal places, we set the precision as

```
cout << setiosflags(ios::fixed);
cout << setprecision(3);
cout << "[" << x << "]" << endl;
cout << "[" << y << "]" << endl;
```

and now the output will be

```
[5.000]
[21.556]
```

Finally, we can align the decimal points (see figure 4.7) by specifying the width using the `setw` manipulator

```
cout << setiosflags(ios::fixed);
cout << setprecision(3);
cout << "[" << setw(8) << x << "]" << endl;
cout << "[" << setw(8) << y << "]" << endl;
```

and then the output will be

```
[   5.000]
[  21.556]
```

Table 4.1 summarizes the common manipulators defined in the header file `<iomanip.h>`.

4.3 Character-based input

We use the predefined `istream` object `cin` for getting input values into a program. The `cin` object accepts input values from the keyboard. So a user can see what has been entered, a program that uses the `cin` object will display the characters pressed on the keyboard as the value is entered. We call this process *echo printing*, and it appears on the cout

Table 4.1 Output format manipulators

Manipulators	Descriptions
setw(N)	Display the next value using N spaces. Default value is normally 1 for most compilers. When the value to be displayed requires more than the designated N spaces, the number will be displayed using the minimum spaces necessary to fully display the value.
setprecision(N)	Display the following values using N decimal places. Default value is normally 6 for most compilers.
setiosflags(FLAGS)	Set the flags in FLAGS, which is a list of flags separated by the vertical bar |. The following are the most common flags.

Flags	Descriptions
ios:: fixed	Display the value in fixed-point format.
ios:: scientific	Display the value in scientific notation.
ios:: left	Display the value left-justified in the allocated spaces.
ios:: right	Display the value right-justified in the allocated spaces.

window. The istream object cin accepts any primitive data type. The input operator >> (two greater-than symbols put together) is used with the cin object to input values.

Let's modify the program Volume from the previous section to illustrate the use of the cin object. Instead of having assigned values for the base, height, and width within the program, this program will read in those values.

```
// Program Volume3:   A program that computes the volume of
//                    a triangular prism using the formula
//                    (1/2) * b * h * w. The values for b, h,
//                    and w are read from the cin object.

#include <iostream.h>

void main()
{
    float b, h, w, volume;

    cin >> b; //read b,
    cin >> h; //       h,
    cin >> w; // and w

    volume = 0.5 * b * h * w;

    cout << "Volume of triangular prism with" << endl;
    cout << "base   b = " << b << endl;
    cout << "height h = " << h << endl;
    cout << "width  w = " << w << endl;
    cout << "is         " << volume;
}
```

These can be stated equally as
cin >> b >> h >> w;

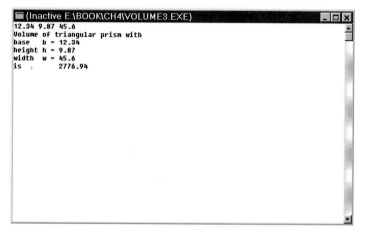

Figure 4.8 Screen result of Volume3 program

Figure 4.8 shows the result of executing the program with the input `12.34, 9.87,` and `45.6`.

Notice that the three inputs are separated by a single space and the <RETURN> key (also called <ENTER>) is pressed after the last number. The separator doesn't have to be a single space. You can put as many spaces as you wish between the numbers. Instead of spaces between the values, it is also acceptable to press the <RETURN> key (you may press more than once). The space and the <RETURN> key are called *separators* because they are used as markers to separate input values. In addition to separating input values, you may also enter any number of spaces and <RETURN> keys before the first number. If you press the <RETURN> key once after each number, then the window will look like figure 4.9.

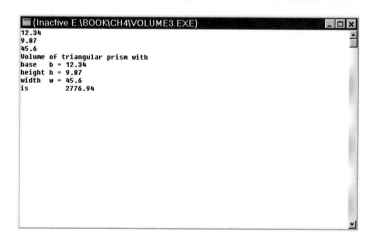

Figure 4.9 Screen with <RETURN>s after each number

Notice also that the three values must be entered in the proper sequence, since the first number read is assigned to the variable b, the second number to the variable h, and the last number to the variable w. Users can easily forget the proper order of entering the input values, thereby resulting in wrong answers. To avoid this problem,we recommend prompting the user with an appropriate message so that he or she knows which value to enter. We can modify the input portion of the above program with such prompts, in the following manner:

```
cout << "Enter the value for the base: ";
cin >> b;

cout << "Enter the value for the height: ";
cin >> h;

cout << "Enter the value for the width: ";
cin >> w;

cout << endl << endl; //insert two blank lines
```

We terminate the prompts with colons so the user can tell that the program is expecting a data value to be entered. Executing the modified program (and assuming that the <RETURN> key is pressed after entering each of the three inputs) will produce the window as shown in figure 4.10.

Just as we can cascade output operators for different data types in a single output statement, we can also cascade input operators for different data types in a single input statement. For example, the following code reads two integers and two real numbers.

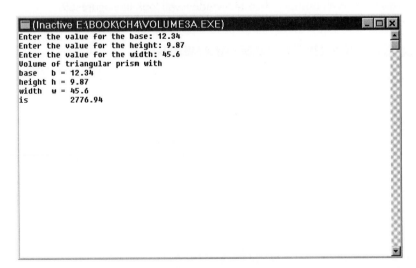

Figure 4.10 Output of Volume3 program with prompts

```
int i, j;
float x, y;
cin >> i >> x >> j >> y;
```

We must enter values in the sequence int, float, int, and float. Since we can assign an integer to a floating-point variable, entering four integer values would also be acceptable.

4.4 Sample program

We will end this chapter with a sample program for computing the sum and average of given real numbers. Since we have not yet mastered the technique necessary to write a program that will compute the sum and average of N real numbers for $N \geq 1$, we will restrict this program to 5 real numbers. (We will write a program that can compute the sum and average of any N real numbers in the next chapter.) The overall flow of the program for the restricted version is as follows:

1 Display the opening message.

2 Ask the user to enter five real numbers v, w, x, y, and z.

3 Compute the sum.

$$sum \ = \ v + w + x + y + z$$

4 Compute the average.

$$avg \ = \ \frac{sum}{5}$$

5 Print out the results.

Here is the complete program.

```
//Program Statistic:    A program that computes the sum and
//                      average of five real numbers.

#include <iostream.h>

void main()
{
    float v, w, x, y, z;
    float avg, sum;

    //opening message
```

```
      cout << "This program will compute the sum and average"
               << endl;
      cout << "of five real numbers you enter." << endl;
      cout << endl << endl;

      cout << "Now, please enter five numbers" << endl;
      cout << "Press the <Return> key after " << endl;
      cout << "you entered five numbers" << endl;

      cin >> v >> w >> x >> y >> z;

      //compute the sum
      sum = v + w + x + y + z;

      //compute the average
      avg = sum / 5;

      //print out the results
      cout << endl << endl;
      cout << "The sum is     " << sum << endl;
      cout << "The average is " << avg;
   }
```

4.5 Exercises

For all of the programming exercises, use the cin and cout objects for input and output.

1 Assuming the declarations

```
float F = 23.4567;
int   I = 675;
```

determine the output for the following statements:

a. cout << F << I;

b. cout << setprecision(5) << F << I;

c. cout << setprecision(10) << F << I;

d. cout << setioflags(ios:right) << setw(10) << F << I;

e. cout << setioflags(ios:right) << setw(10)
         << F << setw(10) << I

2 Assuming the declaration

```
float F = -123.45678;
```

experiment with the manipulators setw, setprecision, and setiosflags to see how these manipulators affect the negative real numbers.

3 Determine the values assigned to the variables I and F with the following statements. Assume the variables I and F are integer and float, respectively, and the input values

```
123    345.5
```

are entered. If the value cannot be assigned because of an error, explain the problem.

a. cin >> I >> F:

b. cin >> F >> I;

c. cin >> I;
    cin >> F;

d. cin >> F;
    cin >> I;

4 Write a program that reads in a temperature in degrees Celsius and prints out the temperature in Fahrenheit. The formula for this conversion is

$$F = \frac{9}{5}C + 32$$

5 The hypotenuse c of a right triangle can be determined from the smaller sides a and b of the right triangle using the Pythagorean Theorem:

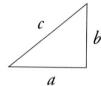

$$c = \sqrt{a^2 + b^2}$$

Write a program that accepts as inputs the lengths of the two smaller sides of a right triangle and prints out the hypotenuse of the triangle. The square root function sqrt is defined in the header file <math.h>.

6 The number of diagonals D in a polygon of N sides is given by the formula

$$D = \frac{1}{2}N^2 - \frac{3}{2}N$$

Example:

$$D = \frac{1}{2}(5)^2 - \frac{3}{2}(5)$$

$$= 12.5 - 7.5 = 5$$

> Diagonals are shown in the dotted lines.

Write a program that prints out the number of diagonals for a given polygon of N sides.

7 Write a program that reads the purchase price of an item and the cash payment amount and prints out the change in dollars, quarters, dimes, nickels, and pennies. Both the purchase price and the cash payment amount are entered as integer values in cents. For example, if the input is

```
1249    1500
```

then the output would be

```
Dollars:    2
Quarters:   2
Dimes:      0
Nickels:    0
Pennies:    1
```

(*Hint:* Use the integer division and remainder operations.)

8 Write a program that reads two integers and prints out their product in a format using commas. For example, if the input is

```
345    9864
```

then the output should be

```
3,403,080
```

(*Hint:* Print out the value in pieces, that is, print out 3, then comma, then 403, and so forth.)

9 Write a program that reads two positive three-digit integers and prints their product in the long format shown below. For the inputs 567 and 876, for example, the output would be

```
           567
   ×       876
   --------
          3402
         3969
        4536
   ---------
        496692
```

(*Hint:* Use the manipulators setw and setiosflags for formatting the output. Use the integer remainder and division operators to extract the multiplier's digits in the 100s, 10s, and 1s positions.)

chapter 5

Repetition control flow

When a computer executes a program, it executes the statements, one by one, in the sequence in which they appear in the program. This process is called *sequential control flow*. When a statement is being executed by the computer, we say that the statement has *control*. Thus control flows from statement to statement. However, to write a non-trivial program, sequential control flow is not enough. We need additional control flows. In this chapter we explain *repetition control flow*, a process that allows a program to execute a sequence of statements repeatedly. You will learn two other control flows in chapters 6 and 8.

5.1 Repetition control flow—for *loops*

The following program draws the pinwheel shown in figure 5.1.

```
// Program Pinwheel: A program to draw a pinwheel.

#include "Turtles.h"

void main ( )
```

```
{
    TurtlemyTurtle;

    myTurtle.Init (306, 216);

    myTurtle.Move(50); myTurtle.Move(-50); myTurtle.Turn(60);
    myTurtle.Move(50); myTurtle.Move(-50); myTurtle.Turn(60);
    myTurtle.Move(50); myTurtle.Move(-50); myTurtle.Turn(60);
    myTurtle.Move(50); myTurtle.Move(-50); myTurtle.Turn(60);
    myTurtle.Move(50); myTurtle.Move(-50); myTurtle.Turn(60);
    myTurtle.Move(50); myTurtle.Move(-50); myTurtle.Turn(60);

    myTurtle.Done();
}
```

Each of the six vanes of the pinwheel is drawn by one of the six lines that cause the turtle to move ahead 50 pixels, move back 50 pixels, and then turn 60 degrees.

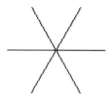

Figure 5.1 Pinwheel

Figure 5.2 Puffball

Consider modifying the program PinWheel by adding more lines so that the modified program draws the "puffball" shown in figure 5.2. The number of vanes in the puffball is 90. (We hope nobody really attempts to count them.) Therefore, a program for the puffball would need to repeat the following statements 90 times:

```
myTurtle.Move(50);
myTurtle.Move(-50);
myTurtle.Turn(4);   // Turn 4 degrees , 4 X 90 = 360
```

Although the program editor you are using may allow you to copy selected statements 90 times without too much effort, you must be wondering if there is an easier way to program a turtle to draw the puffball. The answer, of course, is "yes". Here is a puffball program that utilizes repetition control flow with a C++ for statement. The for statement is also called a *for loop*.

```
// Program Puffball:   A program to draw a puffball
//                     by using a for statement.
```

```
#include "Turtles.h"

void main( )
{
    TurtlemyTurtle;
    int count;

    myTurtle.Init(306, 216);

    for (count = 1; count <= 90; count = count + 1) {

        myTurtle.Move(50);
        myTurtle.Move(-50);
        myTurtle.Turn(4);

    } //end for

    myTurtle.Done();
}
```

These three statements are executed 90 times.

Let's study how the `for` statement works. Notice that it contains a sequence of three statements surrounded by curly braces. This sequence of statements is executed 90 times. The number of repetitions depends on how you specify the control expression of a `for` statement. When a `for` statement is encountered, the number of repetitions is determined as shown in figure 5.3.

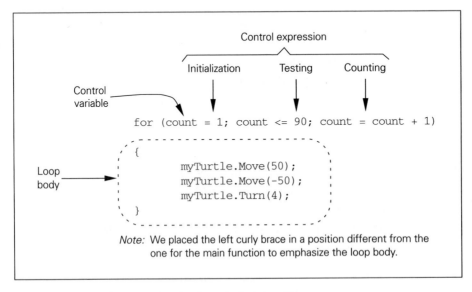

Figure 5.3 Repetition control expression of a for statement

1 The initialization expression is executed. You may put any valid C++ expression here, but we usually initialize the value of the control variable to some value. (In the expression above, the control variable count is initialized to 1.)

2 The testing expression is evaluated. If the testing expression evaluates to FALSE, then execution of the for statement is terminated; otherwise, the loop body is executed.

3 The counting expression is evaluated. Again, any valid expression may be placed here, but we usually change the value of the control variable. (In the example, the control variable count is incremented by 1.) We modify the control variable, and the testing expression eventually gets evaluated to FALSE, thus terminating the for statement.

4 Repeat the procedure starting at step 2.

The control flow of the for statement is depicted graphically in figure 5.4.

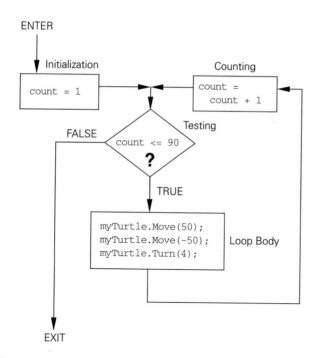

Figure 5.4 Control flow of the for statement

Here are some additional examples of control expressions:

```
//execute the loop for i = 100, 102, 104, ..., 198
for ( i = 100; i < 200; i = i + 2 )
```

```
//execute the loop for k = 50, 49, ..., 1
for ( k = 50; k >= 1; k = k - 1)

//execute the loop for cnt = -10, -9, ..., 0
for (cnt = -10; cnt < 1; cnt = cnt + 1)
```

C++   C++ counting operators ++ (increment) and -- (decrement) can be used for a more concise counting expression. Instead of

```
count = count + 1
```

we may use

```
count++
```

to state the control expression as

```
for (count = 1; count <= 90; count++ )
```

The loop body of a `for` statement can be any C++ statement. For example, to print "Hello, world." 10 times, we write

```
for (cnt = 1; cnt <= 10; cnt = cnt + 1)
    cout << "Hello, world." << endl;
```

Notice that the statement has no curly braces. They are required only if the loop body is composed of multiple statements (identified by the syntax category *compound-statement* in the following production rules). Although it is not required, you may use curly braces even for a single-statement loop body. To make the structure consistent, some programmers prefer to use curly braces for all loops. The following syntax of the `for` statement summarizes these points:

> *for-statement*
>> **for** (*initialization*$_{opt}$; *testing*$_{opt}$; *counting*$_{opt}$) *statement*

> *initialization*
>> *expression*

> *testing*
>> *expression*

> *counting*
>> *expression*

statement

    expression-statement

    compound-statement

    for-statement

    ...

> These three dots mean that there are more syntax categories. We will list more later in the chapter as we discuss additional types of statements.

expression-statement

    expression $_{opt}$ **;**

compound-statement

    { *statement-list* $_{opt}$ **}**

statement-list

    statement

    statement-list   *statement*

When using a `for` statement, we must make sure that execution will eventually terminate. For example, the following loop will be executed for an infinite number of times (unless you do something inside the loop to terminate it).

```
for ( i = 1; i < 2; i = i - 1)
```

Do you see why? The control variable starts with the value of 1, and the counting expression

```
i = i - 1
```

decrements it by 1 after each execution of the loop body. So the control variable `i` becomes 1, 0, -1, -2, and so forth. It never reaches 2, and thus the execution gets into an infinite loop. We must also be careful not to include a statement inside the loop body that affects the control variable. The following is an infinite loop:

```
for ( i = 1; i <= 10; i = i + 1) {
   ...
   i = i - 1;
   ...
}
```

Let's try another example. The following MoveAndTurn program illustrates an interesting use of a for statement. The program contains a for loop in which a turtle moves and turns each time through the loop. Depending on the length of a move and the angle of a turn the turtle can display a wide range of intricate and interesting designs.

```
// Program MoveAndTurn:  A program that draws an interesting
//                       pattern

#include "Turtles.h"

void main( )
{
    TurtlemyTurtle;
    int count;

    myTurtle.Init( 306, 216);

    for ( count = 1; count <= 50; count = count + 1) {
        myTurtle.Move(100);
        myTurtle.Turn(110);
    }

    myTurtle.Done();
}
```

```
myTurtle.Move(2*count);
myTurtle.Turn(90);
```

```
myTurtle.Move(count);
myTurtle.Turn(45);
```

```
myTurtle.Move(100);
myTurtle.Turn(110);
```

Figure 5.5 MoveAndTurn figures

The figures in figure 5.5 were drawn by MoveAndTurn. Underneath each figure are the calls to Move and Turn which drew it.

You can also change the number of times the loop body is executed. Figures 5.5 and 5.6 show some other figures drawn by MoveAndTurn and the for loops that drew them. Notice that the control variable of the for statement is used inside the loop in some of the examples, such as:

```
myTurtle.Move(2 * count)  and  myTurtle.Turn(count / 3)
```

In the first two of the three examples in figure 5.5, the control variable count is used to compute a distance in the Move call, and in the last example in figure 5.6, it is used to compute an angle in the Turn call. Using the control variable inside the loop is fine and causes no problem.

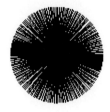

```
for (count=1; count <= 200; count = count + 1){
    myTurtle.Move(100);
    myTurtle.Turn(179);
}
```

```
for (count=1; count <= 12; count = count + 1){
    myTurtle.Move(100);
    myTurtle.Turn(150);
}
```

```
for (count=1; count <= 100; count = count + 1){
    myTurtle.Move(3);
    myTurtle.Turn(count / 3);
}
```

Figure 5.6 MoveAndTurn figures

5.2 Repetition control flow—`while` loops

Consider the following program, which is a slightly modified version of Volume3, which we wrote in Chapter 4.

```
// Program Volume3a:  A program to compute the volume of a
//                    triangular prism using the formula
//                    (1/2) * b * h * w. The values for b, h,
//                    and w are read from the cin object.

#include <iostream.h>

void main()
{
    float b, h, w, volume;

    cout << "Type in base, height, and width" << endl;
    cin >> b >> h >> w;

    volume = 0.5 * b * h * w;

    cout << "Volume of triangular prism with" << endl;
    cout << "base   b = " << b << endl;
    cout << "height h = " << h << endl;
    cout << "width  w = " << w << endl;
    cout << "is          " << volume;
}
```

This program computes the volume of a triangular prism with the given values of base, height, and width. Notice the program is capable of computing only one volume. If we wish to calculate the volume of another triangular prism, we must execute the program again. Instead of repeatedly executing the program, we can add a repetition control flow to the program. Then we can execute the program once and compute as many volumes as we desire. We will first rewrite the program using a `for` loop.

We begin with an outline of the modified program. As code becomes more complex, it gets much harder to understand the whole program immediately, just by reading it. A standard practice is to provide some high-level view of the program that captures its basic control flow. An outline of a program that provides such an overview is called *pseudocode*. Pseudocode is not real code, but it is a useful way to express your thinking process while designing a program. The following is a pseudocode of the modified program.

```
get N; // the number of times to repeat the for loop
for (cnt = 0; cnt < N; cnt = cnt + 1) {
```

```
        get b, h, w;
        compute the volume;
        output the result;

    } //end for
```

We first request the user to type in the number of times the computation is to be repeated. If, for example, the user enters 5, then the program is repeated five times and five volumes are computed (provided all inputs are entered, of course). The following is the complete program.

```
// Program Volume4:  A program to compute the volume of a
//                   triangular prism using the formula
//                   (1/2) * b * h * w. The values for b, h,
//                   and w are read from the cin object.
//                   Repeat the computation for N times.

#include <iostream.h>

void main()
{
    float b, h, w, volume;
    int cnt, N; //# of times to repeat the computation

    cout << "How many times do you want to compute?" << endl;
    cin >> N;

    for (cnt = 0; cnt < N; cnt = cnt + 1) {
        cout << "Type in base, height, and width" << endl;
        cin >> b >> h >> w;

        volume = 0.5 * b * h * w;

        cout << "Volume of triangular prism with" << endl;
        cout << "base    b = " << b << endl;
        cout << "height h = " << h << endl;
        cout << "width  w = " << w << endl;
        cout << "is          " << volume << endl << endl;
    } //end for
}
```

Although the program can now be used to compute as many volumes as we wish, it has one major limitation. We must know or arbitrarily decide how many times we want to repeat the computation. Some systems allow you to terminate a program that uses the cout object by closing the cout window. So we can enter a large number for N, much larger than we actually intend to repeat, and simply close the cout window whenever we want to stop the program. However, it is never a good idea to write a program that assumes specific features of a particular system, especially when we have a more natural and elegant solution that works for all systems.

A looping requirement of the sample program is to repeat the computation until the user wants to quit. Therefore, we need a control flow that allows us to specify the execution of a sequence of statements until a certain condition arises. This type of looping can be implemented by the `while` statement. The `while` statement is also called a *while loop*. Let's use a `while` statement to rewrite the program.

The pseudocode is as follows:

```
prompt the user to continue or not;

while (user says continue) {

    get b, h, w;
    compute the volume;
    output the result;

    prompt the user to continue or not;
} //end while
```

We will require the user to enter the number 1 to continue and 2 to stop the repetition. Notice that the numbers 1 and 2 have no special meaning. Any two numbers will do, for example, 5 and 6 would work just as well. So the "number entered equals to 2" is a condition that terminates the repetition, and thus the program.

Here is the complete program:

```
// Program Volume5:  A program to compute the volume of
//                   a triangular prism using the formula
//                   (1/2) * b * h * w. The values for b, h,
//                   and w are read from the cin object.
//                   Repeat the computation until the user
//                   enters 2 at the prompt.

#include <iostream.h>

void main()
{
    float b, h, w, volume;
    int answer;
    const int YES = 1;

    cout << "Do you want to begin the computation?" << endl;
    cout << "(1 - yes; 2 - no) " << endl;
```

```
        cin >> answer;

        while (answer == YES) {
            cout << "Type in base, height, and width" << endl;
            cin >> b >> h >> w; //read b, w, & h

            volume = 0.5 * b * h * w;

            cout << "Volume of triangular prism with" << endl;
            cout << "base    b = " << b << endl;
            cout << "height h = " << h << endl;
            cout << "width  w = " << w << endl;
            cout << "is         " << volume << endl << endl;
                                        //leave double spaces

            cout << "Do you want to continue?" << endl;
            cout << "(1 - yes; 2 - no) " << endl;

            cin >> answer;

        } //end while
    }
```

Let's look at the `while` statement of the program, shown in figure 5.7.

Unlike the `for` statement, in which the loop body is executed for a fixed number of times by the use of control variable and counting, the loop body of the `while` statement is executed repeatedly until the evaluation of the *logical expression* becomes FALSE. The

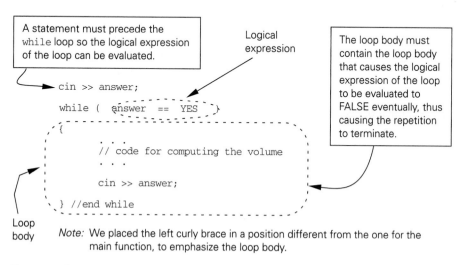

Note: We placed the left curly brace in a position different from the one for the main function, to emphasize the loop body.

Figure 5.7 The while statement

C++ expressions we have seen so far are all arithmetic. An *arithmetic expression*, when evaluated, results in a numerical value. For example, 5 + 7 is an arithmetic expression that evaluates to the numerical value 12. In contrast, a *logical expression* results in a logical value—TRUE (1) or FALSE (0). For example, assuming the values of variables x and y are 10 and 20, respectively, the logical expressions

```
x >= 5
x == 10
x + y <= 35
```

are all TRUE, while the logical expressions

```
y <= x + 5
y <= 10
x == 14
```

are all FALSE. The symbols <=, >=, and == mean "is less than or equal to," "is greater than or equal to," and "is equal to," respectively. These symbols are called *relational* or *comparison* ope*rators*. Notice that in C++, a single equal sign = is an assignment and a pair of equal signs == is a comparison.

Beware   Be careful not to confuse the C++ operators = and ==. One is for assignment (=), and the other is for comparison (==). For example:

```
a = 1
```

assigns an integer value 1 to a, while

```
a == 1
```

tests whether a is equal to 1 or not.

These relational operators are discussed in detail in the next section. The execution of a while statement proceeds as follows:

1   The logical expression is evaluated.

2   If the result of evaluation is FALSE, then the execution of the while statement is complete. Otherwise, the loop body is executed.

3   The procedure is repeated again, starting at step 1.

The control flow of the while statement is shown graphically in figure 5.8.

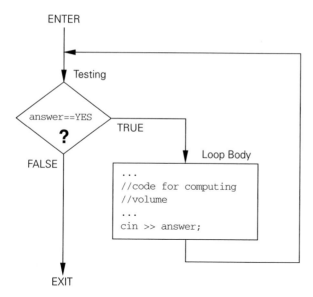

ENTER

Testing

answer==YES

?

TRUE

FALSE

Loop Body

```
. . .
//code for computing
//volume
. . .
cin >> answer;
```

EXIT

Figure 5.8 Control flow of the while statement

Let's trace the execution of this `while` statement. In figure 5.9, we will assume the user enters 1 twice and then enters 2. Notice that, strictly speaking, the user does not have to enter 2 to stop the repetition, because any value other than 1 will cause the logical expression `answer == YES` to be evaluated to FALSE.

```
cin >> answer;     ◄─────

while (  answer  ==  YES   ) {

        . . .
        // code for computing
        // the volume
        . . .

        cin >> answer;    ◄─────
} //end while
```

(1) `cin >> answer` is executed; assume 1 is entered.

(2) `answer == YES` is TRUE, so the loop body is executed. (The last statement inside the loop body
          `cin >> answer`
is executed; assume 1 is entered.)

(3) `answer == YES` is TRUE, so the loop body is executed. (The last statement inside the loop body
          `cin >> answer`
is executed; assume 2 is entered.)

(4) `answer == YES` is FALSE, so the execution of the `while` statement is done; the statement that follows the `while` statement, if any, is executed next.

Figure 5.9 Execution of the while statement

The syntax of the `while` statement is

> *while-statement*
>> **while**   (*logical-expression*   )   *statement*

and *statement* now includes *while-statement*

> *statement*
>> *expression-statement*
>> *compound-statement*
>> *for-statement*
>> *while-statement*
>> . . .

The syntax rule for *logical-expression* is given in the next section.

5.3 Logical expressions

In Chapter 3 we explained C++ arithmetic expressions that result in a numerical value when evaluated. Another kind of C++ expression is a logical expression that, when evaluated, has one of only two possible values—TRUE or FALSE. A logical expression, such as `answer == 1`, evaluates to TRUE or FALSE, depending on the value of `answer`. In the previous section we showed you how to use simple logical expressions in the `while` statement. We will now explain in detail the syntax and semantics of C++ logical expressions.

Just as arithmetic expressions are made up of meaningful combinations of arithmetic operators and operands, logical expressions are made up of meaningful combinations of

Table 5.1 Relational operators

Operator	Description	Sample expression	Result[*] (for x = 10, y = 3)
<	is less than	x < y	0
<=	is less than or equal to	x <= 4 * y	1
>	is greater than	y > 0	1
>=	is greater than or equal to	x / 5 >= y	0
==	is equal to	x == y	0
!=	is not equal to	x != y	1

[*]In C++, 0 represents FALSE and 1 represents TRUE.

relational operators, logical operators, and operands. The *relational operators* compare two numerical values, such as x < y. Six relational operators are shown in table 5.1. For the sample logical expressions listed there, we assume the values 10 for x and 3 for y. Notice that each relational operator takes two operands, one on each side. Also notice that operands may be simple expressions like a single literal or identifier (e.g., 0, x, or y), or they may be more complex arithmetic expressions (e.g., x / 5 + c).

Notice that in the result column the numerical values 0 and 1 are used. In C++, the numerical values 0 and 1 are used to represent FALSE and TRUE, respectively.

Beware   We already noted the difference between = and ==. You may think that the compiler is intelligent enough to distinguish the mistake between the assignment and comparison. For example, you may think the compiler will detect the following as invalid.

```
while ( answer = 1 ) {
. . .
cin >> answer;
}
```

Unfortunately, no compiler error is given for the above because an arithmetic expression (*expression*) is one type of logical expression (*logical-expression*), as will be shown by the production rules given at the end of this section. The code will execute but in a manner completely different than we intend. So be very careful to distinguish the two. For the explanation of the logic, please refer to the following C++ note.

C++   When a C++ arithmetic expression is evaluated, it will result in a value. For example, the result of an arithmetic expression 5 + 7 is the value 12 . Since

```
answer = 1
```

is an expression (review the syntax rule for *expression* on in chapter 4), it will result in a value when evaluated. The value 1 is assigned to answer, and the whole expression will be evaluated to 1. Since the value 1 represents TRUE

```
while ( answer = 1 ) {
. . .
cin >> answer;
}
```

will end up in an infinite loop because the expression answer = 1 is always TRUE.

The logical operators are the second type of operators used in logical expressions. They are AND, OR, and NOT. In C++, we use the symbols && for AND, || for OR, and ! for NOT. These logical operators are used to express more complex logical expressions. The logical expression

```
x < a && x > b
```

is TRUE (1) if both x < a and x > b are TRUE. The meanings of the logical operators are explained in table 5.2.

The logical expression A && B is TRUE only when both A and B are true. The logical expression A || B is TRUE when either one or both of A and B are true. The logical expression !A reverses the logical value of A—TRUE to FALSE or FALSE to TRUE.

Logical expressions, like arithmetic expressions, are evaluated each time they are encountered, using the current values of the variables in them. As for arithmetic expressions, well-defined rules dictate the order of evaluation of logical expressions. A logical expression is evaluated in the following order:

1 Expressions within parentheses are always evaluated before any operators outside parentheses.

2 Arithmetic expressions.

3 Relational operators.

4 NOTs.

5 ANDs.

6 ORs.

7 From left to right, unless specified by one of the other rules 1–6.

Table 5.2 Logical operators and their semantics

A	B	A || B	A && B	! A
0	0	0	0	1
0	1	1	0	1
1	0	1	0	0
1	1	1	1	0

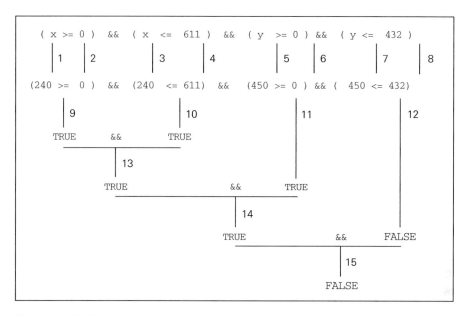

Figure 5.10 Evaluation sequence of logical expression based on the given rules

According to these rules, the logical expression in figure 5.10 would be evaluated in 15 steps, assuming that the value of x is 240 and the value of y is 450.

Steps 1 through 8 used rules 1 and 2; steps 9 through 12 used rules 1 and 3; and steps 13 through 15 used rules 5 and 7.

The following are the production rules for logical expressions.

> *logical-expression*
>> *expression*
>> *expression   relational-operator   expression*
>> (*logical-expression*)
>> ! *logical-expression*
>> *logical-expression logical-operator logical-expression*
>
> *logical-operator*
>> &&
>> ||
>
> *relational-operator*
>> < | <= | != | == | >= | >

(*Note: expression* was defined in chapter 4.)

5.4 Sample program: computing the sum and average

In section 4.4, we promised to write a program that computes the sum and average of N real numbers. We will do this using the repetition control we have learned in this chapter. The basic idea is to continue reading real numbers and adding them to the running sum as they are entered. We also need to keep track of how many real numbers are entered. Here is the pseudocode:

```
cnt = 0;
sum = 0;

read number;
while (number != 0) {

    sum = sum + x; // compute the running sum
    cnt = cnt + 1; // keep track the count of numbers read

    read number;   // get the next number
}
```

The program will continue reading input values until the user enters a 0. We are assuming that 0 is not one of the N real numbers. If the number 0 is one of the possible numbers we must include for computing the sum and average, then we need another method to stop the repetition. (See Exercise 4 at the end of the chapter.) The following listing is the complete program.

```
//Program Statistic2:  A program to compute the sum and average
//                     of N real numbers.
//
//  Note: At least one number must be entered.

#include <iostream.h>

void main()
{
    int    count = 0;
    float number, avg, sum = 0;

    //opening message
    cout << "This program computes the sum and " << endl;
    cout << "average of N real numbers you enter." << endl;
```

```
        cout << "Please press <Return> after each number." << endl;
        cout << "Enter 0 when you are done entering numbers."
                                                        << endl;

        cout << endl << endl;

        cout << "Now, please enter Number " << count+1 << ": ";
        cin  >> number;

        while ( number !=0 ) {

            //compute the running sum and count;
            sum = sum + number;
            count = count + 1;

            //get the next number
            cout << "Now, please enter Number " << count+1 << ": ";
            cin  >> number;
        }

        //compute the average
        avg = sum / count;

        //print out the results
        cout << endl << endl;
        cout << "Sum : " << sum << endl;
        cout << "Average : " << avg;
    }
```

Notice that the user must enter at least one number for this program to work correctly. The program will crash if the user enters 0 without entering any *real* number (pun intended). Do you know why? You will learn how to handle this case in the next chapter.

5.5 *Repetition control flow—* do-while *loops*

The do-while statement is very similar to the while statement. Both repeatedly execute a loop body until a certain condition is met. The major difference is that the while statement evaluates the condition before executing the loop and the do-while statement evaluates the condition after executing the loop. Therefore, the do-while statement always executes its loop body at least once, but the while statement will skip the loop body altogether if the condition is FALSE to begin with. The difference is very clear if we compare the graphical representation of the do-while statement's control flow (see figure 5.11) to the one for the while statement in section 5.2.

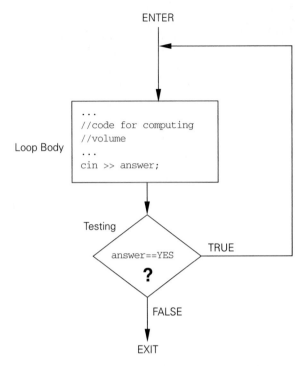

ENTER

Loop Body

```
. . .
//code for computing
//volume
. . .
cin >> answer;
```

Testing

answer==YES

?

TRUE

FALSE

EXIT

Figure 5.11 Control flow of do-while statement

Here is the syntax of the do-while statement:

do-while-statement
> **do**   *statement*   **while**   (*logical-expression*   )   **;**

Consider the program Volume5 from section 5.2 on page 102. The program can be terminated without doing any computation if the user enters 0 at the very first prompt. If we want the program to perform at least one computation, then we can rewrite the program using the do-while loop, as shown in the next program:

```
// Program Volume6:  A program to compute the volume of
//                   a triangular prism using the formula
//                   (1/2) * b * h * w. The values for b, h,
//                   and w are read from the cin object.
//                   Perform the computation at least once.
//                   Repeat the computation until the user
//                   enters 0 at the prompt.

#include <iostream.h>
```

```
void main()
{
    float b, h, w, volume;
    int answer;
    const int YES = 1;

    do {
        cout << "Type in base, height, and width" << endl;
        cin >> b >> h >> w; //read b, w, & h

        volume = 0.5 * b * h * w;

        cout << "Volume of triangular prism with" << endl;
        cout << "base   b = " << b << endl;
        cout << "height h = " << h << endl;
        cout << "width  w = " << w << endl;
        cout << "is         " << volume << endl << endl;

        cout << "Do you want to continue?" << endl;
        cout << "(1 - yes; 2 - no) " << endl;

        cin >> answer;

    } while (answer == YES); //end do-while
}
```

5.6 Nested loops

If you look very carefully at the production rules for the syntax categories *statement*, *for-statement*, *while-statement*, and *do-while-statement*, you will notice that repetition control statements (i.e., for, while, and do-while) can be nested in other repetition control statements. Consider, for example, the derivation of a for statement:

for-statement
===> **for** (*initialization*$_{opt}$; *testing*$_{opt}$; *counting*$_{opt}$) *statement*

> This statement can be replaced with any valid statement, including another for statement.

===> **for** (*initialization*$_{opt}$; *testing*$_{opt}$; *counting*$_{opt}$) *for-statement*

===> **for** (*initialization*$_{opt}$; *testing*$_{opt}$; *counting*$_{opt}$)
            for (*initialization*$_{opt}$; *testing*$_{opt}$; *counting*$_{opt}$) *statement*

===> . . .

Let's first look at the example of nested `for` loops. Here's a program that draws seven squares using nested `for` loops.

```
// Program Tunnel:   A program that draws
//                   seven nested squares.

#include "Turtles.h"

void main( )
{
        Turtle      myTurtle;
        int         i, j;

        myTurtle.Init (306, 216);

        // seven squares, big to small
        for (i = 8; i >= 2; i = i - 1) {

                myTurtle.PenUp();
                myTurtle.GoToPos(306 - (i*10 / 2),
                                 216 + (i*10 / 2) );
                myTurtle.PenDown();

                //draw four sides of a square
                for (j = 1; j <= 4; j = j + 1) {

                        myTurtle.Move(i*10);
                        myTurtle.Turn(90);

                } // end inner

        } // end outer

        myTurtle.Done();
}
```

Outer Loop Body

Inner Loop Body

The outer `for` loop is executed seven times (for i = 8, 7, 6, ..., 2). Each time the outer `for` loop is executed, the inner `for` loop is executed four times (for j = 1, 2, 3, 4), one for each of the four sides of a square. Thus the inner loop is executed 28 times (4 x 7). Notice that the control variable i is decremented from 8 to 2, instead of a count down from 7 to 1, because of its intended use in the `GoToPos` function call. We will be seeing more examples of nested `for` statements later in the book.

In the next section we will write a sample program that utilizes nested repetition control loops.

5.7 Sample program: ManySquares

Let's summarize the concepts we have learned in this chapter by writing an improved square-drawing program. Program AnySquare (all versions) draws only one square and then quits. A better program will allow the user to draw many squares of different sizes. Of course, you can draw many squares of different sizes by running AnySquare over and over again, but running the program repeatedly would draw only one square in a window. What we are trying to achieve here is to draw many squares in a single window. The pseudocode of the program is as follows:

```
while ( user wants to continue ) {
    get size;
    draw the square;
}
```

We will use a new GUI object called *YesNoBox* for asking the user whether to continue. Executing

```
YesNoBox prompt;
prompt.Ask("Do you want a square?");
```

will display a simple window with the YES and NO buttons (see figure 5.12).

If the user clicks the YES button, the `Ask` function will return TRUE (1). If the user clicks the NO button instead, then the `Ask` function will return FALSE (0).

Here's the program and its object diagram (see figure 5.13):

```
// Program ManySquares:  A program to draw a square repeatedly
//                       until the user wants to quit.
//
//  Note:  All squares remain on the window, i.e. a previously
//         drawn square is not erased when a new square is drawn.
#include "Turtles.h"
```

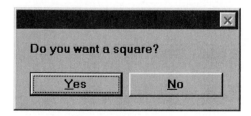

Figure 5.12 YesNoBox GUI object

```
#include "GUIObj.h"
void main( )
{
    Turtle          myTurtle;
    YesNoBox        prompt;
    IntTypeIn       inputBox;
    int             size, i;

    myTurtle.Init(0, 0); //initialize turtle;
                         //any position will do

    while ( prompt.Ask("Do you want a square?") ) {
        // YES button is clicked,
        // so draw another square

        size = inputBox.GetInt("Type in the square size",
                            "Size (< 432):");

        myTurtle.PenUp(); //move to center
        myTurtle.GoToPos(306 - size / 2,
                        216 + size / 2 );

        myTurtle.PenDown(); //now draw the square
        for (i = 1; i <= 4; i = i + 1) {
        myTurtle.Move(size);
        myTurtle.Turn(90);
        } // end for

    } //end while

    myTurtle.Done();
}
```

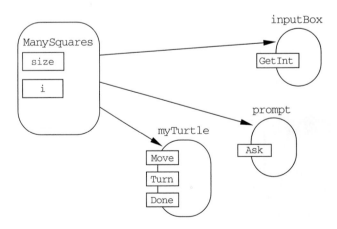

Figure 5.13 ManySquares object diagram

5.8 Sample program: drawing a circle and round-off error

Let's write another sample program using a repetition control. We will write a program that draws circles of a specified radius at a specified position (see figure 5.14). Given input x, y, and r, the program will draw a circle with radius r, whose center is at location (x,y). In developing this program, we will encounter and solve a problem commonly known as *round-off error.*

Let's start with some mathematics. The total distance a Turtle must travel is the circumference of a circle, which is

$$circumference = 2\pi r$$

for a circle with radius *r.* We will make the Turtle travel this total distance in 360 segments. By moving

$$\frac{2\pi r}{360}$$

pixels in each segment and turning 1 degree after each segment, the Turtle can draw a circle with the circumference 2πr. Since the center of a circle is at (x,y), the Turtle begins its drawing from location (x+r,y).

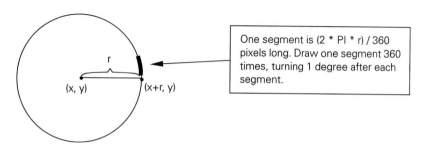

One segment is (2 * PI * r) / 360 pixels long. Draw one segment 360 times, turning 1 degree after each segment.

Figure 5.14 Drawing a circle

Here's one way to express this idea in code:

```
const float PI = 3.14159;

PenUp();              //first move to the starting
GoToPos(x+r, y);      //point without drawing and
TurnTo(90);           //turn upward before moving
PenDown();

for (int i = 1; i <= 360; i = i+1) {

    Move( (2 * PI * r) / 360 );
    Turn ( 1 );

}
```

Although logically correct, the example is not acceptable C++ code. There is a problem of type mismatch in the argument for the Move function. The argument to the Move function must be an integer, but we are passing the result of the expression

```
(2 * PI * r) / 360
```

which is a float. If an arithmetic expression contains only integer values, then the expression will evaluate to an integer. However, if an expression contains both int and float values, then the expression will result in a float value. We explained the mixed-mode arithmetic expression in section 3.4. The expression above contains the float data value PI, and thus the result will be a float value, which causes a type mismatch. To eliminate the type mismatch, we convert the result of the expression to an integer. In C++, we can convert a float data value to an integer as

```
int ( <arith exp> )
```

Table 5.3 lists some conversion examples. Type conversion is called *type casting* in C++. Notice that integer type casting simply cuts off the fractional part. For this program, we want to round off values to the nearest integer. Rounding off a real number can be done easily by adding 0.5 and then converting it, as shown in the next statement.

Table 5.3 Conversion examples

Expression	Result
int(3.567);	3
x = 2.34; int(x + 2.1);	4
int(0.99999)	0

```
int ( x + 0.5 )
```

If the fractional part of x is greater than or equal to 0.5, then it will be rounded to the smallest integer greater than x. And if the fractional part of x is less than 0.5, then it will be rounded to the largest integer smaller than x. With this adjustment, the looping portion of the code now becomes

```
for (int i = 1; i <= 360; i = i+1) {

    Move( int( (2 * PI * r) / 360 + 0.5 ) );
    Turn ( 1 );

}
```

The code is now correct, but has an efficiency problem. Since the result of the expression

```
int( (2 * PI * r) / 360 + 0.5 )
```

does not change, it is very inefficient to repeat it 360 times. To eliminate such redundant and wasteful computation, we put the expression outside of the loop.

We are now ready to complete the program.

```
//Program Circle:  A program that draws a circle of radius r
//                 and whose center is at (x,y).

#include "Turtles.h"
#include "GUIObj.h"

void main ( )
{
    IntTypeIn inputBox;
    YesNoBox  prompt;
    Turtle    myTurtle;

    const float PI = 3.14159;
    float dist;
```

```
int    i, r, x, y;

myTurtle.Init(0, 0); //initialize turtle;
                        //any position will do

while ( prompt.Ask("Do you want a circle?") ) {
    // YES button is clicked,
    // so draw another circle

    r = inputBox.GetInt("Type in the radius",
                        "Radius:");
    x = inputBox.GetInt("Type in the center (x,y)",
                        "x:");
    y = inputBox.GetInt("Type in the center (x,y)",
                        "y:");

    myTurtle.PenUp();            //first move to the starting
    myTurtle.GoToPos(x+r, y);    //point without drawing and
    myTurtle.TurnTo(90);         //turn upward before moving
    myTurtle.PenDown();

    dist = int( (2 * PI * r) / 360 + 0.5 );

    for (i = 1; i <= 360; i = i+1) {
        myTurtle.Move( dist );
        myTurtle.Turn ( 1 );
    }
}

myTurtle.Done();
}
```

When we execute the program with the input values in table 5.4 we would expect to see a window such as the one in figure 5.15. In reality, when the program is executed with the above input values, we encounter the window shown in figure 5.16.

What happened? A *round-off error* is the culprit. Since we are rounding off to the nearest integer, a small margin of error has entered into our computation. We tried three circles with radii 50, 60, and 70. We certainly expect them to be of different sizes. In fact, as shown in table 5.5, the circumferences (and accordingly, the segment lengths in float) are different, showing that they are indeed circles of different sizes. However, when the segment lengths were converted into integers, they all

Table 5.4 Circle input values

Radius r	Center x	Center y
50	306	216
60	306	216
70	306	216

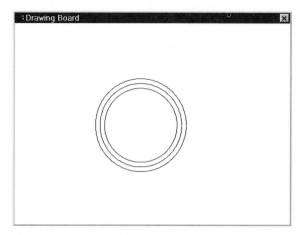

Figure 5.15 Expected program results

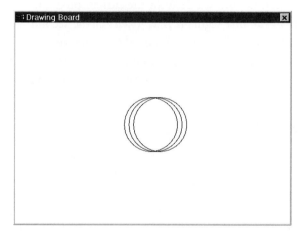

Figure 5.16 Actual program results

became 0. Thus, they became equally sized circles. (The shift to the right is due to the difference in the starting points.)

Table 5.6 shows the effect of round-off errors on different radii. You will notice that for the first five circles, the integer segment length is 0, and therefore no circles will be drawn. The remaining nine circles all have the integer segment length of 1, and thus they will all be drawn the same size.

To write a program that draws the circles precisely, we have to somehow compensate for the round-off error. Consider, for example, that the "real" distance to move is 0.6 for each segment. Currently, we would convert this to 1 and move one pixel 360

Table 5.5 Circle program measurements

Radius	Circumference	Segment length (float)	Segment length (int)
r	$2\pi r$	$\dfrac{2\pi r}{360}$	$int\left(\dfrac{2\pi r}{360} + 0.5\right)$
50	314.15899658	0.87266392	1
60	376.99081421	1.04719663	1
70	439.82260132	1.22172940	1

times. Since we overcompensate 0.4 for each segment, the total margin of error is $360 \times 0.4 = 144$. To reduce this margin of error, we can keep track of over- and under-compensation after each move and adjust the following moves accordingly. For example, after the two moves, we should have moved 0.6 + 0.6 = 1.2. With the current program, the actual distance covered by the turtle in the first segment is 1. Then for the second segment, the turtle must move only 0.2, because it has already moved 0.4 more than it should have moved in the first segment (1 − 0.4). Since a turtle can move only in integer amounts, 0.2 is converted to 0 and no distance is actually covered for the second segment.

Table 5.6 Effect of round-off errors on different radii

Radius	Circumference	Segment length (float)	Segment length (int)
r	$2\pi r$	$\dfrac{2\pi r}{360}$	$int\left(\dfrac{2\pi r}{360} + 0.5\right)$
5	31.41589928	0.08726639	0
10	62.83179855	0.17453277	0
15	94.24770355	0.26179916	0
20	125.66359711	0.34906554	0
25	157.07949829	0.43633196	0
30	188.49540710	0.52359831	1
35	219.91130066	0.61086470	1
40	251.32719421	0.69813108	1
45	282.74310303	0.78539753	1
50	314.15899658	0.87266392	1
55	345.57489014	0.95993030	1
60	376.99081421	1.04719663	1
65	408.40670776	1.13446307	1
70	439.82260132	1.22172940	1

Table 5.7 Compensation for round-off errors

Move #i	Total distance	Actual distance moved at Move #i	Next distance to be moved (Float) at Move #i	Under- or over-compensation	Real distance	Total real distance
	sum(A)	A = int(B)	B = (old B-A) + C	B - A	C	sum(C)
1	1	1	0.6		0.6	0.6
				-0.4		
2	1	0	0.2	+ — 0.6		1.2
				+0.2		
3	2	1	0.8	+ — 0.6		1.8
				-0.2		
4	2	0	0.4	+ — 0.6		2.4
				+0.4		
5	3	1	1.0	+ — 0.6		3.0
				0.0		
6	4	1	0.6	+ — 0.6		3.6
				-0.4		
					0.6	

In the third segment, the turtle has to adjust for the under-compensation of 0.2. We continue in this fashion, keeping track of under- and over-compensation and adjust the successive moves accordingly. Table 5.7 shows the general idea. Notice that overcompensation is represented as a negative number and undercompensation as a positive number.

The following is the modified program that adjusts for the round-off errors. We use three variables dist, nextDist, and actualDist for keeping track of the real distance to cover (this value will not change), the distance supposed to be covered in the next segment, and the actual distance covered in the next segment, respectively. These three variables correspond to the sixth, fourth, and third columns in the preceding table.

```
//Program Circle2:  A program that draws a circle of radius r
//                  and whose center is at (x,y). The program
//                  draws a correct size circle by
//                  adjusting for the round-off errors.
```

```
#include "Turtles.h"
#include "GUIObj.h"

void main ( )
{
    IntTypeIn      inputBox;
    YesNoBox       prompt;
    Turtle         myTurtle;

    const float PI = 3.14159;
    float dist, nextDist;
    int   i, r, x, y, actualDist;

    myTurtle.Init(0, 0); //initialize turtle;
                         //any position will do

    while ( prompt.Ask("Do you want a circle?") ) {
        // YES button is clicked,
        // so draw another circle.

        r = inputBox.GetInt("Type in the radius","Radius:");
        x = inputBox.GetInt("Type in the center (x,y)","x:");
        y = inputBox.GetInt("Type in the center (x,y)","y:");

        myTurtle.PenUp();           //first move to the starting
        myTurtle.GoToPos(x+r, y);   //point without drawing and
        myTurtle.TurnTo(90);        //turn upward before moving
        myTurtle.PenDown();

        nextDist = dist = (2 * PI * r) / 360 + 0.5;

        for (i = 1; i <= 360; i = i+1) {
        actualDist = int(nextDist);
        myTurtle.Move( actualDist );
        myTurtle.Turn ( 1 );
        nextDist = (nextDist - actualDist) + dist;
        }
    }
    myTurtle.Done();
}
```

Some of you may be wondering why we do not change the Move function to accept a float value, so we can make a call like

```
myTurtle.Move(3.8)
```

You may think that having such a function will eliminate the need for type casting and allow the original code to be executed as is, but it will not work. It does not make sense to pass a noninteger value to the function. The argument we pass to the `Move` function specifies the number of pixels, but pixels do not have fractional units. The argument must be a whole number, a multiple of 1, because a pixel is the smallest unit of line drawing we can make on a computer screen. You either draw a full pixel or not; you cannot draw half a pixel.

In this sample program, we used integer conversion to illustrate the round-off error problem, but the problem can occur even if we are dealing strictly with `float` or `double` data values. A computer will use a fixed number of bytes for representing a real number. For instance, suppose one computer can represent up to 12 decimal places. To store a real number that has more than 12 decimal places in this computer, the number must be rounded off to the nearest 12th decimal place. Therefore, any two numbers differing in the 13th or successive decimal places will be stored as the same number in memory. The sample program presented here shows the round off error at the 0th decimal place (i.e., a whole number) instead of the 12th decimal place. Fortunately, in many software applications, the data types `float` and `double` are sufficient to represent numbers as precisely as they need to be represented.

5.9 Exercises

1   In the program Tunnel (section 5.6), the inner `for` loop is executed 28 times. Fill in the following table that shows the values of the control variables of both loops (i for the outer loop, j for the inner) for each of the 28 executions of the inner loop. The first two columns are already filled in for you.

Execution #	1	2	3	4	5	6	7	8	9	10	11	12	13	14
i	1	1												
j	1	2												

Execution #	15	16	17	18	19	20	21	22	23	24	25	26	27	28
i														
j														

2 Determine the output for the following code fragments:

```
a. int i = 0;
   int j = 0;
   for (i = 10; i  < 10; i = i + 2) {
       j = j + 2 * i;
   }
   cout << j;
```

```
b. int i = 0;
   int j = 500;
   for (i = 10; i > 0; i = i - 2) {
       j = j -  i * i;
   }
   cout << j;
```

```
c. int k = 0;
   for (i = 0; i < 10; i = i + 1) {
     for (j =0; j < 10; j = j + 2) {
       k = k +  i * j;
   }
   cout << k;
```

```
d. int i = 20;
   int j = 1;
   while (i > 1) {
       j = j * i - 1;
       i = i - 5;
   }
   cout << j;
```

```
e. int i = 1;
   int j = 1;
   while (i < 10) {
       j = j * i;
       i = i + 3;
   }
   cout << j;
```

```
f. int i = 2;
   int j = 1;
   do {
       j = j + i;
       i = i * i;
   } while (i < 100);
   cout << j;
```

3 Rewrite the following for statement using the while and do-while statements.

```
for (cnt = 1; cnt < 20; cnt = cnt + 1)
    cout << cnt << endl;
```

4 The program to compute the sum and average of *N* real numbers we wrote in this chapter uses an input of 0 to terminate the program. Modify the program so it will compute the sum and average of any *N* real numbers, including 0.

5 Modify the program Tunnel so the user can enter the number of squares to be drawn.

6 Write a program that computes the nth factorial n!, which is defined as

$$n! \ = \ n \times (n-1) \times (n-2) \times \ldots \times 2 \times 1$$

The program may use either graphical or character-based input and output.

7 Write a program that prints out a table of temperatures in both Fahrenheit and Celsius. The program accepts the starting and ending Fahrenheit temperatures and the increment value. For example, with the inputs −10, 70, and 10 for the starting and ending Fahrenheit temperatures and the increment value, respectively, the program will print out the following table:

Fahrenheit	Celsius
-10	-23.352
0	-17.792
10	-12.232
20	-6.672
30	-1.112
40	4.448
50	10.008
60	15.568
70	21.128

Use cin and cout for this program. The formula for computing the Celsius equivalent for a given Fahrenheit is

$$C = \frac{5}{9}(F - 32) \cong 0.556(F - 32)$$

8 Write programs to draw the following figures. Each figure can be drawn with five lines and each program should have a for statement whose loop body is executed once for each line.

a.

b.

c.

d.

9 Write a program that will draw rows and columns of 20 × 20-pixel squares. Use an IntTypeIn box to accept the number of rows and columns from a user. For example, if the user specifies five rows and seven columns, then your program should draw the following:

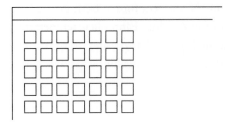

Draw the array of squares using nested `for` statements.

```
for each row r
    for each column c
        draw a square at row r column c
```

Draw a square with a `for` statement, also.

10 Write a program that draws a pine tree using the repetition control learned in this chapter.

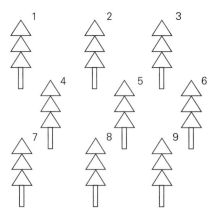

You have to repeat the code for drawing a triangle three times.

11 Write a program that draws a pine forest by drawing N, $1 \leq N \leq 9$, pine trees. The following is the output when the input N is 9. The number above the tree shows the order of drawing. The program does not display the numbers.

12 Write a program that draws a Chinese character for a forest. Notice that a forest contains three trees (see exercise 10 in chapter 2).

chapter 6

Selection control flow

Repetition control flow (see chapter 5) allows program segments to be executed repeatedly. Without it, no useful and practical programs can be realized. If every statement in a program is executed only once, computer programs cannot perform very meaningful functions. The second control flow that is indispensable in writing useful and practical programs is selection control flow. In this chapter you will learn two types of statements that allow selection control flow.

6.1 Selection control flow—if statement

We will begin our study of selection control flow by reviewing program Quad, which we wrote in chapter 3 to compute the solutions for a given quadratic equation.

```
//Program Quad:  Find two real number solutions for the
//               quadratic equation Ax² + Bx + C = 0.

#include "GUIObj.h"
#include <math.h>
```

```
void main ()
{
    float A, B, C, x1, x2, sqrtOfDiscriminant;
    FloatTypeInfloatInpBox;
    OKBoxmsgBox;

    //get three inputs
    A = floatInpBox.GetFloat("INPUT","Type in value for A");
    B = floatInpBox.GetFloat("INPUT","Type in value for B");
    C = floatInpBox.GetFloat("INPUT","Type in value for C");

    //compute the sqrt of a discriminant and two solutions
    sqrtOfDiscriminant = sqrt( B*B - 4*A*C );
    x1 = (-B + sqrtOfDiscriminant) / (2 * A);
    x2 = (-B - sqrtOfDiscriminant) / (2 * A);

    //display the results
    msgBox.Display(x1);
    msgBox.Display(x2);
}
```

The program will work properly only if the relationship

$$B^2 \geq 4AC$$

holds because it is designed to compute only the real number solutions. If this relationship does not hold, then there will be no real number solutions. The solutions will be two complex numbers. In this chapter we will limit our discussion to real number solutions. For the program to work properly for real number solutions, users must enter values for A, B, and C to make the preceding relationship TRUE. Instead of requiring users to enter valid values, a better program would allow users to enter any real numbers and then warn them of any input errors, that is, if any of the values entered violates the relationship. If users are required to enter valid values, by the time they can determine that the values for A, B, and C are indeed valid, much of the computation already will have been done (by the users), so running the program is not of much benefit.

We need a selection control flow to write a program that checks the validity of inputs. The logic of the modified program is as follows:

1 Read A, B, and C.
2 Do step 3 if $B^2 < 4AC$; otherwise, do step 4.
3 Display the message "No real number solutions exist."
4 Compute and display solutions.

Here is the complete program:

```
//Program Quad2:  A program to find two real number solutions
//                for the quadratic equation Ax² + Bx + C = 0.

#include "GUIObj.h"
#include <math.h>

void main ()
{
    float A, B, C, x1, x2, sqrtOfDiscriminant;
    FloatTypeIn  floatInpBox;
    OKBox        msgBox;

    //get three inputs
    A = floatInpBox.GetFloat("INPUT","Type in value for A");
    B = floatInpBox.GetFloat("INPUT","Type in value for B");
    C = floatInpBox.GetFloat("INPUT","Type in value for C");

    //test the input
    if (B*B < 4*A*C) { //then

        msgBox.Display("No real number solutions exist.");
    }
    else {

        //compute the sqrt of a discriminant and two solutions
        sqrtOfDiscriminant = sqrt( B*B - 4*A*C );
        x1 = (-B + sqrtOfDiscriminant) / (2 * A);
        x2 = (-B - sqrtOfDiscriminant) / (2 * A);

        //display the results
        msgBox.Display(x1);
        msgBox.Display(x2);

    } //end if
}
```

Execution of the if statement proceeds as follows (see figure 6.1).

1 The logical expression is evaluated.

2 If the result is TRUE, then the TRUE part is executed; this step completes the execution of the if statement.

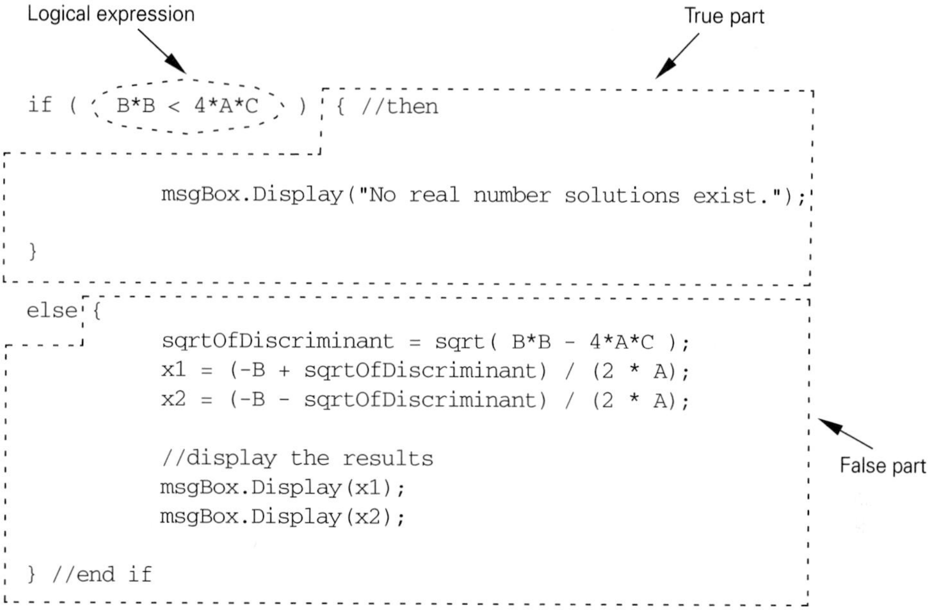

Logical expression
True part
if (B*B < 4*A*C) { //then
msgBox.Display("No real number solutions exist.");
}
else {
sqrtOfDiscriminant = sqrt(B*B - 4*A*C);
x1 = (-B + sqrtOfDiscriminant) / (2 * A);
x2 = (-B - sqrtOfDiscriminant) / (2 * A);
//display the results
msgBox.Display(x1);
msgBox.Display(x2);
} //end if
False part

Figure 6.1 Execution of the if statement

ENTER
B*B < 4*A*C
?
TRUE
msgBox.Display
("No real number solutions exist.");
FALSE
sqrtOfDiscriminant = sqrt(B*B - 4*A*C);
x1 = (-B + sqrtOfDiscriminant) / (2 * A);
x2 = (-B - sqrtOfDiscriminant) / (2 * A);
msgBox.Display(x1);
msgBox.Display(x2);
EXIT

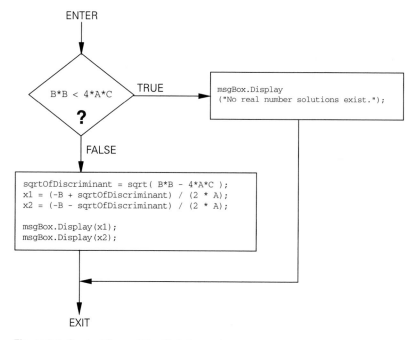

Figure 6.2 Control flow of the if statement

3 If the result is FALSE, then the FALSE part is executed; this step completes the execution of the if statement.

Graphically, the if statement can be visualized as shown in figure 6.2.
Here is the syntax of the if statement:

> *if-statement*
>   `if`   (*logical-expression*   )   *statement*   *false-part*$_{opt}$

> *false-part*
>   `else`   *statement*

The TRUE and FALSE parts may contain any valid statements, including another if statement. Nested if statements become necessary when we have multiple testing conditions to check. Let's look at the sample program Quad2. When $B^2 = 4AC$ is TRUE, the equation has only one real number solution, so it is redundant to compute both x1 and x2 is redundant, because they are equal. Also, we do not want to display the same values twice when x1 and x2 are equal. We can improve the program by using nested if statements. Here is the modified program:

Note   According to the syntax rule of the *statement,* the loop body of the repetition control statements needs to be surrounded by curly braces only if it is a compound statement (i.e., a sequence of statements). As the above syntax rules show, the same rule applies to the TRUE and FALSE parts of the if statement. For example, it is not necessary to write

```
if (a < b) {
    min = a;
}
else
    min = b;
}
```

Instead, we can write

```
if (a < b)
    min = a;
else
    min = b;
```

In general, we use the curly braces only when they are necessary. In some situations, however, we use the curly braces even when they are not necessary, to show the flow of control clearly, thus making the code easier to read and understand.

```
//Program Quad3:  A program to find two real number solutions for
//                the quadratic equation Ax² + Bx + C = 0. The
//                program does not display a unique solution
//                twice.

#include "GUIObj.h"
#include <math.h>

void main ()
{
     float          A, B, C, x1, x2, sqrtOfDiscriminant;
     FloatTypeIn    floatInpBox;
     OKBox          msgBox;

     //get three inputs
     A = floatInpBox.GetFloat("INPUT","Type in value for A");
     B = floatInpBox.GetFloat("INPUT","Type in value for B");
     C = floatInpBox.GetFloat("INPUT","Type in value for C");

     //test the input
     if (B*B < 4*A*C) { //then

               msgBox.Display("No real number solutions exist.");
     }
     else { //either one or two solutions exist

          if (B*B == 4*A*C) {//then one solution

               // compute and display one solution
               x1 = -B / (2 * A);
               msgBox.Display(x1);
          }
          else {//two solutions

               //compute and display two solutions
               sqrtOfDiscriminant = sqrt( B*B - 4*A*C );
               x1 = (-B + sqrtOfDiscriminant) / (2 * A);
               x2 = (-B - sqrtOfDiscriminant) / (2 * A);
               msgBox.Display(x1);
               msgBox.Display(x2);

          } //end inner if

     } //end outer if
}
```

Boxes alongside the code:

$$\boxed{\begin{array}{c} \text{0 solutions} \\ B^2 < 4AC \end{array}}$$

$$\boxed{\begin{array}{c} \text{1 solution} \\ B^2 = 4AC \end{array}}$$

$$\boxed{\begin{array}{c} \text{2 solutions} \\ B^2 > 4AC \end{array}}$$

The logical expression $B*B == 4*A*C$ of the inner if statement determines whether the equation has one or two solutions. Notice that the logical expression $B*B == 4*A*C$

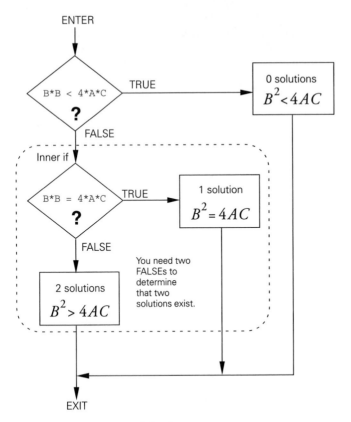

Figure 6.3 Control flow of Quad3 program

alone does not determine the number of solutions. In other words, this expression being FALSE does not necessarily imply two solutions. Notice that this logical expression is tested inside the else part of the outer if statement; that is, it is tested after the outer logical expression B*B < 4*A*C has been determined to be FALSE. This control flow is shown in diagram form in figure 6.3.

The program now distinguishes three cases by using the nested if statements, and carries out the tasks appropriate for each case. Although the program is doing what we want it to do, we will make slight modifications to it to highlight a few points. The first modification is to eliminate the recomputation of identical expressions.

```
//Program Quad4:  A program to find two real number solutions
//                for the quadratic equation Ax² + Bx + C = 0.
//                Duplicate computation is eliminated in this
//                program.
```

```
#include "GUIObj.h"
#include <math.h>

void main ()
{
    float A, B, C, x1, x2, discriminant, sqrtOfDiscriminant;
    FloatTypeInfloatInpBox;
    OKBox    msgBox;

    //get three inputs
    A = floatInpBox.GetFloat("INPUT","Type in value for A");
    B = floatInpBox.GetFloat("INPUT","Type in value for B");
    C = floatInpBox.GetFloat("INPUT","Type in value for C");

    discriminant = B*B - 4*A*C;

    //test the input
    if (discriminant < 0) { //then

        msgBox.Display("No real number solutions exist.");
    }
    else { //either one or two solutions exist

        if (discriminant == 0) {//then one solution

            // compute and display one solution
            x1 = -B / (2 * A);
            msgBox.Display(x1);
        }
        else {//two solutions

            //compute and display two solutions
            sqrtOfDiscriminant = sqrt( discriminant );
            x1 = (-B + sqrtOfDiscriminant) / (2 * A);
            x2 = (-B - sqrtOfDiscriminant) / (2 * A);
            msgBox.Display(x1);
            msgBox.Display(x2);

        } //end inner if

    } //end outer if
}
```

Compute once

and use multiple times

The expression B*B - 4*A*C is computed once and reused multiple times in the program. Notice the logical expressions in the if statements have changed as a result of this modification. In general, elimination of duplicate computations improves its performance, especially when the duplication appears inside the loop body of a repetition control statement. However, we should not be overzealous in trying to eliminate every redundant computation. If the elimination makes a program less readable or does not improve the performance of the program measurably, then we should leave the duplication in the program. For example, eliminating the duplication of the expression 2*A would probably make the program less readable, and since the cost of recomputing 2*A is negligible, the duplication is not eliminated.

The second, and final, modification to the program is the use of an alternative format of the `if` statement. The following is the modified program.

```
//Program Quad5: A program to find two real number solutions
//                for the quadratic equation Ax² + Bx + C = 0. The
//                program uses an alternative style for the if
//                control statement.

#include "GUIObj.h"
#include <math.h>

void main ()
{
     float A, B, C, x1, x2, discriminant, sqrtOfDiscriminant;
     FloatTypeIn floatInpBox;
     OKBox        msgBox;

     //get three inputs
     A = floatInpBox.GetFloat("INPUT","Type in value for A");
     B = floatInpBox.GetFloat("INPUT","Type in value for B");
     C = floatInpBox.GetFloat("INPUT","Type in value for C");

     discriminant = B*B - 4*A*C;

     //test the input
     if (discriminant < 0) { //then

          msgBox.Display("No real number solutions exist.");
     }
     else { //either one or two solutions exist

          // compute and display the first solution

          sqrtOfDiscriminant = sqrt( discriminant );
          x1 = (-B + sqrtOfDiscriminant) / (2 * A);
          msgBox.Display(x1);

          if (discriminant > 0) {//then the second solution
```

Get 1st solution

$$B^2 \geq 4AC$$

138   CHAPTER 6   SELECTION CONTROL FLOW

Get 2nd solution
$$B^2 > 4AC$$

```
//compute and display the second solution

x2 = (-B - sqrtOfDiscriminant) / (2 * A);
msgBox.Display(x2);

        } //end inner if

    } //end outer if

}
```

The control flow for the modified program Quad5 is shown diagramatically in figure 6.4.

In program Quad4, when the outer `if` test is determined to be FALSE, we immediately test the second `if`. Depending on the result, we compute either one or two solutions. Each of the TRUE and FALSE parts of the second `if` is used exclusively to compute either one or two solutions. Now consider the modified program. In program Quad5, when the outer `if` test is determined to be FALSE, instead of testing the second

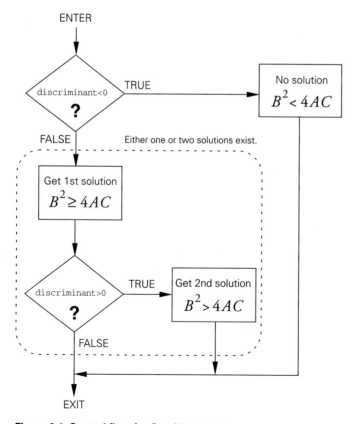

Figure 6.4 Control flow for Quad5 program

`if`, we immediately compute the first solution, because we know the equation has at least one solution. Then we test the second `if` to see if the equation has a second solution; and if so, we compute it.

The inner `if` statement

```
if (discriminant > 0) {//then the second solution

    //compute and display the second solution

    x2 = (-B - sqrtOfDiscriminant) / (2 * A);
    msgBox.Display(x2);

} //end inner if
```

has no `else` part, which is, of course, valid because the `else` part is optional. (See the production rule on page 134.) We use this alternative format of the `if` statement when we want a sequence of statements to be executed if some condition is TRUE and no statements to be executed if the condition is FALSE.

We can summarize the execution of an `if` statement as follows:

1 The logical expression is evaluated.

2 If the result is TRUE then the TRUE part is executed; this step completes the execution of the `if` statement.

3 If the result is FALSE and there is a FALSE part, then it is executed; this step completes the execution of the `if` statement.

4 If the result is FALSE and there is no FALSE part, then the execution is complete.

6.2 *Multiple selections*

In the previous section we saw an (inner) `if` statement nested in another (outer) `if` statement. In some situations we may need to nest not one but many `if` statements. If we wish to derive a letter grade from a given test score based on table 6.1, then we need to nest multiple `if` statements.

Here's a program that nests multiple `if` statements.

Table 6.1 Sample test scores and letter grades

Test score	Letter grade
$90 \leq X \leq 100$	A
$80 \leq X < 90$	B
$70 \leq X < 80$	C
$60 \leq X < 70$	D
$X < 60$	F

CHAPTER 6   SELECTION CONTROL FLOW

```
//Program Grade:  A program to compute a letter grade for
//                a given test score.

#include "GUIObj.h"
#include <math.h>

void main ()
{
    float       X;
    FloatTypeIn floatInpBox;
    OKBox       msgBox;

    //get input
    X = floatInpBox.GetFloat("Test Score","Enter X:");

    //test the input

    if (X < 60) {

        msgBox.Display("It is F.");
    }
    else { // X is 60 or higher

        if (X < 70) {

            msgBox.Display("It is D.");
        }
        else { // X is 70 or higher

            if (X < 80) {

                msgBox.Display("It is C.");
            }
            else { // X is 80 or higher

                if (X < 90) {

                msgBox.Display("It is B.");
                }
                else { // X is 90 or higher

                msgBox.Display("It is A.");
                }
            }
        }
    }

}
```

When the nesting becomes too deep, you may have some trouble reading the code. Since the TRUE and FALSE parts contain only one statement in the preceding code, we can eliminate the curly braces and rewrite the `if` statements as

```
if (X < 60)

    msgBox.Display("It is F.");

else
    if (X < 70)

        msgBox.Display("It is D.");

    else
        if (X < 80)

        msgBox.Display("It is C.");

        else
            if (X < 90)

            msgBox.Display("It is B.");

        else

    msgBox.Display("It is A.");
```

Ordinarily, we indent the TRUE (then) and FALSE (else) parts to show the structure of the code clearly. Another way to make the code a little more readable is to align the `else if` instead of indenting the `else` parts, as shown here:

```
if (X < 60)

    msgBox.Display("It is F.");

else if (X < 70)

    msgBox.Display("It is D.");

else if (X < 80)

    msgBox.Display("It is C.");

else if (X < 90)

    msgBox.Display("It is B.");

else

    msgBox.Display("It is A.");
```

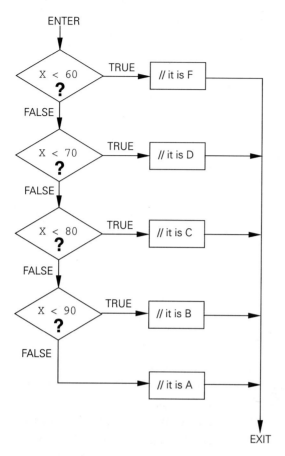

ENTER

X < 60 ? — TRUE → // it is F

FALSE

X < 70 ? — TRUE → // it is D

FALSE

X < 80 ? — TRUE → // it is C

FALSE

X < 90 ? — TRUE → // it is B

FALSE

// it is A

EXIT

Figure 6.5 Control flow for Grade program

The control flow for the testing is, of course, the same in either style (see figure 6.5).

In most cases, aligning else if statements is the preferred style when the inner if statements are nested in the else part of the outer if statements. However, consider the following code fragment for determining the maximum of three input values.

```
if ( x < y)

    if (y < z)
        max = z       ;// x < y < z
    else
        max = y       ;// x < z <= y or z <= x < y

else
```

```
    if (x < z )
        max = z      ;// y <= x < z
    else
        max = x ;   // y <= z <= x or z <= y <= x
```

Aligning the `else if` would make the code fragment look like

```
if ( x < y)

    if (y < z)
        max = z ;   // x < y < z
    else
        max = y ;   // x < z <= y or z <= x < y

else if (x < z )

    max = z ;       // y <= x < z
else

    max = x ;       // y <= z <= x or z <= y <= x
```

which does not help much to clarify the logic of the code as it did in the earlier example. It is hard to say which is a better style; in fact, personal preferences may be the deciding factor in many situations. We should not follow any one style blindly, but strive to select the style that conveys the meaning of the code as clearly as possible.

Another situation in which we must be careful using multiple `if` statements is when we have a "dangling else." Consider the following statement written without any indentation.

```
if ( x < y) if (y < z)cout << "Scherzo"; else cout << "Waltz";
```

Will the compiler process this as

```
if ( x < y) {
    if (y < z)
        cout << "Scherzo";
    else
        cout << "Waltz";
}
```

Interpretation 1

or as

```
if ( x < y) {
```

```
        if (y < z)
            cout << "Scherzo";
    }                                   ┌──────────────────┐
    else                                │ Interpretation 2 │
        cout << "Waltz";                └──────────────────┘
```

Notice that the indentation is an aid for human programmers: the indentation of code has no meaning to the compiler. The compiler will process the code as follows: Without any curly braces to specify the structure for nesting, an `else` is matched with the nearest `if` preceding it. Therefore, the statement

```
if ( x < y) if (y < z)cout << "Scherzo"; else cout << "Waltz";
```

is equivalent to

```
if ( x < y) {
    if (y < z)
        cout << "Scherzo";          ┌──────────────────┐
    else                            │ Interpretation 1 │
        cout << "Waltz";            └──────────────────┘
}
```

If you want interpretation 2, then you would have to use the curly braces to specify the structure of nesting explicitly.

6.3 Sample program: drawing many squares

Let's summarize the techniques presented in this chapter by writing a program that allows the user to draw many squares of different sizes. The program uses both the selection and repetition controls. It is an extension of program ManySquares in section 5.7. The logic of this program is

```
while ( user wants to continue ) {
    get size;
    adjust size if too big or too small;
    draw the square;
}
```

while the logic for the original ManySquares is

```
while ( user wants to continue ) {
```

```
        get size;
        draw the square;
    }
```

The modified program incorporates a test to check that the specified size of a square is not too small or too large. If the specified size is outside the range of allowable sizes, the program adjusts the size. Here is the modified program:

```
// Program ManySquares2:  A program that draws squares of
//                        different sizes until a user wants
//                        to stop. It adjusts the size if it
//                        too small or too large.

#include "Turtles.h"
#include "GUIObj.h"

void main( )
{
    TurtlemyTurtle;
    YesNoBoxprompt;
    OKBoxmsgBox;
    IntTypeIninputBox;
    int size, i, response;
    const intMAX = 432, MIN = 2, YES = 1,
        CENTER_X = 306, CENTER_Y = 216;

    myTurtle.Init(0,0); //initialize turtle, any position is ok

    response = prompt.Ask("Do you want a square?");
    while ( response == YES ) {
        // the YES button is clicked,
        // so draw another square

        size = inputBox.GetInt("Square Size",
                               "Type in the square size");

        if (size > MAX) {//too big
            size = MAX;
            msgBox.Display("Too big. Adjust to maximum.");
        }

        else if (size < MIN) { //error
            size = MIN;
            msgBox.Display("Too small. Adjust to minimum.");
        }

        myTurtle.PenUp(); //move to the center
```

Repeat until the user clicks the NO button.

Adjust the size if the input is bigger than the maximum.

Adjust the size if the input is smaller than the minimum.

```
myTurtle.GoToPos(   CENTER_X - size / 2,
                    CENTER_Y + size / 2);

myTurtle.PenDown(); //now draw the square
for (i = 1; i <= 4; i = i+1 ) {
    myTurtle.Move(size);
    myTurtle.Turn(90);
} // end for

response = prompt.Ask("Do you want another square?");

} //end while

myTurtle.Done();
}
```

Its diagram is shown in figure 6.6.

C++ programs follow two general approaches for handling input errors. The first is to adjust an erroneous input value. This approach is used in the preceding sample program. The second approach is to continue asking a user for input values until he or she enters a valid value. Let's modify the original program ManySquares using this second approach (see figure 6.7). We will list only the relevant portion of the program. The rest of the program is the same as the program ManySquares2.

Which is the better approach? In general, the second approach is preferable for an *interactive I/O*, where a user interacts directly with a program. That is, a user provides an input and reads an output while executing a program. If an input error occurs, then the program can ask the user to correct the input values. We have seen only this type of

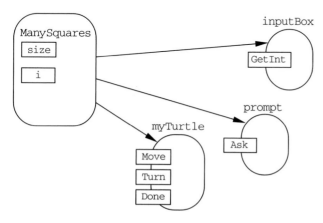

Figure 6.6 ManySquares2 object diagram

C++ Because the values 1 and 0 are interpreted as TRUE and FALSE in C++, respectively, and the Ask function returns 1 or 0, you can write

```
while ( prompt.Ask("Continue?") ){
        ...
    }
```

instead of

```
    response = prompt.Ask("Continue?");
    while ( response == YES ){
        ...
        response = prompt.Ask("Continue?");
    }
```

The benefit of the first approach is its conciseness. The benefit of the second approach is its ability to allow the use of various messages such as

```
    response = prompt.Ask("Start?");
    while ( response == YES ){
        ...
        response = prompt.Ask("Repeat Again?");
    }
```

```
while ( response == YES ) {
    // the YES button is clicked,
    // so draw another square

    size = inputBox.GetInt("Square Size",
            "Type in the square size");

    while (size < MIN || size > MAX) {
        msgBox.Display("Invalid size. Please try again.");
        size = inputBox.GetInt("Square Size",
            "Type in the square size");
    }

    myTurtle.PenUp(); //move to the center
    myTurtle.GoToPos(CENTER_X - size / 2,
                     CENTER_Y + size / 2);

    myTurtle.PenDown(); //now draw the square
    for (i = 1; i <= 4; i = i+1 ) {
        myTurtle.Move(size);
        myTurtle.Turn(90);
    } // end for

    response = prompt.Ask("Do you want another square?");

} //end while
```

MODIFIED PART
The while statement keeps repeating until the user enters a valid size.

Figure 6.7 Revised ManySquares program

interaction. In a *noninteractive I/O*, more commonly known as *batch processing*, the user and the program do not interact directly. Rather, the program is designed to get an input from sources such as computer files or physical devices connected to a computer. (We will examine noninteractive I/O using files in chapter 16.) A program can also read input from a monitoring device such as an oscilloscope. With noninteractive I/O, we cannot use the second approach because there is nobody to prompt to correct the input values. We must use the first approach if we want the program to continue the processing of the remaining input values. In some cases, we must terminate the program whenever an input error occurs.

6.4 Sample program: computing statistical values

In chapter 5 we wrote a program to compute the sum and average of N input values. We will extend the program to also determine the maximum and minimum of N input values. The structure of the modified program is similar to the structure of program ManySquares we wrote in the previous section. Let's start with a pseudocode.

```
cnt = 1;

read number;              //set min and max to the first
max = min = sum = number;   //number read

while (user wants to continue) {

    cnt = cnt + 1; // keep track the count of numbers read
```

```
        read number;   // get the next number

        sum = sum + number; // compute the running sum
        if (number > max)

             max = number; //found a new maximum

        else if (x < min)

             min = number; //found a new minimum
    }

    avg = sum / cnt;
    print out sum, avg, min, max;
```

The user must enter at least one real number. Unlike the program Statistic2 in chapter 5, this program can accept any real number including 0. Notice that the first number entered is assigned to min and max. It is not correct to assign max to 0, for example, because the user may be entering negative real numbers also. If the user enters negative numbers only, then the program would erroneously print out 0 as the maximum. Here is the complete program:

```
//Program Statistic3:  A program to compute the sum, average,
//                     minimum, and maximum of N real numbers.
//
// Note: At least one number must be entered.

#include <iostream.h>

void main()
{
    int    count = 1, answer;
    float number, avg, sum, min, max;
    const int YES = 1;

    //opening message
    cout << "The program will compute the sum, average"<<endl;
    cout << "max, and min of N real numbers you enter."
            << endl << endl;
    cout << "Please press <Return> after each number." << endl;
    cout << endl << endl;

    cout << "Now, please enter Number " << count << ": ";
    cin  >> number;
    min = max = sum = number;
```

```
    cout << "More number? (1 - yes;0 - no)" << endl;
    cin  >> answer;

    while ( answer == YES ) {

        count = count + 1;

        //get the next number
        cout << "Now, please enter Number " << count << ": ";
        cin  >> number;

        //compute the running sum
        sum = sum + number;

        if (number > max)   //found new max

            max = number;

        else if (number < min) //found new min

            min = number;

        cout << "More number? (1 - yes;0 - no)" << endl;
        cin  >> answer;
    }

    //compute the average
    avg = sum / count;

    //print out the results
    cout << endl << endl;
    cout << "Sum :      " << sum << endl;
    cout << "Average : " << avg << endl;
    cout << "Min :      " << min << endl;
    cout << "Max :      " << max << endl;
}
```

6.5 Selection control flow—
`switch` *statement*

Our next program computes the volumes of a triangular prism, a sphere, a cylinder, and a cone. The program first prompts a user to specify one of the shapes and then computes the volume of the selected shape. The program repeats until the user wants to quit. The overall logic of the program is

```
    while (user wants to continue) {
        get shape;

        if (shape is triangular prism) {
            compute the volume of a triangular prism
        }
        else if (shape is sphere) {
            compute the volume of a sphere
        }
        else if (shape is cylinder) {
            compute the volume of a cylinder
        }
        else if (shape is cone) {
            compute the volume of a cone
        }
    }
```

The user enters a numerical value to select the choice—1 for a triangular prism, 2 for a sphere, 3 for a cylinder, and 4 for a cone. If the user enters any other value, the program displays an error message. Using the control statements we have learned so far, we can write the following program:

```
// Program Volumes:  A program to compute the volumes of
//                   four shapes - triangular prism, sphere,
//                   cylinder, and cone.

#include <iostream.h>

void main()
{
    float     base, height, width, radius, volume;
    int       answer, shape;
    const int YES = 1,
              TRIANGULAR_PRISM = 1,
              SPHERE = 2,
              CYLINDER = 3,
              CONE = 4;
    const floatPI = 3.14159;

    cout << "Do you want to begin the computation?" << endl;
    cout << "(1 - yes; 2 - no) " << endl;
    cin >> answer;

    while (answer == YES) {

        cout << "Select shape:1. Triangular prism" << endl;
        cout << "2. Sphere" << endl;
```

```
                    cout << "          3. Cylinder" << endl;
                    cout << "          4. Cone" << endl << endl;
                    cout << "Enter 1, 2, 3, or 4" << endl;
                    cin >> shape;

                    if (shape == TRIANGULAR_PRISM) {

                        cout << "Type in base, height, and width" << endl;
                        cin >> base >> height >> width;

                        volume = 0.5 * base * height * width;

                        cout << "Volume of triangular prism with" <<endl;
                        cout << "base   = " << base << endl;
                        cout << "height = " << height << endl;
                        cout << "width  = " << width << endl;
                        cout << "is          " << volume << endl << endl;
                    }
                    else if (shape == SPHERE) {

                        cout << "Type in radius" << endl;
                        cin >> radius;

                        volume = (4.0/3.0) * PI * radius*radius*radius;

                        cout << "Volume of sphere with" << endl;
                        cout << "radius   = " << radius << endl;
                        cout << "is          " << volume << endl << endl;
                    }
                    else if (shape == CYLINDER) {

                        cout << "Type in radius and height" << endl;
                        cin >> radius >> height;

                        volume = PI * radius*radius * height;

                        cout << "Volume of cylinder with" << endl;
                        cout << "radius   = " << radius << endl;
                        cout << "height   = " << height << endl;
                        cout << "is          " << volume << endl << endl;
                    }
                    else if (shape == CONE) {

                        cout << "Type in radius and height" << endl;
                        cin >> radius >> height;

                        volume = (1.0/3.0) * PI * radius*radius * height;

                        cout << "Volume of cone with" << endl;
```

width

height

base

radius

height

radius

height

radius

```
            cout << "radius    = " << radius << endl;
            cout << "height    = " << height << endl;
            cout << "is          " << volume << endl << endl;
        }
        else {

            cout << "Improper selection." << endl;
            cout << "Must be one of 1, 2, 3, or 4" << endl;
        }

        cout << "Do you want to continue?" << endl;
        cout << "(1 - yes; 2 - no) " << endl;
        cin >> answer;

    } //end while
}
```

Now let's look at the structure of the `if` statement.

```
if (shape == TRIANGULAR_PRISM) {

    //code for computing the volume of a triangular prism

}
else if (shape == SPHERE) {


    //code for computing the volume of a sphere

}
else if (shape == CYLINDER) {


    //code for computing the volume of a cylinder

}
else if (shape == CONE) {

    //code for computing the volume of a cone

}
else {

    //error message

}
```

When we have a multiple selection whose logical expressions contain equality testing (==) against constant values, we can express it more succinctly using a switch statement. Using a switch statement, the preceding nested if statement becomes the code shown in figure 6.8.

The execution of the switch statement works as follows:

1 The switch expression is evaluated and compared with each constant of the case labels in order.

2 If one of the constants is equal to the value of the switch expression, control is passed to the matching case block and the first statement in the case block is executed next. Then the subsequent statements are executed in sequence until the end of the switch statement or the break statement is encountered.

3 If there is no match and there is a default label, then control is passed to the default case block.

4 If there is no match and there is no default label, then no case block is executed (i.e., no statement in the switch statement is executed).

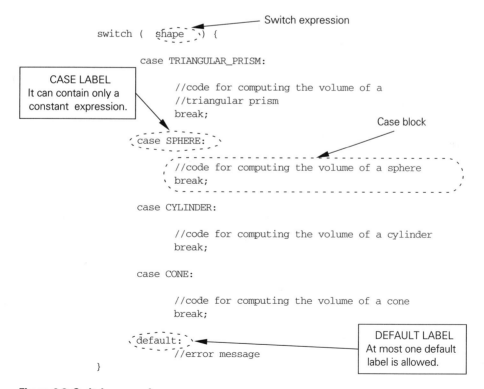

Figure 6.8 Switch expression

No two constants in the `case` labels may be the same, and the maximum number of `default` labels is one. Also, the curly braces are not necessary to surround the `case` block. The `case` and `default` labels do not alter the control flow, so you need an explicit `break` statement to exit from the `switch` statement after executing a `case`. For example, the following code

```
branch = 2;
switch (branch) {

    case 1: cout << "one" << endl;

    case 2: cout << "two" << endl;

    case 3: cout << "three" << endl;

    case 4: cout << "four" << endl;

    case 5: cout << "five" << endl;
}
```

will print out

```
two
three
four
five
```

In other words, after control is passed to the statement

```
cout << "two" << endl;
```

in the matching case label `case 2:`, control is then passed in sequence to the subsequent `case` labels. If we desire to execute only the matching `case` block, we must include a `break` statement at the end of a `case` block, as shown in the following example:

```
switch (branch) {

    case 1:   cout << "one" << endl;
              break;

    case 2:   cout << "two" << endl;
              break;

    case 3:   cout << "three" << endl;
              break;

    case 4:   cout << "four" << endl;
              break;
```

```
case 5:    cout << "five" << endl;
           break;    //break is actually not necessary here,
                     //because this is the last case.
}
```

Figure 6.9 shows the difference between the two statements.

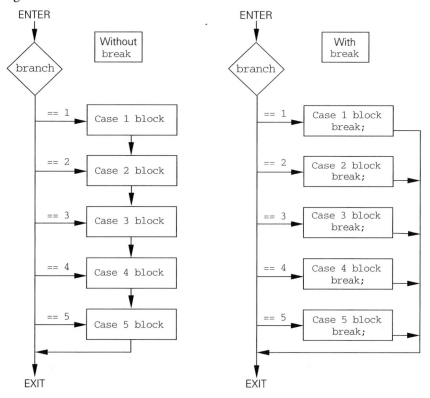

Figure 6.9 Switch statement with and without break statements

A case block may have more than one case label. Suppose, for example, we wish to print out "excellent" for the scores of 8, 9, or 10; "good" for the scores of 4, 5, 6, or 7; and "try harder" for all others. We can use the following switch statement:

```
switch (score) {
    case 8: case 9: case 10: cout << "excellent"; break;
    case 4: case 5: case 6: case 7: cout << "good"; break;
    default: cout << "try harder";
}
```

The following rules are the syntax rules of the `switch` statement. The syntax category *statement* now includes two additional categories—*switch-statement* and *labeled-
statement*—and one additional statement.

statement

. . .

switch-statement
labeled-statement
break

. . .

switch-statement
switch (*expression*) *statement*

labeled-statement
case *constant-expression* **:** *statement-list*
default **:** *statement-list*
constant-expression
identifier
constant

We end this section with a modified version of program Volumes that uses a `switch`
statement.

```
// Program Volumes2:   Computes the volumes of four shapes -
//                     triangular prism, sphere, cylinder,
//                     and cone. Uses a switch statement.

#include <iostream.h>

void main()
{
```

```
float        base, height, width, radius, volume;
int          answer, shape;
const int    YES = 1,
             TRIANGULAR_PRISM = 1,
             SPHERE = 2,
             CYLINDER = 3,
             CONE = 4;
const float PI = 3.14159;

cout << "Do you want to begin the computation?" << endl;
cout << "(1 - yes; 2 - no) " << endl;
cin >> answer;

while (answer == YES) {

    cout << "Select shape: 1. Triangular Prism" << endl;
    cout << "              2. Sphere" << endl;
    cout << "              3. Cylinder" << endl;
    cout << "              4. Cone" << endl << endl;
    cout << "Enter 1, 2, 3, or 4" << endl;
    cin >> shape;

    switch ( shape ) {

        case TRIANGULAR_PRISM:

            cout << "Type in base, height, and width"
                    << endl;
            cin >> base >> height >> width;

            volume = 0.5 * base * height * width;

            cout << "Volume of triangular prism with"
                    <<endl;
            cout << "base   = " << base << endl;
            cout << "height = " << height << endl;
            cout << "width  = " << width << endl;
            cout << "is          " << volume <<endl<<endl;
            break;

        case SPHERE:

            cout << "Type in radius" << endl;
            cin >> radius;

            volume = (4.0/3.0) *PI*radius*radius*radius;

            cout << "Volume of sphere with" << endl;
            cout << "radius   = " << radius << endl;
            cout << "is          " << volume <<endl<<endl;
```

```
                    break;

        case CYLINDER:

                cout << "Type in radius and height" << endl;
                cin >> radius >> height;

                volume = PI * radius*radius * height;

                cout << "Volume of cylinder with" << endl;
                cout << "radius    = " << radius << endl;
                cout << "height    = " << height << endl;
                cout << "is           " << volume <<endl<<endl;
                break;

        case CONE:

                cout << "Type in radius and height" << endl;
                cin >> radius >> height;

                volume = (1.0/3.0) *PI*radius*radius*height;

                cout << "Volume of cone with" << endl;
                cout << "radius    = " << radius << endl;
                cout << "height    = " << height << endl;
                cout << "is           " << volume <<endl<< endl;
                break;

        default:
                cout << "Improper selection." << endl;
                cout << "Must be one of 1, 2, 3, or 4"<<endl;

    } //end switch

    cout << "Do you want to continue?" << endl;
    cout << "(1 - yes; 2 - no) " << endl;
    cin >> answer;

  } //end while
}
```

6.6 *Making programs more general*

In developing computer programs, one of our goals is to make them as general as possible. We say that one program is more general than another if we can use it in a larger number of situations than the other. For example, we say a program that computes the sum of any *N* real numbers is more general than one that computes the sum of any five real numbers. Notice that the generality of a program is a relative issue. We do not have a definition to determine whether a program is general or not. We can only say that, relatively speaking, one program is more general than another program.

In this section, we present one example that shows how to make a program more general. Consider the sample program ManySquares2 we wrote earlier in the chapter. With the declarations

```
const int  MAX = 432,
           CENTER_X = 306,
           CENTER_Y = 216;
```

we are making the assumptions that the center of the turtle object's drawing board is at coordinate (306,216) and the maximum possible size of a square is 432 pixels. These assumptions limit the usefulness of the program. The program is not as general as it can be. Let's see why.

When we introduced the `Turtle` object in chapter 2, we described a drawing board with a width of 433 pixels and a height of 612 pixels. We mentioned the actual dimensions of the drawing board to make the discussion concrete and easy to follow, and we wrote the sample programs with this assumption to simplify the programs. In writing real programs, however, we should not make such assumptions. Although we cannot eliminate all assumptions, we must aim not to make assumptions that can be eliminated easily with a little care in design.

Let's first see why making the above assumptions is not a good idea. Consider what happens if we need to change the size of the drawing board. For instance, we may want to adjust the size of the drawing board according to the size of a computer monitor. We may, for example, make the drawing board 960 × 800 pixels for a large monitor. All of the programs we have written so far need to be modified so they will run correctly on the 960 × 800 pixels drawing board.

One may argue that we could replace the constant values and compile the program again. The problem with this approach is that we have to maintain different versions of the same program: one program for a drawing board of size 612 × 433, another program for a drawing board of size 960 × 800, and so forth. We have to give each version a unique name, even though they are all essentially the same program.

A better solution is to write one program that works properly for a drawing board of any size. How can we make such a general program? We can do so by not making any assumption about the dimensions of a drawing board in a program. A `Turtle` object is responsible for drawing figures, so we will let it tell us the size of its drawing board. The turtle has two functions `GetWidth` and `GetHeight`, which return the width and the height of its drawing board in pixels. Using these two functions, we can modify the program ManySquares2 so that it is capable of drawing squares on a drawing board of any dimension. This adaptability is made possible by not making any assumption about the dimension of a drawing board and by getting this information from the `Turtle` object. The modified program is much more general than the original version.

```
// Program ManySquares3: A program that draw squares of
//                       different sizes until a user wants
//                       to stop. The squares are drawn at
//                       the center of a drawing board of
//                       any dimension.

#include "Turtles.h"
#include "GUIObj.h"

void main ( )
{
        Turtle       myTurtle;
        YesNoBox     prompt;
        OKBox        msgBox;
        IntTypeIn    inputBox;
        int          size, i, response, width, height,
                     MAX, CENTER_X, CENTER_Y;
        const int    MIN = 2, YES = 1;

        myTurtle.Init(0,0); //initialize turtle, any position is ok

        width  = myTurtle.GetWidth();//get the dimension
        height = myTurtle.GetHeight();//of drawing board

        if (height > width)    //the largest square cannot be
            MAX = width;       //bigger than the smaller of
        else                   //width and height
            MAX = height;

        CENTER_X = width  / 2;
        CENTER_Y = height / 2;
        response = prompt.Ask("Do you want a square?");
        while ( response == YES ) {
            // the YES button is clicked,
            // so draw another square

            size = inputBox.GetInt("Square Size",
                                "Type in the square size");

            if (size > MAX) {//too big
                size = MAX;
                msgBox.Display("Too big. Adjust to maximum.");
            }
```

Note these are not constants anymore.

Note how the variables are set.

```
        else if (size < MIN) { //error
            size = MIN;
            msgBox.Display("Too small. Adjust to minimum.");
        }

        myTurtle.PenUp(); //move to the center
        myTurtle.GoToPos(CENTER_X - size / 2,
            CENTER_Y + size / 2);

        myTurtle.PenDown(); //now draw the square
        for (i = 1; i <= 4; i = i+1 ) {
            myTurtle.Move(size);
            myTurtle.Turn(90);
        } // end for

        response = prompt.Ask("Do you want another square?");

    } //end while

    myTurtle.Done();
}
```

6.7 Exercises

1   Consider the example of multiple selections on section 6.2. Suppose 80% of the input has values between 90 and 100. Then 80% of the time, we need to execute four tests (X < 60, X < 70, X < 80, and X < 90) to determine that an input value is between 90 and 100. We can improve the performance by rearranging the sequence of testing so only one test is necessary to determine that an input value is between 90 and 100. Modify the program so that the testing is done in the reverse order (i.e., test for A, then B, then C, and so on).

2   Write a wage calculation program that accepts the hours worked and the hourly rate as inputs, and compute the total wage according to the following formula:

Hours worked	Wage
hours ≤ 40	rate * hours
40 < hours ≤ 60	rate * 40 + 1.5 * rate * (hours - 40)
hours > 60	rate * 40 + 1.5 * rate * 20 + 2.0 * rate * (hours - 60)

3 Write a change-calculation program that accepts the change as input (0...99) and prints out the change in quarters, dimes, nickels, and pennies using the `if` statements. Repeat the computation until a user wants to stop.

4 Are the code segments on the left side equivalent to the corresponding segments on the right side?

```
if (a > b)                          if (a > b || c < d)
    if (c < d)                          cout << "one";
        cout << "one";              else
else                                    cout << "two";
    cout << "two";
```

```
if (a > b)                          if (a > b) {
    if (c < d)                          if (c < d)
        cout << "one";                      cout << "one";
else                                }
    cout << "two";                  else
                                        cout << "two";
```

```
if (a > b)                          switch (a > b) {
    cout << "one";                      case 1:
else                                        cout << "one";
    cout << "two";                          break;
                                        case 0:
                                            cout << "two";
                                    }
```

5 Write a grade calculation program that accepts a class level and test score and computes the grade according to the following formula:

Class level	Test score	Grade
1, 2, 3, 4	score ≥ 60 score < 60	pass fail
5, 6, 7, 8	score ≥ 75 score < 75	pass fail
9, 10, 11, 12	score ≥ 90 score < 90	pass fail

Print out an appropriate error message for invalid class level and test score values.

CHAPTER 6   SELECTION CONTROL FLOW

6 Determine the output for the following `if` statements. They are purposely written in a poorly indented manner.

a)
```
int x = 1, y = 0;
    if (x > 0)
        if (y != 0)
            cout << y;
    else
        cout << x;
        cout << y;
```

b)
```
int x = 1, y = 0;
    if (x != 0)
        if (y == 0)
            cout << y;
            cout << x;
        else
            if (y == x)
                cout << x;
        else cout << y;
```

c)
```
int x = 1, y = 0;
    if (x > 1)
        cout << y;
    else if (y == 0)
        cout << x;
        cout << y;
        if (x != 1) cout<< x;
    else if (y = 1) cout<< y;
    else cout << x;
```

d)
```
int x = 1, y = 0;
    if (x > 1)
        cout << y;
    else if (y == 0)
        if (x != 1) cout << x;
        else if (y = 1) cout << y;
    else cout << x;
```

7 Rewrite the `if` statements in exercise 6 with properly indented `if` statements.

8 Rewrite the program Statistic3 in section 6.4 using GUI objects.

9 What is the difference between the next two code segments? They do the same thing, but which one does it more efficiently? Notice that the code on the left has two `if` statements without the `else` parts, while the code on the right has one `if` statement with the `else` part containing a nested `if` statement.

```
if (number > max)

    max = number;

if (number < min)

    min = number;
```

```
if (number > max)

    max = number;

else if (number < min)

    min = number;
```

10 Modify the program ManySquares so the user has an option of changing the pen color before drawing each new square. Allow the user to specify six different colors: 1 – black, 2 – blue, 3 – green, 4 – cyan, 5 – red, and 6 – magenta. You can change a `Turtle` object's pen color by calling its `ChangePenColor` function with the argument BLACK, BLUE, GREEN, CYAN, RED, or MAGENTA. For example, to change the pen color of myTurtle to red, you call

```
myTurtle.ChangePenColor(RED);
```

11 Write a program that reads a sequence of positive integers and determines how many times it reads the value 20. The program terminates when a user enters a negative number. For the input

```
12   3   4   20   4   3   20   14   98   11   20   20   -1
```

the program will output 4.

chapter 7

Nonnumerical data

In addition to the numerical data types we studied in chapter 3, nonnumerical data types are indispensable in writing useful and practical computer programs, such as word processing and database programs. Word processing programs allow the user to create documents that contain text and diagrams, while database programs allow the user to create files that contain information such as names, addresses, and phone numbers. Both of these kinds of programs process nonnumerical data; therefore, we need a computer programming language that allows the use of nonnumerical data types in writing such programs. In this chapter, we will study two types of nonnumerical data that we can use in writing C++ programs.

7.1 The `char` *data type*

The data type `char` is used to represent a single character in C++. Typically, a value of type `char` occupies 1 byte (8 bits) of memory, and it is encoded using a specific coding convention, such as ASCII (American Standard Code for Information Interchange) or EBCDIC (Extended Binary Coded Decimal Interchange Code). Table 7.1 lists 128 characters (not all of them are printable) along with their ASCII codes.

Table 7.1 ASCII

CODE	CHAR	CODE	CHAR	CODE	CHAR	CODE	CHAR
0	NUL	32	Space	64	@	96	'
1	SOH	33	!	65	A	97	a
2	STX	34	"	66	B	98	b
3	ETX	35	#	67	C	99	c
4	EOT	36	$	68	D	100	d
5	ENQ	37	%	69	E	101	e
6	ACK	38	&	70	F	102	f
7	BEL	39	'	71	G	103	g
8	BS	40	(	72	H	104	h
9	HT	41	)	73	I	105	i
10	LF	42	*	74	J	106	j
11	VT	43	+	75	K	107	k
12	FF	44	,	76	L	108	l
13	CR	45	-	77	M	109	m
14	SO	46	.	78	N	110	n
15	SI	47	/	79	O	111	o
16	DLE	48	0	80	P	112	p
17	DC1	49	1	81	Q	113	q
18	DC2	50	2	82	R	114	r
19	DC3	51	3	83	S	115	s
20	DC4	52	4	84	T	116	t
21	NAK	53	5	85	U	117	u
22	SYN	54	6	86	V	118	v
23	ETB	55	7	87	W	119	w
24	CAN	56	8	88	X	120	x
25	EM	57	9	89	Y	121	y
26	SUB	58	:	90	Z	122	z
27	ESC	59	;	91	[	123	{
28	FS	60	<	92	\	124	l
29	GS	61	=	93	]	125	}
30	RS	62	>	94	^	126	~
31	US	63	?	95	_	127	DEL

If you look at the code for the character *A* in this table, you will see it is 65. Since every-thing is binary in a computer, the ASCII representation of the character *A* is stored as the binary equivalent of 65, which is 0100 0001. You might want to review the discussion on data representation in chapter 1. Not all 128 ASCII characters can be printed. Codes 0 through 31 and code 127 are nonprinting characters. They are used for control purposes

Table 7.2 Nonprinting control characters

Control characters	ASCII code	Meaning
NUL	0	Null
HT	9	Horizontal tab (effect of pressing the tab key)
CR	13	Carriage return (effect of pressing the return key)
LF	10	New line (*LF* stands for line feed)
ESC	27	Escape (effect of pressing the esc key)
BEL	7	Bell
BS	8	Backspace (effect of pressing the del key)

in data transmission and keyboard input. Some of the more commonly used control characters are listed in table 7.2.

Since there are 8 bits to a byte, it is possible to store $2^8 = 256$ distinct values in 1 byte, ranging from 0000 0000 to 1111 1111. But there are only 128 distinct ASCII codes, so we really don't need 8 bits. In fact, 7 bits ($2^7 = 128$) would be enough to represent the 128 ASCII codes. Then why are we using eight bits? The reason is the addressing scheme used in computer memory. A byte is the smallest unit of memory that we can address and access (i.e., we can fetch 1 byte, 2 bytes, and so forth, but not $1\frac{1}{2}$ or $\frac{3}{4}$ bytes). Since we need to use only 128 values for the ASCII codes, many computer vendors use the extra 128 values for special purposes. For example, PC-compatible machines utilize the extra values for representing graphic symbols primarily employed in drawing graphical images such as boxes.

Let's consider how we declare and use character data. Declaring a character variable is essentially the same as declaring the other data types we have already seen. For example, the declaration

```
charch1, ch2 = 'A', ch3 = 'x';
```

declares three character variables `ch1`, `ch2`, and `ch3`. The variables `ch2` and `ch3` are initialized to the values `'A'` and `'x'`, respectively. The single quotes denote a character constant. For nonprintable characters, we must use a special notation called an escape sequence. For example, the tab character (HT) is denoted as `'\t'`. The statement

```
cout << 15 << '\t' << 25;
```

will result in the output shown in figure 7.1.

Figure 7.1 Escape sequence output

Table 7.3 Common escape sequences

Code	Escape sequence	Meaning
0	\0	Null
8	\b	Backspace
9	\t	Tab
10	\n	New line
12	\f	Form feed (next page)
13	\r	Carriage return
39	\'	Single quote
92	\\	Backslash

C++ Escape sequences for control characters not listed in this table must be represented by their octal values (base-8 numbers). For example, the code for the vertical tab (VT) is decimal 11, so the escape sequence for VT in octal notation is \13 since $1 \times 8 + 3 = 11$.

The backslash symbol (\) is called the *escape character*. Table 7.3 shows some common escape sequences.

Let's write a program that illustrates the use of character data. The program Volumes2 from section 6.2 used the switch statement for determining the shape of the volume to be computed. An integer input was used to determine the shape: 1 – triangular prism, 2 – sphere, 3 – cylinder, and 4 – cone. We will modify the program so the user enters a character to specify the shape: *T* or *t* – triangular prism, *S* or *s* – sphere, *Y* or *y* – cylinder, and *O* or *o* – cone. The flow of the switch statement is as follows:

```
char shape;
...
cin >> shape;
switch (shape) {

    case 'T':
    case 't': //compute the volume of a triangular prism
            break;

    case 'S':
    case 's': //compute the volume of a sphere
            break;
```

```
            case 'Y':
            case 'y': //compute the volume of a cylinder
                        break;

            case 'O':
            case 'o': //compute the volume of a cone

            default: //error. wrong character is entered

    }
```

Here is the complete program:

```
// Program Volumes3: A program to compute the volumes of
//                   four shapes — triangular prism, sphere,
//                   cylinder, and cone. Uses a switch
//                   statement with a character input.

#include <iostream.h>

void main()
{
    float         base, height, width, radius, volume;
    int           answer;
    char          shape;  ◄─────────  data type
    const int     YES = 1;              char
    const float   PI = 3.14159;

    cout << "Do you want to begin the computation?" << endl;
    cout << "(1 - yes; 2 - no) " << endl;
    cin >> answer;

    while (answer == YES) {

        cout << "Select shape: T. Triangular Prism" << endl;
        cout << "              S. Sphere" << endl;
        cout << "              Y. Cylinder" << endl;
        cout << "              O. Cone" << endl << endl;
        cout << "Enter T, S, Y, or O" << endl;
        cin >> shape;

        switch ( shape ) {

            case 'T':
            case 't':

                cout << "Type in base, height, and width"
                     << endl;
```

```
            cin >> base >> height >> width;

            volume = 0.5 * base * height * width;

            cout << "Volume of triangular prism with"
             <<endl;
            cout << "base   = " << base << endl;
            cout << "height = " << height << endl;
            cout << "width  = " << width << endl;
            cout << "is         " << volume <<endl<<endl;
            break;

    case 'S':
    case 's':

            cout << "Type in radius" << endl;
            cin >> radius;

            volume = (4.0/3.0) * PI*radius*radius*radius;

            cout << "Volume of sphere with" << endl;
            cout << "radius   = " << radius << endl;
            cout << "is         " << volume <<endl<<endl;
            break;

    case 'Y':
    case 'y':

            cout << "Type in radius and height" << endl;
            cin >> radius >> height;

            volume = PI * radius*radius * height;

            cout << "Volume of cylinder with" << endl;
            cout << "radius   = " << radius << endl;
            cout << "height   = " << height << endl;
            cout << "is         " << volume <<endl<<endl;
            break;

    case 'O':
    case 'o':

            cout << "Type in radius and height" << endl;
            cin >> radius >> height;

            volume = (1.0/3.0) * PI*radius*radius*height;

            cout << "Volume of cone with" << endl;
            cout << "radius   = " << radius << endl;
```

```
                        cout << "height    = " << height << endl;
                        cout << "is           " << volume <<endl<< endl;
                        break;

               default:
                        cout << "Improper selection." << endl;
                        cout << "Must be one of T, S, Y, or O"<<endl;

       } //end switch

       cout << "Do you want to continue?" << endl;
       cout << "(1 - yes; 2 - no) " << endl;
       cin >> answer;

   } //end while
}
```

The user can enter either lower- or uppercase letters in selecting a shape. Since the cylinder and cone have the same first letter, we used *Y* or *y* for selecting the cylinder and *O* or *o* for the cone. Another possibility is to let the user enter the first two letters of the cylinder and cone. Since the program does not distinguish lower- and uppercase letters, any one of *CY, Cy, cY,* or *cy* is acceptable for selecting the cylinder and any one of *CO, CO, cO,* or *co* for selecting the cone. We will list a modified switch statement of the program here.

```
           char ch;
           ...
           cin >> ch;
           switch (ch) {

                case 'T':
                case 't': //compute the volume of a triangular prism
                            break;
                    case 'S':
                    case 's': //compute the volume of a sphere
                            break;

                    case 'C':
                    case 'c': // is it a cylinder or a cone?

                        cin >> ch; //read the second character
                        if (ch == 'Y' || ch == 'y') {
                            //compute the volume of a cylinder
                        }
                        else if (ch == 'O' || ch == 'o') {
                            //compute the volume of a cone
```

You can use another switch statement here instead. See exercise 2 at the end of this chapter.

```
        }
        else {
            //error. wrong second character is entered
        }
        break;

    default: //error. wrong character is entered

}//end switch
```

The program requires the user to enter one character for specifying the triangular prism and the sphere, and two characters for specifying the cylinder and the cone. To make the input routine consistent, we could allow the user to enter two characters for specifying all four shapes. For example, we use two character variables, say ch1 and ch2, for the first and second characters, respectively, and perform the tests on these two variables to determine the shape. We will discuss this approach in the next section.

We stated that a value of type char typically occupies 1 byte of memory. Although 1 byte is enough to represent all the characters of English, it is not enough for some languages whose character set is very large, such as Chinese or Japanese. Character codes for Japanese and Chinese require 2 bytes, and they use their own standard coding schemes similar to ASCII. Why should we be aware of such differences? After all, not many of us will be writing programs that manipulate Chinese or Japanese characters. We mention this fact as a case study of *program portability.* We say a program is *portable* if it can be executed on different operating systems with no changes. An activity to modify a program so it will run on a different operating system is called *porting.*

One way to develop portable programs is not to use any operations or assumptions that apply only to a particular operating system. Here's an example. We use the I/O manipulator endl to insert a line break in the output. In the MS–Windows environment

```
cout << 15 << '\r' << '\n' << 25;
```
◄── Can also be expressed as
`cout << 15 << "\r\n" << 25;`

is equivalent to

```
cout << 15 << endl << 25;
```

However, in the Macintosh environment, you need only '\n'. If you use both '\r' and '\n' (as in the first example), the statement will not work correctly. Therefore, the statement

```
cout << 15 << '\r' << '\n' << 25;
```

works differently on Mac and PC platforms. Programs that use such system-specific operations must be modified if we wish to port them to different operating systems. If we use the I/O manipulator `endl`, no modification is necessary because the compilers for the Mac and PC define the I/O manipulator accordingly (`"\r\n"` for PC, and `"\n"` for Mac).

Another way to develop portable programs is to use standard functions that come with the compiler, such as the standard functions for mathematical computations (`sin`, `cos`, etc.), string manipulations, and character manipulations. Each compiler implements these standard functions in a way appropriate to the operating system on which it runs. The implementation may be different, but the way we use the functions in our programs is the same (thus, the name *standard*). We just have to use the correct header file (e.g., the header file for the Mac, if we want to run the program on a Mac). So by using the standard functions, we can make a program portable; the program code can run unmodified on Macs or PCs. We will discuss standard character functions in the next section.

7.2 Standard character functions

To illustrate the use of ASCII characters further, let's write a simple program that will read in characters and count the number of letters (A, ... , Z, a, ... , z) and digits (0, ... , 9) that occur in the input. The program continues until the pound (#) key is entered. Its pseudocode is

```
alphaCount = 0; digitCount = 0;
read character ch;
while (ch is not '#') {
    if (ch is letter)
        alphaCount = alphaCount + 1;
    else if (ch is digit)
        digitCount = digitCount + 1;

    read character ch;
}

output alphaCount and digitCount;
```

The key point for this program is how to determine whether the input character `ch` is a letter or digit, which we can do in two ways. The first way is to check the character's ASCII code. Based on the ASCII codes, the following relationships hold. (Refer to table 7.1 on page 168).

```
'0'<'1'<...<'9'<'A'<'B'<...<'Y'<'Z'<'a'<'b'< ... <'y'<'z'
```

We can write the `if` statement as

```
if ( (ch >= 'A' and ch <= 'Z') or (ch >= 'A' and ch <= 'Z') )

    alphaCount = alphaCount + 1;

else if (ch >= '0' and ch <= '9')

    digitcount = digitCount + 1;
```

Notice that we cannot write the first test as

```
if (ch >= 'A' and ch <= 'z')
```

because there are six nonalphabetic characters between Z and a.

The second way to determine whether the input character is a letter or digit is to use the standard character functions. These functions are defined in the header file `<ctype.h>`. Table 7.4 lists some of the useful character functions.

Table 7.4 Some useful character functions in <ctype.h>[*]

Function	Meaning
isalpha(ch)	Returns nonzero (TRUE) if ch is a letter. Otherwise returns 0 (FALSE).
isdigit(ch)	Returns nonzero if ch is a digit. Otherwise returns 0 .
isalphanum(ch)	Returns nonzero if ch is a letter or a digit. Otherwise returns 0.
islower(ch)	Returns nonzero if ch is a lowercase letter. Otherwise returns 0.
isupper(ch)	Returns nonzero if ch is an uppercase letter. Otherwise returns 0.
isprint(ch)	Returns nonzero if ch is a printable character. Otherwise returns 0. *Note:* A space is a printable character.
iscntrl(ch)	Returns nonzero if ch is a control character. Otherwise returns 0.
ispunct(ch)	Returns nonzero if ch is a printable character that is not a space, letter, or digit. Otherwise returns 0.
isspace(ch)	Returns nonzero if ch is a space (32), line feed (10), tab (9), form feed (12), carriage return (13), or vertical tab (11). Otherwise returns 0.
toupper(ch)	Returns the corresponding uppercase letter if ch is a lowercase letter. Otherwise returns ch.
tolower(ch)	Returns the corresponding lowercase letter if ch is an uppercase letter. Otherwise returns ch.
toascii(ch)	Returns the ASCII code of ch.

[*]Your compiler may not support all of the functions listed here.

Using the standard character functions, the `if` statement becomes

```
if ( isalpha(ch) )

    alphaCount = alphaCount + 1;

else if ( isdigit(ch) )

    digitcount = digitCount + 1;
```

The following listing is the complete program (with the standard character functions).

```
//Program Count: A program that reads characters and
//               counts the occurrence of letters and digits.

#include <iostream.h>
#include <ctype.h>

void main ( )
{
    int alphaCount = 0, digitCount = 0;
    char ch;
    const char poundSign = '#';

    cout << "Input:" << endl;
    cin >> ch;
    while (ch != poundSign) {

        if ( isalpha(ch) )

            alphaCount = alphaCount + 1;

        else if ( isdigit(ch) )

            digitcount = digitCount + 1;
        //end if

        cin >> ch;
    }

    cout << endl << endl;
    cout << "# of alphabets: " << alphaCount << endl;
    cout << "# of digits:    " << digitCount << endl;
}
```

C++ provides various conversion functions for converting data of one type to another. We call type conversion *type casting*. We can type cast an integer value x to a character by using the expression

```
char ( x )
```

Table 7.5 lists examples of integer-to-character type casting.

Let's write a program that will accept an integer from the user and display the corresponding character if the integer entered is the ASCII code for a printable character. We use an IntTypeIn object for entering an integer. The program will display the message Nonprintable character is entered for values that correspond to the nonprintable characters. The program will also display an error message for the values outside the range 0–127. The user clicks the No button on a YesNoBox box to terminate the program. We will use an OKBox object for displaying the character.

Table 7.5 Integer-to-character type casting

X	char (X)
64	'A'
13	'\r'
54	'6'
97	'a'

Here is the pseudocode:

```
do {
    input code;
    if (code is between 0 and 127, inclusive) {

        convert code to character ch;

        if (ch is printable)
            display the character;
        else
            display "Non-printable character is entered";
        //end if
    }
    else
        display the error message;

} while (user wants to continue);
```

And here is the program:

```
// Program ASCII:  A program that displays a character of
//                 a given ASCII code.
#include "GUIObj.h"
#include <ctype.h>
```

```
void main ( )
{
    IntTypeIn       inputBox;
    OkBox           msgBox;
    YesNoBox        prompt;
    int             code, response;
    char            ch;
    const int       YES = 1;

    do {
        code = inputBox.GetInt( "Input Box",
                                "Type an ASCII code [0-127]");

        if (code >= 0 && code <= 127) {

            ch = char(code);

            if ( isprint(ch) )
                msgBox.Display(ch);

            else
                msgBox.Display(
                    "Non-printable character is entered");
        }
        else

         msgBox.Display("Error:Input value is out of range");

        //end if

        response = prompt.Ask("Continue?");
    } while (response == YES);
}
```

Figure 7.2 shows the object diagram.

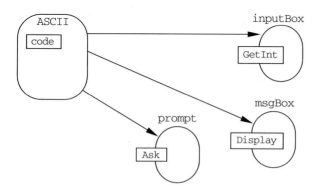

Figure 7.2 Program ASCII object diagram

7.3 String data

We have already used string data. For example, the messages we displayed in OKBox and IntTypeIn GUI objects were all string data. In this section, we will consider string data in more detail.

So far our usage has been limited to string literal constants. Many of you may be expecting something such as:

```
string   str1, str2;
int      age;
...
str1 = "Hi, my name is Iris, and I'm 11." ;
str2 = "How old are you?";
age  = inputBox.GetInt( str1, str2);
...
```

for string variables. This is a reasonable and logical expectation, but C++ does not have a data type called *string*. Instead, C++ represents string data as an array, or sequence, of characters.

Consider the declaration

```
char str[10];
```

that declares the variable str to be an array of characters. For simplicity, we will use the term *string variable*, instead of the correct but long expression *variable of type array of characters*. Also, we will use the terms *character array* or *string* instead of *array of characters*. The integer value inside the bracket denotes the size of the string. The value of 10 in the preceding declaration means that the string has 10 slots, addressed from 0 to 9, and will result in the diagram shown in figure 7.3.

If we initialize the string variable in the declaration as

```
char str[10] = "Hello";
```

then the result is shown in figure 7.4.

Figure 7.3 Character array str

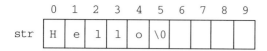

Figure 7.4 Hello string

The NUL character '\0' in slot 5 signals the end of the string. Every string in C++ must be terminated by the NUL character. Since one slot is occupied by the NUL character, we can store at most $N-1$ "real" characters in a string variable with the declared size N. The declared size of the variable str in the above example is 10, so we can store at most nine real characters. It would be an error to initialize a string variable to a string that has more characters than the declared size of the variable. For instance, the initialization

```
cbar str[10] = "This is too long";
```

would result in a compile error. Another common mistake programmers make in using C++ string data is not distinguishing a single character from a string with one character in it. Remember that a literal character constant is enclosed in single quotes, whereas a literal string constant is enclosed in double quotes. Figure 7.5 illustrates the difference. The variable ch is of type char, while the variable str is of type array char.

Notice that the individual slots of a string are indexed, or addressed, from 0 to 1 minus the declared size of the string. This index is used to refer to an individual character in the string. To refer to the fourth character of str, for example, we say str[3], as shown in figure 7.6.

The syntax rule for a character array is

character–array–declaration
      char   *identifier*   **[**   *constant*   **]**   *string–initializer*$_{opt}$

string–initializer
      =   *string–constant*

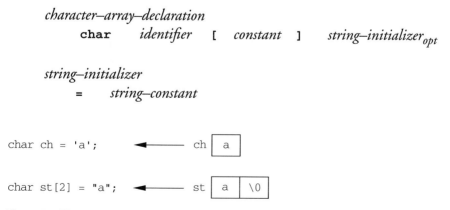

Figure 7.5 Literal character and literal string constants

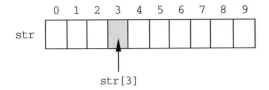

Figure 7.6 Fourth character of str

An expression like

        str[3]

is called an *indexed expression,* and it is used to manipulate a string on a character-by-character basis, as figure 7.7 illustrates.

  Let's write a program that prints out a given string using an OKBox for each word. For this program we define a word to be a sequence of characters separated by a blank space. Executing the program for the input

        "OK. Here's a string."

will result in figure 7.8.

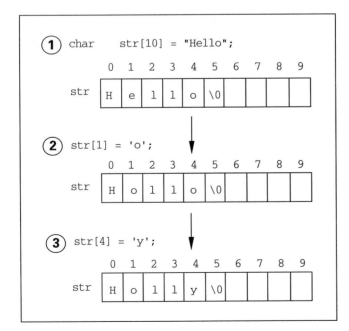

Figure 7.7 Indexed expression

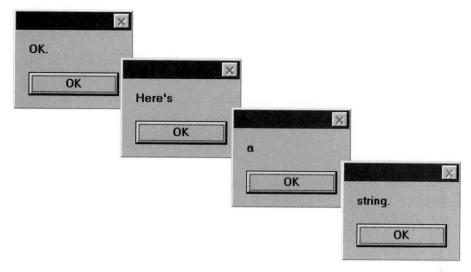

Figure 7.8 OK box used for each word of string

Its pseudocode is

```
do {
    if (next char == space or end-of-string marker)
        display the next word;
    else
        append next char to the end of current word;
} while (not end of string )
```

And the complete program is as follows:

```
//Program Dissect:   A program that divides a given
//                   string into individual words.

#include "GUIObj.h"

void main()
{
    // str is the string variable containing the string
    // wd is the string variable to contain a word
    OKBox       msg;
    char        str[30] = "OK. Here's a string.";
    char        word[10];
    const char  END_MARKER = '\0';
    const char  BLANK= ' ';
```

```
int i = -1, j = -1;
do {
    j = j + 1; i = i + 1;

    if (str[i] == BLANK || str[i] == END_MARKER) {

        word[j] = END_MARKER;
        msg.Display(word);
        j = -1; //reset the counter for the next word

    }
    else
        word[j] = str[i];

} while (str[i] != END_MARKER);
}
```

7.4 Standard string functions

In the previous example, we initialized the string variable str with the string "OK. Here's a string." at the time of declaration:

```
char str[30] = "OK. Here's a string.";
```

The preceding statement is valid, but the following is not.

```
char str[30];
str = "This is a string";
```

C++ does not allow you to assign a whole string to a string variable. We must either assign characters individually such as

```
char str[10];
str[0] = 'H';
str[1] = 'e';
str[2] = 'l';
str[3] = 'l';
str[4] = 'o';
str[5] = '\0';
```

or use one of the standard string functions. Table 7.6 lists five frequently used functions. Please refer to your compiler for other string functions. For the functions to work correctly, arguments must be NUL-terminated strings.

To see how these functions work, we can use the strcpy function to assign a string value to a string variable. The code

Table 7.6 Standard string functions

Function	Usage
strcpy(string1, string2)	Copies string2 to string1. string1 must be large enough to hold all of the characters in string2. The original value of string1 is destroyed.
strlen(string)	Returns the size of a string, that is, the number of characters in the string, excluding the NUL character.
strcmp(string1, string2)	Compares string1 and string2 and returns a negative, zero, or positive value depending on whether string1 is less than, equal to, or greater than string2 in alphabetical order.
strcat(string1, string2)	Appends string2 to the end of string1. string1 must be large enough to hold both string1 (before appending) and string2.
strdup(string)	Returns a duplicate copy of string. The original string remains unchanged.

```
char str[10];
strcpy(str, "Hello");
```

assigns the string "Hello" to the string variable str.

The strlen function returns the size of a string, that is, the number of characters in the string. Assuming the above string str, then

```
strlen(str)
```

will return 5 because the string "Hello" has five characters. The function determines the size of a string by counting the number of characters from the first position to the position that contains the NUL character. So if we assign the NUL character explicitly somewhere in the middle of a string as in this example:

```
strcpy(str, "Bonjour");
str[4] = '\0';
strlen(str);
```

the strlen function returns 4.

The strcmp function compares two strings and returns a result according to the following rule:

$$
\text{strcmp(str1,str2)} = \begin{cases} \text{negative} & \text{if str1} < \text{str2} \\ 0 & \text{if str1} = \text{str2} \\ \text{positive} & \text{if str1} > \text{str2} \end{cases}
$$

Table 7.7 Strcmp function results

Comparison	Result	Comment
`strcmp("Hello", "Hillo");`	Negative	The second character e is less than *i*.
`strcmp("Hello","hello");`	Negative	Uppercase letters are smaller than lower-case letters in alphabetical order.
`strcmp("Hello","Helloo");`	Negative	If two strings have the same prefix, then the longer string is larger than the shorter string.
`strcmp("Hello","H5llo");`	Positive	Digits are smaller than letters in lexico-graphic order.
`strcmp("Hello","Hello");`	0	Must be exactly same for the function to return 0.

Some examples are shown in table 7.7.

The `strcat` function concatenates two strings. For example, the code

```
char str1[10] = "Turtle";
char str2[10] = "Power";
strcat(str1, str2);
```

will cause `str1` to become `"TurtlePower"`. The variable `str2` remains unchanged. If `str1` is an empty string, then the `strcat` function has an effect of assigning the value of `str2` to `str1`; that is, it is equivalent to `strcpy`.

Beware In C++ the numeral 0 is treated as FALSE. For example, the logical expression (x == 15) returns 0 if x is not equal to 15 (i.e., the result is FALSE). The `strcmp` function returns 0 if two strings are equal, so the following will not output equal:

```
if (strcmp(s1,s1))
    cout << "equal";
else
    cout << "not equal";
```

But the following will:

```
if (strcmp(s1,s1) == 0)
    cout << "equal";
else
    cout << "not equal";
```

The `strdup` function returns a duplicate copy of a string. For example, the following code will print out `HelloHello`.

```
char str2[10] = "Hello";
cout << strdup(str2) << str2;
```

Notice that

```
cout << str2 << str2;
```

would result in the same output, but the first code fragment prints two distinct strings (they just happen to contain the same sequence of characters), while the second one prints the same string twice.

Let's write a program to illustrate the use of these string functions. The program reads a word and appends it to an output string if the length of the word is between five and ten characters and it falls between `"GUIObj"` and `"Turtle"` in alphabetical order. The program displays the output string and then stops when the input word is `"STOP"`. In addition to the string functions, the program will use a `StringTypeIn` object for inputting a word and an `OKBox` object for displaying the output string. The output string can consist of a maximum of 50 characters, so the program will also stop when the number of characters in the output string reaches the maximum. The maximum is set to 50 characters because an `OKBox` is not appropriate for displaying a very long string.

The overall flow of the program can be expressed as

```
done = FALSE;
do {
    get the next word;

    if word != "STOP" {
        size = strlen(word); //length of word

        if ( (size is between 5 and 10) &&
             (word is between "GUIObj" and "Turtle"))

            if strlen(outString) + size <= 50
                strcat(outString,word); //append word
            else
                done = TRUE; //overflow so stop
            //endif
    } //endif
    else
        done = TRUE; //input is "STOP" so stop
} while (not done);
```

```
print out outString;
```

And here's the complete program:

```
//Program String:    A program to illustrate the use of
//                    standard string functions.

#include "GUIObj.h"
#include <string.h>

void main ( )
{
    int            size, done;
    const int      MAX = 50;
    char           outString[MAX+1] = "",
                   word[25];
    StringTypeIn   strInputBox;
    OKBox          msg;
    const int      FALSE = 0, TRUE = 1;

    done = FALSE;
    do {
        strcpy(word,
               strInputBox.GetString("String Input",
                                     "Type in a word") );

    if (strcmp( word, "STOP") != 0) { //not equal
        size = strlen( word );

        if ( (size >= 5 && size <= 10) &&
             (strcmp( word, "GUIObj" ) >= 0 &&
              strcmp( word, "Turtle") <= 0) )

            if (strlen( outString ) + size <= MAX)
                strcat( outString, word );
            else
                done = TRUE; //overflow so stop
            //endif
        //endif
    }
    else
        done = TRUE; //input is "STOP" so stop
    } while (!done);

    msg.Display(outString);
}
```

New GUI object for string input

You need to initialize it to an empty string for the function strcat work properly.

WARNING! If FALSE and TRUE are already defined by the compiler, this statement will cause a compilation error. Remove this statement in such cases.

We use a new GUI object called StringTypeIn, a cousin of IntTypeIn, for reading in a string. By executing

```
StringTypeIn        strInputBox;
char                word[25];
strInputBox.GetString("String Input Box","Please type in");
```

the user will see a dialog on the screen as shown in figure 7.9.

When the user types in a string and clicks the OK button, the string is returned from the GetString function. As mentioned earlier, an assignment statement such as

```
word = strInputBox.GetString("Input Box","Type in a word");
```

does not work with a string. Thus we use the string copy function strcpy as

```
strcpy(word,
       strInputBox.GetString("String Input","Type in a word"));
```

to assign the string entered via strInputBox to the variable word.

The string outputString is initialized to an empty string at the time of declaration. This is necessary for the statement

```
strcat( outString, word );
```

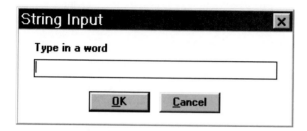

Figure 7.9 Screen result of StringTypeIn

to work correctly when it is executed for the first time. The function strcat requires NUL-terminated strings for both arguments. Without initialization, outString would not be a NUL-terminated string.

Some of you may have noticed that the character and string functions are somewhat different from the functions we have seen so far. We have been using functions that belong to an object. For example, the GetString function we use in the preceding program is a function that belongs to a StringTypeIn object. Unlike GetString, the character and string functions introduced in this chapter do not belong to any object-which is allowed in C++. Since they do not belong to any object, we do not use the dot notation to call them. The dot notation is necessary only if we use functions that belong to an object. We will learn more about objects and functions in the following chapters.

7.5 Sample program: detecting palindromes

Let's review what we have learned in this chapter by writing a program that detects a *palindrome*. A *palindrome* is a word, phrase, verse, or sentence that reads the same backward or forward. For example, *madam, dad, noon,* and *redivider* are all single-word palindromes and *Madam, I'm Adam* is a multiword palindrome. (Punctuation, cases, and blank spaces are ignored.) We will write two programs: one for detecting single-word palindromes and another for detecting multi-word palindromes. We first write a simplified version that detects single-word palindromes. The program reads in a word and displays a message to inform the user whether the word is a palindrome. The diagram in figure 7.10 shows our approach.

We start our comparisons from both ends of a string. The total number of comparisons is approximately half the length of the string. If a comparison results in an inequality, then the string cannot be a palindrome, so the program stops immediately. Putting these ideas together, we have the following:

```
n = length of input word;
i = 0;
midpoint = n/2 -1;

while ( i <= midpoint && word[i] == word[n-1-i] )

    i= i + 1; //move to the next comparison

//end while

if (i > midpoint)       //all comparisons were made & they
                        //were all equal
```

```
        display "it is a palindrome";

    else
        display "it is not a palindrome";
```

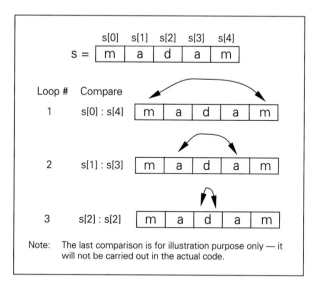

Figure 7.10 Palindrome program description

The complete program is listed below. We use standard GUI objects for the string input and message display. Be sure to verify that the program works correctly for words having odd or even numbers of characters. Also verify that *Madam,* for example, is not recognized as a palindrome by the following program, because the lower and uppercase letters are considered different.

```
//Program Palindrome:     A program that reads a word and
//                        determines whether the word is a
//                        palindrome.

#include "GUIObj.h"
#include <string.h>

void main ( )
{
    int            i, n, midpoint, response;
    char           word[25];
    StringTypeIn   strInputBox;
    OKBox          msgBox;
    YesNoBox       prompt;
```

```
        const int        YES = 1;

do {
    strcpy(word,
            strInputBox.GetString("String Input",
                                   "Type in a word") );

    n = strlen( word );
    midpoint = n/2 - 1;
    i = 0;

    while (i <= midpoint && word[i] == word[n-1-i])

        i = i + 1;

    //end while

    if (i > midpoint)

        msgBox.Display("It is a palindrome.");

    else

        msgBox.Display("It is NOT a palindrome.");
    //end if

    response = prompt.Ask("Continue?");
} while (response == YES);
}
```

Another approach to writing the palindrome program is to first make a new string that is the reverse of the input word and then use the string function strcmp to see if the words are equal. If they are, then the input word is a palindrome. This approach is left as exercise 7 at the end of the chapter.

Now let's write the second version, which detects multiword palindromes. More interesting palindromes consist of multiple words that read the same forward and backward when punctuation and spaces are ignored. The following examples are all palindromes.

Was it a rat I saw?

A man, a plan, a canal, Panama!

Madam, I'm Adam.

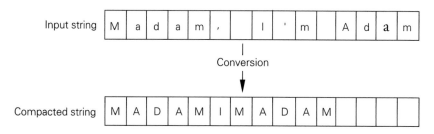

Figure 7.11 Palindrome conversion description

We can easily modify the first program to detect these more complicated palindromes by having it delete all but the alphabetic characters and by converting all alphabetic characters to uppercase before comparison. The conversion works as shown in figure 7.11.

We can delete nonalphabetic characters by copying the alphabetic characters of the potential palindrome into another string, one character at a time. Here is the pseudocode:

```
Get a potential multi-word palindrome.
For (each character in the potential palindrome)
    if (the character is alphabetic) then
        convert it to uppercase and
        copy it into a string called compact;
//end for

n = length of compact;
i = 0;
midpoint = n/2 - 1;

while (i <= midpoint && compact[i] == compact[n-1-i])
    i = i+1; //move to the next comparison
//end while

if (i > midpoint)
    display "it is a palindrome";
else
    display "it is not a palindrome";
//end if
```

For this program we will use the standard character functions for testing whether the input character is alphabetic and for converting the character to uppercase. These standard character functions are located in <ctype.h>. Here is the complete program:

```
//Program Palindrome2:      A program that reads multiple words and
//                          determines whether they are a palindrome.

#include "GUIObj.h"
#include <string.h>
#include <ctype.h>

void main ( )
{
    int             i, j, n, midpoint, size, response;
    char            inputString[255], compactedString[255];
    StringTypeIn    strInputBox;
    OKBox           msgBox;
    YesNoBox        prompt;
    const int       YES = 1;

    do {
        strcpy(inputString,
                strInputBox.GetString("String Input",
                                    "Type in a sentence") );
        size = strlen(inputString);
        j = 0; strcpy(compactedString,"");

        //construct the compacted string
        for ( i = 0; i < size; i = i+1)

                if ( isalpha(inputString[i]) ) {

                    compactedString[j] = toupper(inputString[i]);
                    j = j + 1;

                } //end if
        //end for

        //now test for palindrome
        compactedString[j] = '\0'; //append NUL so strlen works
        n = strlen( compactedString );
        midpoint = n/2 - 1;
        i = 0;

        while ( i <= midpoint &&
            compactedString[i] == compactedString[n-1-i] )

            i = i + 1;

        //end while

        if (i > midpoint)
```

Since we are not using the strcpy function, we must append the NUL character explicitly.

```
        msgBox.Display("It is a palindrome.");
    else

        msgBox.Display("It is NOT a palindrome.");
    //end if

        response = prompt.Ask("Continue?");
    } while (response == YES);
}
```

The standard character function `isalpha` returns nonzero (TRUE) if the character is alphabetic. Otherwise, it returns 0 (FALSE). The function `toupper` converts a given character to uppercase if the given character is a lowercase letter. Otherwise, it returns the given character unchanged.

7.6 Exercises

1   Program ASCII in this chapter accepts an integer ASCII code. Modify the program so it will accept a character as its input.

2   We used the following control flow for the modified program Volumes3 earlier in the chapter.

```
char ch;
...
cin >> ch;
switch (ch) {

    case 'T':
    case 't': //compute the volume of a triangular prism
                break;

    case 'S':
    case 's': //compute the volume of a sphere
                break;

    case 'C':
    case 'c': // is it a cylinder or a cone?

                cin >> ch; //read the second character
                if (ch == 'Y' || ch == 'y') {
                    //compute the volume of a cylinder
                }
                else if (ch == 'O' || ch == 'o') {
                    //compute the volume of a cone
                }
```

You can use another `switch` statement here instead.

```
            else {
                //error. wrong second character is entered
            }
            break;

    default: //error. wrong character is entered

}//end switch
```

Replace the if statement with another switch statement in the third case of the switch statement. Then notice the two places for printing out an error message. Since we print out two different messages, this code is correct. However, as an exercise, let's assume that we want to print out one message only, inside the default case. Modify the if statement so the control will flow into the default case when an invalid second character is entered.

3 In program String in section 7.4, we used the following nested if statements:

```
if ( (size >= 5 && size <= 10) &&

    (strcmp(word,"GUIObj") >= 0 &&
     strcmp(word,"Turtle") <= 0) )

    if (strlen( outString ) + size <= 255)
        strcat( outString, word );
    else
        done = TRUE;
    //endif
//endif
```

Why is it wrong to rewrite the above in the following manner?

```
if ( (size >= 5 && size <= 10) &&

        (strcmp( word, "GUIObj") >= 0 &&
         strcmp( word, "Turtle") <= 0) &&

  (strlen( outString ) + size <= 255) )

      strcat( outString, word );

  else

      done = TRUE;

  //endif
```

4 Write a program that will accept a string with a StringTypeIn and then display that string in an OKBox with all of the letters of the string converted to uppercase.

5 Write a program that will accept a series of strings. The entered strings will be concatenated into a single string. When a user terminates the input by entering STOP, the program will display the concatenated string in an OKBox. Remember that an OKBox can display a string of 255 characters or less.

6 Write a program that will accept a string str and then display a string consisting of every third character from str. Include the blanks and punctuation marks when you count. If the program accepts the string

```
A line stay's so. Hop, at rest Ryan!
```

then it should output

```
let's party!
```

7 Modify the program Palindrome by creating a new string reverseWord, which is the reverse of the input string word, and then check for a palindrome by comparing these two strings.

8 Write a program to compare two strings without using the string function strcmp. The program compares the characters one at a time using the indexed expression.

9 Write a program to compute the length of a string without using the string function strlen.

10 Write a program to input a word and draw a Chinese character equivalent to the given word. The program can accept the following words. (The equivalent Chinese characters are listed below the words.)

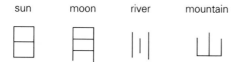

sun   moon   river   mountain

11 Determine the output for the following code:

a)
```
char s[10] = "";
strcat(s,"Papageno");
s[2] = 'g';
s[4] = s[6];
s[5] = s[7] = 'i';

cout << s;
```

b)
```
char s[10]; int j,n;
strcpy(s,"Konishiki");
n = strlen(s);
for (j=0; j < n; j = j+2)
    s[j] = toupper(s[j]);

cout << s;
```

c)
```
char s[10];
strcpy(s,"C");
strcat(s,"++");
strcat(s, strdup(s));
strcat(s, strdup(s));

cout << s;
```

d)
```
char s[10] = "VIVALDI";
int i, n;
n = strlen(s);
for ( i=n, i>0, i = i-1)
     if (ascii(s[i]) < 76)
          s[i] = 'e';

cout << s;
```

chapter 8

Functions

We have written programs using existing objects, such as `Turtle`, `OKBox`, and `IntTypeIn`, and standard functions, such as character and string functions provided in the `<ctype.h>` and `<string.h>` header files. As the programs we develop become more complex, however, it is not enough to use predefined objects and standard functions. In fact, we have to know how to define our own functions and objects. In this and the next three chapters, we explain the fundamentals of defining and using functions and objects.

We will begin our study of functions by defining the two types: object functions and nonobject functions. Object functions belong to objects; for example, the function `Display` belongs to the `OKBox`. Nonobject functions, such as the string function `strcpy`, do not belong to any objects. In object-oriented programming, we emphasize the use of object functions over nonobject functions. Indeed, some object-oriented programming languages do not allow any nonobject functions at all. We will begin our study of objects and functions with nonobject functions. Mastering nonobject functions is a prerequisite to understanding objects and object functions. In the following discussion, we will use the term *function* to mean both nonobject and object functions, unless we state otherwise.

We define functions for two purposes: code reuse and program decomposition. We say that a function is *reusable* if it can be used in different programs. If a function can be used only in a single program or in a very limited number of programs, then it has a very low degree of reusability. The standard functions all have a very high degree of reusability. The second use of a function is program decomposition for improved program readability. All of the functions we have written so far are the main functions of the programs. Since we have been using predefined objects and standard functions, our main functions have been rather short. As we write more difficult and complex programs, we cannot simply write larger and larger main functions. When main functions (or any functions) get too large, their meanings become obscure. In other words, the functions are not very readable. One possible method to ensure readability is to decompose large functions into smaller ones. Instead of writing a program as one gigantic main function, we can write it as a collection of smaller functions. We call this type of program construction *modular*. Modular construction is indispensable in writing complex programs. Well-designed functions are highly reusable and facilitate a modular construction of a program.

8.1 Function basics

Let's begin with the basics of defining a function. We will write a program that prints out the average of three real numbers. The program uses a function that computes the average of three real numbers.[*] The program calls this function three times to illustrate different ways of passing values to the function.

```
//Program Average:   A program to compute the
//                   average of three real numbers
//                   using a function.

#include <iostream.h>

float Average ( float num1,
                float num2,
                float num3)
{
    float result;
    result = (num1 + num2 + num3) / 3.0;
    return result;
}
```

Function definition

---

[*] A function to compute the average of three real numbers is not very reusable. A more truly reusable average function would compute the average of any N real numbers, for $N \geq 1$. The purpose here is pedagogic, to learn how to define and use a function so that we will be able to write truly reusable functions later.

```
void main()
{
    float x = 10.0, y = 20.0, z = 40.0;
    int i;

    cout << Average(5.0,17.0,30.0) << endl;
    cout << Average(x,y,z) << endl;
    cout << Average(x+10,2*y,x-5) << endl;

}
```

Function
calls

Now let's look at the function definition.

The function definition contains two parts: the function prototype and the function body (see figure 8.1). The *prototype* of a function specifies its data type, name, and input parameters. The data type of a function is the data type of a value returned by the function. The Average function returns the average of three real numbers, so its data type is declared as float. If a function returns no value, then its data type must be declared as void. Any valid identifier can be a function name. A *function parameter*, or *parameter* for short, defines an input to a function. Each parameter must have a data type, and each parameter must be declared individually. So, for example, the prototype

```
float Average (float x, y, z)
```

is not valid. The *function body* is a sequence of statements.

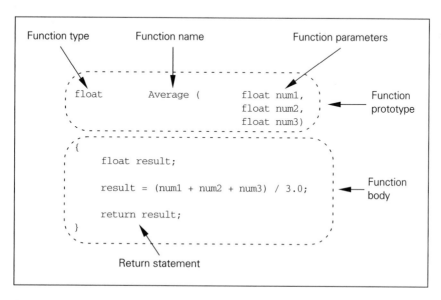

Figure 8.1 The function definition

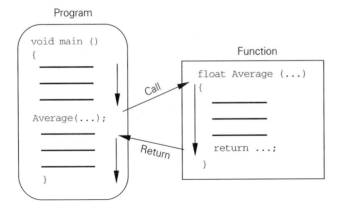

Program

void main ()
{
Average(...);
}

Call

Return

Function

float Average (...)
{

return ...;
}

Figure 8.2 Function call control flow

Let's trace the control flow of the program. Execution of the program starts from the first statement of the main function. It continues until a statement containing the function call is executed, which causes control to be transfered to the called function. When the function is called from the program (main function), execution of the program's statements is temporarily suspended while the statements of the called function are executed. In addition to transferring control, three real numbers are passed to the function. When the return statement in the function is executed, the result and control are returned to the main function, and the execution of the statements in the main function is resumed.

Figure 8.2 illustrates the *function call control flow,* the third control flow (the other two are the repetition and selection control flows) that alters the sequential execution of a program. The arrows in the diagram show the control flow in the program.

If a function does not return a value, then its body must contain at least one return statement. For the Average function, the return statement

```
return result;
```

causes control and the value of the variable result to be returned to the calling statement. A function can contain more than one return statement. When any one of the multiple return statements is executed, control is immediately returned to the calling statement. Consider, for example, the following function that returns the larger of the two integer numbers passed to the function (written without using the if–then–else construction to illustrate the effect of a return statement).

```
int Max ( int x, int y)
{
    if (x > y)

        return x;

    return y;
}
```

This statement is executed only if y ≥ x.

If x is larger than y, then the statement `return x;` is executed, which causes control and the value of x to be returned to the calling statement. Since control is passed back to the calling statement, no other statements in the function will be executed. So the statement `return y;` is executed only when y is greater than or equal to x.

If a function is of type `void`, then the `return` statement is optional. If a `void` function contains no `return` statement, then control is automatically returned to the calling statement after the final statement in the function is executed.

Any expression (including an empty expression) is allowed in the `return` statement. For example, the following expressions are all valid.

```
return 1;
return x+y;
return;
```

Now let's study how input values are passed to the `Average` function. The main program has three function calls:

```
... Average( 5.0, 17.0, 30.0 )...
... Average( x, y, z )       ...
... Average( x+10, 2*y, x) ...
```

When this function call is executed, function parameters num1, num2, and num3 receive the values 5.0, 17.0, and 30.0, respectively.

An expression inside the parentheses of a function call is called an *argument* of the function. The number of arguments in the function call and the number of parameters listed in the corresponding function definition must match.* A function call to the `Average` function should therefore have three arguments. The arguments and parameters are matched by position, that is, the leftmost argument corresponds to the leftmost

---

* One way to define a C++ function that eliminates this restriction is to list a varying number of arguments in a function call. We will limit our discussion here to the most basic form of the function definition where this restriction applies.

parameter, the next argument corresponds to the next parameter, and so on. The matched arguments and parameters must have assignment-compatible data types. For example, it is invalid to match a `float` argument with a `char` parameter, because you cannot assign a `float` to a `char` variable. Similarly, it is valid to match an integer argument to a `float` parameter, but not vice versa.

Figure 8.3 illustrates the mechanism of passing values to the function and returning a value from the function.

Values are passed from the arguments to the parameters, but not in the other direction. In other words, changing the values of the parameters inside the function will not affect the values of the matching arguments in the function call. For example, figure 8.4 shows the output of the next program.

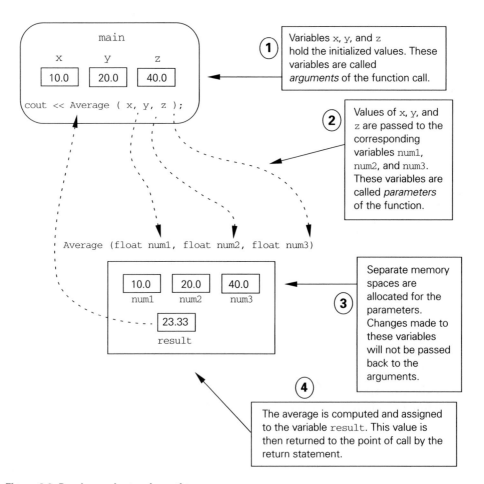

Figure 8.3 Passing and returning values

```
2
4
6
2
4
```

Figure 8.4 Program output

```cpp
#include <iostream.h>

int sum (int i, int j)
{
    int result;
    result = i + j;
    i = 30; j = 60;
    return result;
}

void main()
{
    int a = 2, b = 4;
    cout << a << endl << b << endl;
    cout << sum(a,b) << endl;
    cout << a << endl << b << endl;
}
```

> Changing the values of i and j will not affect the values of a and b.

This mode of passing only the values of arguments to the matching parameters in a one-way direction is called *pass-by-value*. We will explain other ways of passing arguments to a function in the next chapter.

Notice that a function call is treated just like any another expression. For example, the following expressions are all valid.

```cpp
x = Average( 1, 100, y) + Average( a, b, c);

for (i = 1; i < Average(34,39,44); i = i + 1)
    cout << "test";

if (Average(x,y,z) < 1599) cout << "okay";

Average(2.5, 3.5, 4.5);
```

For the sample code above to be semantically valid also, the variables and the functions must be type compatible. For example, the following expression is invalid semantically because of type incompatibility — you cannot assign float data to a char variable.

```
char c;

c = Average(12.3, 34.5, 67.8); //Invalid
```

If a function does not return a value (i.e., it is a void function), the function call to this function cannot be within another expression. The function call, however, is valid as a statement.

```
void function one(int x, int y)
{
    ...
}

if (a < b )
    one(a,b);                          Valid
else
    c = one(a,b);

                                       Not valid
```

We will conclude this section with the syntax of the function definition, the function call, and the return statement. We first modify the syntax categories *statement* and *expression* to include the new categories *return-statement* and *function-call.*

> *statement*
>   ...
>   *return-statement*
>
> *expression*
>   ...
>   *function-call*

The categories *return-statement* and *function-call* are defined as

> *return-statement*
>   **return**   *expression*   ;
>
> *function-call*
>   *identifier*   (*expression-list* $_{opt}$)
>
> *expression-list*
>   *expression*

expression ,   expression-list

The category *function–definition* is defined as

function–definition
     function–prototypefunction–body

function–signature
     function–type–specifier   function–name   (parameter–list$_{opt}$)

function–name
     identifier

function–type–specifier
     void
     type–specifier

parameter–list
     type–specifieridentifier
     type–specifier   identifier ,   parameter–list

function–body
     {   *statement*   **}**

8.2 Multifile program organization

With the sample program Average in section 8.1, we placed both the function `Average` and the main function in the same file. To reuse this function in another program, we must copy the code to another file that contains the main function of a new program. This process is not practical. To make functions readily available for reuse by different programs, without tedious copying, we put the functions in a separate header file, in the same way that standard functions are organized. For instance, the string functions (`strcpy`, `strcat`, etc.) are placed in a single header file. To use any of these functions in our programs, all we have to do is to include this header file in the programs.

    Let's put the `Average` function in a separate header file. For this example we have only one function in the header file; however, in a more realistic setup, we can expect a header file to contain many functions. First we place the function definition in a header file named `"stat.h"` (see figure 8.5).

```
float Average (        float num1,
                       float num2,
                       float num3)
{
        float result;
        result = (num1 + num2 + num3) / 3.0;
        return result;
}
```

Figure 8.5 Header file "stat.h"

Then we modify the program.

```
//Program Average2:   A program to compute the average of
//                    three real numbers by using a function
//                    defined in a separate header file.

#include <iostream.h>
#include "stat.h"

void main()
{
    float x = 10.0, y = 20.0, z = 40.0;
    int i;

    cout << Average(5,17,30) << endl;
    cout << Average(x,y,z) << endl;
    cout << Average(x+10,2*y,x-5) << endl;

}
```

To use the `Average` function in other programs, we just add the following `include` statement in them:

```
#include "stat.h"
```

Because a single program is built from multiple files, we call such program organization *multifile program organization*. One of the major benefits of multifile program organization is the ease of modification. When we have to modify the `Average` function, we need to change only one copy in the header file. Had we duplicated the code in individual programs, we would have to modify every copy of the function. This task is tedious, and we may not even locate all the copies.

8.3 Decomposing a program with functions

The second purpose for using functions is program decomposition to improve the program readability. Let's look at an example. The following program is Volumes3, from chapter 7.

```
// Program Volumes3:    A program to compute the volumes of
//                      four shapes - triangular prism, spheres,
//                      cylinder, and cone. Uses a switch
//                      statement with a character input.

#include <iostream.h>

void main()
{
    float          base, height, width, radius, volume;
    int            answer;
    char           shape;
    const int      YES = 1;
    const float    PI = 3.14159;

    cout << "Do you want to begin the computation?" << endl;
    cout << "(1 - yes; 2 - no) " << endl;
    cin >> answer;

    while (answer == YES) {

        cout << "Select shape: T. Triangular Prism" << endl;
        cout << "                S. Sphere" << endl;
        cout << "                Y. Cylinder" << endl;
        cout << "                O. Cone" << endl << endl;
        cout << "Enter T, S, Y, or O" << endl;
        cin >> shape;

        switch ( shape ) {

            case 'T':
            case 't':

                cout << "Type in base, height, and width"
                        << endl;
                cin >> base >> height >> width;

                volume = 0.5 * base * height * width;

                cout << "Volume of triangular prism with"
                        <<endl;
```

```
            cout << "base   = " << base << endl;
            cout << "height = " << height << endl;
            cout << "width  = " << width << endl;
            cout << "is        " << volume <<endl<<endl;
            break;

        case 'S':
        case 's':

            cout << "Type in radius" << endl;
            cin >> radius;

            volume = (4.0/3.0) * PI*radius*radius*radius;

            cout << "Volume of sphere with" << endl;
            cout << "radius   = " << radius << endl;
            cout << "is        " << volume <<endl<<endl;
            break;

        case 'Y':
        case 'y':

            cout << "Type in radius and height" << endl;
            cin >> radius >> height;

            volume = PI * radius*radius * height;

            cout << "Volume of cylinder with" << endl;
            cout << "radius   = " << radius << endl;
            cout << "height   = " << height << endl;
            cout << "is        " << volume <<endl<<endl;
            break;

        case 'O':
        case 'o':

            cout << "Type in radius and height" << endl;
            cin >> radius >> height;

            volume = (1.0/3.0) * PI*radius*radius*height;

            cout << "Volume of cone with" << endl;
            cout << "radius   = " << radius << endl;
            cout << "height   = " << height << endl;
            cout << "is        " << volume <<endl<< endl;
            break;

        default:
            cout << "Improper selection." << endl;
```

```
            cout << "Must be one of T, S, Y, or O"<<endl;

        } //end switch

        cout << "Do you want to continue?" << endl;
        cout << "(1 - yes; 2 - no) " << endl;
        cin >> answer;

    } //end while
}
```

The length of this main function is approaching the size limit of a function that is easily comprehensible. When a function gets too large, following its logic becomes difficult. The main function of Volumes3 performs four tasks; it computes volumes of triangular prisms, spheres, cylinders, and cones. To improve the clarity of this function, we can decompose it into smaller functions, one function for each of the four tasks.

The first function, which computes the volumes of triangular prisms, is defined as

```
void tri_prism ()
{
    cout << "Type in base, height, and width" << endl;
    cin >> base >> height >> width;

    volume = 0.5 * base * height * width;

    cout << "Volume of triangular prism with" << endl;
    cout << "base   = " << base << endl;
    cout << "height = " << height << endl;
    cout << "width  = " << width << endl;
    cout << "is        " << volume << endl << endl;
}
```

The function `tri_prism` has the simplest structure: no value is passed to it nor returned from it. The other three functions are similarly defined as

```
void sphere ()
{
    cout << "Type in radius" << endl;
    cin >> radius;

    volume = (4.0/3.0) * PI * radius*radius*radius;

    cout << "Volume of sphere with" << endl;
    cout << "radius   = " << radius << endl;
    cout << "is        " << volume << endl << endl;
```

```
    }
void cylinder ()
{
    cout << "Type in radius and height" << endl;
    cin >> radius >> height;

    volume = PI * radius*radius * height;

    cout << "Volume of cylinder with" << endl;
    cout << "radius    = " << radius << endl;
    cout << "height    = " << height << endl;
    cout << "is          " << volume <<endl<<endl;
}
void cone ()
{
    cout << "Type in radius and height" << endl;
    cin >> radius >> height;

    volume = (1.0/3.0) * PI * radius*radius * height;

    cout << "Volume of cone with" << endl;
    cout << "radius    = " << radius << endl;
    cout << "height    = " << height << endl;
    cout << "is          " << volume << endl << endl;

}
```

To decompose the program further, let's define three functions for handling input and output.

```
void getAnswer()
{
    cout << "Do you want to continue/begin the computation?"
         << endl;
    cout << "(1 - yes; 0 - no) " << endl;
    cin >> answer;
}
void getShape()
{
    cout << "Select shape: T. Triangular Prism" << endl;
    cout << "              S. Sphere" << endl;
    cout << "              Y. Cylinder" << endl;
    cout << "              O. Cone" << endl << endl;
    cout << "Enter T, S, Y, or O" << endl;
    cin >> shape;
}
void errorMessage()
{
    cout << "Improper selection." << endl;
```

```
        cout << "Must be one of T, S, Y, or O"<<endl;
    }
```

Using these functions, the main function becomes

```
    void main()
    {
        getAnswer();

        while (answer == YES) {

            getShape();

            switch ( shape ) {

                case 'T':
                case 't':       tri_prism();
                                break;

                case 'S':
                case 's':       sphere();
                                break;

                case 'Y':
                case 'y':       cylinder();
                                break;

                case 'O':
                case 'o':       cone();
                                break;

                default:        errorMessage();

            } //end switch

            getAnswer();

        } //end while
    }
```

The switch statement is now much more simplified, showing the general outline of the statement concisely and clearly.

Function call.

Control is passed from the main function to the called function .

Notice that the break statements remain in the main function, not in the four shape functions. The break statement must be enclosed in a selection or repetition control flow statement, such as switch, while, do, or for, because its purpose is to terminate the execution of the enclosing control flow statement. However, a function call is not a text replacement.[*] A compiler does not replace a function call statement with the body of the function. A function call is a transfer of control to the statements in the called function, as explained previously, and the statements inside the function body do

A C++ function can be designated as `inline`. The compiler processes an `inline` function by replacing each call to the function with the body of this function. If the function call contains arguments, then the matching arguments replace the parameters in the function body. For example, the following code

```
void main()
{
    int a = 5, b = 7;
    cout << sum(a, b),
    cout << sum(2, 40);
    cout << sum(a, 10);
}
```

becomes

```
void main()
{
    int a = 5, b = 7;
    cout << a + b;
    cout << 2 + 40;
    cout << a + 10;
}
```

if the function sum is declared `inline` as

```
inline int sum(int i, int j)
{
    return i + j
}
```

The amount of time required to execute a function call is more than the amount of time required to execute a nonfunction call statement. Since the `inline` function is handled by text replacement, not by a function call, executing `inline` functions is faster than regular, that is, noninline, functions. However, `inline` functions are not appropriate for functions with complex function bodies.

not affect the statements in the calling function (i.e., a function that contains the function call statement). Putting a `break` statement inside the shape functions therefore has no effect on the `switch` statement in the main function. (In fact, a compiler will generate a syntax error message.)

Now this main function looks very much like the pseudocode given in chapter 7 that shows an outline of the program. This organization gives programmers a high level overview—a big picture—of the program by looking at its main function. Providing a

---

* A function is a text replacement when the function is *inline*. Please see the C++ note.

clear overview of the logic of a program is an important part of developing easy to read and easy to maintain programs. Although we have been studying only about writing programs so far, maintaining existing programs (i.e., modifying, updating, or extending their features) is one of the most costly and time-consuming programming tasks. We discuss additional aspects of software development in chapter 17.

We can discover how each subtask is accomplished by reading the individual functions. This type of *functional decomposition* is one way to manage complexity. It is not difficult to appreciate the advantages of functional decomposition. Imagine writing a complete program as one huge main function. Would you prefer to read a main function that is five pages long, or to read a main function that provides a high level overview?

When the second level functions (the main function is the first level function) are themselves long and complex, then they are decomposed further into third level functions. The decomposition process thus continues in a hierarchy.

Now that all the pieces are defined, let's compose the whole program. In the following complete program, please pay close attention to the relative positions of variable declarations, function definitions, and the main function. One key point to remember here is that a function and a variable must be defined before being used.

```
// Program Volumes4:   A program to compute the volumes of
//                     four shapes — triangular prism, spheres,
//                     cylinder, and cone — by using functions.

#include <iostream.h>

float          base, height, width, radius, volume;
int            answer;
char           shape;
const int      YES = 1;
const float    PI = 3.14159;

void tri_prism ()
{
    cout << "Type in base, height, and width" << endl;
    cin >> base >> height >> width;

    volume = 0.5 * base * height * width;

    cout << "Volume of triangular prism with" << endl;
    cout << "base   = " << base << endl;
    cout << "height = " << height << endl;
    cout << "width  = " << width << endl;
    cout << "is        " << volume << endl << endl;
}
```

```cpp
void sphere ()
{
    cout << "Type in radius" << endl;
    cin >> radius;

    volume = (4.0/3.0) * PI * radius*radius*radius;

    cout << "Volume of sphere with" << endl;
    cout << "radius    = " << radius << endl;
    cout << "is        " << volume << endl << endl;
}
void cylinder ()
{
    cout << "Type in radius and height" << endl;
    cin >> radius >> height;

    volume = PI * radius*radius * height;

    cout << "Volume of cylinder with" << endl;
    cout << "radius    = " << radius << endl;
    cout << "height    = " << height << endl;
    cout << "is        " << volume <<endl<<endl;
}
void cone ()
{
    cout << "Type in radius and height" << endl;
    cin >> radius >> height;

    volume = (1.0/3.0) * PI * radius*radius * height;

    cout << "Volume of cone with" << endl;
    cout << "radius    = " << radius << endl;
    cout << "height    = " << height << endl;
    cout << "is        " << volume << endl << endl;
}
void getAnswer()
{
    cout << "Do you want to continue/begin the computation?"
            << endl;
    cout << "(1 - yes; 0 - no) " << endl;
    cin >> answer;
}
void getShape()
{
    cout << "Select shape: T. Triangular Prism" << endl;
    cout << "              S. Sphere" << endl;
    cout << "              Y. Cylinder" << endl;
    cout << "              O. Cone" << endl << endl;
    cout << "Enter T, S, Y, or O" << endl;
```

```
        cin >> shape;
    }
    void errorMessage()
    {
        cout << "Improper selection." << endl;
        cout << "Must be one of T, S, Y, or O"<<endl;
    }
    //MAIN FUNCTION
    void main()
    {
        getAnswer();

        while (answer == YES) {

            getShape();

            switch ( shape ) {

                case 'T':
                case 't':   tri_prism();
                            break;

                case 'S':
                case 's':   sphere();
                            break;

                case 'Y':
                case 'y':   cylinder();
                            break;

                case 'O':
                case 'o':   cone();
                            break;

                default:    errorMessage();

            } //end switch

            getAnswer();

        } //end while
    }
```

8.4 Local and global variables

The purpose of the program Volumes4 in the previous section is to illustrate program decomposition. Because we defined the functions purely for program decomposition and used *global variables*, these functions are not reusable. Let's explore why.

The following is the `tri_prism` function:

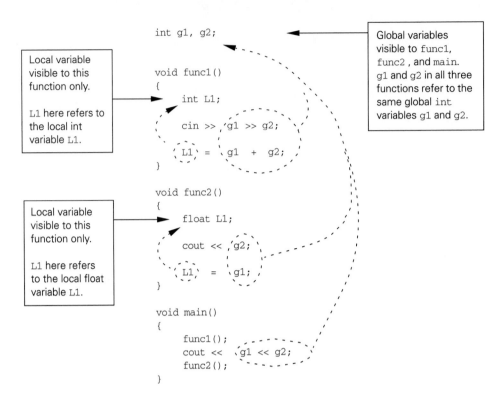

Figure 8.6 Local and global variables

```
void tri_prism ()
{
    cout << "Type in base, height, and width" << endl;
    cin >> base >> height >> width;

    volume = 0.5 * base * height * width;

    cout << "Volume of triangular prism with" << endl;
    cout << "base   = " << base << endl;
    cout << "height = " << height << endl;
    cout << "width  = " << width << endl;
    cout << "is          " << volume << endl << endl;
}
```

The function uses the four variables base, height, weight, and volume. Since every variable in a C++ program must be declared before it is used, these four variables must be declared somewhere before they are used. Where were they declared? As we can see from the program listing, they were all declared at the beginning of the program. A variable or

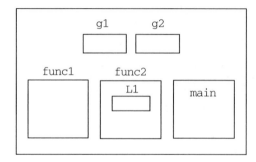

Figure 8.7 Memory allocation for the variables

a constant that is used inside the function body but declared outside of the function body is called *global*. A variable or a constant declared inside the function body is called *local*. The variable `result` in the `Average` function in program Average (section 8.1) is a local variable. In the remainder of this section, we refer only to global and local variables, but the discussion applies to global and local constants as well.

The difference between local and global variables is the visibility, or scope, of the variables. A global variable is visible to all functions that follow the declaration. A local variable is visible only to the function where it is declared. The diagram in figure 8.6 illustrates the difference.

Notice that the statement `cout << g2;` is valid in `func2` because `g2` is a global variable and its value is already assigned in `func1`. (`func1` is called before `func2` from the main function.) Memory allocation for the variables and their visibility are shown in figure 8.7. The rectangle that surrounds the variable shows its visibility. That is, `g1` and `g2` are visible to `func1`, `func2`, and `main`. The function `func1` has a local variable `L1` visible only to it. The function `func2`, likewise, has a local variable `L1` visible only to it.

Since local and global variables are distinct, with separate memory spaces allocated to them, giving local and global variables the same name will cause no conflict. For example, consider the program and the corresponding memory-allocation diagram in figure 8.8. Variable `var1` in `func1` refers to the local variable, and `var1` in `func2` refers to the global variable. We know `var1` in `func1` refers to the local variable because it is declared in the same function; that is, a variable refers to the closest declaration.

Global variables allow functions to share data without passing values to the individual functions. The shape functions, for example, share four global variables. Because only one copy is necessary for each variable, less memory space is required than passing values to the functions using the pass-by-value scheme. At first, using global variables rather than passing values to the functions may seem advantageous because the use of global variables seems cleaner and simpler. However, with a little more thought, we should realize that this

```
float var1 ;

void func1()
{
    int var1;
    var1 = 10;
}

void func2()
{
    var1 = 55.0;
}

void main()
{
    func1();
    func2();
}
```

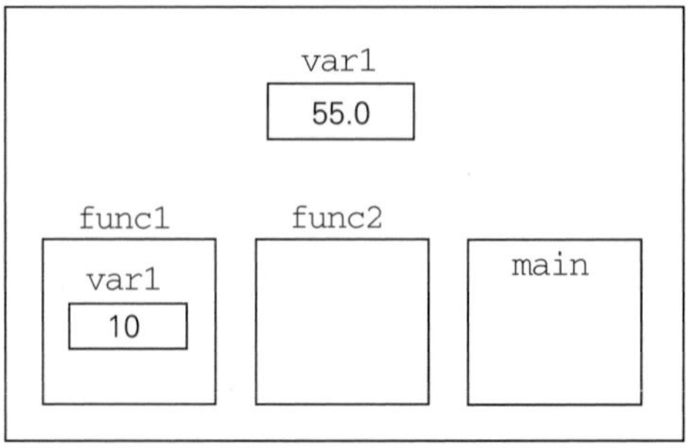

Figure 8.8 Program with memory allocation diagram

alleged advantage is really not good enough to compensate for its major disadvantage. Global variables severely limit the reuse of functions. For instance, one of the reasons the shape functions are not reusable is their use of the global variables. The `Average` function, on the other hand, is much more reusable because it does not use global variables. (It uses only the local variable and the three parameters passed to the function.) A function is *self-contained* if it does not rely on anything that is declared outside of it. A self-contained function uses only local variables and passed arguments. Notice that an argument passed to a function is local to the function. Since self-contained functions do not rely on anything outside of them, we can easily integrate them into different programs. In contrast, if a function relies on global variables, then to reuse it , we must make sure to incorporate the declaration for these global variables into new programs. With a self-contained function, everything necessary for executing the function is right within the function.

Another difficulty in reusing functions that are not self-contained is a potential conflict in integrating them. For example, consider the two sets of functions in figure 8.9.

The first set contains functions for getting input, computing the area of triangles, and computing the volume of triangular prisms. The second set contains functions for computing the area of rectangles and computing the volume of rectangular prisms. What would happen if we try to reuse the functions for computing the volumes of rectangular and triangular prisms? We need to incorporate all five functions in addition to the global variables. Moreover, we have to make sure that the functions are called together. For example, we need to call `getData` and `tri_area` before calling the function

```
int width, height, length,            int width, height, length,
    area, volume;                         area, volume;

void getData()                        void rect_area()
{                                     {
    cin >> width >> height                cin >> width >> height;
        >> length;                        area = width*height;
}                                     }

void tri_area()                       void rect_volume()
{                                     {
    area = 0.5*width*height;              cin   >> length;
    cout << area;                        volume
}                                            = area*length;
                                      }
void tri_volume()
{
    volume = length * area;
}
```

Figure 8.9 Integrating functions

tri_volume. If they are not called together, and a call to rect_area is made in between, then the function tri_volume would not work, because the global variables would be overwritten by different values. For this particular example, remembering to call three functions together may not be seem so hard. However, imagine a situation where we have to incorporate 10 or 20 of these types of functions. It would be an unnecessary burden for programmers to sort out all the constraints to use the functions correctly. We can easily avoid this problem with self-contained functions.

Yet another difficulty in reusing functions that are not self-contained is a potential naming conflict. Suppose we want to reuse the function tri_volume in another program. Since the function relies on the global variables width, height, length, area, and volume, we cannot use these variables for any other purpose. For instance, if we have already written a progam that uses the identifiers height and width to represent some other data, then we cannot incorporate the tri_volume function in this program without modifying the identifiers height and weight.

Design Guideline Avoid using global variables and constants for the functions that are intended to be reused in other programs later. If you use global variables, then avoid using common names for them, to reduce the chance of naming conflicts.

8.5 Sample program

Let's rewrite Volumes4 by utilizing the concepts we have discussed in this chapter. Our first task is to extract a portion of the program that can be reused in other programs into a separate header file. Computing volumes of various geometric shapes is something that we can reuse in many different programs, so we will define functions for computing volumes of various geometric shapes and save them in the "volumes.h" header file as shown in the following code:

File "volumes.h"

```
const float    v_PI = 3.14159;

//tri_prism: compute the volume of triangular prism
float tri_prism (float base, float height, float width)
{
    return  0.5 * base * height * width;
}

//rect_prism: compute the volume of rectangular prism
float rect_prism (float base, float height, float width)
{
    return  base * height * width;
}

//sphere: compute the volume of sphere
float sphere (float radius)
{
    return  (4.0/3.0) * v_PI * radius*radius*radius;
}

//cylinder: compute the volume of cylinder
float cylinder (float radius, float height)
{
    return  v_PI * radius*radius * height;
}

//cone: compute the volume of cone
float cone (float radius, float height)
{
    return  (1.0/3.0) * v_PI * radius*radius * height;
}
```

In defining a reusable function, try to avoid using any global variables or constants. If you must use them, then avoid using common names. In the "volumes.h" header file, we used a global constant v_PI. Had we used the more common name PI instead, then we would have a greater chance of naming conflicts. Although a programmer is unlikely to use the identifier PI for anything other than to represent the mathematical constant π, one programmer could be using the constant with different precision, say eight decimal places as opposed to the five decimal places we used. So the name could result in a conflict.

We have several possible solutions for resolving the naming-conflict problem. The first solution is not to use the global constant in our header file and to use the literal constant only inside individual functions. This solution is not a good one because modifying the value is cumbersome. We would have to locate every occurrence of the literal constant if we wanted to change the value for PI. The second solution is to name the global constant with some uncommon name that has a very small chance of resulting in a naming conflict. For example, we can use the header file name as a prefix to the global constants and variables. With this approach, the global constant PI is named volumes_h_PI. Or we could use a shortened version such as v_PI, which we did for our header file. The third solution is to force the programmer to rename the constant PI as something else, for example, pi or Pi. The fourth solution is to define a new object (in this case, for computing volumes of geometric shapes), a technique we explain in chapters 10 and 11.

Using the "volumes.h" header file, we can rewrite the program as

```
// Program Volumes5:    A program to compute the volumes of
//                      four shapes - triangular prism, spheres,
//                      cylinder, and cone — by using functions
//                      from the header file "volumes.h".

#include <iostream.h>
#include "volumes.h"

void tri_prism ()
{
    float base, height, width;

    cout << "Type in base, height, and width" << endl;
    cin  >> base >> height >> width;

    cout << "Volume of triangular prism with" << endl;
    cout << "base   = " << base << endl;
    cout << "height = " << height << endl;
    cout << "width  = " << width << endl;
    cout << "is         " <<
              tri_prism(base,height,width) << endl << endl;
}

void sphere ()
{
```

```
    float radius;

        cout << "Type in radius" << endl;
    cin  >> radius;

    cout << "Volume of sphere with" << endl;
    cout << "radius   = " << radius << endl;
    cout << "is          " <<
                sphere(radius) << endl << endl;
}

void cylinder ()
{
    float radius, height;

    cout << "Type in radius and height" << endl;
    cin  >> radius >> height;

    cout << "Volume of cylinder with" << endl;
    cout << "radius   = " << radius << endl;
    cout << "height   = " << height << endl;
    cout << "is          " <<
                cylinder(radius,height) <<endl<<endl;
}

void cone ()
{
    float radius, height;

    cout << "Type in radius and height" << endl;
    cin  >> radius >> height;

    cout << "Volume of cone with" << endl;
    cout << "radius   = " << radius << endl;
    cout << "height   = " << height << endl;
    cout << "is          " <<
                cone(radius,height) << endl << endl;
}

int getAnswer()
{
    int answer;
    cout << "Do you want to continue/begin the computation?"
            << endl;
    cout << "(1 - yes; 0 - no) " << endl;
    cin >> answer;
    return answer;
}
```

```
char getShape()
{
    char selection;
    cout << "Select shape: T. Triangular Prism" << endl;
    cout << "              S. Sphere" << endl;
    cout << "              Y. Cylinder" << endl;
    cout << "              O. Cone" << endl << endl;
    cout << "Enter T, S, Y, or O" << endl;
    cin >> selection;
    return selection;
}

void errorMessage()
{
    cout << "Improper selection." << endl;
    cout << "Must be one of T, S, Y, or O"<<endl;
}

//MAIN FUNCTION
void main()
{
    int          reply;
    char         selectedShape;
    const int    YES = 1;

    reply = getAnswer();

    while (reply == YES) {

        selectedShape = getShape();

        switch ( selectedShape ) {

            case 'T':
            case 't':    tri_prism();
                         break;

            case 'S':
            case 's':    sphere();
                         break;

            case 'Y':
            case 'y':    cylinder();
                         break;

            case 'O':
            case 'o':    cone();
                         break;
```

```
                    default:errorMessage();

                } //end switch

            reply = getAnswer();

        } //end while
    }
```

The functions from `"volumes.h"` are used in the four functions `tri_prism`, `sphere`, `cylinder`, and `cone`. As before, the purpose of these four functions is not reuse, but program decomposition for better readability.[*] We also changed the functions `get-Answer` and `getShape`. Instead of using a global variable, we modified the functions to return a value. Now the main function is a little easier to understand. The earlier main function had the structure

```
        void main()
        {
            getAnswer();

            while (answer == YES) {

                getShape();

                switch ( shape ) {

                    . . .
                } //end switch
            }
        }
```

This main function uses two variables `answer` and `shape`, but does not indicate where these variables are set. In other words, looking at the main function does not tell us when and where values are assigned to these variables. Of course, we have functions named `getAnswer` and `getShape`, so it is not that hard to guess where the values are set, but the names of functions are not always good indicators. A better way is to show clearly how these variables are set. After modifying the functions `getAnswer` and `get-Shape`, the main function becomes

```
        void main()
```

---

[*] We will make further improvements to these four functions in chapter 10 so they will become more reusable.

```
{
    . . .
    reply = getAnswer();

    while (reply == YES) {

        selectedShape = getShape();

        switch ( selectedShape ) {

            . . .

        } //end switch

        reply = getAnswer();

    } //end while
}
```

which clearly shows how the variables are set and used in the main function.

Notice that two different functions have the same name in this program. Although the same identifiers are used for two different functions, their respective function prototypes are different, so no ambiguity results. For instance, the function call `tri_prism()` will not be confused with the function call `tri_prism(base, height, width)`, because they have different prototypes.

8.6 Exercises

1 Write a function that accepts the number of quarters, dimes, nickels, and pennies, and returns the value in cents.

2 Write a function that returns the minimum of the three parameters passed to it. Write another function that returns the maximum.

3 Write two functions `ToFarenheit` and `ToCelsius` that convert Celsius to Fahrenheit, and vice versa. The conversion formulas are

$$C = \frac{5}{9}(F - 32) \qquad F = \frac{9}{5}C + 32$$

4 Determine the output for the following programs.

a.
```
#include <iostream.h>

int j = 4;

int func1 (int i)
{
    int result;
    result = i + j;
    i = 30; j = 60;
    return result;
}

void main()
{
    int a = 2;
    cout << a << endl
            << j << endl;
    cout << func1(a) <<endl;
    cout << a << endl
            << j << endl;
}
```

b.
```
#include <iostream.h>

int j = 4;

int func1 (int i)
{
    int j;
    j = 2 * i;
    return j;
}

void main()
{
    int a = 2;
    cout << j << endl;
    cout << func1(a) <<endl;
    cout << j << endl;
}
```

c.
```
int g1 = 1, g2 = 2;

void func1()
{
    int L1;
    L1  = g1 + g2;
    cout << L1 << endl;
}

void func2()
{
    float L1 = 3.0;
    g2 = 4;
    cout <<  g2 + L1;
}

void main()
{
    func1();
    cout << g1 << g2;
    func2();
}
```

d.
```
void func1(int g1, int g2)
{
    int L1;
    L1  = g1 + g2;
    cout << L1 << endl;
}

void func2(int g2)
{
    float L1 = 3.0;
    cout <<  g2 + L1;
    g2 = 5;
}

void main()
{
    int g1 = 1, g2 = 2;
    func1(g2, g1);
    func2(g2);
    cout << g1 << g2;
}
```

5 Define a header file `"areas.h"` that contains functions for computing the areas of triangles, rectangles, parallelograms, and circles.

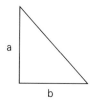

$$Area = \frac{1}{2} \cdot a \cdot b$$

$$Area = a \cdot b$$

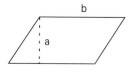

$$Area = a \cdot b$$

$$Area = \pi \cdot r^2$$

6 Extend the program Volumes5 so it will also compute the areas of triangles and squares by using the functions from the header file areas.h created in the previous exercise. Notice that the function in the header areas.h computes the areas of rectangles, but for this program, we want to compute the areas of squares.

7 Write a program that draws a pine tree by defining and using two functions: one for drawing a triangle and another for drawing a rectangle.

8 Write a function that draws the Chinese character for a tree.

The function should be capable of drawing the character in different sizes. The size of the character is specified by passing the height of the character as an argument to the function. The character is drawn proportional to the specified height. Use this function to write a program that draws a forest.

9 Rewrite the program Volumes5 using GUI objects for the program's user interface.

10 A *Fibonacci sequence* is a sequence of numbers

```
1, 1, 2, 3, 5, 8, 13, 21, 34, . . .
```

where each number, except the first two, is the sum of the preceding two numbers. Write a function that uses a repetition control flow to compute the *N*th Fibonacci number, $N \geq 1$. For example, Fib(1) = 1, Fib(2) = 1, Fib(6) = 8, and so forth. Use this function to write a program to print out the first 20 Fibonacci numbers.

11 Using the function as defined in exercise 10 is very inefficient, because it does the same calculation repeatedly. For instance, when you make the function call Fib(20), the function will compute the nineteenth Fibonacci number, but this number was actually computed before by calling Fib(19). A faster way to compute the *N*th Fibonacci number F_N is to use the formula

$$F_N = \frac{1}{\sqrt{5}}\left[\left(\frac{1 + \sqrt{5}}{2}\right)^N - \left(\frac{1 - \sqrt{5}}{2}\right)^N\right]$$

Redo exercise 10 using the new function for computing the *N*th Fibonacci number. Run both programs and see if you notice any difference in the execution speed. *Note:* The square root function is available in the <math.h> header file.

chapter 9

Passing pointers and references to functions

We learned the basics of defining and using functions in the previous chapter. In this chapter we continue the discussion of functions with a more in-depth look at the different ways of passing arguments to a function. There are three modes of passing arguments: *pass-by-value*, *pass-by-pointer*, and *pass-by-reference*. We explained pass-by-value in the previous chapter. With this mode the value of an argument is passed to the corresponding parameter of a function, and a local copy of the passed value is created. Pass-by-value is the default mode of passing an argument and the one used most frequently. In some situations, however, the pass-by-value mechanism is inadequate. We introduce two additional passing mechanisms in this chapter. We first explain the concept of a pointer and how a pointer is passed to a function, and then we explain the concept of a reference and how the reference is passed to a function.

231

9.1 Pointers

To understand pass-by-pointer, we must first understand the term *pointer*. We stated in chapter 1 that computer memory is divided into units of bytes, and each byte is assigned a unique address. We use this address to access data in memory. For example, if we declare

```
char     ch;
int      num;
```

then the C++ compiler will allocate certain numbers of bytes each for ch and num. Figure 9.1 shows one possible situation, in which ch is allocated 1 byte at address 1402 and num is allocated 4 bytes at address 1403. Here we use decimal number addresses for simplicity. In an actual computer, the addresses are, of course, binary numbers. Two values are actually associated with any C++ variable—its address and its contents. We haven't used the address of a variable explicitly before. Whenever we used variables in expressions, we were referring to their contents. But implicitly the compiler has been dealing with their addresses all along. Otherwise, the content would not have been stored in a memory location.

When a variable appears in an expression, we are referring to its contents. To refer to its address, we need a special *address operator*. The address operator is denoted by the ampersand symbol &. Assuming the memory setup shown in the diagram, the expression

```
msg.Display(ch);   // msg is an OKBox
```

will print out 'A', while the expression

```
msg.Display(int(&ch))   //OKBox can print int also
```

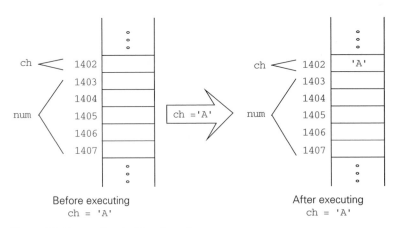

Figure 9.1 Bytes allocated for ch and num

will print out `1402`. Notice that we must make an explicit conversion to an integer by saying `int(&ch)` because the expression `&ch` is not an `int`, but a pointer to a character (i.e., it is of type `char *`; see the following discussion). Even though a pointer is an address, which is a numerical value, its type is not an `int`, so it must be converted to an `int` before being passed as an argument to the `Display` function.

The address operator can be read as "the address of." The address of a memory location is a numerical value, and thus, can be stored in another memory location. Consider figure 9.2, where the address of `ch` is stored in a memory location beginning at `1345`. Notice that the diagram implies that the address `1402` fits in a single byte. However, in reality, we normally use 4 or 8 bytes to store memory addresses. We draw the diagram this way to keep it simple and easy to follow.

We need a variable to refer to the memory location; let's name this place `p`. We know `ch` is of type `char` because its content is a character value. What about `p`? What kind of value are we putting there? It is a memory address, but we don't have a data type called "memory address." When a variable contains a memory address, we must declare it as a pointer type. In addition, we must specify the data type of the data stored in the memory location referred to by this memory address. For the example above, since `p` contains the memory address of a location whose content is a character type, we declare `p` as a pointer to character data, or a *char pointer* for short. If the content is some other data type, say an integer, then `p` would be declared as an *int pointer*, and so forth. The following declares two pointers, one `char` pointer and one `int` pointer:

```
char      *p;
int       *q;
```

The symbol * is called a *dereference operator*. It tells us that `p` is a pointer whose content is the address of a memory location that contains character data and `q` is a pointer whose content is an address of a memory location that contains integer data.

Assuming the declarations

```
char      ch = 'A';
int       num = 789;
int       *q;
char      *p;
```

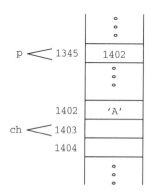

Figure 9.2 Memory location

Table 9.1 Sample expressions involving pointers

Expression	Meaning
`q = &num;`	`q` gets the address 1403.
`msg.Display (*q);` `msg.Display (num);`	Both output the value 789.
`p = &ch;`	`p` contains the address 1402.
`msg.Display (*p);` `msg.Display (ch);`	Both output the value 'A'.
`p = ch;` `q = num;`	Error—incompatible types.
`*p = 'Z';`	Content at memory location 1402 is now changed to 'Z'.

with `ch` and `num` at memory locations 1402 and 1403, respectively, table 9.1 shows sample expressions involving pointers.

The last expression needs special attention. Notice that both `*p` and `ch` refer to the exact same location. In other words, whether you say

```
*p = 'Z';
```

or

```
ch = 'Z';
```

the content of memory location 1402 will change to 'Z'.

At this point the pointer variable may seem like a roundabout way of accessing data in memory. The use of a nonpointer variable seems to be a simpler and better way to access a memory location. The pointer variable is, however, much more powerful and flexible than a nonpointer variable. With a nonpointer variable, you can access only one location, but with a pointer variable, you can access multiple memory locations. For instance, in the example above, the variable `ch` is tied to one and only one memory location, 1402, whereas `p` can be used to access many different memory locations by changing its content. Consider figure 9.3, where `ch1` and `ch2` are `char` variables and `p` is a `char` pointer.

Given the configuration of the initial state S_0, executing the sequence of statements

```
*p  =  'B';
 p  = &ch2;
*p  =  'Y';
```

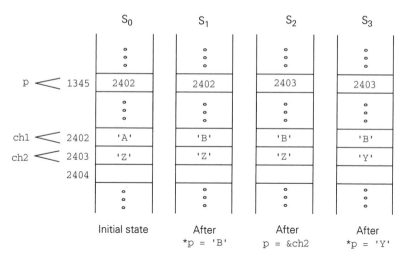

	S_0	S_1	S_2	S_3

p < 1345

ch1 < 2402
ch2 < 2403
2404

Initial state   After   After   After
*p = 'B'   p = &ch2   *p = 'Y'

Figure 9.3 Memory locations of p, ch1, and ch2

will result in state S_3. We have changed the contents of two memory locations using the single pointer variable p. So by changing the contents of p, we can access many different locations via the pointer variable p, whereas with nonpointer variables such as ch1 and ch2, we can access only fixed locations. The use of a pointer variable to access a memory location is called *indirect addressing* because we access a memory location indirectly through the content of a pointer, instead of directly accessing the memory location tied to a nonpointer variable.

By using simple arithmetic operations such as addition and subtraction, we can write expressions involving pointer variables that allow us to refer to (point to) many

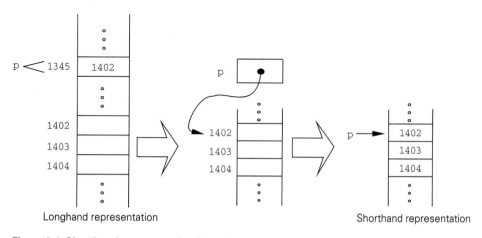

Longhand representation   Shorthand representation

Figure 9.4 Shorthand representation for pointers

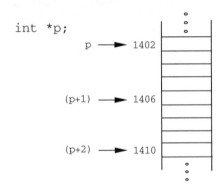

```
int *p;
```

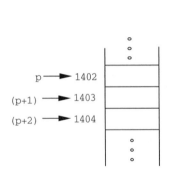

Figure 9.5 Arithmetic expressions with pointers to character data

Figure 9.6 Arithmetic expressions with pointers to integer data

different memory locations. Before we give an example, we will first introduce a shorthand representation for pointers, as shown in figure 9.4. Using this representation, we can show the effects of simple arithmetic expressions involving pointers (see figure 9.5). By adding 1 to p, we can refer to the memory location one position beyond the one pointed to by p. By adding two to p, we refer to two positions down from p. In general, the expression (p+i) refers to the ith position from p. In the preceding example, we made an implicit assumption that a character occupies 1 byte, which is always true if ASCII representation is used. The number of bytes allocated for one position depends on the data value that occupies that position. So, for example, if an integer takes up 4 bytes of memory and p is an integer pointer, then our diagram looks like figure 9.6.

We could use a pointer variable instead of a character array to manipulate string data. With the following declaration and assignment statement

```
char str[4] = "Zen";
char *p;

p = &str[0];
```

we have this situation shown in figure 9.7.

Remember that a variable with an arrow indicates a pointer, so you need a dereference operator to access the contents (e.g., *p refers to 'Z'). A variable without an arrow means a nonpointer variable, so you access the content directly (e.g., str[0] refers to

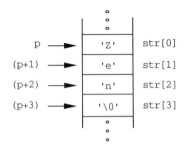

Figure 9.7 Manipulating string data using pointer variable

'z'). Using pointer arithmetic, we can easily rewrite the program that prints out each word of a given string using one OKBox per word (section 7.3). Here is the program fragment using pointer arithmetic.

```
char str[30] = "OK. Here's a string.";
char    word[10];
OKBox   msg;
int     i = -1, j = -1;
char    *p;

p = &str[0]; // set p to the address of first character

do {
    j = j+1; i = i+1;
    if (*(p+i) == ' ' || *(p+i) == '\0') {
        word[j] = '\0';
        msg.Display(word);
        j = -1; //reset counter for next word
    }
    else
        word[j] = *(p+i); //NOTE: *p + i will not work

} while (*(p+i) != '\0');
```

We used pointer arithmetic to refer to elements of str. We can do the same for word. Notice that we used the expression *(p+i), not *p + i, because the precedence of the dereference operator is higher than the precedence for the addition operator. The expression *p + i adds the value of i to the content of memory location referred to by p. Also notice that the value of p does not change; that is, it still refers to the same memory location at the end of execution. If we do not have to leave p pointing to the first position, then we can do the same without the variable i as follows:

```
char str[30] = "OK. Here's a string.";
char    word[10];
OKBox   msg;
int     j = -1;
char    *p;

p = &str[0]-1; // set p to the address one before the
               // address of first character

do {
    j = j+1; p = p+1;   //notice the pointer arithmetic on p
    if (*p == ' ' || *p == '\0') {
        word[j] = '\0';
```

```
        msg.Display(word);
        j = -1;            //reset counter for next word
    }
    else
        word[j] = *p;

} while (*p != '\0');
```

In the first example, the value of p never changes; it always contains the address of str[0]. In the second example, when the execution is completed, p contains the address of the location containing the character '\0'.

We will see more examples using pointers in the later chapters.

9.2 Pass-by-pointer passing

To describe how pass-by-pointer works, we start with an example. Suppose we want to write a function that exchanges the values of two variables. Such a function is useful in writing sorting algorithms for arranging *N* numbers in a particular order (sorting algorithms are covered in detail in chapter 18). For example, the following code

```
int x = 89, y = 45;
cout << x << " " << y << endl;
swap(x,y);
cout << x << " " << y;
```

will print out

```
89 45
45 89
```

The values of x and y have been exchanged. The following definition, which utilizes the pass-by-value passing mechanism, will not work.

```
void swap ( int a, int b)
{
    int temp = a;
    a = b;
    b = temp;
}
```

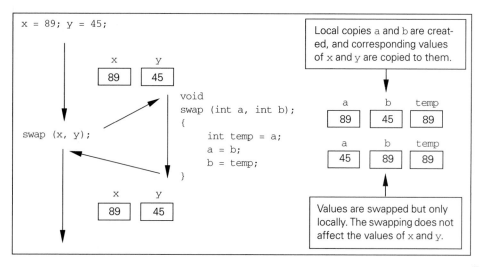

Figure 9.8 Pass-by-value passing mechanism

Why not? It won't work because the pass-by-value passing mechanism makes a local copy of the passed argument, and anything we do to the local copy will not affect the value of the argument. Figure 9.8 illustrates this situation.

We can get the desired result by using the pass-by-pointer passing mechanism. The function is written as

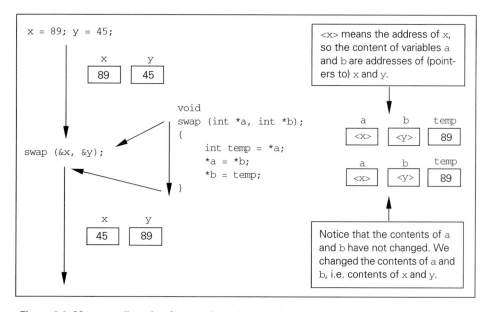

Figure 9.9 Memory allocation for pass-by-value passing mechanism

```
void swap ( int *a, int *b)
{
    int temp = *a;
    *a = *b;
    *b = temp;
}
```

The parameters are a and b, which are pointers to integers, as signified by the asterisks in front of them.

and called as

```
int x = 89, y = 45;
```

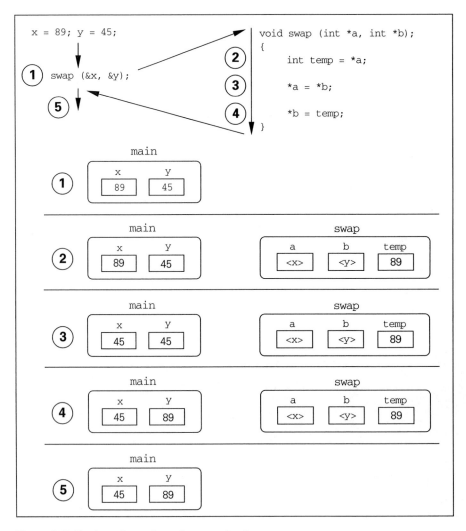

Figure 9.10 Review of pass-by-pointer mechanism

```
cout << x << " " << y << endl;

swap(&x, &y);

cout << x << " " << y;
```

The addresses, or pointers, to integers are passed, not the integers themselves.

Figure 9.9 shows the memory allocation for the pass-by-pointer passing mechanism.

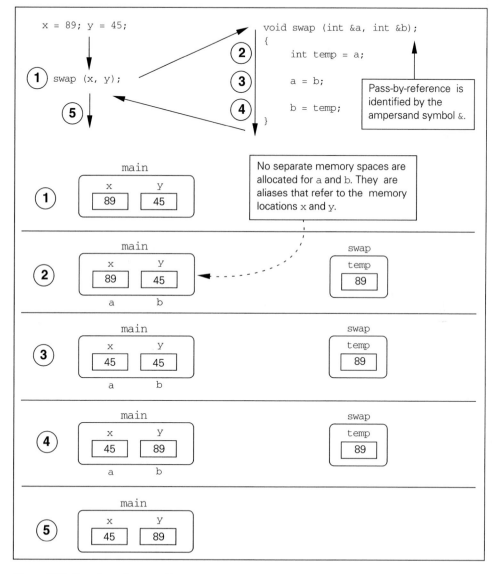

Figure 9.11 Pass-by-reference diagram

The pass-by-pointer mechanism is really not a distinct passing mechanism. Rather it is a pass-by-value mechanism where we pass an address (a pointer) instead of data values. We use the distinct name pass-by-pointer and treat it as a distinct parameter passing mechanism because of its special nature compared to the ordinary pass-by-value scheme in which we pass nonpointer data values such as `int` and `float`. The function parameters a and b contain the addresses of x and y. We access and swap the contents of x and y indirectly via a and b, using the dereference operator *. Figure 9.10 reviews this example in detail and shows each statement in the function affects the contents of x and y.

9.3 Pass-by-reference passing

We can also implement the `swap` function using pass-by-reference. With the pass-by-reference passing mechanism, we are passing references to memory locations instead of passing values, that is, contents of memory locations. References and pointers to memory locations are similar in concept, but they differ in how they are treated in passing arguments to a function. When the reference to a memory location is passed, both the argument and the function parameter refer to the same memory location. No separate memory spaces are allocated for the function parameters. Figure 9.11 illustrates pass-by-reference.

The calling statement is the same as the one for pass-by-value. The body of the function is also the same as the one for the function using pass-by-value. The only difference is the declaration of the function parameters. We denote a pass-by-reference parameter by attaching the ampersand symbol & in front of the parameter. This symbol signifies that we are not creating a separate memory location for storing the passed value, but rather adding a new name for the memory location of the passed argument. This new name is called *alias*.

9.4 Sample program: solving quadratic equations

In chapter 6 we wrote several versions of a program that solves quadratic equations of the form

$$Ax^2 + Bx + C = 0$$

Let's rewrite the program Quad5 (section 6.1) to illustrate the use of pass-by-reference. Here we repeat Quad5.

```
//Program Quad5:    A program to find solutions of the
//                  quadratic equation Ax² + Bx + C = 0. The
//                  program uses an alternative style for the if
//                  control statement.

#include "GUIObj.h"
#include <math.h>

void main ()
{
    float A, B, C, x1, x2, discriminant, sqrtOfDiscriminant;
    FloatTypeIn    floatInpBox;
    OKBox          msgBox;

    //get three inputs
    A = floatInpBox.GetFloat("INPUT","Type in value for A");
    B = floatInpBox.GetFloat("INPUT","Type in value for B");
    C = floatInpBox.GetFloat("INPUT","Type in value for C");

    discriminant = B*B - 4*A*C;
    //test the input
    if (discriminant < 0) { //then

        msgBox.Display("No real number solutions exist.");
    }
    else { //either one or two solutions exist

        // compute and display the first solution

        sqrtOfDiscriminant = sqrt( discriminant );
        x1 = (-B + sqrtOfDiscriminant) / (2 * A);
        msgBox.Display(x1);

        if (discriminant > 0) {//then the second solution

            //compute and display the second solution

            x2 = (-B - sqrtOfDiscriminant) / (2 * A);
            msgBox.Display(x2);

        } //end inner if

    } //end outer if
}
```

Get 1st solution
$B^2 \geq 4AC$

Get 2nd solution
$B^2 > 4AC$

We will use two functions in the new program: one to get three inputs for A, B, and C, and another to compute the solutions for x. Let's start with the one for getting three input values:

```
void GetInputs(float &A, float &B, float &C)
{
    FloatTypeIn  floatInpBox;

    A = floatInpBox.GetFloat("INPUT","Type in value for A");
    B = floatInpBox.GetFloat("INPUT","Type in value for B");
    C = floatInpBox.GetFloat("INPUT","Type in value for C");
}
```

Notice that unlike the swap function shown earlier, no values are passed into this function. The function parameters are used only to return values, a valid use of pass-by-reference parameters.

The function for computing one or two possible solutions requires three input values for A, B, and C, and returns two values for the two possible solutions. For the first three values, we use pass-by-value, and for the last two values, we use pass-by-reference. In addition to returning the values for the two possible solutions, the function must also let the caller know whether the equation has zero, one, or two solutions. We can return this information as the result of the function. Here's how.

```
int GetSolutions(float A, float B, float C,
                 float &x1, float &x2)
{

    float discriminant, sqrtOfDiscriminant;

    discriminant = B*B - 4*A*C;

    if (discriminant < 0) { //then no solution

        return 0;
    }
    else { //either one or two solutions exist

        sqrtOfDiscriminant = sqrt( discriminant );
        x1 = (-B + sqrtOfDiscriminant) / (2 * A);

        if (discriminant == 0) {// only one solution exists
        return 1;
        }
        else {//the second solution exists

            x2 = (-B - sqrtOfDiscriminant) / (2 * A);
            return 2;

        } //end inner if

    } //end outer if
```

Putting everything together, we have Quad6.

```
//Program Quad6:    A program to find solutions of
//                  quadratic equation Ax² + Bx + C = 0. The
//                  program uses functions with both pass-by-value
//                  and pass-by-reference parameters.

#include "GUIObj.h"
#include <math.h>
void GetInputs(float &A, float &B, float &C)
{
    FloatTypeIn  floatInpBox;

    A = floatInpBox.GetFloat("INPUT","Type in value for A");
    B = floatInpBox.GetFloat("INPUT","Type in value for B");
    C = floatInpBox.GetFloat("INPUT","Type in value for C");
}
int GetSolutions(float A, float B, float C,
                 float &x1, float &x2)
{

    float discriminant, sqrtOfDiscriminant;

    discriminant = B*B - 4*A*C;

    if (discriminant < 0) { //then no solution

        return 0;
    }
    else { //either one or two solutions exist

        sqrtOfDiscriminant = sqrt( discriminant );
        x1 = (-B + sqrtOfDiscriminant) / (2 * A);

        if (discriminant == 0) {// only one solution exists
            return 1;
        }
        else {//the second solution exists

            x2 = (-B - sqrtOfDiscriminant) / (2 * A);
            return 2;

        } //end inner if

    } //end outer if
}
//MAIN FUNCTION
void main ()
{
    float      A, B, C, x1, x2;
    int        noOfSolutions;
```

```
OKBox        msgBox;

GetInputs(A, B, C);

noOfSolutions = GetSolutions(A, B, C, x1, x2);

switch (noOfSolutions) {

    case 0:

      msgBox.Display("No real number solutions exist.");
      break;

    case 1:

      msgBox.Display(x1);
      break;

    case 2:

      msgBox.Display(x1);
      msgBox.Display(x2);
      break;

    } //end switch
}
```

9.5 Exercises

1 For each of the following code segments, determine the output. Assume the memory location for the variable num is 1402. Identify any statement for which you cannot determine the output, and explain why.

a.
```
int num = 123;
int *pnum;

pnum = &num;
cout << *pnum << endl;
num = num + 5;
cout << *pnum << endl;
```

b.
```
int num = 123;
int *pnum;

*pnum = num;
cout << *pnum << endl;
num = num + 5;
cout << *pnum << endl;
```

c.
```
int num = 123;
int *pnum;

pnum = &num;
cout << num << endl;
cout << &num << endl;
cout << pnum << endl;
cout << *pnum << endl;
```

d.
```
int num = 123;
int *pnum;

*pnum = num;
cout << num << endl;
cout << &num· << endl;
cout << pnum << endl;
cout << *pnum << endl;
```

2 Which of the following code segments are semantically invalid? Which are syntactically valid, but do not make sense?

```
int     num;
int     *q;
```

a. `num = 1234;`

b. `q = num = 3;`

c. `&q = 112;`

d. `*q = 112;`

e. `&num = q;`

f. `q = 334;`

g. `num = *q + 223;`

h. `*q = num;`

3 Modify functions `GetInputs` and `GetSolutions` of the program Quad6 by using pass-by-pointer parameters.

4 The `GetSolutions` function in program Quad6 returns an integer giving the number of solutions found for the given quadratic equation. Another method to return this number would use a reference parameter. The function signature for the new function is

```
void GetSolutions (float A, float B, float C,
                   float &x1, float &x2, int &noOfSolutions)
```

Rewrite the `GetSolutions` function using this function prototype. Rewrite Quad6 using the modified `GetSolutions` function.

5 Write a function that accepts a value in cents between 0 and 99 and returns the number of quarters, dimes, nickels, and pennies. The result of the function should be 1 if the input value is valid and 0 otherwise.

6 Write a function that accepts five integers and returns the maximum and minimum numbers.

7 Write a function that accepts three integers and returns the integers in ascending order. For example:

```
int i = 14; int j = 128; int k = 34;
Arrange(i,j,k);
cout << i << endl << j << endl << k;
```

will print out

```
14
34
128
```

8 Using `char` pointers, write a program that reads in a string and prints out the number of vowels and consonants.

9 Write a function that accepts a string and returns the number of characters in the string; do not count the blank spaces and punctuation marks. Use the pass-by-pointer passing mechanism with a pointer to character as a parameter for receiving the string value. The function prototype is

```
int CountChar (char *p)
```

Refer to the sample code given at the end of section 9.1 for implementing this function. A call to the function can be made as

```
char str[20] = "I love C++";
cout << CountChar(str);
```

10 Write a function that accepts a string and returns the number of words in the string. Words are separated by blank spaces or punctuation marks.

11 Write a function that accepts three temperatures in Fahrenheit and converts them into Celsius. The function should contain exactly three parameters. The formula for conversion is given in exercise 3 in chapter 8.

chapter 10

Defining objects

New words or new meanings for old words are continually being added to natural languages. As our society becomes more and more complex, we need new vocabularies to describe new ideas, devices, and discoveries. The fluid and dynamic nature of language facilitates the evolution of our society. When we look back at the history of computer programming languages, we realize that the earlier programming languages were very limited. Much like an early human society with only a limited vocabulary, early programming languages had only a very small number of data types and control structures. As the demands for more complex software arose, programming languages were improved to meet them. One improvement was the addition of the *object*. Grafting an object concept onto a programming language allows the programming language to be fluid and dynamic. The object concept extends the power of programming languages by allowing programmers to add new objects that encapsulate both data and processes. In this chapter we will explain the mechanics of defining new objects.

10.1 Defining a Volume object

In section 8.5, we created the `volumes.h` header file, which contains a set of functions for computing volumes of various geometric shapes. We mentioned that a naming conflict could arise from the use of global constants and variables defined in the header files. One of the four possible solutions to the naming conflict problem is to define an object that encapsulates functions and data (constants and variables). We will explain the basic mechanics of defining a new object in this section. We will define a new object called `Volume` that encapsulates the functionality of computing volumes of various geometric shapes.

As we begin to define new objects, we must also distinguish between the *object type* and the *object instance*. Up until now, we have been using only preexisting objects, so such a distinction was not necessary. An *object type*, or *class*, is a generic description or definition of objects. An *object instance* is a specific, individual object of an object type. Every object is an instance of exactly one object type. Consider the following declarations:

```
OKBox   msg;
Turtle  myTurtle;
```

`OKBox` and `Turtle` are object types, or classes; `msg` and `myTurtle` are object instances of the object types `OKBox` and `Turtle`, respectively. We use the expression *define an object* to mean *define a new object type* or *define a new class*. And we use the expression *declare an object* to mean *create a new object instance*. An object type must be defined prior to creating any object instance of that type. Object definition is done only once, but object declaration can be done more than once, either by declaring more than one object in a single declaration or by using more than one declaration.

Defining an object is the act of specifying a mold for making actual objects. Using housing construction as an analogy, defining an object is equivalent to making a blueprint for a house. Just as having a blueprint does not imply the existence of an actual house, defining an object does not imply the existence of any actual object instance.

When we need to identify clearly the object type X of an object instance y, we say either "y is an X object" or "y is an instance of the object type X." For example, in the declaration above, we say "myTurtle is a Turtle object," or "myTurtle is an instance of

> **Note** An *object type*, or *class*, is a generic description, or definition, of objects. An *object instance*, or more simply, an *object*, is a specific, individual object of an object type. Every object is an instance of exactly one object type.

the object type Turtle." Similarly, we say "msg is an OKBox object," or "msg is an instance of the object type OKBox." When we refer to an arbitrary instance of the object type X, we say "an X object." For example, when we say "a Turtle object can draw a line" or "use a Turtle object to draw a square," we are referring to an instance of the object type Turtle.

The following defines a new object type Volume:

```cpp
class Volume {

public:

    //constructor
    Volume( ) : PI(3.14159)
    {
    }

    //tri_prism: compute the volume of a triangular prism
    float tri_prism (float base, float height, float width)
    {
        return  0.5 * base * height * width;
    }

    //rect_prism: compute the volume of a rectangular prism
    float rect_prism (float base, float height, float width)
    {
        return  base * height * width;
    }

    //sphere: compute the volume of a sphere
    float sphere (float radius)
    {
        return  (4.0/3.0) * PI * radius*radius*radius;
    }

    //cylinder: compute the volume of a cylinder
    float cylinder (float radius, float height)
    {
        return  PI * radius*radius * height;
    }

    //cone: compute the volume of a cone
    float cone (float radius, float height)
    {
        return  (1.0/3.0) * PI * radius*radius * height;
    }
private:
    const float  PI;

}; //end of Volume
```

Figure 10.2 Object diagram for Volumes6

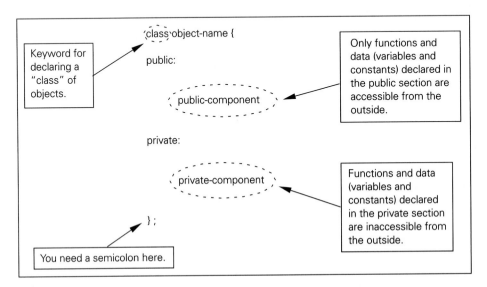

Figure 10.1 General syntax of an object definition

And here's a simple example of computing the volume of a cone using a `Volume` object, assuming its definition is stored in the header file `Volumes.h`.

```
//Program Volumes6:   A simple program to illustrate the use of
//                    a Volume object.

#include "Volumes.h"
#include <iostream.h>

void main()
{
    Volume vol;
    float result;

    result = vol.cone(2.0, 34.5);
```

```
        cout << result;
    }
```

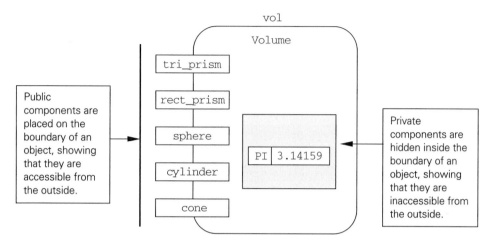

Figure 10.3 Accessibility of object components

The object diagram for the program is shown in figure 10.1.

The general syntax of an object definition is shown in figure 10.2.

An object definition contains two basic components: *private* and *public*. Everything that is declared within the public section is accessible to the users of an object, and everything that is declared within the private section is inaccessible to the users of an object. Figure 10.3 shows the way we depict the accessibility of object components.

Suppose we have the following definition:

```
class Dog {
public:
    int wgt;
    . . .
private:
    int age;
    . . .
};

Dog fifi;
```

Then, the expression

```
fifi.age = 10; // NOT valid
```

is not valid, while

```
fifi.wgt = 15; //valid
```

is valid, because the variable wgt is public and age is private.

The Volume object has one private constant PI that is shared by its functions. Since the constant PI is hidden inside the private section of the Volume object and is inaccessible from the outside of the object, there can be no naming conflict. The following sample program illustrates this point.

```
//Program Volumes7:    A program to illustrate inaccessibility of
//                     the private components of an object
//                     from the outside of the object.

#include "Volumes.h"
#include <iostream.h>

void main ()
{
    float PI = 3.141593, volume, area;
    Volume vol;

    volume = vol.sphere(3.44);
    area = PI * 3.44 * 3.44;

    cout << volume << "  " << area;
}
```

> PI here refers to the local variable and does not conflict with the Volume object's private constant PI.

In C++, object functions are called *member functions,* and object data (both variables and constants) are called *data members.* A member function is also called an *object method.* Data members are declared and used within the object definition just like nonobject variables, and constants are declared and used in a program. Data initialization is, however, done differently. Unlike nonobject variables and constants, which are initialized at the point of declaration, data members are initialized in a special function called a *constructor.* The name of a constructor function must be the same as the name of the object. Let's look at the portion of the Volume object definition that deals with the data member declaration and initialization (see figure 10.4).

Initialization of data members is done in the function prototype of a constructor. Instead of using the assignment operator, initialization is specified using the following syntax:

data-member   (*initial-value*   )

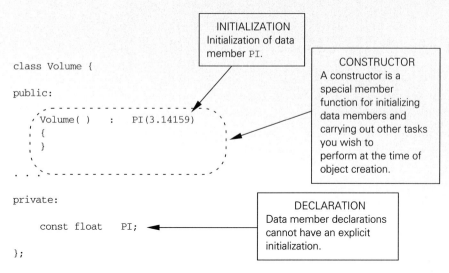

Figure 10.4 Data member declaration and initialization

If the program has multiple initializations, then they are separated by commas, as shown in the following example. Three data members—one constant and two variables—are initialized here:

```
class Sample {

    public:

    Sample( ) : one(45), two(2.33), three('a')
    {
    }

.  .  .

    private:

        const int    one;
        float        two;
        char         three;
};
```

Since `two` and `three` are variables, another valid way to assign values to them is to use assignment statements inside the function body, such as

```
    Sample( ) : one(45)
    {
```

```
        two = 2.33;
        three = 'a';
    }
```

Notice that the assignment statement for initialization is valid only for variables. For constants, we must use the initialization expression inside the function prototype.

Unlike other member functions, a constructor function is not explicitly called. The constructor function is implicitly called at the point of declaration. For example, in the following sample program, the constructor is called when vol is declared.

```
#include "Volumes.h"
#include <iostream.h>

void main()
{
    Volume vol;

    float result;

    result = vol.cone(2.0, 34.5);

    cout << result;
}
```

An implicit function call to the constructor function at the point of object declaration.

An explicit call to the member function.

Once the object type is defined, many instances of the object type may be declared. For example, we may have three Volume objects by declaring

```
#include "Volumes.h"

...
Volume vol1, vol2, vol3;
```

What do we gain by creating multiple Volume objects? Actually, whether we use vol1, vol2, or vol3, as long as we enter the same input values, you would get the same result for the volumes. So what's the point in having multiple Volume objects? Since they all behave identically, isn't it sufficient to have just one Volume object? Well, consider a situation where we want to compute volumes with a varying degree of precision for PI. For certain computations, we may not require high precision, so PI = 3.14 may suffice. For other computations, we need higher precision, say PI = 3.141593. By making a slight modification to the definition of the Volume object, we will be able to create Volume objects with varying degrees of precision.

First we modify the constructor so we can assign different values to the constant PI at object declaration time. Here's the modified definition of the Volume object.

```
class Volume {

public:

    //constructor
    Volume(float x) : PI(x)
    {
    }
```

A modified constructor. Notice a parameter is added to the function.

```
    //tri_prism: compute the volume of a triangular prism
    float tri_prism (float base, float height, float width)
    {
        return  0.5 * base * height * width;
    }

    //rect_prism: compute the volume of a rectangular prism
    float rect_prism (float base, float height, float width)
    {
        return  base * height * width;
    }

    //sphere: compute the volume of a sphere
    float sphere (float radius)
    {
        return  (4.0/3.0) * PI * radius*radius*radius;
    }

    //cylinder: compute the volume of a cylinder
    float cylinder (float radius, float height)
    {
        return  PI * radius*radius * height;
    }

    //cone: compute the volume of a cone
    float cone (float radius, float height)
    {
        return  (1.0/3.0) * PI * radius*radius * height;
    }

private:
    const float  PI;

}; //end of Volume
```

Using this modified Volume object, we can write a program, that computes the volume of a cone with two different precisions for the constant PI.

```
//Program Volumes8:    A program that computes the volumes by
//                     using Volume objects with different
//                     precisions for PI.
```

```
#include "Volumes.h"
#include <iostream.h>

void main()
{
    Volume lo_precision_vol(3.14), hi_precision_vol(3.141593);

    float lo_result, hi_result;

    lo_result = lo_precision_vol.cone(2.0, 34.5);
    hi_result = hi_precision_vol.cone(2.0, 34.5);

    cout << lo_result << "   " << hi_result;
}
```

We made one modification to the Volume object. The constructor was modified to accept an input parameter as in

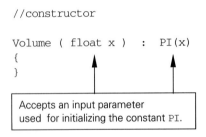

```
//constructor

Volume ( float x )   :   PI(x)
{
}
```

Accepts an input parameter used for initializing the constant PI.

The initial values are passed to the two objects at the time of declaration in

```
Volume lo_precision_vol(3.14), hi_precision_vol(3.141593);
```

Instead of using the Volume objects defined above, this program could be written using nonobject shape functions. It would be a much more tedious and error-prone process because you have to keep resetting the global constant PI to the desired precision. (See exercise 1 at the end of the chapter.)

An object may have multiple constructors. For example, the Volume object may have two constructors, as in following example:

```
class Volume {

public:

    //constructor #1
```

```
      Volume() : PI(3.14)
      {
      }

      //constructor #2
      Volume(float x) : PI(x)
      {
      }

 . . .

private:
    const float  PI;

}; //end of Volume
```

Since the two constructors have different function prototypes, there is no conflict. In the example, a declaration with an input value calls the second constructor, and one without any input value calls the first constructor.

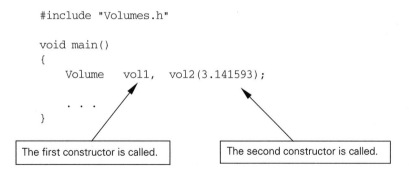

```
#include "Volumes.h"

void main()
{
    Volume   vol1,  vol2(3.141593);

      . . .
}
```

The first constructor is called.

The second constructor is called.

We end this section with the syntax rules for class definition.

class-definition
    class-heading   {   *member-list* $_{opt}$ }   ;

class-heading
    class   *identifier*

member-list
    member-definition   *member-list*

member-definition
    constructor-definition
    function-definition
    data-member-declaration
    `public`   `:`
    `private`   `:`

constructor-function
    function-definition
    function-signature   `:`   *member-initializers*   *function-body*

member-initializers
    initializer
    initializer `,`   *member-initializers*

initializer
    identifier   `(`   *expression*   `)`

data-member-declaration
    type-specifier   *data-member-list*   `;`
    `const`   *type-specifier*   *data-member-list*   `;`

data-member-list
    identifier
    identifier `,`   *data-member-list*

10.2 Defining a `Person` *object*

As another example of defining an object type, let's define a `Person` object. Suppose we wish to develop a program that maintains an address book containing names and phone numbers. What kinds of objects do we need? The first thing we need is a way to keep track of a person's name and phone number. We can define a `Person` object to keep track of this information. We will deal only with this `Person` object here. Later in the book, as you learn more concepts, we will develop a full-fledged address book program with additional types of objects.

    A `Person` object is defined as follows:

```
#include <string.h>
class Person {

public:
    Person ( )                                    //constructor #1
    {
        name[0] = '\0';
        phone[0] = '\0';
    }

    Person (char *inpName, char *inpPhone)    //constructor #2
    {
        strcpy(name,inpName);
        strcpy(phone,inpPhone);
    }

    void SetName(char *pName)
    {
        strcpy(name, pName);
    }

    void SetPhone(char *pPh)
    {
        strcpy(phone, pPh);
    }

    char *GetName()
    {
        return strdup(name); //return the duplicate copy
    }

    char *GetPhone()
    {
        return strdup(phone); //return the duplicate copy
    }

private:
    charname[25];
    charphone[11];

}; //end of definition
```

Here's a short example using a Person object.

```
Person x;
OKBoxmsg;
```

```
...
x.SetName("John Smith");
x.SetPhone("408-123-2233");
msg.Display(x.GetName());
msg.Display(x.GetPhone());
...
```

The `Person` object has two constructors. The first constructor is

```
Person ( )
{
    name[0] = '\0';
    phone[0] = '\0';
} //constructor
```

It initializes the two data members to a NUL-terminated string. As already mentioned, the name of a constructor function must be the same as the name of the object type. Although it is not a requirement, defining at least one constructor function is a good practice to ensure that the proper initialization is carried out. Without a constructor function, the system will perform a default initialization, which may or may not be what we expect. To be certain that the object is initialized as we desire, we should define our own constructor. The `Person` object also has the following second constructor

```
Person (char *inpName, char *inpPhone)
{
    strcpy(name,inpName);
    strcpy(phone,inpPhone);
}
```

This constructor is useful if we want to initialize a `Person` object at the point of declaration. For example:

```
Person mrY("Amadeus Mozart", "408-222-3333");
```

creates a new `Person` object `mrY` and initializes its `name` and `phone` to `"Amadeus Mozart"` and `"408-222-3333"`, respectively.

Now let's look at the function that assigns a passed string to the data member name.

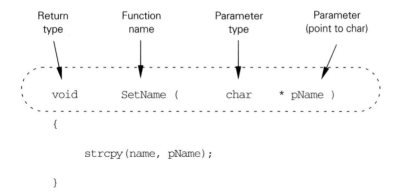

The return type is declared to be void because the function does not return a value. The function has one parameter, which is a pointer to char, and uses the pass-by-pointer passing mechanism.[*] Notice that the SetName function uses the standard string function strcpy for copying the passed parameter to the data member name.

The inverse of SetName is GetName which returns the value of the data member name. The function is defined as

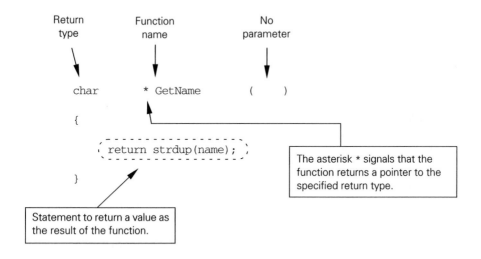

---

[*] You can use other techniques to pass an array of characters, but passing a pointer to char is the most flexible and works well for both passing and returning an array of characters.

This function returns a pointer to char, which we can see by the asterisk placed in front of the function name. This is similar to declaring a variable to be a pointer to char. For example, consider the following:

```
char    *p;        // p is a pointer to char

char    *func();   //func is a function that
                   //returns a pointer to char
```

The asterisk does not have to be adjacent to a parameter. The preceding two declarations can also be written as

```
char*p;

char*func();
```

In fact, the asterisk may appear anywhere between the type name and variable or function name. But be aware that

```
char*p, q;
```

is not equivalent to

```
char *p, *q;
```

Rather, it is equivalent to

```
char*p; char q;
```

In the GetName function, we return a pointer to a character; that is, we use a pointer expression to return string data. The standard string function strdup makes a duplicate copy of a string and returns the address of the first character of the duplicate string. The GetName function therefore returns the address of the first character of a duplicate copy of name. We do not return the address of the first character of name itself; if we do, then the caller of this function could inadvertently modify the original value. This event could happen if we passed back the address of the original data. To avoid this potential problem, we make a copy and return the address of this copy. In this way, the caller has no direct access to the original data, and the original data is safe from outside interference. (See exercise 3 at the end of this chapter.)

10.3 Interface and implementation files

In the previous section, we presented the definition of the `Person` object as if it were stored in a single file. Although this option is a valid and viable for a very short definition, normal practice is to separate the definition into two files—the interface and implementation files. The interface file contains just the specification of the object, that is, a list of data members and member functions without the implementation code. The implementation code for the member functions is stored in the implementation file. For example, the interface and implementation files for the `Person` object might look like figure 10.5.

Notice that in the implementation file, the member function names are all preceded by the class name `Person` and double colons. The double colon is called the *scope resolution operator*, and it is required for the compiler to recognize that these functions are defined for the `Person` object. In the original single-file version of our object definition, the specification and implementation were both contained within the scope of the `class` declaration, where the scope of a `class` begins with the left brace and ends with the matching right brace (see figure 10.6).

Since we are now putting the implementation code in a separate file, all the member functions require the scope resolution operator.

The syntax category *function–name* is updated to

> *function–name*
>   *identifier*
>   *identifier*   ::   *identifier*

to accommodate scope resolution.

For the rest of the book, we will define new objects using interface and implementation files. One reason for organizing the object definition this way is to make the definition more readable. Consider reading the interface file for the `Turtle` object. If we had included everything for the `Turtle` object in one big file, it would be much too difficult to understand. As users of the `Turtle` object, we do not need to read the implementation. All we really need to know is the list of public function prototypes provided in the interface file[*]. Since the file is much smaller and presents its public components concisely, it is much easier to read and comprehend.

---

[*] This file actually contains more than we really need to know. For instance, we don't have to know about the data members and member functions mentioned in the private component because we do not have direct access to them anyway. The private component is listed in the interface file to facilitate efficient compilation.

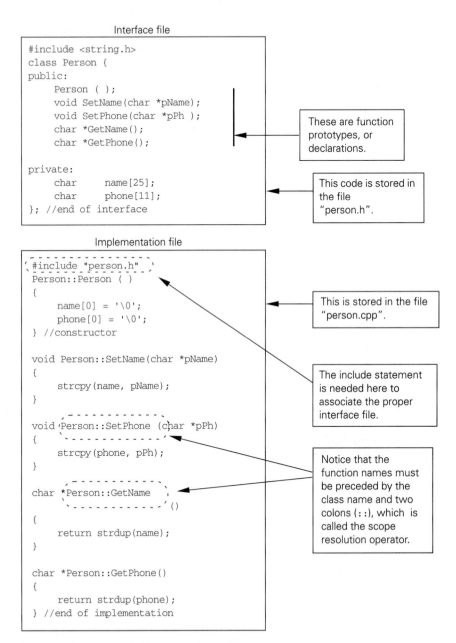

Figure 10.5 Interface and implementation files

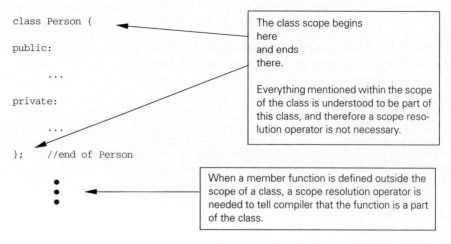

```
class Person {

public:

    ...

private:

    ...

};    //end of Person
        •
        •
        •
```

The class scope begins
here
and ends
there.

Everything mentioned within the scope
of the class is understood to be part of
this class, and therefore a scope resolution operator is not necessary.

When a member function is defined outside the
scope of a class, a scope resolution operator is
needed to tell compiler that the function is a part
of the class.

Figure 10.6 Beginning and ending braces

10.4 Defining a Fraction object

In this section, you will find out how to define a new object type, fraction. So far, you have learned about numerical data types, such as int, float, and double, and nonnumerical data types, such as char. We call these data types *primitive data types* because they are part of a programming language. With older programming languages, we are limited to using only primitive data types, which is a severe restriction. In developing more complex programs, we need many different kinds of data and objects, and primitive data types alone are not enough.

As a simple illustration, let's suppose that we need to develop a program that uses fractions. Without a means to define new types of data, we must represent a fraction using existing data types. For instance, we could use an array of two integers to represent a fraction. The first element is for the numerator, and the second for the denominator. This implementation, however, is awkward and unnatural. We would not be able to express the addition of two fractions A and B as A + B, for example. With C++ and other object-oriented programming languages, we can define a new object type called fraction. And by doing so, we would be able to treat fraction objects just as we treat the values of primitive data types. For example, just as we can write an integer expression

```
(a + b) / c
```

for integers a, b, and c, we could write the same expression if a, b, and c were fraction objects. After we define an object fraction, we could say something like

```
f1 = (f2 + f3) / (f4 - f5);
```

provided that fractions `f2` through `f5` are initialized properly.

Instead of immediately presenting the full definition of a `fraction` object in its final form, we will define the object incrementally, concentrating on one topic at a time. Let's begin with the portion of the definition that allows us to initialize, assign, and retrieve the fraction data.

```
// INTERFACE - fraction.h

#include <stdlib.h>

class fraction {

public:

    fraction ( ); //constructor #1

    fraction (int n, int d); //constructor #2

    int numerator ( ); //return the numerator

    int denominator ( ); //return the denominator

    void assign (int n, int d); //assign values for numerator
                                //and denominator

    //other functions are defined here

private:

    int num, denom;

};
```

The corresponding implementation portion is

```
// IMPLEMENTATION - fraction.cpp

#include "fraction.h"

fraction::fraction ()
{
    num =0;
    denom = 1;
}

fraction::fraction (int n, int d)
```

```
{
    num = n;
    denom = d;
}

int fraction::numerator( )
{
    return num;
}

int fraction::denominator( )
{
    return denom;
}

void fraction::assign (int n, int d)
{
    num = n;
    denom = d;
}
```

A `fraction` object has two private data members, `num` and `denom`, to store its numerator and denominator. For example, a `fraction` object representing the fraction 1/3 would look like the diagram in figure 10.7.

Using the first constructor function, a `fraction` object can be declared as

```
fraction f, g, h;
```

and we can assign values as:

```
f.assign ( 1, 3 );
g.assign ( 2, 5 );
h.assign ( 9, 4 );
```

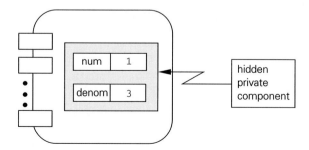

Figure 10.7 A fraction object

The body of the function `assign` contains simple assignment statements for setting the object's data members. The numerator and denominator values are accessed by the two functions using

```
f.numerator(); //returns the numerator 1
f.denominator(); //returns the denominator 3
```

The second constructor function will allow us to initialize the values at the time of declaration. For example:

```
fraction f(1,3), g(2,5), h(9,4);
```

Now let's look at the arithmetic operations for fractions. We will explain only the addition operation here. The other three arithmetic operations are implemented in a similar manner. With the final form of definition for the `fraction` object, we will be able to write an expression such as

```
x + y
```

to add two `fraction` objects x and y. But first, as an intermediate step, we will define a function called add. The function prototype for add is

```
fraction add (fraction f);
```

Once this function is defined fully, we can do the following:

```
fraction x ( 1, 2 ), y ( 3, 4 ), result;

result = x.add(y); //or y.add(x) since addition is commutative
```

Now let's look at the function body for add. The addition of two fractions is performed according to the following formula

$$\frac{a}{b} + \frac{c}{d} = \frac{a \cdot d + c \cdot b}{b \cdot d}$$

and the code for implementing the add function follows:

```
fraction fraction::add (fraction f)
```

```
{
    fraction sum;

    sum.num = num * f.denom + f.num * denom;

    sum.denom = denom * f.denom;

    return sum;
}
```

Let's trace the add function for the execution of the statement

```
x.add(y);
```

The original values of x and y should not change, and therefore, the first thing we do inside the add function is to declare a new fraction object sum. We then compute the numerator and denominator of sum. After the values are computed, we return the value of sum and the function is terminated. We have to pay special attention to how the object's internal data members are accessed. We are dealing with three fractions, x, y, and sum. Fraction y is an argument to the function, and its value is accessed inside the function as f. We call fraction x the *owner object,* or *owner,* of the function because we are executing its add function. Fraction sum is the result of adding x and y. Data members (and functions) are accessed inside an object's function just by their names, that is, without dot notation. Figure 10.8 illustrates the situation.

Inside the add function, we use dot notation to access the numerator and denominator of fractions sum and f. Since the data members num and denom are both private, they are not accessible from the outside of objects. However, access to the private data members is allowed if access is made from an object of the same object type using dot notation.

Let's write a simple program to test the add function.

```
//Program Fraction:    A simple program to test the
//                     fraction object.

#include "fraction.h"
#include <iostream.h>

void main()
{
    fraction f(1,2), g(1,4), result;

    result = f.add(g);
```

```
    cout << result.numerator() << "/"
            << result.denominator();
}
```

If you run the above program, you will get the result 6/8. The answer is correct, but not in the simplified form we normally would expect. That is, we would like to get the result 3/4.

To reduce a fraction to its simplest form, we need to identify the greatest common divisor of its numerator and denominator. The greatest common divisor of two integers A and B can be determined by the following algorithm:

1 Set DIV equal to the smaller of the absolute values of A and B. If DIV == 0, then stop.

2 Attempt dividing A and B by DIV. If DIV divides both A and B perfectly, then stop. DIV is the greatest common divisor.

3 Decrement DIV by 1. If DIV == 1, then stop. Otherwise, repeat step 2.

We will define a function gcd for computing the greatest common divisor of the numerator and denominator. We place this gcd function in the private section of the object, since the function is intended for internal use. Its implementation is given at the

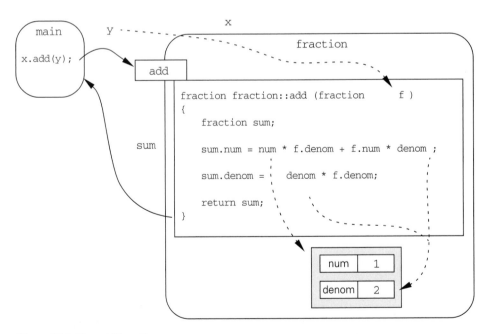

Figure 10.8 The add function

end of the chapter. We should remind you that the algorithm provided here is not very efficient. In fact, it is quite inefficient, but we will use it here because it is simple and easy to understand. The *Euclidean algorithm* is better for computing the greatest common divisor of two integers. (See exercise 6 at the end of this chapter.)

With the gcd function in place, we can simplify a fraction by first finding the greatest common divisor of the numerator and denominator and then dividing them by this number. Then

$$\frac{a/gcd\,(a,b)}{b/gcd\,(a,b)}$$

is the simplified form of the fraction $\frac{a}{b}$.

We will call the function that reduces a fraction to its simplest form reduce. Its definition is

```
fraction fraction::reduce(fraction f)
{
    int div = gcd(f.num,f.denom);

    if (div != 0) {
        f.num    = f.num / div;
        f.denom = f.denom / div;
    }

    return f;
}
```

The following shows how the add function uses the reduce function:

```
fraction fraction::operator+ ( fraction f )
{
    fraction sum;

    sum.num   = num * f.denom +  f.num * denom;
    sum.denom = denom * f.denom;

    return reduce(sum);
}
```

Figure 10.9 illustrates how the reduce function is used. Notice that the reduce function of the fraction object x is used, not the reduce function belonging to sum. In other words, x is the owner object here. The fraction object sum is passed as an argu-

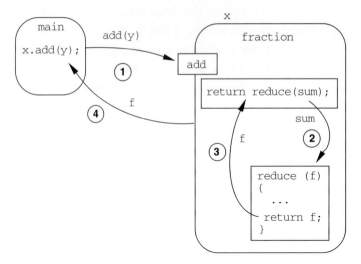

Figure 10.9 The reduce function

ment to the `reduce` function of the fraction object x. Also notice that the reduced `fraction` object is returned first to the `add` function and then returned to the main function.

We need to cover only one more topic before we can list the final version of the object type `fraction`. We need to define a function so we can write an expression

```
x + y
```

instead of

```
x.add(y)
```

The following is the final version of the addition operation:

```
fraction fraction::operator+ ( fraction f )
{
    fraction sum;

    sum.num   = num * f.denom +  f.num * denom;
    sum.denom = denom * f.denom;

    return reduce(sum);
}
```

The only difference between the two version of addition function is that the name of the function is changed from `add` to `operator+`. Because the name of the function is `operator+`, we can call the function using the syntax

```
x.operator+(y);
```

In addition, we can make a function call to `operator+`, using the shorthand notation

```
x + y;
```

The plus (+) and other symbols are used for multiple purposes in C++. For example, when the compiler sees the expression

```
x + y
```

it will perform an integer addition if the operands `x` and `y` are integers. It will perform `float` division if either one of the operands is a `float` data type. In other words, the plus symbol has multiple meanings, and the compiler will determine the meaning from the types of the operands. We call operators with multiple meanings *overloaded operators*. What we did above was to overload the plus operator with one more meaning, namely, the addition of two fractions. Therefore, when the compiler encounters the expression

```
x + y
```

and `x` and `y` are `fraction` objects, the compiler will correctly execute the `operator+` function defined for the `fraction` object.

Table 10.1 lists the operators that can be overloaded. Notice that the word *operator* is a reserved word.

To allow the definition of functions with overloaded operators as their names, the syntax category *function–name* is modified to

> *function–name*
>   *identifier*
>   *identifier*   `::`   *identifier*
>   **operator**   *operator*
>   *identifier*   `::`   **operator**   *operator*

Table 10.1 C++ operators that can be overloaded

+	–	*	/	%
^	&	|	~	!
,	=	<	>	<<
>>	<=	>=	==	&&
||	++	--	+=	-=
*=	/=	%=	^=	&=
|=	!=	<<=	>>=	->
[]	()	new	delete	

The syntax category *operator* is any one of the operators listed in table 10.1.

We are now ready to present the final version of the fraction object definition. We include the reduce function only in the final version.

"fraction.h"

```
#include <stdlib.h>

class fraction {

public:

    fraction ( );

    fraction (int n, int d);

    int numerator ( );
        /* returns the numerator of an owner */

    int denominator (  );
        /* returns the denominator of an owner */

    fraction operator+ ( fraction f );
        /* returns the sum of an owner and f */

    fraction operator- ( fraction f );
        /* returns the difference of an owner and f */

    fraction operator/ ( fraction f );
        /* returns the quotient of an owner divided by f */

    fraction operator* ( fraction f );
        /* returns the product of an owner and f */

private:

    int num, denom;

    int gcd ( int a, int b);
        /* returns the greatest common divisor of a and b */

    fraction reduce ( fraction f );
        /* reduces f into the simplest form */

};
```

```
#include "fraction.h"

fraction::fraction ( )
{
}

fraction::fraction (int n, int d)
{
     num   = n;
     denom = d;
}

int fraction::numerator ( )
{
     return  num;
}

int fraction::denominator ( )
{
     return denom;
}

fraction fraction::operator+ ( fraction f )
{
     fraction sum;

     sum.num   = num * f.denom +  f.num * denom;
     sum.denom = denom * f.denom;
     return reduce(sum);
}

fraction fraction::operator- ( fraction f )
{
     fraction diff;

     diff.num   = num * f.denom -  f.num * denom;
     diff.denom = denom * f.denom;
     return reduce(diff);
}

fraction fraction::operator/ ( fraction f )
{
     fraction quotient;

     quotient.num = num * f.denom;
     quotient.denom = denom * f.num;
     return reduce(quotient);
}
fraction fraction::operator* ( fraction f )
{
     fraction product;

     product.num   = num * f.num;
     product.denom = denom * f.denom;
     return reduce(product);
}

//Private functions

int fraction::gcd ( int a, int b)
{
     int div;

      if (abs(a) > abs(b))
```

```
           div = abs(b);
      else
           div = abs(a);

      if (div != 0)
           while ( (a % div != 0   || b % div != 0)    //div does not divide
                      &&                                //a or b perfectly
                      div != 1 )                        //and div is not 1 yet
           {
                div = div - 1

           } //end while

      // At this point either div == 1 or div divides both
      // a and b perfectly

      return div;
}
fraction fraction::reduce ( fraction f  )
{
      int div = gcd(f.num, f.denom);

      if (div != 0) {
           f.num   = f.num / div;
           f.denom = f.denom / div;
      }
      return f;
}
```

We will conclude this chapter with a program that tests the overloaded operators defined for the fraction object.

```
//Program Fraction2:    A simple program to test the operators
//                      defined for the fraction object.

#include "fraction.h"
#include <iostream.h>

void main()
{
    fraction f(1,2), g(1,4), result;

    result = f + g;
    cout << result.numerator() << "/"
            << result.denominator() << endl;

    result = f - g;
    cout << result.numerator() << "/"
            << result.denominator() << endl;

    result = f * g;
    cout << result.numerator() << "/"
```

```
                    << result.denominator() << endl;

        result = f / g;
        cout << result.numerator() << "/"
                    << result.denominator() << endl;

    }
```

10.5 Exercises

1 Write two versions of a program that prints out the volumes of geometric shapes using three different precisions for PI — 3.14, 3.1415, and 3.141593. Use Volume objects for the first version and nonobject shape functions (from chapter 8) for the second version. Output from the program should resemble the following output, but real values will replace the Xs and Ys. Use cout for output.

```
    cone            radius = XXXXX          height = XXXX
                PI=3.14         PI=3.1415           PI=3.141593
                ----------------------------------------
                YYYYYY          YYYYYYY             YYYYYYYY

    cylinder        radius = XXXXX          height = XXXX
                PI=3.14         PI=3.1415           PI=3.141593
                ----------------------------------------
                YYYYYY          YYYYYYY             YYYYYYYY
```

2 Modify the Person object to include an age attribute (data member). Write functions to set and get the age attribute values and modify the constructor function accordingly.

3 Suppose the getName function of the Person object is changed to the following:

```
    char *GetName()
    {
        return name; //return the address of the original data
    }
```

What will be the output of the following program? Is it what you expect? Compare the results with executing the same program with the correct Person object.

```
#include "GUIObj.h"
#include "Person.h"

void main()
{   .
    Person p; OKBox msg;
    char *str;

    p.SetName("John");
    str = p.GetName();
    msg.Display(str);
    str[2] = 'i';
    msg.Display(str);
}
```

4 Extend the `fraction` object by adding new operations +=, -=, /=, and *=.

5 Add a new function `init` to the `fraction` object that assigns a numerator and denominator to a fraction. Its function prototype is

```
void init ( int num, int denom);
```

Using the `init` function, you can assign 1/4 to a fraction `f` as follows:

```
fraction f;
f.init ( 1, 4);
```

6 The algorithm provided in the chapter for determining the greatest common divisor of two integers is not efficient, but it is easy to understand. A better, faster way to determine the greatest common divisor is the Euclidean algorithm. It works as follows:

```
To find the greatest common divisor of integers A and B
(assume A ≥ B):

    let Q = A / B and R = A % B; // Q - quotient, R - remainder

    if R = 0 then stop, B is the gcd;

    let A = B and B = R;

    repeat the procedure;
```

Write an object function gcd using the Euclidean algorithm. Why is the gcd function based on the Euclidean algorithm faster than the gcd function given in the chapter?

7 Define a new object String. A String object will have at least two private data members str and length. The variable str is a character array, and the variable length is of type int for keeping track of the number of characters plus the NUL character. Add a function + (an overloaded operator), which concatenates two String objects and returns the result. Add a second function = (another overloaded operator), which assigns string data to a String object. With a properly defined String object, you could do the following:

```
String u, v, w;
OKBox msg;

u = "Hello ";
v = "world!";
w = u + v;
msg.Display(w);
```

8 Define a new object called Date. A Date object will have at least three private data members for year, month, and day. You should add standard access functions for reading and setting values for year, month, and day. Add a constructor function that lets programmers assign values at the time of declaration. Add a subtraction operation that computes the number of days between the two given dates. To simplify the implementation of the subtraction operation, you may require that the two dates have the same year. For example, the following code displays 119.

```
Date   d1(94, 7, 7);
Date   d2(94, 3, 10);
OKBox  msg;

msg.Display(d1 - d2);
```

9 Define a new object called Name. A Name object will have at least three private data members for the first, middle, and last names. Add one function GetFullName that returns the full name (e.g., Johann Sebastian Bach) and another function Get-ShortName that returns the name with initials (e.g., J. S. Bach). Don't forget to define the standard access functions for getting and setting the first, middle, and last names individually. You should also add a constructor to assign three values at the time of declaration, as in this statement:

```
      Name jsb("Johann", "Sebastian", "Bach");
```

10 Define a new object called Money. Add operations for adding and subtracting two
    Money objects. Remember that Money should maintain only two decimal places.

11 Define a new object called Complex for representing complex numbers. An
    expression of the form $a + bi$, where $i^2 = -1$, is called a *complex number*. The value
    a represents the real number part, and the value b represents the imaginary part of the
    complex number. Four arithmetic operations for complex numbers are defined as

$$\text{Addition:} \quad (a + bi) + (c + di) = (a + c) + (b + d)i$$

$$\text{Subtraction:} \quad (a + bi) - (c + di) = (a - c) + (b - d)i$$

$$\text{Multiplication:} \quad (a + bi) \times (c + di) = (ac - bd) + (ad + bc)i$$

$$\text{Division:} \quad \frac{a + bi}{c + di} = \frac{ac + bd}{c^2 + d^2} + \frac{bc - ad}{c^2 + d^2}i$$

$$\text{provided} \quad c^2 + d^2 \neq 0$$

You need to define a constructor, a function to assign values, and functions to
return the real number and imaginary number parts of a complex number. You
may want to define an additional constructor.

12 Using the Complex object defined in exercise 11, write a program that solves qua-
    dratic equations. The program will find a complex number solution when a dis-
    criminant is negative.

chapter 11

Defining objects using inheritance

In any object-oriented programming language, there are two ways to define a new object type. Either you define a new object type from scratch or you define a new object type by extending or modifying an existing object type using a mechanism called *inheritance*. In the preceding chapter we learned how to define a new object type without inheritance, that is, to define a new object type from scratch. Some languages allow one to define new objects,[*] but we do not call these languages object-oriented unless they support inheritance. The degree and type of inheritance supported by object-oriented programming languages vary widely. The inheritance mechanism supported by C++ is one of the most powerful among the currently available object-oriented programming languages. We will describe inheritance in this chapter.

---

[*] These languages do not use the term *object*. They call user-defined objects *abstract data types*.

11.1 *Creating a* SmartTurtle *by inheritance*

Suppose we want to write a program that draws a very small galaxy—say eight stars arranged as follows:

A star can be formed by drawing five lines of equal length, turning 144 degrees after each one, as shown in the following:

```
// draw a star with each side 30 pixels long
Turtle t;
int i;
for ( i = 1; i <= 5; i=i+1 ) {
    t.Move(30);
    t.Turn(-144);
}
```

We are using –144 because we want to turn 144 degrees clockwise (with positive 144, we would end up drawing the star upside down). Now, to draw the whole galaxy of eight stars, we define a function for a single star and call this function eight times. The function can be defined as

```
void Star (Turtle t, int x, int y)
{
    t.PenUp();
    t.GoToPos(x,y);
    t.PenDown();
    t.TurnTo(0);

    int i;
    for ( i = 1; i <= 5; i++) {
        t.Move(30);
        t.Turn(-144);
    }
}
```

> Move the turtle to the desired position first and set the turtle to face the correct direction.

The last two parameters designate the (x, y) coordinate of a starting point. Using this function, the desired program can be written as

```
void main()
{
    Turtle myTurtle;

    myTurtle.Init(0,0);

    Star(myTurtle, 100, 50);  //draw the top three stars
    Star(myTurtle, 150, 50);
    Star(myTurtle, 200, 50);

    Star(myTurtle, 125,100);  //draw the middle two stars
    Star(myTurtle, 175,100);

    Star(myTurtle, 100,150);  //draw the bottom three stars
    Star(myTurtle, 150,150);
    Star(myTurtle, 200,150);

    myTurtle.Done();
}
```

Another approach to writing this program is to add the function Star to a descendant of Turtle. We define a new object type called a SmartTurtle by deriving it from a Turtle.

Some readers may be wondering why we do not change the Turtle object itself. In other words, we could add a new function to the definition of the Turtle object. However, we don't want to modify the Turtle for at least two reasons. First, the source code may not be available. Instead of having both Turtle.h and Turtle.cpp, we may have only the compiled version (i.e., Turtle.obj). Without the source code, we cannot modify the object. Second, and more importantly, even if the source code is available, the Turtle object is shared by many programmers; if every programmer started making additions to the object, it would become unmanageable. For instance, if one programmer makes an addition to the Turtle, say, adding the function Star, then nobody else can add a new function having the same name. Moreover, if the Turtle were to include every functionality needed by all programmers, it would become too huge to be useful. Each programmer would end up using only a very small portion of the object. We want an object to be clean and lean, with 100 percent or at least a very large portion of it useful to a large number of programmers. A much better approach to adding functionality is to allow programmers to have their own extended versions of Turtle objects into which they can put the desired additional functionality.

The following program defines a new object type SmartTurtle and uses it to draw a galaxy of eight stars.

```
// Program Galaxy: A program that draws eight stars.

#include "Turtles.h"

class SmartTurtle : public Turtle {

public:

        void Star (int x, int y)
        {
            PenUp();
            GoToPos(x,y);
            PenDown();
            TurnTo(0);

            int i;
            for ( i = 1; i <= 5; i=i+1){
                Move(30);
                Turn(-144);
            }
        }
};


void main()
{
        SmartTurtle myTurtle;

        myTurtle.Init(0, 0);

        myTurtle.Star(100, 50);
        myTurtle.Star(150, 50);
        myTurtle.Star(200, 50);

        myTurtle.Star(125,100);
        myTurtle.Star(175,100);

        myTurtle.Star(100,150);
        myTurtle.Star(150,150);
        myTurtle.Star(200,150);

        myTurtle.Done();
}
```

Defining a new object type SmartTurtle as an extension of Turtle. One additional function Star is defined for this object.

Declaring myTurtle as a SmartTurtle. myTurtle can do everything a Turtle can do, as well as draw a star.

Notice the syntax for calling an object function.

The program first defines a new object type called SmartTurtle as an extension of a Turtle. The Turtle is called a *base class*, or *base object type*, and the SmartTurtle is called a *derived class*, or *derived object type*. A base class is also called a *parent class*, and a derived class is called a *child class*. A child class can be a parent class of another class, and thus, the classes formulate a *class inheritance hierarchy*. The syntax for defining a new object with inheritance is essentially identical to the syntax for defining an object without inheritance, except for the identification of a base object type from which the new object type is derived.

The SmartTurtle object is defined as follows:

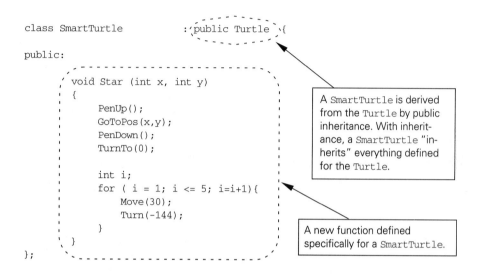

```
class SmartTurtle          : public Turtle {

public:

        void Star (int x, int y)
        {
              PenUp();
              GoToPos(x,y);
              PenDown();
              TurnTo(0);

              int i;
              for ( i = 1; i <= 5; i=i+1){
                   Move(30);
                   Turn(-144);
              }
        }
};
```

A SmartTurtle is derived from the Turtle by public inheritance. With inheritance, a SmartTurtle "inherits" everything defined for the Turtle.

A new function defined specifically for a SmartTurtle.

The first line

```
        class SmartTurtle : public Turtle {
```

shows that the newly defined object SmartTurtle is derived from the Turtle using *public inheritance*. There are two types of inheritance: public and private. *Public inheritance* means the inherited public components of a parent object are accessible to the users of a child object. For example, because a SmartTurtle is a publicly inherited object, the following is valid:

```
        SmartTurtle myTurtle;
        ...
        myTurtle.Turn(90);
```

In other words, every command we can use with a Turtle, we can also use with a SmartTurtle. We illustrate public inheritance in figure 11.1.

If the reserved word *public* is missing from the object definition or the reserved word *private* is explicitly stated in the object definition, then the inheritance is *private*.

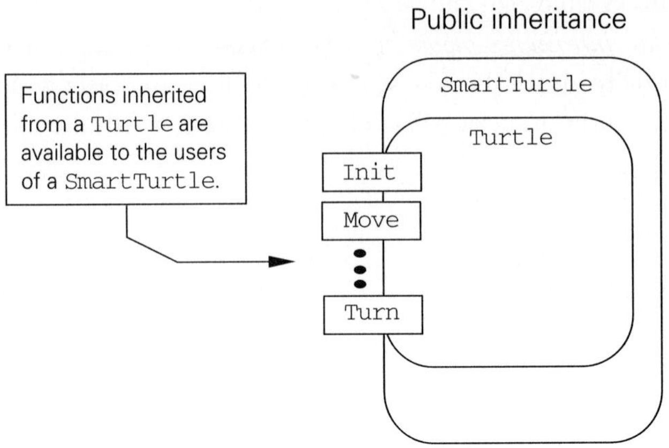

Public inheritance

Figure 11.1 Public inheritance

Private inheritance means the inherited public components of a parent object are inaccessible to the users of a child object. So, for example, if we had the object definition

```
class SmartTurtle : Turtle {
```

or

```
class SmartTurtle : private Turtle {
```

then the code

```
SmartTurtle myTurtle;
...
myTurtle.Turn(90);
```

would be invalid.

We illustrate private inheritance in figure 11.2.

Remember that a private component is hidden from the users of an object and, therefore, invisible and inaccessible to them, while a public component is visible to users and, therefore, accessible to them. Similarly, private inheritance hides the inherited pubic components from the users of a derived object, while public inheritance makes the inherited public components visible to users. Notice that a private component of a base object is always inaccessible to the users of a derived object, regardless of whether inheritance is private or public.

The syntax for an object definition needs to be modified to accommodate object definition using inheritance. The syntax category *class-heading* is modified to

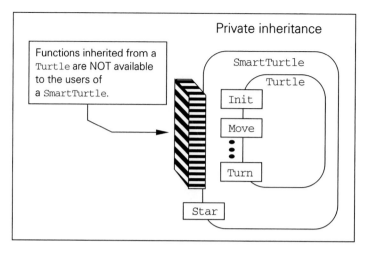

Figure 11.2 Private inheritance

class-heading
    class   *identifier*   *base-specifier* $_{opt}$

base-specifier
    :   *access-specifier* $_{opt}$ *identifier*

access-specifier
    public
    private

Now let's look at the function Star.

```
void Star (int x, int y)
{
    PenUp();
    GoToPos(x,y);
    PenDown();
    TurnTo(0);

    int i;
    for ( i = 1; i <= 5; i++) {

        Move(30);
        Turn(-144);
    }
}
```

Notice that dot notation was not used for the function calls.

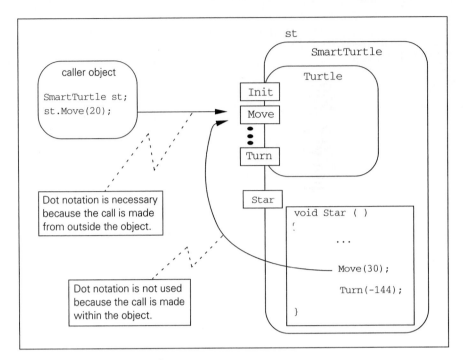

Figure 11.4 Use of dot notation

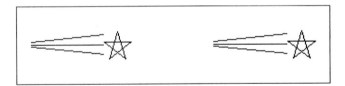

Figure 11.3 Shooting stars

When a call to an object function is made from one of the object's own functions, dot notation is not used. We use dot notation only when we are invoking an object function from outside the object. Figure 11.3 illustrates the difference between the two.

As a review of what we have learned so far in this section, let's add one more function to SmartTurtle; the new function draws a line between two arbitrary points. This new function, called Line, will take four parameters, the x and y coordinates of two points. We can use the Line function (and the Star function) in a program to draw some "shooting stars" (see figure 11.4).

```
// Program ShootingStars: A program that draws two
//              shooting stars.
```

```cpp
#include "Turtles.h"

class SmartTurtle : public Turtle {

public:

    void Star (int x, int y)
    {
        PenUp();//move to a starting point
        GoToPos(x,y);   //without drawing
        PenDown();
        TurnTo(0);
        int i;
        for ( i = 1; i <= 5; i=i+1) {
            Move(30);
            Turn(-144);
        }
    }

    void Line (int x1, int y1, int x2, int y2)
    {
        PenUp();
        GoToPos(x1, y1);//draw a line from (x1,y1)
        PenDown();//to (x2,y2)
        GoToPos(x2, y2);
    }
};

void main()
{
    SmartTurtle myTurtle;
    int a = 100, b = 92;
    myTurtle.Init(0, 0);

    myTurtle.Star(100, 100);//shooting star #1
    myTurtle.Line(20, a    , 100, b);
    myTurtle.Line(20, a + 3, 100, b + 11);
    myTurtle.Line(20, a + 5, 100, b + 22);

    myTurtle.Star(300, 100); //shooting star #2
    myTurtle.Line(220, a    , 300, b);
    myTurtle.Line(220, a + 3, 300, b + 11);
    myTurtle.Line(220, a + 5, 300, b + 22);

    myTurtle.Done();
}
```

11.2 Sample program: two-dimensional graph

As another illustration of inheritance, let's write a program that draws a two-dimensional graph like the one shown in figure 11.5.

For this program we will define a new object type TwoDGraph, a descendant of Turtle. We will first explain how this object is used, and at the end of this section, we will present its implementation. Here is the interface:

```
#include "Turtles.h"

class TwoDGraph : private Turtle
{
 public:

    TwoDGraph();

    void Done();

    void SetXScale(int units);
    //Change the scale on the X-axis

    void SetYScale(int units);
    //Change the scale on the Y-axis

    void Plot(int x1, int y1, int x2, int y2);
    //Draws a line from (x1,y1) to (x2,y2)


  private:

    void DrawAxis();
    //Draw the X- and Y-axis

    int XOrigin, YOrigin, // X, Y coordinates for the origin
    XMax, // # of pixels on the X-axis
    YMax; // # of pixels on the Y-axis

    int XUnit, //number of pixels per one unit on X
    YUnit; //number of pixels per one unit on Y

};
```

A private inheritance. A user of TwoDGraph cannot use the Turtle functions.

Notice that private inheritance is used here, which makes the public functions and data members of the Turtle object unavailable to the users of the descendant object TwoDGraph. As designers of TwoDGraph, we want to reuse the functionalities of

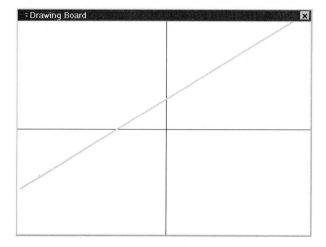

Figure 11.5 Two-dimensional graph

the `Turtle` object in implementing `TwoDGraph`, but we do not want the users of our `TwoDGraph` object to call the functions of `Turtle`. If we define it using public inheritance, we cannot prohibit the user of a `TwoDGraph` object from calling `Turtle`'s functions, which could result in the `TwoDGraph` object not working correctly.

Using the `TwoDGraph` object, a graph will be drawn with its origin (0,0) positioned at the center of a window. The axes are drawn in black, and the graph is drawn in green. The `Plot` function, which accepts four parameters representing the X and Y coordinates of the starting and ending points, draws a line between two given points. For example, assuming `graph` is a `TwoDGraph` object, the function call

```
graph.Plot(0, 0, 3, 2)
```

will draw the green line (shown as dotted) in figure 11.6.

The tick marks in this diagram are for reference only—they are not drawn in the actual program. We draw the complete graph by calling the `Plot` function repeatedly. Before we call the `Plot` function, we must set the scales for both axes. For example, for one graph we may want to draw the graph with the X-axis ranging from −10 to +10 and the Y-axis from −20 to +20. For another graph we may want to set the

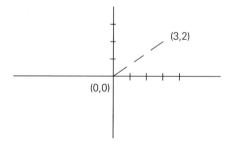

Figure 11.6 Drawing a line from (0,0) to (3,2) with a function call graph.

ranges as –5 to +5 and –15 to +15. The two functions that set the scales for the X-axis and Y-axis are SetXScale and SetYScale. The integer argument to these two functions specifies the total number of units. For example, calling the function

```
graph.SetXScale(30)
```

will set the X-axis range as –15 to +15. Finally, a TwoDGraph object's Done function must be called at the end of the program.

Let's look at a sample program that uses a TwoDGraph object for drawing a linear function Y = X + 5.

```
//Program Graph: A program to draw the graph of a
//                function Y = X + 5

#include "TwoDGph.h"                    ◄──── TwoDGraph's definition is in the
                                              separate file TwoDGph.h. This
int func(int x)                               technique allows a TwoDGraph
{                                             object to be incorporated easily
    return x + 5;                             into different programs.
}

void main()
{
    TwoDGraph graph;
    int oldX, X, oldY, Y;

    graph.SetXScale(40); // 40 units on the X-axis
    graph.SetYScale(50); // 50 units on the Y-axis

    oldX = -20;
    oldY = func(oldX);//set the starting point

    for (X = -20; X <= 20; X = X+2) {

        Y = func(X);

        graph.Plot(oldX, oldY, X, Y); // draw a line from
                // (oldX,oldY) to
                // (X, Y)
        oldX = X;
        oldY = Y;
    } //end for
}
```

Now let's study how the object is implemented. Its implementation file is

```
#include "TwoDGph.h"

TwoDGraph::TwoDGraph()
{
    XMax = GetWidth();   //the window's width is XMax pixels;
    XOrigin = XMax/2;    //position the center of graph;
    XUnit = 1;           //set default value;
    YMax = GetHeight();
    YOrigin = YMax/2;
    YUnit = 1;

    DrawAxis();
    ChangePenSize(2);
    ChangePenColor(GREEN);
}

void TwoDGraph::Done()
{
    Turtle::Done();
}
```

This statement calls the parent `Turtle` object's Done function.

```
void TwoDGraph::DrawAxis()
{

    PenUp();
    GoToPos(   0, YOrigin);
    PenDown();
    GoToPos(XMax, YOrigin); //draw the X-axis

    PenUp();
    GoToPos(XOrigin,    0);
    PenDown();
    GoToPos(XOrigin, YMax); //draw the Y-axis

}

void TwoDGraph::SetXScale(int units)
{
    XUnit = XMax / units;   //X axis is divided into units
                            //so each unit will have XUnit
                            //number of pixels
}

void TwoDGraph::SetYScale(int units)
{
    YUnit = YMax / units;   //Y axis is divided into units
                            //so each unit will have YUnit
                            //number of pixels

}

void TwoDGraph::Plot(int x1, int y1, int x2, int y2)
```

```
{
    PenUp();                        //convert the starting point
    x1 = XOrigin + x1*XUnit;        //from the user-defined coord
    y1 = YOrigin - y1*YUnit;        //to the pixel coord & move
    GoToPos(x1,y1);                 //to it with pen up (no drawing)

    PenDown();                      //convert the ending point
    x2 = XOrigin + x2*XUnit;        //from the user-defined coord
    y2 = YOrigin - y2*YUnit;        //to the pixel coordinate & move
    GoToPos(x2,y2);                 //to it with pen down(draw line)
}
```

The constructor function initializes the data members, draws the axes by calling the private function DrawAxis, and sets the pen size and color for drawing a graph. The variables XMax and YMax contain the window's width and height in pixels. The variables XOrigin and YOrigin store the pixel point (x,y) that corresponds to the origin (0,0) of the graph. Figure 11.7 illustrates this relationship.

A constructor function of the parent is automatically called before a constructor of a descendant object is called. Therefore, the declaration for a new TwoDGraph object, such as

```
TwoDGraph graph;
```

will cause two constructors—Turtle() and TwoDGraph()—to be invoked. If an object has more than one ancestor, then all of the constructors are called from the oldest to the newest objects in the inheritance hierarchy. The following diagram shows an inheritance hierarchy where Person is the oldest ancestor and Student is the next-oldest

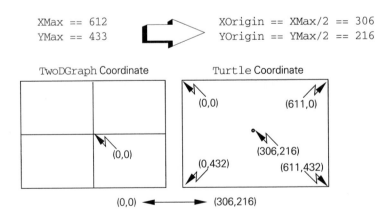

Figure 11.7 Mapping of TwoDGraph coordinates to Turtle coordinates

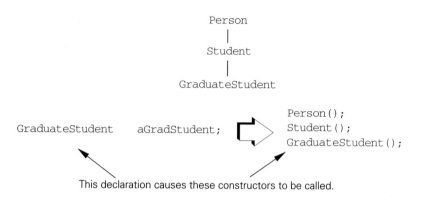

Figure 11.8 GraduateStudent declaration

ancestor for GraduateStudent. Assuming the constructors are defined for each object type, the declaration

    GraduateStudent aGradStudent;

will result in calling the constructors Person(), Student(), and GraduateStudent() in order (see figure 11.8).

The Plot function first moves to the point (x1, y1) with the pen up and then draws a line to the point (x2, y2) with the pen down. Since the arguments x1, y1, x2, and y2 are given in user-specified TwoDGraph coordinates (e.g., a point (3,2) on the two-dimensional plane with 40 units on the X-axis and 50 units on the Y-axis), and the Turtle function GoToPos requires the parameters in pixel coordinates, we must convert the values in TwoDGraph coordinates to the corresponding values in pixel coordinates. Figure 11.9 illustrates the conversion process (assuming a drawing board size of 612 × 433 pixels).

11.3 Objects and code reuse

We learned two ways to draw a star in section 11.1. First, we defined a nonobject function, and then we defined a new object type SmartTurtle with a function for drawing a star. Which way is better? The answer depends largely on whether we expect to reuse the code or not.

If a function is used in only one program, then a simple nonobject approach will suffice. In other words, if we have no intention of reusing this function in other programs, then we have no compelling reason to take the object-oriented approach. However, if we intend to reuse the function in other programs, then the object-oriented approach is generally more beneficial. Why?

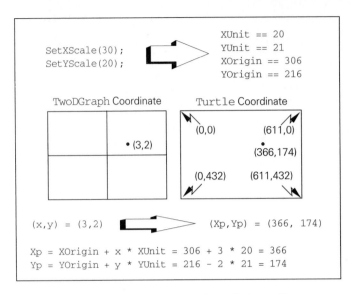

Figure 11.9 Conversion from TwoGraph to pixel coordinates

Before we answer that question, we should emphasize that if we are really talking about one function only, the differences between the two approaches are negligible. So let's consider the case of TwoDGraph in the following discussion. If we had not defined a TwoDGraph object, the program would have been very awkward because of nonobject functions and global variables. (See exercise 9 at the end of this chapter.) It may be possible to use no global variables, but in such case we would end up passing many arguments to the functions in an awkward manner. We identified this type of problem in section 8.5.

The use of an object-oriented approach does not automatically guarantee reusable objects. We must design them properly. There is no easy rule to say whether an object is properly designed, but certain features support reusability. Highly reusable objects are self-contained and logically defined. Being *self-contained* means everything you need is contained in the object. For example, self-contained objects do not use global variables. Being *logically defined* means an object contains only the necessary and sufficient functions and data members for a single, well-defined functionality. For example, a Turtle object does not contain a function for converting a Fahrenheit temperature to Celsius. In other words, a logically defined Turtle object contains only functions that are relevant to its line-drawing functionality.

An object, in addition to being self-contained and logically defined, must be encapsulated. An object is *encapsulated* if its internal workings are protected from the outside interference. Let's consider an example. Figure 11.10 illustrates that the data members

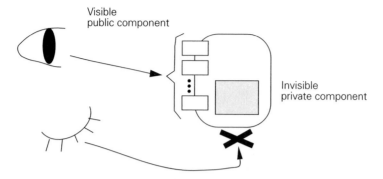

Visible
public component

Invisible
private component

Figure 11.10 Encapsulated object

and functions defined in the private section are protected from outside interference by the object's outer boundary. The public functions (and data members, if any) defined in the public section will be visible and accessible from outside, illustrated as rectangles sitting on the object's outer boundary. Because the private section is hidden and never directly accessed by external objects, we are able to change the content of the private section without affecting external objects. The ability to change the contents of the private section without affecting external objects greatly enhances the degree of program

```
class Student {                       class Student {

public:                               public:
     char      name[30];                   char *getName()
                                           {
     ...                                        return strdup(name);
};                                         }
                                           ...
                                      private:
                                           char      name[30];
                                           ...
                                       };
                                       ...
...

main()                                main()
{                                     {
     OKBox        m;                       OKBox        m;
     Student bernie;                       Student      bernie;
     ...                                   ...
     m.Display( bernie.name );             m.Display( bernie.getName() );
     ...                                   ...
}                                     }

        VERSION B (bad)                       VERSION G (good)
```

Figure 11.11 Alternative definitions of a Student object

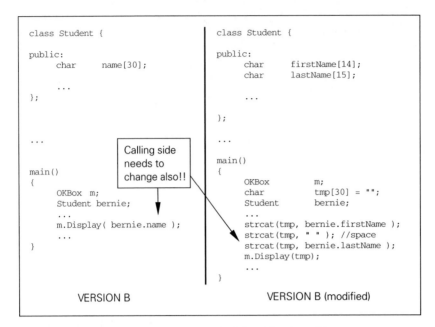

```
class Student {

public:
     char      name[30];

     ...
};



...



main()
{
     OKBox  m;
     Student bernie;
     ...
     m.Display( bernie.name );
     ...
}
```

Calling side
needs to
change also!!

```
class Student {

public:
               char      firstName[14];
               char      lastName[15];

     ...

};


...


main()
{
     OKBox          m;
     char           tmp[30] = "";
     Student        bernie;
     ...
     strcat(tmp, bernie.firstName );
     strcat(tmp, " " ); //space
     strcat(tmp, bernie.lastName );
     m.Display(tmp);
     ...
}
```

VERSION B   VERSION B (modified)

Figure 11.12 Effect of changing the poorly defined Student object

modifiability and extensibility, meaning that a programmer can modify or extend an existing program with little or no change to the existing code.

Consider the two alternative definitions of a Student object shown in figure 11.11. (Only the portion relevant to the discussion is shown.)

In version B, the data member name is made public. In contrast, it is hidden in version G, but the public function is provided to access the data member. Which one is the more properly encapsulated object? Version G, of course. But why?

Consider that there is a requirement change in the problem such that we must now store the name as the first and last names. First let's look at the modifications we have to make for version B (see figure 11.12). Making the required change requires us also to change the calling statements in the main program. Although the consequences may not be obvious in this small example, a single change in the Student object like the one above may require changes to hundreds of statements. For example, if a statement such as

        m.Display(bernie.name)

is made hundreds of times, the person who modifies the Student object definition must also change all of those statements. Just finding all of the occurrences of the offending

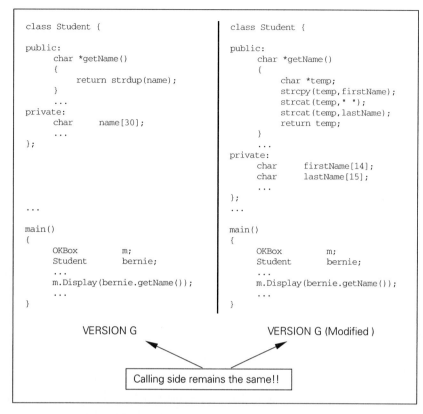

```
class Student {                          class Student {

public:                                  public:
      char *getName()                          char *getName()
      {                                        {
          return strdup(name);                     char *temp;
      }                                            strcpy(temp,firstName);
      ...                                          strcat(temp," ");
private:                                           strcat(temp,lastName);
      char      name[30];                          return temp;
      ...                                      }
};                                             ...
                                         private:
                                               char      firstName[14];
                                               char      lastName[15];
                                               ...
                                         };
                                         ...
...
                                         main()
main()                                   {
{                                              OKBox       m;
      OKBox       m;                           Student     bernie;
      Student     bernie;                      ...
      ...                                      m.Display(bernie.getName());
      m.Display(bernie.getName());             ...
      ...                                }
}
```

VERSION G   VERSION G (Modified)

Calling side remains the same!!

Figure 11.13 Modifying the properly encapsulated object definition will not affect the calling program

statements is not an easy task.* What we have seen here is that a small change could potentially cause havoc if the object is not properly encapsulated.

Now let's look at the changes needed in version G (see figure 11.13). All of the changes are contained within the Student object's definition. It doesn't matter how many calls are made from outside; no change is required outside of the Student object's definition. This desirable situation is attained by not changing the public interface; that is, the function getName remains the same. Once you make something public, you cannot change it without affecting external objects. One design guideline toward proper encapsulation is not to put data members in the public section.

---

* If you have experience using a word processor, you may argue for using the "global replace" function to replace all occurrences of the above text with the new text. Global replace may work for some cases, but not always, because without looking at the context where the text occurs, we really cannot determine whether the text should be replaced. In short, you cannot trust any automatic "global replacer" tool to work 100 percent of the time.

Determining that an object is properly encapsulated is not an easy matter. We have introduced you to the importance of encapsulation in this section and shown you a glimpse of what can happen with a poorly encapsulated object. We shall revisit these design topics again in chapters 15 and 17.

11.4 Exercises

1 Add the following functions to a SmartTurtle:

a. Square(x, y, size) —

   Draws a square with sides size long centered at (x,y).

b. Rectangle(x,y,wide,high) —

   Draws a rectangle with width wide and height high, centered at (x,y).

c. Triangle(x1,y1,x2,y2,x3,y3) —

   Draws a triangle with corners at (x1,y1), (x2,y2), and (x3,y3).

Store the interface and implementation of a SmartTurtle in "SmTurtle.h" and "SmTurtle.cpp", respectively.

2 Modify the Star method of the `SmartTurtle` in Galaxy2 so that it takes another parameter specifying the size of a star to be drawn. Then modify Galaxy2 itself so that it draws a galaxy that looks like this:

3 Write a program to place 50 stars at random positions on the screen. Your stars should range in size from 5 to 105 pixels.

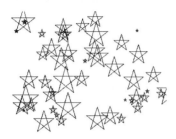

4 Write a program StringArt that draws the following design:

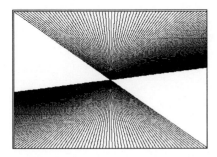

The design has 200 lines in all, with a line starting every 10th pixel along the top of the drawing board and ending every 10th pixel from the right along the bottom of

the drawing board. *Hint:* One line is drawn by the calling the SmartTurtle's Line
function as

```
t.Line(10*i, 0, 611 - 10*i, 432);
```

Make this call 200 times to draw 200 lines. We assume the coordinates for the bot-
tom-right corner are 611 and 432. By changing the parameters to the Line function,
you can easily come up with different designs. Some interesting variations are

```
t.Line(0, 0, 611 - 10*i, 432);
t.Line(10*i, 0, 611, 10*i);
t.Line(0, 0, 611, 10*i);
```

5   Write a new function for SmartTurtle that draws a puffball of a specified size centered at a specified position on the screen. Use that function in a program to draw a
small patch of dandelions. The previously defined Line function could be used to
draw the stems.

6   Write a program that draws a house surrounded by pine trees.

What should be the level of abstraction? Is it better to define a descendant of `Turtle` that knows how to draw a house? Or is it better to draw a house by directing a `Turtle` to draw squares and triangles? For this exercise define an object that knows how to draw a house and a pine tree. This object can be a descendant of `SmartTurtle` defined in exercise 1. The object uses the functions `Rectangle` and `Triangle` in drawing a house and a pine tree. Pine trees may be drawn at random positions.

7   In Chapter 5 we drew a circle by computing the length of each segment from a given radius and drawing the segment 360 times, rotating 1 degree after each segment is drawn. There is a better way to draw a circle, which can be generalized to draw different, more interesting figures. We can compute the (x,y) coordinates from the radius r and angle θ using the following formula:

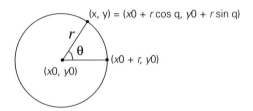

To draw a complete circle, we can let θ range from 0 to 360 with an increment of 5 degrees (an increment less than 5 degrees is probably too small.) The loop may look something like

```
x = x0 + r; y = y0; // (x0,y0) is the center
PenUp();
MoveTo(x, y);
PenDown();

for (theta = 0 ; theta <= 360; theta = theta + 5) {
    x = x0 + r * cos (theta);
    y = y0 + r * sin (theta);
    MoveTo(x, y);
}
```

Since the sine and cosine functions available in the standard library <math.h> can only accept angles expressed in radians, and since the `MoveTo` function can only accept integers, we adjust the preceding code as follows:

```
x = x0 + r; y = y0; // (x0,y0) is the center
```

```
PenUp();
MoveTo( int(x), int(y) );
PenDown();

for (theta = 0 ; theta <= 360; theta = theta + 5) {
    radian = 2 * PI * theta / 360;
    x = x0 + r * cos (radian);
    y = y0 + r * sin (radian);
    MoveTo( int(x), int(y) );
}
```

This new approach can be used to draw much more interesting figures. With circles, the radius *r* remains constant. Changing the values for *r* while making a 360-degree turn allows us to draw many interesting figures. First we change the code to

```
x = x0 + r; y = y0; // (x0,y0) is the center
PenUp();
MoveTo( int(x), int(y) );
PenDown();

for (theta = 0 ; theta <= 360; theta = theta + 5) {
    radian = 2 * PI * theta / 360;

    r = compute( radian ); //r is computed from a radian

    x = x0 + r * cos (radian);
    y = y0 + r * sin (radian);
    MoveTo( int(x), int(y) );
}
```

The function compute may be defined as

```
float compute ( float radian)
{
    const int C = 30; //try different values for C
    float result;

    result = C * sin(radian) * cos(radian) * cos(radian);

    return result;
}
```

Design and implement SmarterTurtle using the preceding idea. The SmarterTurtle is a descendant of a Turtle; that is, drawings are done by using the pixel coordinates. Experiment with the following equations:

a. `result = C * sin (N * radian) where N = 1, 2, 3, ...`

b. `result = C / (1 - cos(radian))`

c. `result = sqrt ( C * C * cos(2*radian) )`

d. `result = C * radian`

8 Redo exercise 7 by defining a `SmarterTurtle` as a descendant of a `TwoDGraph`; that is, drawings are done using the user-specified coordinates.

9 Redo the program Graph1 in section 11.2 without defining a `TwoDGraph` object; that is, use only nonobject functions. You may or may not need global variables, depending on how you define your nonobject functions.

10 Extend the `TwoDGraph` object so tick marks are drawn for both the X-axis and Y-axis.

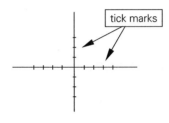

chapter 12

Event-driven programming

So far we have been using very simple GUI objects, such as `IntTypeIn` and `OKBox`, or the standard `ostream` and `istream` objects `cout` and `cin`. These objects are easy for beginners to use, but they are not powerful enough to develop a program that requires the type of sophisticated user interface that we have come to expect from today's computer programs. In this chapter we will introduce new GUI objects, most notably `EditWin` and `Menu`, that allow us to implement such an interface. To become proficient in using these advanced GUI objects, you must first understand a style of programming called *event-driven programming*. We will begin this chapter with an introduction to events and event-driven programming.

12.1 Event loops

The user interface of GUI programs consists of windows, menus, buttons, and other interface objects. The user may select a menu item, click on a button, change the size of a window, and so on while interacting with the program. Each of these user actions generates an *event*. An *event-driven program* is a program in which designated code is executed in response to an event.

Events generated as a result of user actions are queued in a list called a *event queue.* An event-driven program contains a control code called an *event processing loop,* or more simply, an *event loop,* to process the events in the event queue. An event loop is a cycle of fetching the next event in the event queue, translating the retrieved event into the internal messaging format, and dispatching the translated message to an appropriate object in the program for processing. Although each system has a slightly different implementation, the basic idea is the same, and the event loop looks something like the following:

The event queue is similar in structure to people waiting in a queue, say, for an ATM machine. There are many different types of events. Some of the more obvious ones are mouse events, menu events, and keyboard events. Each type of event carries information about its details. For example, with keyboard events, in addition to the event type, there is information on which key was pressed, whether any modifier key (CTRL, SHIFT, etc.) was pressed, and so forth.

Notice that the event loop itself does not process an event. The event loop only dispatches the translated messages. When the DispatchMessage function is executed, the intended receiver of the message is identified and the message is sent to it. The intended receiver may or may not be able to process the message. If this receiver cannot handle the message, it will forward the message to the next object in line, much like military officers following the chain of command.

Figure 12.1 illustrates the chain of command. Let's suppose we have a window called TestWin that contains a button called TestBtn. Let's assume that the mouse is pressed on the TestBtn button. The chain of command is the TestBtn button, TestWin window, and then the program's main window. The main window of our GUI programs is always the window with the title *Sample Application.*

The actual chain of command differs with each system, but is very similar to what we describe here. The message is first dispatched to the TestBtn button where the event occurred. If this button object can handle the event, that is, if the object has a function to process this message, the button object will handle it and the chain stops. If the

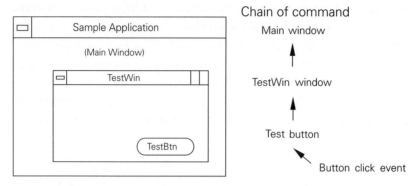

Figure 12.1 Chain of command; how the event is passed from one object to another

object cannot handle the event, then the message is transferred to the TestWin window object. If this window object can handle the event, then it will. Otherwise, the message is again transferred to the next object in the chain of command, which in this case is the program's main window. Finally, the program's main window will process it.

We use a two-stage approach to handle events. The event loop handles the first by fetching, translating, and dispatching events to objects. Each receiver object in the chain of command takes its turn in handling the event. The first object in the chain of command that can process the event will do so. Some of our predefined objects are already programmed to handle certain types of events, but at this point those functions do nothing because the respective function bodies do not contain any code. We can customize the content of the function bodies for whatever processing we wish to carry out. We will give examples of this customization later in the chapter.

12.2 Editor windows

In this section we will introduce a new GUI object, EditWin, a simplified, general-purpose editor. The object is like an entire page of paper on which the user can type and the program can write information. Thus far, we have seen GUI programs that accept data from the user through IntTypeIn and StringTypeIn objects and display written information to the user by means of OKBox objects. A more typical GUI program involves considerably more communication between the user and the program. For example, instead of typing in a simple integer value, we may want the user to type a long list of students' examination grades into a program that computes the average score. We certainly could use the IntTypeIn object repeatedly to get the grade information, but this procedure is tedious and error prone. Likewise, we could use an OKBox object repeatedly for display, but this would take too long to display even a few lines of text. What we need is an `EditWin` capable of allowing the user to input a large amount of data and the program to display a large amount of data.

As a simple example of an `EditWin`, let's look at a program that writes out the first two lines of Shakespeare's Sonnet 18. The program listed below will declare an instance of `Edit-Win`, initialize it, and then write the first two lines. The user can close the window normally by double-clicking the close box. Clicking the OK and Cancel buttons would not do anything. We will add the code for processing the button-clicking events in the next section.

```
//Program Sonnet: A program that prints out the first two
//  lines of Sonnet 18.

#include "GUIObj.h"

void main ()
{
    EditWinew;

    ew.Init(50,50,400,250);
    ew.WriteLine("Shall I compare thee to the summer's day");
    ew.WriteLine("Thou art more lovely and more temperate");
    ew.Done();
}
```

When the program is executed, the window in figure 12.2 appears on the screen.

The arguments to the `Init` function set the window's upper-left corner to (50,50) and the width and height to 350 and 250. Try running the program with different values to see the differences in the window's appearance. If any of the four values is not valid, the window is displayed with the default location and dimension. The two `WriteLine` func-

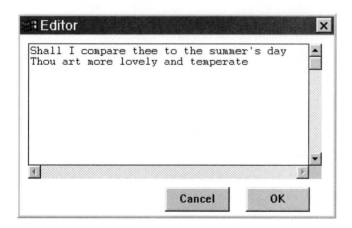

Figure 12.2 Program Sonnet screen capture

Table 12.1 Functions defined for EditWin

Function	Description
`Init (int x, int y,` `int w, int h)`	Initializes an editor window `w` pixels wide and `h` pixels high, with the upper left corner at the coordinates (x,y). The window contains two buttons: OK and Cancel.
`Done()`	Initiates an event loop. The window is displayed, and events are processed.
`WriteLine ( char *str )`	Writes a given string `str` to the `EditWin`. A line delimiter is also written.
`Write ( char *str )`	Writes a given string `str` to the `EditWin`.
`ReadLine ( int lineNo )`	Returns the string at line `lineNo`. If the line is longer than 255 characters, only the first 255 characters are returned.

`Read ( int lineNo,`
`int charPos,`
`int length)`
	Returns a string `length` characters long, starting at position `charPos` in line `lineNo`.

`ReadAll ( )`	Returns the entire content of the `EditWin`. The maximum number of characters that can be returned is 2,048.
`DeleteLine ( int lineNo)`	Deletes the string at line `lineNo`.

`Delete (int lineNo,`
`int charPos,`
`int length)`
	Deletes a string `length` characters long, starting at position `charPos` in line `lineNo`.

`InsertLine (int lineNo,` `char *str)`	Inserts a string `str` in line `lineNo`.

`Insert (int lineNo,`
`int charPos,`
`char *str)`
	Inserts a string `str` starting at position `charPos` in line `lineNo`.

`Clear ( )`	Erases the entire contents of the `EditWin`.
`GetNumLines ()`	Returns the number of lines in the `EditWin`.
`OK ()`	Executed in response to a mouse-click event on the OK button. The function does nothing as a response. It is intended to be overridden in a descendant class.
`Cancel ()`	Executed in response to a mouse-click event on the Cancel button. The function does nothing as a response. It is intended to be overridden in a descendant class.
`SetTitle (char *str)`	Sets the window's title to `str`.
`SetOkLabel (char *str)`	Sets the OK button's label to `str`.
`SetCancelLabel (char *str)`	Sets the Cancel button's label to `str`.

tions write two lines of text. Finally, the Done function sets the event loop in motion. The Done function must be placed at the end of the code. Without it, the event loop will not run properly, and the window will not appear. Try running the program without the Done function call to see what happens.

As you can see from figure 12.2 above, an EditWin object has an editing area with horizontal and vertical scroll bars and OK and Cancel buttons. The editing area supports full editing capabilities. Using a keyboard, you can insert, delete, select, copy, cut, and so on.

Table 12.1 describes the functions of an EditWin object. This information is extracted from the file GUIObj.h.

We can describe an EditWin as analogous to an entire sheet of paper on which the user and the program can write text, except that the paper is as wide as it needs to be to hold the longest line written on it and as long as it needs to be to hold all the lines written on it. The information in an EditWin that extends too far to the right or below the

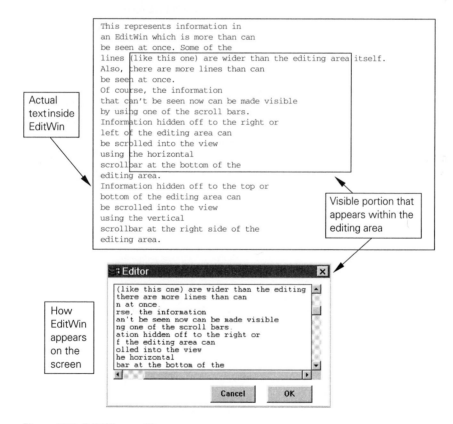

Figure 12.3 EditWin scrolling

Figure 12.4 Program ThreeLines screen capture

visible editing area can be scrolled into view using one of the scroll bars. Figure 12.3 explains this concept.

Information in an EditWin object is one big string. Although you can enter as many characters as you want into an EditWin, the maximum number of characters you can retrieve from an EditWin is limited to 2K(= 2,048) characters.[*]

The single string of information is divided into lines by line delimiters. A *line delimiter* is either a single character <CR> or a character pair <CR><LF>, depending on the type of computer. (Windows/DOS uses <CR><LF>, while Macintosh uses <LF>, for example.) <CR> is a carriage return character, and <LF> is a line feed character. In the following discussion, we assume the line delimiter is the <CR><LF> pair. This line delimiter is appended to the end of any string passed to the Writeline function. If the line delimiter is found in a string passed to Writeline, then the part of the string before the delimiter will appear on one line and the part following the delimiter will appear on the next line. For example, the following program displays the EditWin shown in figure 12.4. Notice that <CR> is ASCII value 13 and <LF> is ASCII value 10. They are represented in C++ by the characters \r and \n, respectively.

```
//Program ThreeLines:  A program to illustrate the WriteLine
//                      function of an EditWin.

#include "GUIObj.h"

void main ()
{
    EditWin ew;
    ew.Init(50, 50, 400, 300);

    ew.WriteLine( "Line 1\r\nLine 2\r\nLine 3");

    ew.Done();
}
```

---

[*] The value is set to 2K, because an EditWin object is not intended to handle a very large number of characters. You can make the limit much larger if you wish, but the system determines a physical limit. The system's limit is ordinarily a very large number, such as $2^{32} - 1$ characters.

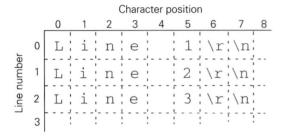

Figure 12.5 Position of characters in an EditWin object

Characters stored in an `EditWin` can be read by the two functions `Read` and `ReadLine`. The `Read` function returns a substring of the `EditWin` object's contents. A substring is referred to by its position and length. The position of a character in the `EditWin` object is specified by its line number and the character position within the line. Figure 12.5 shows how the lines and the character positions are numbered. Notice that the first line and the first character position within a line are both 0. We could have set them to start from 1, but since C++ arrays start from 0, we decided to make the `EditWin`'s numbering scheme consistent with that convention. Notice also that the line number is not related to visibility. For example, the first line that appears on the editing area may be line 4 if the first four lines (numbered 0 through 3) are hidden.

To retrieve the characters `"ne 2"` from the preceding diagram, we execute

```
ew.Read(1, 2, 4)
```

This statement retrieves four characters starting from the second character position on line 1. The following program is an extension of the program ThreeLines; it illustrates the use of the `Read` function. Before reading the explanation that follows the program listing, you may want to figure out for yourself what the program will display when executed.

```
//Program ThreeLines2:  A program to illustrate the use
//                      EditWin's WriteLine function.

#include "GUIObj.h"
#include <string.h>
void main ()
{
    EditWin ew;
    char s[10];
```

```
        ew.Init(50, 50, 400, 300);

        ew.WriteLine( "Line 1\r\nLine 2\r\nLine 3");
        strcpy(s, ew.Read(1,0,6));
        ew.Clear(); //erase the window's contents

        ew.WriteLine(s);
        ew.WriteLine(s);
        ew.WriteLine(s);

        ew.Done();
}
```

Program ThreeLines2 is just like program ThreeLines, until the Read function is called. The Read function retrieves six characters from position (1,0)—line 1, character 0—and returns them so they are copied to the variable s by the standard string function strcpy. The value of s is now "Line 2". After ew is cleared with the Clear function, the three calls to the WriteLine function display the screen shown in figure 12.6.

Figure 12.6 ThreeLines2 screen capture

If we make the last argument of the Read function 8, as in

```
        strcpy( s, ew.Read(1,0,8));
```

the program would then display the screen shown in figure 12.7.

If we read eight characters starting from character position #0, the value of s would be "Line 2\r\n". Then each copy of s written to the EditWin object by the WriteLine function would have two sets of line delimiters, one that was inside s and another appended by the WriteLine function.

Figure 12.7 ThreeLines2 screen capture

We assumed in the text that the line delimiter is a <CR><LF> pair, for the sake of making the discussion and examples concrete and easy to follow. However, making such an assumption in actual programming is dangerous. As stated already, the actual characters used for the line delimiter will depend on the platform. Therefore, the code

```
EditWin ew;
...
ew.Write("hello\r\n");
```

may or may not work. You should always use the provided functions Read, Write, ReadLine, and WriteLine, because they handle platform discrepancies. In other words, we have an EditWin for Windows, an EditWin for Macintosh, and an EditWin for UNIX, and these functions are tailored to the platform specifications. So as long as we use the provided functions correctly, our code will work on any platform by simply using the EditWin corresponding to the platform on which the program is to be executed.

12.3 Event processing

As we mentioned in the previous section, when you click either button of an EditWin window, nothing happens. The bodies of the functions to handle the button click events are empty. They are intended to be overridden in descendant objects. To illustrate this process and to show how some of the other EditWin functions might be used, we will write a program that allows the user to type something into an EditWin and then displays the length of the string when the OK button is clicked. When the Cancel button is clicked, the program will erase the contents of the EditWin. We will derive a new object from EditWin so we can override the OK and Cancel functions. Our derived object is called *CntEditWin*.

```
//Program CountChar:  A program to count the number of
//                    characters entered into an EditWin

#include "GUIObj.h"
#include <string.h>

class CntEditWin : public EditWin {
public:
    void Ok ()
```

```
        {
            char str[MAXSTRLEN]; //MAXSTRLEN defined in GUIObj
            char len[4];

            strcpy(str, ReadAll());
            WriteLine(""); //skip line

            itoa(strlen(str), len, 10);
            WriteLine(len);
        }

        void Cancel ()
        {
            Clear();
        }
    };

    void main ( )
    {
        CntEditWin ew;

        ew.Init(50, 50, 400, 300);
        ew.Done();
    }
```

Notice that the main program is very simple, yet the resulting program is quite complex—a direct benefit of reusing a high-level object. The purpose of the main function is simply to create and run a CntEditWin object. From that point on, the CntEditWin and other objects take over. Various kinds of events and the corresponding responses (inherited from EditWin) are all handled internally by the CntEditWin object. All we have to do is to override the response functions for the two buttons so that the responses can be custom-tailored to our needs.

Let's see how the program works. The main function initializes and displays a CntEdit-Win object. The editing area is initially empty. The user can type data into this CntEditWin window's editing area. For example, one might type the phrase shown in figure 12.8.

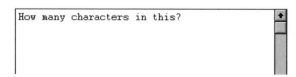

Figure 12.8 Typing into the editing area

Table 12.2 itoa examples

Expression	Value of s
itoa(14, s, 10)	"14"
itoa(14, s, 2)	"1110"
itoa(28, s, 10)	"28"

If the OK button is then clicked, the function Ok is called via the controller's event loop. The Ok function defined for the CntEditWin object retrieves the entire contents of the CntEditWin using the function ReadAll. The result is assigned to a string variable str. The standard string function strlen is used to compute the size of the string (i.e., the number of characters in the string). The size is an integer. Since we can only output a string data value to EditWin, we convert this integer into a string by using another standard function itoa (integer-to-alphabet). The function itoa accepts three parameters: the integer to be converted, the resulting string, and the base. We want to convert this to a decimal, so we supply the value 10. Table 12.2 lists examples of the itoa function.

Figure 12.9 shows the effect of clicking the OK button after the above text is entered. If the user clicks the OK button again, figure 12.10 is displayed. Why? Because this time, when the Ok function is executed and the function ReadAll is

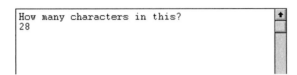

Figure 12.9 Result of clicking the OK button

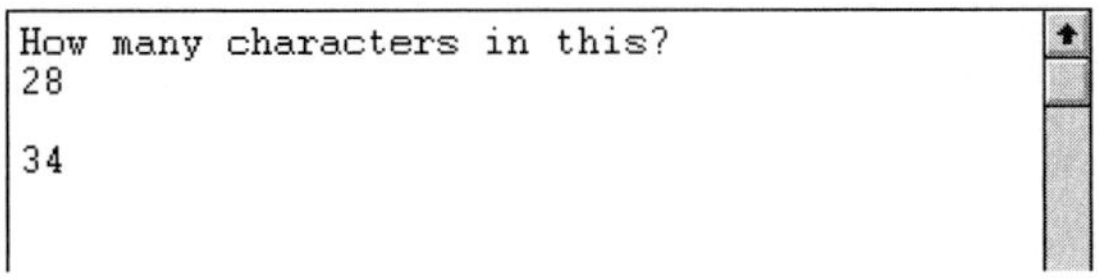

Figure 12.10 Result of clicking OK button again

Figure 12.11 Final results

called, six more characters are in the editing area: the line-delimiter pair "\r\n" appended by the `WriteLine` function, the two characters "28", and another line-delimiter pair written out by the statement `WriteLine(str)`.

The `Cancel` function just clears the editing area. If the user clicks the Cancel button and then clicks the OK button four times, the four lines shown in figure 12.11 will be displayed. Can you tell what happened?

12.4 Grading program

Let's write a somewhat more practical program using an `EditWin` object. Our program will allow the user to type in the names and examination scores for the students in a class and will compute the average score and letter grade for each student. To simplify the program's development, we will restrict it so that it is capable only of computing the average of exactly three midterm exams and a final exam. Furthermore, the program will compute the average by weighting the final exam score twice as heavily as the midterm exam score. Thus, the average will be computed as

$$avg = \frac{(midterm1 + midterm2 + midterm3 + 2 \times final)}{5}$$

The letter grade will be assigned according to the rules shown in table 12.3.

The user is required to type the scores into an `EditWin` according to the format shown in figure 12.12. When the user clicks the OK button, our program will calculate and display the average and letter grade for each student as shown in figure 12.13. We

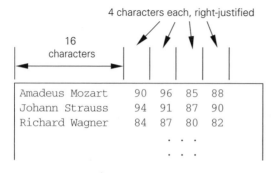

Figure 12.12 Format of scores

Table 12.3 Letter grade rules

Avg	Letter grade
90 <= AVG	A
80 <= AVG < 90	B
70 <= AVG < 80	C
60 <= AVG < 70	D
AVG < 60	F

```
Amadeus Mozart    90  96  85  88  89.40   B
Johann Strauss    94  91  87  90  90.40   A
Richard Wagner    84  87  80  82  83.00   B
                         . . .
                         . . .
```

Figure 12.13 Display of grades for students

will create a new descendant of EditWin called ScoresWindow. The interface of a Score-sWindow, stored in the file "ScoreWin.h", is as follows:

```
#include "GuiObj.h"                    ┌─────────────────────────────┐
#include "util.h"    ◄─────────────────│ Float-to-Alpha conversion   │
#include <string.h>                    │ function ftoa is defined in │
                                       │ "util.h".                   │
                                       └─────────────────────────────┘

class ScoresWindow : public EditWin {
public:

    void Ok();
    void Cancel();

private:

    void GetData(int lineNo, float &mid1, float &mid2,
                    float &mid3, float &final);

    float ComputeAverage(float mid1, float mid2, float mid3,
                    float final);

    char *LetterGrade(float average);

    void PrintResult(int lineNo, char *numGrade,
                    char *letterGrade);

};
```

The outline for the Ok function is

```
for (each line) {
    read in three midterms and one final exam score;
    convert them (string data) into real numbers;
    compute the average and convert it back to string data;
    compute the letter grade for the average;
    insert the results at the end of the line;
}
```

Using the private functions defined above, the Ok function is written as follows in the implementation file "ScoreWin.cpp":

```cpp
void ScoresWindow::Ok()
{
    float mid1, mid2, mid3, final, avg;

    char    grade[2];
    int     lineNo, numLines;

    numLines = GetNumLines();

    for (lineNo = 0; lineNo <= numLines-1; lineNo++) {

        GetData(lineNo, mid1, mid2, mid3, final);

        avg = ComputeAverage(mid1, mid2, mid3, final);

        strcpy(grade, LetterGrade(avg));

        PrintResult(lineNo, ftoa(avg), grade);
                            //ftoa in "util.h"

    }
}
```

We again define the Cancel function to clear the editing area:

```cpp
void ScoresWindow::Cancel()
{
    Clear();
}
```

Now let's implement the four private functions. The GetData function is used to get four data values from one line. The function passes back the data values using reference parameters. Since only string data can be entered or displayed using an EditWin object, we must perform a data conversion so the numerical values can be passed back. We use the standard function atof (alpha-to-float) for converting a string into a real number. Do you know why we don't convert it into an integer?

```cpp
void ScoresWindow::GetData(int lineNo,
                    float &mid1, float &mid2,
                    float &mid3, float &final)
{
    char str[MAXLINE];      //MAXLINE is defined in GUIObj.h

    strcpy( str, Read(lineNo, 16,4));
    mid1  = atof(str);
```

```
        strcpy( str, Read(lineNo, 20,4));
        mid2  = atof(str);

        strcpy( str, Read(lineNo, 24,4));
        mid3  = atof(str);

        strcpy( str, Read(lineNo, 28,4));
        final = atof(str);
}
```

Notice that we simplified the writing of this function by forcing the user to type in the data values in a rigid format. The function can and should be modified, so that the user can enter the data values without following such a rigid format. For example, the user can enter the data values by separating them with commas. See exercise 4 at the end of this chapter.

The ComputeAverage function takes four parameters and returns the average score using the formula presented earlier. It is written as

```
float ScoresWindow::ComputeAverage( float mid1, float mid2,
                                    float mid3, float final)
{
    return (mid1 + mid2 + mid3 + 2*final) / 5;
}
```

The function LetterGrade accepts a real number and returns the corresponding letter grade using the rule stated earlier:

```
char *ScoresWindow::LetterGrade(float average)
{
    if       (average >= 90.0)
         return "A";

    else if (average >= 80.0)
         return "B";

    else if (average >= 70.0)
         return "C";

    else if (average >= 60.0)
         return "D";

    else
         return "F";
}
```

Finally, the `PrintResult` function prints out the two passed strings on the line. Notice the order of output. We print out the letter grade first and then the average grade. Printing is easier this way because we can insert the two strings at the same position. Characters to the right of the insertion point are moved to the right, so the values will be displayed correctly.

```
void ScoresWindow::PrintResult(int lineNo, char *numGrade,
                                    char *letterGrade)
{
    char str[MAXLINE];

    strcpy(str, "  "); strcat(str,letterGrade);
    Insert(lineNo, 32, str);

    strcpy(str, "  "); strcat(str, numGrade);
    Insert(lineNo, 32, str);
}
```

The `ftoa` function is used in the `Ok` function to convert the real number `avg` to a string value before passing it to the `PrintResult` function. The function is defined in the header file `"util.h"` as follows:

```
char *ftoa(float num)
{
    int i, dec, sign, size;
    char str[15], tempstr[15];

    strcpy(tempstr, fcvt(num, 2, &dec, &sign));
    size = strlen(tempstr);

    for (i = 0; i < dec; i=i+1)
        str[i] = tempstr[i];

    str[dec] = '.'; //put the decimal point in the string

    for (i = dec; i <=size; i=i+1)
        str[i+1] = tempstr[i];

    return str;
}
```

The function uses the standard function `fcvt`, which has four parameters. The first two are the values passed to the function: `float` data to be converted into a string and the number of decimal places required in the result. The last two parameters are returned

Table 12.4 Input and output of function

Input		Output		
num	ndig	result	dec	sign
89.9778	2	"8998"	2	0 (positive)
198.988	2	"19899"	3	0
-9.89	3	"9890"	1	1 (negative)

from the function: the number of characters to the left of the decimal point in the converted string, and the sign of the number (0 means positive, and any nonzero number means negative). Notice that the pass-by-pointer scheme is used for the last two parameters. The converted string is the result of a function. Table 12.4 illustrates how the function operates.

Since the result of the function fcvt does not contain the decimal point, the function ftoa needs to include code to insert the required decimal point. In fact, adding the decimal is the sole purpose of the ftoa function. Notice that the ftoa function handles only positive numbers.

With the ScoresWindow object now fully defined, the only task of our main function is to declare and initialize a ScoresWindow object. Frequently in event-driven programming, the only task of a main function is to activate requisite objects. Once the objects are activated, they will take over and respond to the events without any further control from the main function.

```
//Program Grading:  A program that computes the weighted average
//                  and letter grades.

#include "ScoreWin.h"

void main()
{
    ScoresWindow gradeBook;
    gradeBook.Init(50,50,450,350);
    gradeBook.Done();
}
```

12.5 Menu, MenuHandler, *and* MessageHandler *objects*

Next to button events, menu events are probably the ones that occur most frequently. A menu event occurs during program execution when the user makes a menu selection. The program must be written in such a way that this menu event is properly detected and processed by executing a response function. In this section we will discuss the mechanics of processing menu events using Menu objects.

A Menu object is required for each menu of a program. For example, if a program has three menus File, Edit, and View, then we need to create three Menu objects. At the time a new Menu object is declared, we must associate the text, which will be displayed on the screen with this Menu object. The following code declares three Menu objects—fileMenu, editMenu, and viewMenu—with the titles "File", "Edit", and "View".

```
MenufileMenu("File");
Menu        editMenu("Edit");
MenuviewMenu("View");
```

The window in figure 12.13 shows these three menus.

For each menu we declare, we must add individual menu items, or choices. For example, to create the menus and menu choices shown in figure 12.14, we execute:

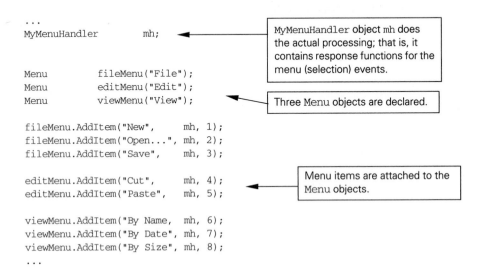

The first parameter of the `AddItem` function is the text to be displayed. The second parameter is the `MyMenuHandler` object (descendant of `MenuHandler`) that processes the menu events. The third parameter identifies the function of `MyMenuHandler` to be executed in response to the selection of the corresponding menu item. The `MyMenuHandler` object is:

"MyMnHnd.h"

```
#include "GUIObj.h"

class MyMenuHandler : public MenuHandler {

public:

        void MenuFunc1();
        void MenuFunc2();
        void MenuFunc3();
        void MenuFunc4();
        void MenuFunc5();
        void MenuFunc6();
        void MenuFunc7();
        void MenuFunc8();

};
```

Note: As the sample programs get more complex, using larger numbers of objects, with each object defined in its interface and implementation files, keeping track of which code belongs to which object gets harder. To provide a clear and easy reference to the source code, we will list the code in a rectangle along with the name of the file where the code is stored.

The menu response functions inside the `MyMenuHandler` must be named `MenuFunc1`, `MenuFunc2`, and so forth. We can have up to `MenuFunc20`. The number we

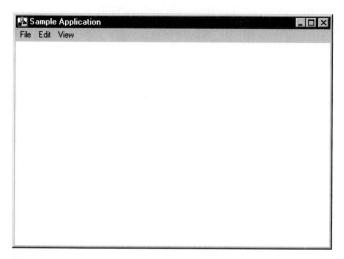

Figure 12.13 A window with three menus attached to it

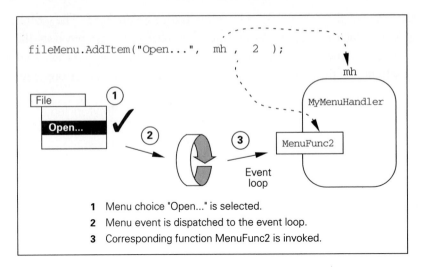

Figure 12.15 MenuFunc2 execution

1 Menu choice "Open..." is selected.
2 Menu event is dispatched to the event loop.
3 Corresponding function MenuFunc2 is invoked.

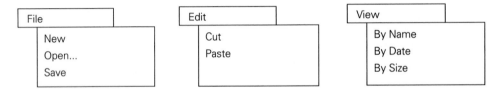

Figure 12.14 Menus with menu choices

pass as the third argument to the `AddItem` function determines which `MenuFunc<x>` function is to be executed. For example, with the statement

```
fileMenu.AddItem("Open", mh, 2);
```

`MenuFunc2` will be executed when the menu item `"Open"` is selected, as illustrated in figure 12.15.

The final task is to write the bodies of the `MenuFunc<x>` functions. For this illustration, we will simply display a message using an `OKBox` to verify that the functions are invoked correctly. The implementation file for the `MyMenuHandler` is defined in figure 12.16.

Now let's run the program. The main program is

```
//Program TestMenu:   A program to illustrate how to use the Menu
//                    object.
```

```
#include "MyMnHnd.h"

void MyMenuHandler::MenuFunc1()
{
    OKBox msg;
    msg.Display("Menu item 'New' is selected.");
}

void MyMenuHandler::MenuFunc2()
{
    OKBox msg;
    msg.Display("Menu item 'Open...' is selected.");
}

void MyMenuHandler::MenuFunc3()
{
    OKBox msg;
    msg.Display("Menu item 'Save' is selected.");
}

void MyMenuHandler::MenuFunc4()
{
    OKBox msg;
    msg.Display("Menu item 'Cut' is selected.");
}

void MyMenuHandler::MenuFunc5()
{
    OKBox msg;
    msg.Display("Menu item 'Paste' is selected.");
}

void MyMenuHandler::MenuFunc6()
{
    OKBox msg;
    msg.Display("Menu item 'By Name' is selected.");
}

void MyMenuHandler::MenuFunc7()
{
    OKBox msg;
    msg.Display("Menu item 'By Date' is selected.");
}

void MyMenuHandler::MenuFunc8()
{
    OKBox msg;
    msg.Display("Menu item 'By Size' is selected.");
}
```

Figure 12.16 MyMenuHandler

```
#include "GUIObj.h"
#include "MyMnHnd.h"

void main()
{
    MyMenuHandler       mh;
    MessageHandler      msgh;

    Menu            fileMenu("File");
    Menu            editMenu("Edit");
    Menu            viewMenu("View");

    fileMenu.AddItem("New",      mh, 1);
    fileMenu.AddItem("Open...",  mh, 2);
    fileMenu.AddItem("Save",     mh, 3);

    editMenu.AddItem("Cut",      mh, 4);
    editMenu.AddItem("Paste",    mh, 5);

    viewMenu.AddItem("By Name",  mh, 6);
    viewMenu.AddItem("By Date",  mh, 7);
    viewMenu.AddItem("By Size",  mh, 8);

    msgh.Start();
}
```

The MesssageHandler object msgh in this program actually starts the event loop for the program. Without this object, menu selections will not be processed properly. (Menus will show up, but an error will occur when you make a menu selection.) Up until now we have hidden this object, because a MessageHandler object does not make much sense without understanding event-driven programming. The programs that use objects such as EditWin and Turtle require an event loop, but the programs we have written so far did not include this MessageHandler object. How was the event loop activated in our earlier programs? Remember that whenever we used an EditWin and a Turtle, we always invoked the function Done.* This function actually did nothing but call the MessageHandler's Start function to activate the event loop. So far, we have never mixed these objects, so there have been no problems. However, when you use these objects in the same program, you do not have to call an individual object's Done function. Rather, you call only one function to activate the event loop. For example, the following is not necessary.

---

* Using other GUI objects, for example, an OKBox or YesNoBox, does not require calling a Done function or using a MessageHandler object because these GUI objects are a special kind of window called a *modal dialog*. Modal dialogs behave differently from windows, and this difference eliminates the need for calling a Done function.

```
...
Turtle t;
EditWin ew;

t.Init(100,100);
t.Move(50);
t.Done();

ew.Init(10,10,300,200);
ew.Write("Hello");
ew.Done();
...
```

You don't need both.

A correct version is

```
...
Turtle t;
EditWin ew;
MessageHandler msgh;

t.Init(100,100);
t.Move(50);

ew.Init(10,10,300,200);
ew.Write("Hello");

msgh.Start();
...
```

12.6 Grading program with menus

Let's add some menus to the program Grading we developed in section 12.4. We will add one menu with five menu items.

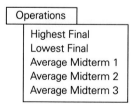

Operations

Highest Final
Lowest Final
Average Midterm 1
Average Midterm 2
Average Midterm 3

Our first step is to define a new descendant of MenuHandler to process menu selections. It searches and displays the highest and lowest final examination scores for the first and second menu choices. It uses an OKBox for the display. Similarly, for the last

```
#include "GUIObj.h"

class GradeMenuHandler : public MenuHandler {

public:

    void SetDisplay(ScoresWindow *sw);
    void MenuFunc1();
    void MenuFunc2();
    void MenuFunc3();
    void MenuFunc4();
    void MenuFunc5();

private:

    OKBox     msg;
    ScoresWindow          *display;
    float ComputeAverage(int num);
};
```

Figure 12.17 GradeMenuHandler

three menu choices, it computes and displays the average of the specified midterm examination. The interface for GradeMenuHandler is shown in figure 12.17.

Before we provide the implementation details for the GradeMenuHandler object, let's look at the main function to see how the objects are declared and put together.

```
//Program Grading2:  The Grading program with menus.

#include "GUIObj.h"
#include "GrMnHnd.h"
#include "ScoreWin.h"

void main()
{
    GradeMenuHandlermh;
    MessageHandler msgh;
    ScoresWindowscorewin;
    MenuopMenu("Operations");

    opMenu.AddItem("Highest Final",    mh, 1); //setup menus
    opMenu.AddItem("Lowest  Final",    mh, 2);
    opMenu.AddItem("Average Midterm 1", mh, 3);
    opMenu.AddItem("Average Midterm 2", mh, 4);
    opMenu.AddItem("Average Midterm 3", mh, 5);

    scorewin.Init(50,50,450,350);   //initialize & pass
    mh.SetDisplay(&scorewin);       //pointer to scorewin and
                                    //connect it to menu
                                    //handler

    msgh.Start();
}
```

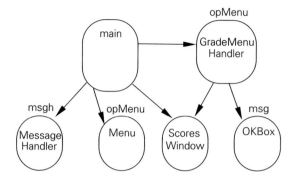

Figure 12.18 Program Grading2 object diagram

The program's object diagram is shown in figure 12.18.

Notice the arrow from mh to scorewin. When a menu choice is selected and the corresponding function of mh is executed, mh needs to request service (i.e., reading a data value) from scorewin. For mh to be able to do this task, the main program calls its Set-Display function to pass a pointer to the scorewin object. The SetDisplay function is defined as

```
void GradeMenuHandler::SetDisplay(ScoresWindow *sw)
{
    display = sw;
}
```

which simply sets its data member display to point to this passed ScoresWindow object. The data member display is a pointer to a ScoresWindow object, not a ScoresWindow object itself. We use the pointer to avoid creating a duplicate ScoresWindow object. Had we declared display as a ScoresWindow object we would have two ScoresWindow objects, but we need only one.[*]

Finding the highest and lowest final examination scores is straightforward. Since the tasks are very similar, we will only explain the function for finding the highest final examination score. The general idea of the function is to request the ScoresWindow object to read the data values down the column for the final examination scores. For each value (an array of characters) returned by the ScoresWindow object, we first convert it to an integer and then compare it to the current maximum. If the number read is larger than the current maximum, we have found a new maximum, so we set the current maximum to this number. The final examination scores are located in the column

---

[*] Even if you have two ScoresWindow objects in your program, both will not show up on the screen unless you call the Init functions for their objects.

positions 28 through 31, so to read this value, we call the `Read` function of the `ScoresWindow` object using

```
(*display).Read(lineNo, 28, 4)
```

where `lineNo` is the line number from which the final examination score is read. Had the `ScoresWindow` object been declared as

```
ScoresWindow   display;
```

we would say

```
display.Read(lineNo, 28, 4);
```

But what we have is a pointer to the `ScoresWindow` object:

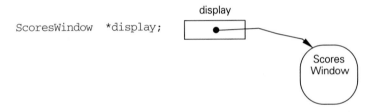

```
ScoresWindow   *display;
```

Therefore, the identifier

```
display
```

is a pointer value, that is, the address where a `ScoresWindow` object is stored. As explained in chapter 9, when we need to access the contents of a memory location referred to by a pointer, we use the dereference operator `*`. Thus to refer to the `ScoresWindow` object, we must say

```
*display
```

Once we have a reference to an object, we can call its function by using the standard dot notation, which will result in

```
*display.Read(lineNo, 28,4);
```

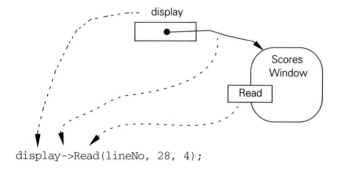

```
display->Read(lineNo, 28, 4);
```

Figure 12.19 Use of the pointer operator

Since the dot operator has a higher precedence than the dereference operator, we must use parentheses to make the dereference operator * execute first. So we write

```
(*display).Read(lineNo, 28,4);
```

This type of dereferencing occurs frequently, so there exists a more concise manner to state the same thing using the pointer operator ->, as in

```
display->Read(lineNo, 28, 4);
```

Figure 12.19 illustrates this concept.

The function for finding the maximum final examination score is as follows:

```
void GradeMenuHandler::MenuFunc1()
{
    int lineNo, numLines, max = 0, num;
    char str[MAXLINE];

    numLines = display->GetNumLines();

    for (lineNo = 0; lineNo < numLines; lineNo = lineNo+1) {

        strcpy(str, display->Read(lineNo, 28, 4));
        num = atoi(str);

        if (num > max) max = num;
    }

    msg.Display(max);
}
```

Now let's see how the averages of the midterms are computed. The function Com-puteAverage computes the average of the specified midterm scores. It is written as

```
float GradeMenuHandler::ComputeAverage(int num)
{
    //num == 1 means midterm 1; 2 means midterm 2;
    // 3 means midterm 3

    int lineNo, numLines, pos, sum = 0;
    char str[MAXLINE];

    pos = 16 + (num-1)*4;
    numLines = display->GetNumLines();

    for (lineNo = 0; lineNo < numLines; lineNo = lineNo+1) {

    strcpy(str, display->Read(lineNo, pos, 4));
    num = atoi(str);
    sum = sum + num;
    }

    return float(sum) / numLines;
}
```

Using the `ComputeAverage` function, the function for computing the average of the first midterm is

```
void MenuFunc3()
{
    float avg;
    avg = ComputeAverage(1);
    msg.Display(avg);
}
```

The other two functions are identical except for the value of argument we pass to the `ComputeAverage` function.

Putting it all together, we have the implementation file `"GrMnHnd.cpp"` for the `GradeMenuHandler`.

"GrMnHnd.cpp"

```
#include "GrMnHnd.h"
#include "GUIObj.h"
#include <string.h>

void GradeMenuHandler::SetDisplay(ScoresWindow *sw)
{
    display = sw;
}

void GradeMenuHandler::MenuFunc1() //maximum final
{
    int lineNo, numLines, max = 0, num;
    char str[MAXLINE];
    numLines = display->GetNumLines();

    for (lineNo = 0; lineNo < numLines; lineNo=lineNo+1){
```

```
            strcpy(str, display->Read(lineNo, 28, 4));
            num = atoi(str);

            if (num > max) max = num;
        }
        msg.Display(max);
}

void GradeMenuHandler::MenuFunc2() //minimum final
{
        int lineNo, numLines, min = 100, num;
        char str[MAXLINE];

        numLines = display->GetNumLines();

        for (lineNo = 0; lineNo < numLines; lineNo=lineNo+1){

            strcpy(str, display->Read(lineNo, 28, 4));
            num = atoi(str);

            if (min > num) min = num;
        }
        msg.Display(min);
}void GradeMenuHandler::MenuFunc3()  //midterm #1 average
{
        float avg;
        avg = ComputeAverage(1);
        msg.Display(avg);
}

void GradeMenuHandler::MenuFunc4()  //midterm #2 average
{
        float avg;
        avg = ComputeAverage(2);
        msg.Display(avg);
}

void GradeMenuHandler::MenuFunc5()  //midterm #3 average
{
        float avg;
        avg = ComputeAverage(3);
        msg.Display(avg);
}

float GradeMenuHandler::ComputeAverage(int num)
{
        //num == 1 means midterm 1; 2 means midterm 2;
        // 3 means midterm 3

        int lineNo, numLines, pos, sum = 0, num;
        char str[MAXLINE];

        pos = 16 + (num-1)*4;
        numLines = display->GetNumLines();

        for (lineNo = 0; lineNo < numLines; lineNo=LineNo+1){

            strcpy(str, display->Read(lineNo, pos, 4));
            num = atoi(str);
            sum = sum + num;
        }

        return float(sum) / numLines;
}
```

12.7 Handling events with SmartTurtle

A `Turtle` object is programmed to process the clicking of the left and right mouse buttons.[*] It has two functions, `LeftButtonClicked` and `RightButtonClicked`, which are invoked from the event loop when a mouse button is clicked. These functions contain no code, so nothing actually happens when the mouse buttons are clicked. They are placeholder functions, so we will be able to create a descendant of `Turtle` and override them if we wish to process mouse button click events.

Let's define `ClickTurtle`, a descendant of `Turtle`. The `ClickTurtle` will draw a star when the left mouse button is clicked and a square when the right mouse button is clicked. Here is the interface file for the `ClickTurtle`.

File "CkTurtle.h"

```
#include "Turtles.h"

class ClickTurtle : public Turtle {

public:
      void LeftButtonClicked ( int x, int y);
      void RightButtonClicked( int x, int y);

private:
      void Star ( int x, int y );
      void Square (int x, int y, int size);
};
```

The implementation file is

File "CKTurtle.cpp"

```
#include "CkTurtle.h"

void ClickTurtle::LeftButtonClicked ( int x, int y)
{
      //draw a star at coordinate (x,y)
      Star(x, y);
}

void ClickTurtle::RightButtonClicked( int x, int y)
{
      //draw a square at coordinate (x,y)
      Square(x, y, 50);
}

void ClickTurtle::Star ( int x, int y )
{
```

---

[*] We use a two-button mouse here. For the Macintosh platform, which has only one button, we use Command-Click to simulate the clicking of the right button. For the UNIX platform, which has three buttons, the middle button is not processed.

```
        PenUp();
        GoToPos(x,y);
        PenDown();
        TurnTo(0);

        int i;
        for (i = 1; i <= 5; i++) {
            Move(30);
            Turn(-144);
        }
    }

void ClickTurtle::Square (int x, int y, int size)
{
        PenUp();
        GoToPos(x,y);
        PenDown();
        TurnTo(0);

        Move(size); Turn(90);
        Move(size); Turn(90);
        Move(size); Turn(90);
        Move(size);
    }
```

The main program declares a ClickTurtle object, initiates it, and calls its Done function.

```
//Program Click: A program to illustrate the processing
//  of mouse click events.

#include "CkTurtle.h"

void main()
{
    ClickTurtleclick;
    click.Init(0, 0);
    click.Done();
}
```

Notice that we do not explicitly call the ClickTurtle's LeftButtonClicked or Right-ButtonClicked functions in the program. We must simply declare a ClickTurtle object click and then initialize and display the click by calling the Init and Done functions.

12.8 Exercises

1 Output on the ScoresWindow will not be aligned if an average score is either a single-digit or three-digit number. Modify the PrintResult function to rectify this problem.

2 Modify the Ok function of the ScoresWindow so that it computes class averages for each midterm and for the final exam. These five averages should be displayed on a separate line below the last student's line. (Skip one line for clarity.).

```
Amadeus Mozart    90  96  85  88  89.4  B
Johann Strauss    94  91  87  90  90.4  A
Richard Wagner    84  87  80  82  83.0  B
Claude Debussy    70  86  75  68  73.4  C
Antonin Dvorak    60  61  57  70  63.6  D
Johann S. Bach    94  97  90  92  93.0  A

AVERAGES          82  86  79  82  82.1
```

3 Make a further modification to the Ok function of the ScoresWindow so that it also counts the number of students receiving each letter grade.

```
Amadeus Mozart    90  96  85  88  89.4  B
Johann Strauss    94  91  87  90  90.4  A
Richard Wagner    84  87  80  82  83.0  B
Claude Debussy    70  86  75  68  73.4  C
Antonin Dvorak    60  61  57  70  63.6  D
Johann S. Bach    94  97  90  92  93.0  A

AVERAGES          82  86  79  82  82.1

      A = 2  B = 2  C = 1  D = 1  F = 0
```

4 Modify the ScoresWindow so that the input can be entered by the user more easily. With the original ScoresWindow, the user must enter the data values at fixed positions. Modify the input routine so the user can enter the data values by separating them with commas.

```
Takanohana,90,96,85,88
Akebono,94,91,87,90
Kaio,84,87,80,82
Musashimaru,70,86,75,68
Terao,60,61,57,70
```

Output should be displayed as

```
Takanohana       90  96  85  88  89.4  B
Akebono          94  91  87  90  90.4  A
Kaio             84  87  80  82  83.0  B
Musashimaru      70  86  75  68  73.4  C
Terao            60  61  57  70  63.6  D
```

Hint: To output a line, erase the whole line first and then print out the formatted line.

5 With the original `ScoresWindow`, after the grades are computed, we can still edit the test scores and click the OK button to recompute the grades. Improve the input routine of the modified `ScoresWindow` from exercise 4 to handle both the original and this modified method of input.

6 Write a menu program to display the following menus (pun intended).:

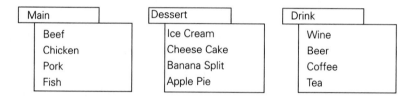

7 Extend the menu program of exercise 6 by adding a descendant of `EditWin` for displaying selected items and their prices. Assign prices that reflect your local market. Notice that the items should be repeated as many times as they are selected (e.g., Ice Cream is repeated twice).

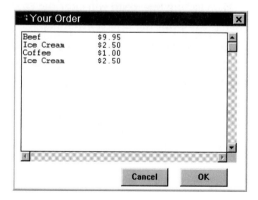

8 Extend the menu program of exercise 7 so that multiple orders of the same item are displayed only once with the correct total. Also, change the labels for the OK and

Cancel buttons to *Total* and *Clear.* When the Total button is clicked, it prints the total price of all ordered items. When the Clear button is clicked, it cancels the order and clears the display.

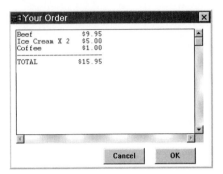

9   Write a program that lets users select a shape from the menu and then draws the selected shape using a `Turtle` or a descendant of a `Turtle`. You can try shapes like triangles, rectangles, polygons, and trees (exercise 12 in chapter 3). Use one `Turtle` for drawing all shapes.

10   Write a program that plays the high-low game. The object (i.e., goal) of the game is to guess the mystery number in the fewest tries. The program generates a mystery number between 1 and 100 using the random number generator in `"util.h"`. The player enters his or her guess via an `EditWin`. When the OK button is clicked, the program replies respectively, `Low`, `High`, or `Bingo` if the entered number is lower than, higher than, or equal to the mystery number. The program keeps track of the number of guesses and prints it when the player guesses right. The program will have menu items `New Game` and `Give Up`. Selecting `New Game` will clear the `EditWin` and start the new game. Selecting `Give Up` will print the mystery number.

11   Define a descendant of `Turtle` called `GridTurtle` that draws a 5 × 5 grid. When the left mouse button is clicked inside a box, it draws a circle within the box. When the right mouse button is clicked inside a box, it draws an X within the box.

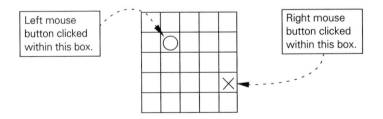

12 Define a descendant of `Turtle` that draws lines as directed by mouse button clicks. Your `Turtle` descendant should respond to a left button click by moving to the point of the click without drawing, and it should respond to a right button click by drawing a line to the point of the click.

13 Modify the `ftoa` function so it will be able to convert negative real numbers to characters.

chapter 13

One-dimensional arrays

An array of characters, which we studied in chapter 7, is just one of the many different types of arrays available in programming languages. An array element does not have to be a character; it can be an integer, a real number, or even an object. In addition, the number of indices, or *subscripts*, for an array is not limited to one; it can have more than one index. An array with more than one index is called a *multidimensional array*. In this chapter we will examine one-dimensional arrays, and in the next chapter we will discuss two- and three-dimensional arrays. Throughout the discussion, we will use the expressions *character array*, *float array*, and so on to mean array of characters, array of `float` data, and so on.

13.1 Numerical arrays

The following code declares an array of three characters and assigns values to it.

```
char str[3];

str[0] = 'H';
str[1] = 'i';
str[2] = '\0';
```

Similarly, the following code declares an array of three integers and assigns numbers to it.

```
int  num[3];

num[0] = 12;
num[1] = 33;
num[2] = 198;
```

There are no differences in the way we declare and access individual members of arrays. The only difference is the data types of individual elements.

Just as simple variables can be initialized, arrays can be initialized with values for their elements. For example, the following declarations result in the arrays already shown.

```
char str[3] = {'H','i','\0'};
int  num[3] = {12, 33, 198};
```

Only arrays of characters can be initialized in an alternative and more concise style. For example, the alternative initialization

```
char str[3] = "Hi";
```

is equivalent to

```
char str[3] = {'H','i','\0'};
```

This shorthand style is the one we have been using so far. The syntax for the array declaration follows

id-declarator
    modifier_{opt} *identifier* *initializer_{opt}*
    modifier_{opt} *identifier* *size-declarator* *array-initializer_{opt}*

size-declarator
    [*constant-expression*   ]

array-initializer
    =   {   *constant-expression-list*   }

constant-expression-list
    constant-expression
    constant-expression ,   *constant-expression-list*

Let's begin our discussion of one-dimensional arrays of numerical data with an example. Suppose we want to input daily temperatures for one week and compute the average temperature for the week. How should we write a program to perform the given task? A program with a simple repetition statement will do the job.

```
float sum = 0.0;
float temperature[7];
int i;

for (i = 0; i < 7; i = i+1) {
    cin >> temperature[i];
    sum = sum + temperature[i];
}

cout << "Average temperature is " << sum / 7;
```

Suppose we also want to compute the number of days whose temperature is higher than the average. How should we write the program? We now have to remember all of the daily temperatures to determine how many days have a temperature higher than the average. Without an array the code would look something like this:

```
int hotDays = 0;
float avg, sum = 0.0;
float temp1, temp2, temp3, temp4, temp5, temp6, temp7;

cin >> temp1 >> temp2 >> temp3 >> temp4 >> temp5
    >> temp6 >> temp7;
```

```
avg = (temp1 + temp2 + temp3 + temp4 + temp5 + temp6 + temp7)/7;

if (temp1 > avg) hotDays = hotDays + 1;
if (temp2 > avg) hotDays = hotDays + 1;
if (temp3 > avg) hotDays = hotDays + 1;
if (temp4 > avg) hotDays = hotDays + 1;
if (temp5 > avg) hotDays = hotDays + 1;
if (temp6 > avg) hotDays = hotDays + 1;
if (temp7 > avg) hotDays = hotDays + 1;
```

This doesn't look good. What if we want to do the same recalculation for one month? One year? Yes, we can do it by using 31, 365, or whatever is the required number of variables, but this method would be impractical. Without an array we cannot use a repetition statement and write a concise program.

Let's see how the same program can be written using a one-dimensional array of float values. Since a week has seven days and temperature can be expressed as a real number, we declare a float array of size 7 for storing seven temperatures from Sunday (temperature[0]) to Saturday (temperature[6]).

```
float temperature[7];
```

Remember that the index for a C++ array always starts at 0. The temperature array with daily temperatures would look like this:

	0	1	2	3	4	5	6
temperature	73.9	70.3	67.4	70.5	76.5	76.0	72.7

A code fragment to input seven temperatures, compute the weekly average temperature, and determine the number of days the temperature is hotter than the weekly average follows:

```
int hotDays = 0;
float avg, sum = 0.0;
float temperature[7];
int i;

for (i = 0; i < 7; i = i+1) {
    cin >> temperature[i];
    sum = sum + temperature[i];
}
```

```
avg = sum / 7;

for (i=0; i < 7; i = i+1)
    if (temperature[i] > avg)
        hotDays = hotDays + 1;
```

Now let's extend the code to compute a monthly average temperature and also the averages for the odd-numbered and even-numbered days. We assume that a month has exactly 31 days. The following code computes the three averages. Notice how the counting variables for the for loops are incremented. Also, to make the indexing for the temperature array natural, we do not use the first position of the array (i.e., temperature[0]). By using positions 1 through 31, we have a natural correspondence in which temperature[i] is a temperature for the ith day of the month.

```
int hotDays = 0;
float sum = 0.0, avg, evenDaysAvg, oddDaysAvg;
float temperature[32];     ◄────── Only positions 1 through 31 are used.

int i;

for (i = 1; i < 32; i=i+1) {
    cin >> temperature[i];
    sum = sum + temperature[i];
}

avg = sum / 31; sum = 0.0;

for (i = 1; i < 32; i=i+2)
    sum = sum + temperature[i];

oddDaysAvg = sum / 16; sum = 0.0;

for (i = 2; i < 32; i=i+2)
    sum = sum + temperature[i];

evenDaysAvg = sum / 15;
```

13.2 Passing array arguments to functions

Now let's examine how to pass an array argument to a function. Passing an array argument is actually not new to us. We have already seen how to pass character arrays to a function by using the pass-by-pointer mechanism. Let's review this with an example. The following is a function to count the number of blank spaces in the passed string.

```
int countSpaces(char *p)
{
    int cnt = 0, i = 0;

    while (p[i] != '\0') {
    if (p[i] = ' ') cnt = cnt + 1;
    i = i+1;
    }

    return cnt;
}
```

The function is called in the following manner:

```
char str[15] = "I love C++";

cout << countSpaces(str);
```

Remember that an array name without an index, for example, str in the above code, refers to the address of the first position of the array.

Now, let's look at how we pass a numerical array. It is actually no different from passing a character array. Here's a function to compute the weekly average temperature.

```
float avgTemp(float *temp)
{
    float sum = 0;
    int i;

    for (i=0; i<7; i=i+1)
    sum = sum + temp[i];

    return sum/7;
}
```

The function is called in the following way:

```
float temperature[7];
int i;

for (i=0; i<7; i=i+1) cin >> temperature[i];

cout << avgTemp(temperature);
```

In this example, we assume the array is of size 7. For the function to be more reusable, we need a little more flexibility. Let's write a function that computes the average of an arbitrary number of `float` values. Unlike the function `avgTemp`, which works on an array of size 7, this function will have to work on an array of arbitrary size. Since the function works on an arbitrary number of array elements, we need some way to detect the end of processing all array elements. We can get this information by placing a special marker at the end of real data values. For this function, we assume that the `float` array will contain the value −1 at the end. For example, if the array has five values, then the sixth position has −1. The value −1 serves the same role as \0 in the character array.

	0	1	2	3	4	5
num	12.3	34.0	33.1	63.9	99.2	−1

Notice that an actual array size can be larger than the number of elements. For example, we could use only 7 positions in an array of size 12:

0	1	2	3	4	5	6	7	8	9	10	11
12.3	34.0	33.1	63.9	99.2	42.3	54.0	−1				

As long as −1 occurs at the end of the real data values, the function will work.

The function is written as

```
float average(float *num)
{
    const float ERROR = -1;

    float sum = 0;
    int   cnt = 0;

    while (num[cnt] != -1) {
        sum = sum + num[cnt];
        cnt = cnt + 1;
    }

    if (cnt == 0) //error
        return ERROR;
    else
        return sum/cnt;
}
```

This function will compute the average of an arbitrary number of `float` values, provided that no real value is –1. This restriction may or may not be a problem. If this restriction causes a problem, we can eliminate it by passing the number of values in the array as the second parameter of the function. The second approach is more common. The function can be modified to

```
float average(float *num, int size)
{
    const float ERROR = -1;

    float sum = 0; int i;

    if (size <= 0)
        return ERROR;
    else {
        for (i=0; i<size; i=i+1)
            sum = sum + num[i];
        return sum/size;
    }
}
```

We can also use an alternative form for specifying an array parameter in the function prototype. For example, instead of declaring a function as

```
float average(float *num)
```

we can declare it as

```
float average(float num[])
```

The way the array `num` is used inside the function is exactly the same in both styles.

Both versions of the function return –1 when an error occurs. This signal could be a problem. If the function deals with positive numbers only, then the average cannot be negative, so returning –1 to signal an error would work fine. However, what if the function must compute the average of any float values? Then the average of float values could be –1. Returning –1 from the function would be ambiguous. In this case, we need to add another parameter to return the status of computation: –1 for error and 1 for success, for example.

13.3 Arrays of objects

An array element can be as simple as a single character or as complex as an object. The following are sample declarations for arrays of objects.

```
Turtle painter[5]; // array of 5 Turtle objects
Person member[100]; // array of 100 Person objects
Student student[25]; // array of 25 Student objects
```

Figure 13.1 illustrates the member array.

We are using the Person object defined in chapter 10. We repeat its interface here (only the public portion):

```
class Person {
public:
    Person ();
    void SetName (char *pName);
    void SetPhone (char *pPhone);
    char *GetName();
    char *GetPhone();
...
};
```

To assign values to the first Person, for example, we say

```
member[0].SetName("Gustav Mahler");
member[0].SetPhone("408-123-9999");
```

This notation shows how the syntax to access an array element and an object function call are combined. The notation is consistent with:

```
Person x;
...
x.SetName(...);
x.SetPhone(...);
```

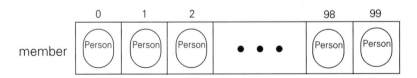

Figure 13.1 The member array

The only difference is how we refer to the individual object—either as x or member[0]. The use of an array of objects allows us to write concise code that deals with many objects. For example, to input information for 100 Person objects, we could simply execute the following code:

```
. . .
StringTypeIninpBox;
charpromptN[15] = "Type in Name:";
charpromptP[15] = "Type in Phone:";
charstr1[15]    = "Person #";
chartitle[17], num[3];
Personmember[100];
. . .
for (int i = 0; i < 100; i = i+1) {

    strcpy(num, itoa(i)); //convert to string;
    strcpy(title,str1);
    strcat(title,num);//construct title string

    member[i].SetName ( inpBox.GetString(title,promptN) );
    member[i].SetPhone( inpBox.GetString(title,promptP) );
}
. . .
```

Even though the program itself becomes concise by the use of an array, we cannot say the same for memory usage. When we declare

```
Person member[100];
```

memory space large enough to store all 100 Person objects is reserved for the program, whether they are actually used or not. So even if our program uses two slots for storing two Person objects, 100 slots are set aside (and 98 slots are wasted). (See figure 13.2.)

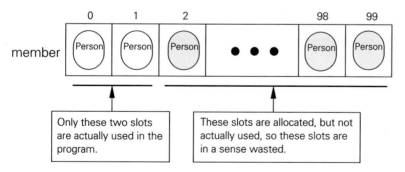

Figure 13.2 Memory space for the total of 100 person objects are allocated for the member array, whether they are used or not

13.4 Array of pointers to objects and dynamic allocation

One way to reduce the amount of memory waste is to use an array of pointers to objects. Consider the following declaration of an array of pointers to `Person` objects:

```
Person  *pMember[100];
```

Figure 13.3 illustrates an array of pointers to `Person` objects in which all 100 `Person` objects are created.

At the time an array of pointers is declared, no memory is allocated for `Person` objects. What we have at the time of declaration is shown in figure 13.4.

Each pointer will normally take up 4 bytes of memory, while each `Person` object could take up a minimum of 27 bytes (i.e., the number of bytes allocated for `name` and `phone` data members), so we save at least 23 bytes for each element of the array. Since we allocate a `Person` object only when needed, this method wastes much less space than the first approach. The discrepancy gets bigger for larger-sized objects. Of course, when the program always uses exactly 100 `Person` objects, then the first approach, an array of `Person` objects, would work better. With the second approach, we end up using memory space for 100 `Person` objects plus 100 pointers to `Person` objects. An array of pointers works well when the number of objects used in a program varies from execution to execution.

We must create a `Person` object each time a new `Person` object is needed after the program starts to run. We call the method of allocating memory while the program is running *dynamic allocation*.

To create an object dynamically, we use the operator called `new`. We create a new `Person` object using

```
new Person;
```

The operator `new` returns a pointer to a newly created `Person` object. To assign this pointer to the first element of `pMember`, we could execute

```
pMember[0] = new Person;
```

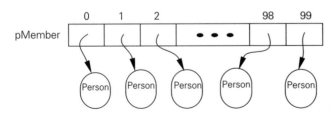

Figure 13.3 State after memory space for 100 Person objects is allocated

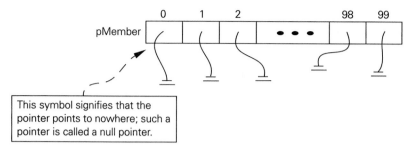

This symbol signifies that the pointer points to nowhere; such a pointer is called a null pointer.

Figure 13.4 State after the array is initially declared

which results in figure 13.5.

Now, to assign data to this newly created `Person` object, we execute

```
(*pMember[0]).SetName ("Gustav Mahler");
(*pMember[0]).SetPhone("408-123-9999");
```

We saw a similar syntax in section 12.6 on page 331 but using a variable, instead of an array element. The syntax is somewhat complicated, so we will explain it again. First, an element of the array `pMember` contains a pointer to a `Person` object, not the `Person` object itself. So, the expression

```
pMember[0]
```

is a pointer value, that is, the address of a memory location, not a `Person` object. As explained in chapter 9, when we need to access the contents of a memory location referred to by a pointer, we use the dereference operator `*`. Thus to access the `Person` object whose address is stored in the first slot of the `pMember` array, we use

```
*pMember[0]
```

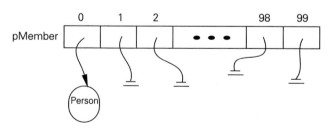

Figure 13.5 Pointer assigned to first element

Once we have a reference to an object, we can call its function using standard dot notation, as

```
*pMember[0].SetName ("Gustav Mahler");   //INCORRECT
```

However, since the dot operator has a higher precedence than the dereference operator, we must use the parentheses to make the dereference operator * execute first. So, we write

```
(*pMember[0]).SetName ("Gustav Mahler");
```

As mentioned in section 12.6, since this type of dereferencing occurs frequently, the above can be expressed in a more concise manner using the pointer operator ->, as in

```
pMember[0] -> SetName ("Gustav Mahler");
```

Figure 13.6 illustrates this concept.

Since we have dynamically allocated the space for a Person object, we must deallocate it, that is, return the space to the system when a Person object is no longer needed. Otherwise, we would end up with a lot of unused and wasted space. We deallocate a Person object using the operator delete. To deallocate the first Person object and reset the pointer to NULL, for example, we execute

```
delete pMember[0];
pMember[0] = NULL;
```

Figure 13.7 shows the effect of deallocating the space.

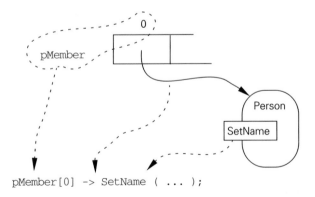

Figure 13.6 Correspondence between the diagram and the actual code

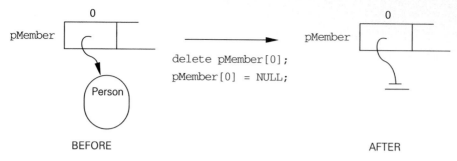

pMember

0

delete pMember[0];
pMember[0] = NULL;

pMember

0

BEFORE

AFTER

Figure 13.7 Deallocation of space

Dynamic allocation (and deallocation) of memory space allows much finer control over the use of memory, resulting in more efficient management of memory space, thanks to the use of pointers.

C++ In C++ we can change the size of an array every time we run the program by dynamically allocating memory space for the array. Assuming the value 10 is entered, the following code

```
Person *p;
int size;
cin >> size;
p = new Person[size];
```

will result in

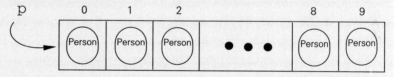

Notice that the variable p is a pointer to the array and that we need a pointer to allocate memory space dynamically. Both pointer and index expressions are valid for referring to an array element. For example, both

```
p[2]
```

and

```
*(p+2)
```

refer to the third element of the array. Although this technique provides a certain amount of flexibility in memory usage, it still requires the user to specify the size, which may or may not be feasible. If the user enters an estimate that is too large, then he or she ends up wasting space anyway.

13.5 Grading program

In this section we will use an array of pointers to objects to implement a sample program. The grading program we introduced in chapter 12 calculated letter grades for students in a class based on the scores of four exams—three midterm exams and a final. Let's write a program similar to that one but add a slightly more sophisticated grading scheme. The new program reads in a name and four exam scores as before. The weighted average score is also computed as before, which is

$$avg = \frac{(midterm1 + midterm2 + midterm3 + 2 \times final)}{5}$$

The letter grade, however, is now computed differently. It is based on the difference between the highest average score and the student's average according to the following rule (see table 13.1). HIGH is the highest average score.

To determine the letter grades, we need to know the highest average score. However, we cannot determine the highest average score unless we first compute the average scores of all students. After we determine the highest average score, we will need to go through the list again to assign letter grades.

To determine the letter grade for a student, we need two numbers: the highest average score, which we have, and the average for that

Table 13.1 Letter grade rules

Avg	Letter grade
HIGH - AVG < 11	A
11 <= HIGH - AVG < 21	B
21 <= HIGH - AVG < 31	C
31 <= HIGH - AVG < 41	D
41 <= HIGH - AVG	F

student, which we don't have. In the process of finding the highest average score, we computed the average score for each student, but we never saved them. We could compute the individual average scores again, but this repetition is obviously inefficient. What we need to do is save the average scores when we compute them the first time. We could save the scores by printing them to the editor window and reading them back when we are ready to determine the letter grades, but using the editor window for such purposes is not a good idea. For example, if we had to clear the window's contents to read in input for other processing, we would lose all the information previously written to the editor window. The editor window is intended for input and output, not for data storage. We should use objects for their intended purposes only. Therefore, we will use an array, not the editor window, to remember not only the average scores but also the other test scores.

We will use three types of arrays. For each `Student` object, we have arrays to keep track of his/her test scores and letter grade. To keep track of students, we will create a

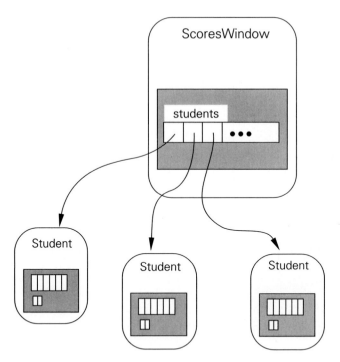

Figure 13.8 Array structure

ScoresWindow, a descendant of an EditWin, that has a data member, which is an array of pointers to Student objects. The structure can be depicted graphically as shown in figure 13.8.

A Student object is created as a descendant of the Person object defined in chapter 10. A Student object is declared as

"Student.h"

```
#include "Person.h"

class Student : public Person {
public:

     void SetScore(int testNumber, float score);
     float GetScore(int testNumber);
     void SetLetterGrade(char grade);
     char *GetLetterGrade();

private:

     float scores[6]; //up to six exam scores
     char  grade[2];  //course grade
};
```

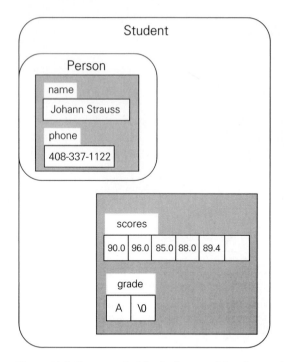

Figure 13.9 Structure inside the Person object for storing information

In addition to the inherited data members, a `Student` object has an array `scores` for storing the exam scores (see figure 13.9) and a variable `grade` for storing the letter grade.

The format for inputting scores is the same as before (see figure 13.10). After the average scores and letter grades are computed, the results are displayed as shown in figure 13.11.

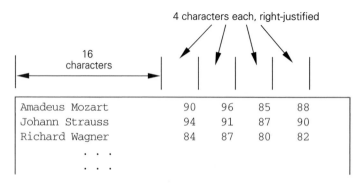

Figure 13.10 Format for input

```
Highest Average:          96.70
Amadeus Mozart            89.40  A
Johann Strauss            90.40  A
Richard Wagner            83.00  B
        . . .
J. S. Bach                79.40  B
```

Figure 13.11 Result of computed scores and grades

The ScoresWindow now has one data member, students, for keeping track of student information. The interface for the ScoresWindow is

"ScoreWin.h"

```
#include "GUIObj.h"
#include "util.h"
#include "Student.h"

class ScoresWindow : public EditWin {
public:

    ScoresWindow();
    void Ok();
    void Cancel();

private:

    void GetData();
    void GetOneStudent(int row);
    void ComputeAvg();
    float FindMaxAvg();
    void AssignGrade(float maxAvg);
    void PrintResult(float maxAvg);

    Student   *students[35];
};
```

The Cancel function remains the same as before. The Ok function is essentially the same as before. The only difference is the new formula for computing the letter grades. The new Ok function is defined as follows:

```
void ScoresWindow::Ok();
{
    float maxAvg;

    GetData();          //read in data & build students array

    ComputeAvg();              //compute the avg for all
    maxAvg = FindMaxAvg();
    AssignGrade(maxAvg);       //assign letter grades
```

```
        PrintResult(maxAvg);
    }
```

The function GetData reads in the complete information on students, reading one line for each student.

```
void ScoresWindow::GetData()
{
    int lineNo, numLines;

    numLines = GetNumLines();

    for (lineNo = 0; lineNo < numLines; lineNo = lineNo+1)
        GetOneStudent(lineNo);
}
```

To process a student's information, GetData calls another function GetOneStudent, which creates a Student object. The function reads the whole line at line number row and assigns data obtained from that line to the newly created Student object. The next open slot of the students array points to this Student object. Notice the syntax for calling the functions of Student.

```
void ScoresWindow::GetOneStudent(int row)
{
    char      str[MAXLINE];
    float     tmp;

    students[row] = new Student;      //allocate memory

    //read values
    students[row]->SetName(Read(row,0,16)); //name

    strcpy( str, Read(row, 16,4));
    tmp  = atof(str);
    students[row]->SetScore(1, tmp); //Midterm 1

    strcpy( str, Read(row, 20,4));
    tmp  = atof(str);
    students[row]->SetScore(2, tmp); //Midterm 2

    strcpy( str, Read(row, 24,4));
    tmp  = atof(str);
    students[row]->SetScore(3, tmp); //Midterm 3
```

```
        strcpy( str, Read(row, 28,4));
        tmp  = atof(str);
        students[row]->SetScore(4, tmp); //final
    }
```

Once the function GetData is done, we have finished reading in the data and building the students array. We are now ready to find the highest average score. We first determine the average scores for all students using the following function:

```
void ScoresWindow::ComputeAvg()
{
    //scan through the students array
    //and compute the average for each student
    int i = 0, j;
    float sum;

    while (students[i] != NULL) {

        sum = 0.0;
        for (j=1; j <= 3; j = j+1)
        sum = sum + students[i]->GetScore(j);

        sum = sum + 2 * students[i]->GetScore(4); //final
        students[i]->SetScore(5, sum / 5); //store the avg

        i = i + 1;
    }
}
```

For each student, we invoke its function GetScore(j) to retrieve the jth test score (the final exam score is the fourth score). The average score thus computed is kept by the Student object as a fifth score. We repeat this process until there are no more students to process. This end condition is tested by

```
        students[i] != NULL
```

where NULL (its value is 0) means no pointer is in the slot, that is, there are no more Student objects to process.

For this code to work correctly, we must initialize the students array. We initialize the data members in the constructor function as follows:

```
        ScoresWindow::ScoresWindow()
        {
            int i;
```

```
        for (i = 0; i < 35; i = i+1)
            students[i] = NULL;
    }
```

We determine the highest average score by going through the average scores for all students:

```
float ScoresWindow::FindMaxAvg()
{
    //scan through the students array
    //and find the maximum average score
    float maxAvg = 0.0, tmp;
    int i = 0;
```

```
    while (students[i] != NULL) {
        tmp = students[i]->GetScore(5); //get the average
                                        //of the next student
        if (maxAvg < tmp)   //found a higher average
            maxAvg = tmp;   //so reassign
        i = i + 1;
    }
    return maxAvg;
}
```

We assign the letter grades by going through the students and evaluating the given formula for each student. The looping structure is the same as that used in the other functions `ComputeAvg` and `FindMaxAvg`.

```
void ScoresWindow::AssignGrade(float maxAvg);
{
    //scan through the students array
    //and assign the letter grade
    int i = 0;
    float avg;
    while (students[i] != NULL) {
        avg = students[i]->GetScore(5);

        if (maxAvg - avg < 11)
            students[i]->SetLetterGrade('A');

        else if (maxAvg - avg < 21)
            students[i]->SetLetterGrade('B');

        else if (maxAvg - avg < 31)
            students[i]->SetLetterGrade('C');

        else if (maxAvg - avg < 41)
            students[i]->SetLetterGrade('D');

        else
            students[i]->SetLetterGrade('F');

        i = i + 1;
    }
}
```

The only remaining function is the printing of the results. Since we print out the highest average score at the first row (row 0), the `i`th student's information is printed on row `i+1`.

```
void ScoresWindow::PrintResult(maxAvg)
{
    //print out the results
    char str[MAXLINE];
    Clear();

    strcpy(str, "Highest Average: ");
    strcat(str, ftoa(maxAvg));
    WriteLine(str);

    int i = 0;
    while (students[i] != NULL) {

        //print one student
        strcpy(str, students[i]->GetName());   //name
        strcat(str, " ");
        strcat(str, ftoa(students[i]->GetScore(5))); //avg
        strcat(str, " ");
        strcat(str, students[i]->GetLetterGrade()); //ltr gr
        WriteLine(str);

        i = i +1;
    }
}
```

The following is the complete implementation for the ScoresWindow object.

"ScoreWin.cpp"

```
#include "ScoreWin.h"

ScoresWindow::ScoresWindow()
{
    int i;
    for (i = 0; i < 35; i = i+1)
        students[i] = NULL;
}

void ScoresWindow::Ok()
{
    float maxAvg;

    GetData();          //read in data & build students array

    ComputeAvg();                   //compute the avg for all
    maxAvg = FindMaxAvg();
    AssignGrade(maxAvg);            //assign letter grades

    PrintResult(maxAvg);
}

void ScoresWindow::Cancel()
{
    Clear();
}
```

```
void ScoresWindow::GetData()
{
      int lineNo, numLines;

      numLines = GetNumLines();

      for (lineNo = 0; lineNo < numLines; lineNo=lineNo+1)
          GetOneStudent(lineNo);
}

void ScoresWindow::GetOneStudent(int row)
{
      char      str[MAXLINE];
      float     tmp;

      students[row] = new Student;//allocate memory

      //read values
      students[row]->SetName(Read(row,0,16));//name

      strcpy( str, Read(row, 16,4));
      tmp  = atof(str);
      students[row]->SetScore(1, tmp); //Midterm 1

      strcpy( str, Read(row, 20,4));
      tmp  = atof(str);
      students[row]->SetScore(2, tmp); //Midterm 2

      strcpy( str, Read(row, 24,4));
      tmp  = atof(str);
      students[row]->SetScore(3, tmp); //Midterm 3

      strcpy( str, Read(row, 28,4));
      tmp  = atof(str);
      students[row]->SetScore(4, tmp); //final
}

void ScoresWindow::ComputeAvg()
{
      //scan through the students array
      //and compute the average for each student
      int i = 0, j;
      float sum;

      while (students[i] != NULL) {
          sum = 0.0;
          for (j=1; j <= 3; j=j+1)
              sum = sum + students[i]->GetScore(j);

          sum = sum + 2 * students[i]->GetScore(4); //final
          students[i]->SetScore(5, sum / 5); //store the avg

          i = i + 1;
      }
}

float ScoresWindow::FindMaxAvg()
{
      //scan through the students array
      //and find the maximum average score
      float maxAvg = 0.0, tmp;
      int i = 0;
      while (students[i] != NULL) {
          tmp = students[i]->GetScore(5); //get the average
                                //of the next student
```

```
            if (maxAvg < tmp)    //found a higher average
                maxAvg = tmp;  //so reassign
            i = i + 1;
        }
        return maxAvg;
    }

    void ScoresWindow::AssignGrade(float maxAvg)
    {
        //scan through the students array
        //and assign the letter grade
        int i = 0;
        float avg;

        while (students[i] != NULL) {
            avg = students[i]->GetScore(5);

            if (maxAvg - avg < 11)
                students[i]->SetLetterGrade('A');

            else if (maxAvg - avg < 21)
                students[i]->SetLetterGrade('B');

            else if (maxAvg - avg < 31)
                students[i]->SetLetterGrade('C');

            else if (maxAvg - avg < 41)
                students[i]->SetLetterGrade('D');

            else
                students[i]->SetLetterGrade('F');

            i = i + 1;
        }
    }

    void ScoresWindow::PrintResult(maxAvg)
    {
        //print out the results
        char str[MAXLINE];
        Clear();

        strcpy(str, "Highest Average: ");
        strcat(str, ftoa(maxAvg));
        WriteLine(str);

        int i = 0;
        while (students[i] != NULL) {

            //print one student
            strcpy(str, students[i]->GetName());  //name
            strcat(str, " ");
            strcat(str, ftoa(students[i]->GetScore(5))); //avg
            strcat(str, " ");
            strcat(str, students[i]->GetLetterGrade()); //ltr gr
            WriteLine(str);

            i = i +1;
        }
    }
```

The implementation of Student is as follows. Notice that we do not have a constructor for Student. The constructor of its parent, Person, is used whenever a new Student object is created. Remember, by default, if a descendant does not have its own constructor, then we use its ancestor's constructor function.

```
#include "Student.h"

void Student::SetScore( int testNumber, float score)
{
    scores[testNumber - 1] = score;
    //subtract one because array index starts from 0
}

float Student::GetScore(int testNumber)
{
    return scores[testNumber - 1];
}

void Student::SetLetterGrade(char grade)
{
    grade[0] = grade;
    grade[1] = '\0';
}

char *Student::GetLetterGrade()
{
    return grade;
}
```

We are now ready for the main function. Once again, its purpose is mainly to declare and activate objects.

```
//Program Grading3:    The grading program with a modified routine
//                     for computing the letter grades.

#include "ScoreWin.h"

void main()
{
    ScoresWindow gradebook;

    gradebook.Init(50, 50, 450, 350);
    gradebook.Done();
}
```

13.6 Enumerated types

The index for a C++ array must be an integer, which is not usually a problem. However, in some cases we would like to have a little more flexibility in indexing an array. C++ has a type called an *enumerated type*, which provides the needed flexibility. Enumerated types are also helpful in writing "self documenting" programs.

An enumerated type consists of an ordered set of values, each named with an identifier. For example, the following type declaration creates a type `CoinType`, which has values `Penny`, `Nickel`, `Dime`, `Quarter`, `HalfDollar`, and `Dollar`.

```
enum CoinType {Penny, Nickel, Dime, Quarter, HalfDollar, Dollar};
```

Similarly, the following declaration creates a type `Fruit` with values `Apple`, `Orange`, and `Cherry`.

```
enum Fruit {Apple, Orange, Cherry};
```

The order of the values is established by their order in the declaration; for example,

```
Penny < Nickel < Dime < Quarter < HalfDollar < Dollar

Apple < Orange < Cherry
```

The compiler achieves this order by assigning the numerical value 0 to `Penny`, 1 to `Nickel`, and so forth. We can also assign specific values to the identifiers; for example:

```
enum CoinType {Penny = 1, Nickel = 5, Dime = 10,
               Quarter = 25,HalfDollar = 50, Dollar = 100}

enum Fruit {Apple = 1, Orange = 3, Cherry = 10};
```

If we merely want to assign values in a sequence with some starting point, then we can use a shortcut. The statement

```
enum Year {freshman = 1, sophomore, junior, senior};
```

is short for

```
enum Year {freshman = 1, sophomore = 2, junior = 3, senior = 4};
```

A very useful enumerated type is

```
enum Boolean {FALSE, TRUE};
```

Once the enumerated type is declared, we can use it like any other type; for example:

```
CoinType change;
Fruit    favorite;
```

```
change = Nickel;
favorite = Cherry;
if (change - Penny > HalfDollar)
    cout << "You have 50 cents or more";
```

We can use an enumerated type to improve the readability of a program that uses an array. Consider the `temperature` array introduced at the very beginning of this chapter. We can write the code for computing the weekly average temperature with the enumerated type `Days` in the following manner:

```
enum Days {Sunday, Monday, Tuesday, Wednesday,
           Thursday, Friday, Saturday};
Days d;
float temperature[Saturday+1];  ◄────  This is equivalent to declaring
                                       float temperature[7];.
                                       Note that Saturday == 6.
sum = 0.0;
for (d = Sunday; d <= Saturday; d = d+1)
    sum = sum + temperature[d];
```

Notice how the enumerated type improves the readability of the code. The enumerated type, when used judiciously, can be very helpful in making programs more readable.

Enumerated values are used mainly to improve program readability; they cannot be used directly for input and output. The following is syntactically valid, but the output will be 3, not `Wednesday`.

```
enum Days {Sunday, Monday, Tuesday, Wednesday,
           Thursday, Friday, Saturday};

Days d = Wednesday;
cout << d;
```

Similarly, we may write

```
cin >> d;
```

in the program, but no value will be assigned to d. If the user enters 1, for example, it is equivalent to saying

```
d = 1;
```

which is not equivalent to

```
d = Monday;
```

In fact, this is an invalid statement because of a type mismatch. Entering the text *Monday* also does not work because of a type mismatch. Notice that if the assignment d = 1 is done within a program, it may work. Even so, the statement does not make logical sense, and therefore, it should be avoided. To be on the safe side, we should always perform an explicit type conversion to avoid type mismatches. An example follows:

```
cin >> i;
d = Day(i);
```

We end this section with syntax rules for the enumerated type.

type-declaration
    ...
        enum identifier {   enumerator-list }

enumerator-list
    enumerator
    enumerator , enumerator-list

enumerator
    identifier
    identifier =   constant-expression

13.7 Exercises

1 Show the output for each of the following code segments:

a.

```
int a[9], i;

for (i = 0; i < 9;  i = i+1)
a[i] = i * i;

for (i = 0; i < 5;  i = i+1)
cout << a[2*i] << endl;
```

b.

```
int a[9], i, temp;

for (i = 0; i < 9;  i = i+1)
a[i] = 2 * i;

for (i = 0; i < 5;  i = i+1) {
temp = a[i];
a[i] = a[8-i];
a[8-i] = temp;
}
for (i = 0; i < 9; i = i+1)
cout << a[i] << endl;
```

c.

```
int a[9], i;

for (i = 8; i >= 0; i = i-1)
a[i] = 9 - i;

for (i = 0; i < 9; i = i+2)
cout << a[i] << endl;
```

2 Write a program that computes the lowest, highest, and average temperatures for each week of the month. Assume the declaration

```
float temperature[32];  //position 0 is not used
```

with `temperature[1]` through `temperature[7]` representing the first week, `temperature[8]` through `temperature[14]` representing the second week, and so forth.

3 Extend the program of exercise 2 to compute the lowest, highest, and average temperatures for each week of the year. For this program assume 52 weeks with exactly seven days for each week. Do not use 52 `for` loops; use two nested `for` loops.

4 Improve the Grading3 program by making it compute the average scores not only for the students but also for each of the three midterms and for one final exam.

5 Add menus to the Grading3 program, using the menu choices of the Grading2 program from chapter 12.

6 Rewrite the Grading1 program in chapter 12 by using the standard `ostream` and `istream` objects `cout` and `cin`, instead of a `ScoresWindow`, for program display and user input. The original Grading1 program used a `ScoresWindow` object for user input, program display, and (primitive) data storage of entered data. With the `cout` and `cin` objects, we can only input and output data; we cannot use either of them for data storage. For this program, use an array of pointers to `Student` objects for data storage. Use one line for entering the student's name and the second line for entering the three midterm and the final exam scores.

7 Extend the program of exercise 6 to include the menu choices of the Grading2 program in chapter 12. The program must also use `cin` for accepting menu choice selections from the user. We have two ways to allow the user to select a menu choice. The first is to prompt the user with menu selections before accepting each new student's information. The outline of a control loop for input follows.

```
enum Choice = {EnterData = 1, HiFinal, LoFinal, Mid1Avg,
    Mid2Avg, Mid3Avg, Quit }
...
choice = prompt();
while (choice != Quit) {

    switch (choice)
        case EnterData: ...
            break;
        case HiFinal: ...
            break;
        case LoFinal: ...
            break;
        case Mid1Avg: ...
            break;
        case Mid2Avg: ...
            break;
        case Mid3Avg: ...
            break;
    }

    prompt();
}
```

The function `prompt` is defined as

```
Choice prompt()
{
    Enum Boolean {FALSE, TRUE};
    Boolean done = FALSE;
```

```
        Choice selection;

        cout << "Please make your selection by pressing" << endl;
        cout << "the number (1..7):" << endl << endl;

        do {
            cout << "1. Enter Data" << endl;
            cout << "2. Find the Highest Final" << endl;
            cout << "3. Find the Lowest Final" << endl;
            cout << "4. Find Midterm 1 Average" << endl;
            cout << "5. Find Midterm 2 Average" << endl;
            cout << "6. Find Midterm 3 Average" << endl;
            cout << "7. Quit program" << endl;

            cin >> selection;
            if (selection < EnterData or selection > Quit) {
                cout << "Error: You must select the number"<<endl;
                cout << "between 1 and 7" << endl << endl;
            }
            else
                done = TRUE;

        } while (not done);

        return selection;
    }
```

A second way to make a menu selection allows the user to enter a control code while data is being entered. The outline of a control loop for input folows.

```
    strcpy(str, readName());

    while (strcmp(str, "\Q") != 0 ){

        if (strcmp(str,"\M") == 0) {
            //prompt the user with menu choices
            //and execute the desired choice
        }
        else {
            //read the next line of data for the student's
            //midterms and final exam scores
        }

        strcpy(str, readName());
    }
```

Every time the program is ready to accept the name of a student, the user can enter the control strings "\Q" or "\M" instead. When the user requests the listing of menu choices, that is, enters "\M", a menu selection prompt, similar to the one given in

Exercise 7, is displayed. The user can request a menu selection prompt any time the program is ready to accept the name of a student. Once the name of a student is entered, the user must complete entering the student's exam scores. The program stops only when the user enters the control string "\Q".

Notice that, from the user's standpoint, the character user interface (CUI) is not as flexible and easy to use as the graphical user interface (GUI).

8 Random numbers are useful in many computer applications involving statistical distributions, probability, and so on. A random number is one drawn at random from a set of numbers such that each of the numbers has an equal probability of being drawn—similar to drawing names out of a hat. Various techniques exist for computing sequences of pseudorandom numbers, and some are better than others. By "better" we mean that the sequences are more random; that is, one cannot detect any bias toward certain numbers over others. Various statistical tests can determine whether a random number generating technique has bias. A simple intuitive test (the digit test) involves the counting of the digits in the different positions of the numbers. For example, if the random number generating technique generates integers in the range 0000–9999, then one might use the technique to generate a few thousand numbers and count the number of occurrences of each digit in each position (see below).

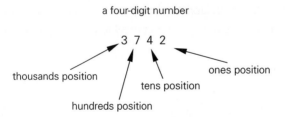

We would expect that if the numbers are truly random, each of the digits 1 through 9 would occur with about equal frequency in each of the four positions. That is, we would have about as many 1s in the thousands position as we would have 2s or 0s or 5s. And we would have about as many ones in the thousands position as we would have 1s (or any other digit) in the tens position or in the hundreds position or in the ones position.

Write a program to apply the digit test to a RandomNumSrc. Your program should draw 10,000 numbers in the range 0–9999 from a RandomNumSrc and count the number of occurrences of each digit in each position. After all the numbers have been drawn, your program should display a table showing the counts. The table might appear as follows:

	Position			
Digit	1	10	100	1000
0	981	958	978	1059
1	980	1018	990	985
2	1015	1020	958	958
3	982	1013	986	977
4	965	989	1011	1033
5	1021	1012	1001	1029
6	1046	980	1022	992
7	995	991	1088	1002
8	987	981	1005	987
9	1028	1038	961	978

9 Indicate which of the following are valid:

```
enum Fruit {apple = 6, banana = 0, peach = 3 };
enum Veggie {carrot, spinach};
int  X;
```

a.
```
Fruit like;
float favorite[7];
```

b.
```
for (like = banana; like <= apple; like = like+1)
     cin >> favorite[like];
```

c.
```
cout << favorite[apple] << endl;
cout << favorite[banana] << endl;
cout << favorite[peach] << endl;
```

d.
```
cout << apple + orange;
```

e.
```
if (carrot > apple) cout << "okay";
```

f.
```
X = carrot;
```

g.
```
X = apple + spinach;
```

10 Use `cout` to write a program that prints out a table of monthly average temperatures in a format similar to the following:

Month	Average temperature
January	40.3
February	43.9
March	50.3
April	54.7
May	54.8
June	60.9
July	75.4
August	78.3
September	70.6
October	58.8
November	56.6
December	45.2

The `temperature` array should be constructed as follows:

```
enum Month {January, February, March, April, May, June, July,
            August, September, October, November, December };

Month month;
float temperature[December+1];

for (month = January; month <= December ; month = month + 1)
    cin >> temperature[month];
```

Note: Enumerated values cannot be printed out directly.

11 Modify the `Plot` function of the `TwoDGraph` object introduced in Exercise 11.2. The modified `Plot` function accepts two arrays of `Point` objects: `startPts` and `endPts`. The function draws a line between `startPts[i]` and `endPts[i]` for i ranging from 0 to the size of the arrays. A `Point` object consists of the x and y coordinate values of a point in a two-dimensional graph.

chapter 14

Multidimensional arrays

Although one-dimensional arrays are suitable for many of our programming needs, they are not always adequate. In some situations we will need to use an array having multiple indices, or subscripts, called a *multidimensional array.* In this chapter, we will examine multidimensional arrays, specifically two- and three-dimensional arrays. You will rarely encounter a situation that requires an array having more than three indices.

14.1 Two-dimensional arrays

Let's start with a simple example of a two-dimensional array. Many different types of information can be expressed nicely in a tabular format using rows and columns. One example of tabular information that we encounter in elementary school is a multiplication table, shown in figure 14.1.

A two-dimensional array is an ideal structure for representing tabular data. Declaring a two-dimensional array is very much like declaring a one-dimensional array. The only difference is the additional indices we declare for the array, that is, a

Columns

	1	2	3	4	5	6	7	8	9
1	1	2	3	4	5	6	7	8	9
2	2	4	6	8	10	12	14	16	18
3	3	6	9	12	15	18	21	24	27
4	4	8	12	16	20	24	28	32	36
5	5	10	15	20	25	30	35	40	45
6	6	12	18	24	30	36	42	48	54
7	7	14	21	28	35	42	49	56	63
8	8	16	24	32	40	48	56	64	72
9	9	18	27	36	45	54	63	72	81

Rows

Figure 14.1 Multiplication table

two-dimensional array has two indices. For a multiplication table we can declare a two-dimensional array as:

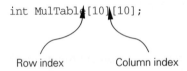

```
int MulTable[10][10];
```

Row index   Column index

We can put the products of two numbers into the table by executing

```
for (i = 1; i < 10; i = i+1)
    for (j = 1; j < 10; j = j+1)
        MulTable[i][j] = i * j;
```

The outer i-loop goes through the rows, and the inner j-loop goes through the columns. Since the column index is the inner loop, the table is filled with values in a row-by-row sequence, as shown below. The numbers in the table (see figure 14.2) show the order of filling.

A keen observer will have noticed that the preceding declaration will result in an extra row and column because array indices in C++ start from 0. However, we did not use (and did not show) row 0 and column 0 in the diagram. If we use a 9 × 9 array, say mult[9][9], then position [i][j] would store the value (i+1)*(j+1), not i*j. We therefore opted to declare a 10 × 10 array with the first column and row unused, to make the indexing simple in this example.

Columns

	1	2	3	4	5	6	7	8	9
1	1	2	3	4	5	6	7	8	9
2	10	11	12	13	14	15	16	17	18
3	19	20	21	22	23	24	25	26	27
4	28	29	30	31	32	33	34	35	36
5	37	38	39	40	41	42	43	44	45
6	46	47	48	49	50	51	52	53	54
7	55	56	57	58	59	60	61	62	63
8	64	65	66	67	68	69	70	71	72
9	73	74	75	76	77	78	79	80	81

(Rows)

Figure 14.2 Table filled in row-by-row sequence

Here's another two-dimensional array:

```
char  name[5][9];
```

Remember that a string is represented as a one-dimensional array of characters in C++. So a two-dimensional array of characters, such as the array name can be used to represent an array of strings. The array name looks like figure 14.3.

We can assign a string value to an individual row using the standard string functions. For example, executing the following statements

```
strcpy(name[0], "Debussy");
strcpy(name[1], "Mozart");
strcpy(name[2], "Verdi");
strcpy(name[3], "Copland");
strcpy(name[4], "Gershwin");
```

will result in figure 14.4.

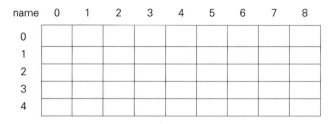

Figure 14.3 Two-dimensional name array

name	0	1	2	3	4	5	6	7	8
0	D	e	b	u	s	s	y	\0	
1	M	o	z	a	r	t	\0		
2	V	e	r	d	i	\0			
3	C	o	p	l	a	n	d	\0	
4	G	e	r	s	h	w	i	n	\0

Figure 14.4 String values assigned to individual rows

Since name is an array, we can manipulate characters individually. Executing

```
cout << name[0][0] << name[0][6] << name[3][3]
        << name[1][3] << name[4][7];
```

will output the screen shown in figure 14.5.

```
Dylan
```

Figure 14.5 Result of manipulating individual characters

Instead of using two-dimensional arrays for representing arrays of strings, we can use arrays of pointers to strings. The declaration

```
char *name[5]
```

declares a one-dimensional array of pointers to char. Since a pointer to char is another way of representing a string, the above is a more memory efficient alternative for representing an array of strings than using a two-dimensional array of characters. Contrast the following statements with the sequence of strcpy statements on the preceding page.

```
name[0] = new char[8];
strcpy(name[0], "Debussy");

name[1] = new char[7];
strcpy(name[1], "Mozart");

name[2] = new char[6];
strcpy(name[2], "Verdi");
```

```
name[3] = new char[8];
strcpy(name[3], "Copland");

name[4] = new char[9];
strcpy(name[4], "Gershwin");
```

Notice that the dynamic allocation of a one-dimensional array of characters is necessary because each `name[i]` is a pointer to a one-dimensional array of characters. The result of the preceding code is shown in the next diagram. In general, dynamic allocation will result in a more efficient usage of memory space than static allocation (i.e., memory space is allocated at the time of declaration). For this example, dynamic allocation does not save any space; in fact, it uses more memory space than declaring the two-dimensional array of characters. Remember that we also must include the number of bytes used for storing pointers in the calculation. Assuming the pointer takes 4 bytes of memory, the following array uses 58 bytes, whereas the `name` array, declared as a two-dimensional array of characters, uses only 45 bytes. In this case, the size of the array is small and all rows contain data. Consider, for example, a 20×8 character array in which only 5 rows are filled with data. The dynamic allocation approach would save space, as shown in figure 14.6.

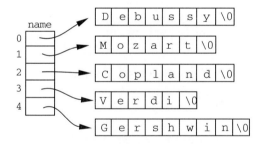

Figure 14.6 Dynamic allocation approach

The following is a sample two-dimensional array of objects. It represents a classroom arrangement of students organized into four rows of desks, with each row having five desks, for a total of twenty desks.

```
Student classroom[4][5];
```

Assuming the `Student` object has a public function `GetName` that returns its name, we can print the names of all students using

```
int row, col;
```

```
for (row = 0; row < 4; row = row+1)
    for (col = 0; col < 5; col = col+1)
        cout << classroom[row][col].GetName() << endl;
```

We end this section with a modified syntax category *size-declarator* to allow the declaration of multidimensional arrays.

size_declarator
> [*constant-expression*]
> [*constant-expression*] *size_declarator*

14.2 `for` *loops and arrays*

`for` loops are very effective in writing concise code for processing arrays. In this section we will present some examples of nested `for` loops manipulating two-dimensional arrays.

Let's use a 5 × 5 array (see figure 14.7) for this example.

In the following code fragments, we will assign numbers 0, 1, 2, ... to the array elements in the order in which they are filled. The numbers in the pictures show the order of filling.

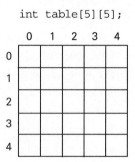

Figure 14.7 5x5 array

	0	1	2	3	4
0	1	2	3	4	5
1	6	7	8	9	10
2	11	12	13	14	15
3	16	17	18	19	20
4	21	22	23	24	25

```
cnt = 0;
for (i = 0; i < 5; i = i+1)
    for (j = 0; j < 5; j = j+1){
        cnt = cnt+1;
        table[i][j] = cnt;
    }
```

	0	1	2	3	4
0	1	6	11	16	21
1	2	7	12	17	22
2	3	8	13	18	23
3	4	9	14	19	24
4	5	10	15	20	25

```
cnt = 0;
for (j = 0; j < 5; j = i+1)
    for (i = 0; i < 5; i = i+1){
        cnt = cnt+1;
        table[i][j] = cnt;
    }
```

	0	1	2	3	4
0	1				10
1		2		9	
2			8 $\cancel{3}$		
3		7		4	
4	6				5

	0	1	2	3	4
0	1	2	3	4	5
1	16				6
2	15				7
3	14				8
4	13	12	11	10	9

```
cnt = 0;
for (i = 0; i < 5; i = i+1){
    cnt = cnt+1;
    table[i][i] = cnt;
}
for (i = 0; i < 5; i = i+1){
    cnt = cnt+1;
    table[i][4-i] = cnt;
}
```

```
cnt = 0;
for (j = 0; j < 5; j = j+1) {
    cnt = cnt +1;
    table[0][j] = cnt;
}
for (i = 1; i < 5; i = i+1) {
    cnt = cnt +1;
    table[i][4] = cnt;
}
for (j = 3; j >= 0; j = j-1) {
    cnt = cnt +1;
    table[4][j] = cnt;
}
for (i = 3; i >= 1; i = i-1) {
    cnt = cnt +1;
    table[i][0] = cnt;
}
```

14.3 Sample program: temperature

Suppose we wish to write a program to compute the average temperatures for each week of the month. We could write a program using a one-dimensional array (see exercise 2 in chapter 13), but a better approach uses a two-dimensional array in which columns represent the days of the week, and rows represent the weeks of the month (see table 14.1).

Table 14.1 Two-dimensional array for days of week and weeks of month

	Sun	Mon	Tue	Wed	Thu	Fri	Sat
wk1	0	0	0	62.0	64.2	64.1	70.5
wk2	65.0	64.4	61.2	60.4	60.9	65.9	65.9
wk3	68.3	66.2	63.0	67.8	67.3	67.3	66.9
wk4	69.9	70.1	72.0	71.5	70.8	70.5	72.0
wk5	70.0	70.3	69.8	69.3	66.9	69.7	0
wk6	0	0	0	0	0	0	0

The table is declared as

```
enum Day  {Sun, Mon, Tue, Wed, Thu, Fri, Sat};
enum Week {wk1, wk2, wk3, wk4, wk5, wk6};
const int EMPTY = 0;

float temperature[wk6+1][Sat+1];
```

The table can accommodate any month of the year. For this table the first of the month is Wednesday, and the thirty-first of the month is Friday. Let's start with an assumption that temperatures will never be 0, so that we can use the value EMPTY (0) to represent an empty entry. Assuming that the values are already entered into the table for all six weeks, we can compute the average temperature for each week by executing the following code:

```
float   avg[wk6+1];
int     cnt;
float   sum;
Week    week;
Day     day;

for (week = wk1; week <= wk6; week = week+1) {
    cnt = 0; sum = 0;

    for (day = Sun; day <= Sat; day = day+1) {
        if (temperature[week][day] != EMPTY) {
            sum = sum + temperature[week][day];
            cnt = cnt + 1;
        }
        avg[week] = sum / cnt;
    }
}
```

To display the daily temperatures and weekly averages (for all six weeks), we can write something like this:

```
cout << setiosflags(ios::fixed);
cout << setprecision(1); //one decimal place

cout << setw(6) << "Sun"
    << setw(6) << "Mon"
    << setw(6) << "Tue"
    << setw(6) << "Wed"
    << setw(6) << "Thu"
    << setw(6) << "Fri"
    << setw(6) << "Sat"
    << setw(6) << "Avg" << endl;
```

```
for (week = wk1; week <= wk6; week = week+1) {
    for (day = Sun; day <= Sat; day = day+1)
        if (temperature[week][day] == EMPTY)
            cout << setw(6) << " ";
        else
            cout << setw(6) << temperature[week][day];

    cout << setw(6) << avg[week] << endl;
}
```

The preceding code will do the job, but not efficiently. The `if` test inside the nested `for` loops introduces an element of inefficiency. Since an array element can either be EMPTY or contain the actual temperature, we must first test for the distinction. Testing inside the `for` loops is unavoidable if any array element can either be EMPTY or contain the actual temperature. However, for this example, the entries of EMPTY occur only at the beginning and at the end. We can avoid the costly `if` test by saving the indices for the first and last day of the month as

```
Day  startDay, endDay;
Week endWeek;
```

For the sample month shown in the preceding diagram, the values are

```
startDay = Wed;
endDay = Fri;
endWeek = wk5;
```

We do not need a variable `startWeek`, because the first week will always be `wk1`. The code for computing the weekly average temperatures can then be written as

```
//assume the starting and ending indices
//are already initialized

//process the first week
cnt = 0; sum = 0.0;
for (day = startDay; day <= Sat; day = day+1) {      First
    sum = sum + temperature[wk1][day];               week
    cnt = cnt + 1;
}
avg[wk1] = sum / cnt;

//process the middle weeks
for (week = wk2; week < endWeek; week = week+1){     Middle
    cnt = 0; sum = 0.0;                               weeks
    for (day = Sun; day <= Sat; day = day+1) {
```

```
        sum = sum + temperature[week][day];
        cnt = cnt + 1;
    }
    avg[week] = sum / cnt;
}

//process the last week
cnt = 0; sum = 0.0;
for (day = Sun; day <= endDay; day = day+1){
    sum = sum + temperature[endWeek][day];
    cnt = cnt + 1;
}
avg[endWeek] = sum / cnt;
```

┌──────────┐
│   Last   │
│   week   │
└──────────┘

We have now avoided costly testing inside the nested loops. In addition, we do not need the constant EMPTY to mark the empty entries; we now know precisely where the actual temperatures occur in the table, since we have saved the indices for the first and last days of the month.

**Program
Guideline**   Avoid testing inside loops if at all possible.

We now design the input routine to complete the program. We use the standard istream object cin for our input routine. We require the user to enter the day of the week for the first day of the month and the number of days in the month. Here's the input routine:

```
cout << "Which day is the first of the month?" << endl;
do {
    cout << "Sun - 0; Mon - 1; Tue - 2" << endl;
    cout << "Wed - 3; Thu - 4; Fri - 5, Sat - 6" << endl;

    cin >> i;
} while (i < 0 || i > 6);

startDay = Day(i);

cout << "How many days are in the month?" << endl;
do {
    cout >> "Enter 28, 29, 30, or 31: ";
    cin >> numOfDays;
} while (numOfDays < 28 || numOfDays > 31);
```

┌───┐
│ Type conversion from int to enum Day.   │
│ Some compilers may let you specify this   │
│ statement as   │
│   startDay = i;   │
└───┘

CHAPTER 14   MULTIDIMENSIONAL ARRAYS

```
week = wk1;
day  = startDay;
cnt = 1;

do {
    do {
        cout << "Temperature for Day #" << cnt << ": ";
        cin >> temperature[week][day];

        day = (day + 1) % 7;
        cnt = cnt + 1;
    } while (day != Sun && cnt <= numOfDays);

    week = week + 1;
} while (cnt <= numOfDays);

endWeek = week - 1;  //incremented one more than necessary
endDay  = day - 1;   //in the above loop, so adjust them here
```

The indices for the last day, endWeek and endDay, are adjusted at the end. We can also use modulo arithmetic to compute the values for these indices, as shown here:

```
incr = (numOfDays - 1) / 7;
endDay = (startDay + incr) % 7;              //modulo operation
endWeek= (startDay + numOfDays - 1) / 7;
```

You can determine that the formulas work correctly later, in exercise 7. We now have all the necessary pieces, and we could complete our program by putting the code segments together and using global variables. Instead, we will complete the program in a rudimentary object-oriented style and wait until the next chatper to discuss further enhancement to it.

First we design a MonthTemp object to encapsulate the functionalities of inputting daily temperatures for a month, computing the weekly average temperatures, and printing out the average temperatures. Its interface and implementation are as follows:

"MonthTmp.h"

```
#include <iostream.h>
#include <iomanip.h>
#include <string.h>

enum Day  {Sun, Mon, Tue, Wed, Thu, Fri, Sat};
enum Week {wk1, wk2, wk3, wk4, wk5, wk6};

class MonthTemp {
```

```
public:
      MonthTemp();
      void ComputeAvg();
      void GetData();
      void PrintResult();
      void SetName(char *str);

private:
      char name[12]; //month name
      float temperature[wk6+1][Sat+1];
      float avg[wk6+1];
      const int EMPTY;

      Day   startDay, endDay;
      Week endWeek;
};
```

```
MonthTemp::MonthTemp():EMPTY(0)
{
      Week week;
      Day  day;
      for (week = wk1; week <= wk6; week = week+1)
            for (day = Sun; day <= Sat; day = day+1)
                  temperature[week][day] = EMPTY;
}

void MonthTemp::ComputeAvg()
{
      int     cnt;
      float sum;
      Day     day;
      Week    week;

      //process the first week
      cnt = 0; sum = 0.0;
      for (day = startDay; day <= Sat; day = day+1) {
            sum = sum + temperature[wk1][day];
            cnt = cnt + 1;
      }
      avg[wk1] = sum / cnt;

      //process the middle weeks
      //process the middle weeks
      for (week = wk2; week < endWeek; week = week+1) {
            cnt = 0; sum = 0.0;
            for (day = Sun; day <= Sat; day = day+1) {
                  sum = sum + temperature[week][day];
                  cnt = cnt + 1;
            }
            avg[week] = sum / cnt;
      }

      //process the last week
      cnt = 0; sum = 0.0;
      for (day = Sun; day <= endDay; day = day+1) {
            sum = sum + temperature[endWeek][day];
            cnt = cnt + 1;
```

```
      }
      avg[endWeek] = sum / cnt;
}
#include "MonthTmp.h"

void MonthTemp::GetData()
{
      Week week;
      Day  day;
      int i, cnt, numOfDays;

      cout << "Which day is the first of the month?" << endl;
      do {
          cout << "Sun - 0; Mon - 1; Tue - 2" << endl;
          cout << "Wed - 3; Thu - 4; Fri - 5, Sat - 6" << endl;

          cin >> i;
      } while (i < 0 || i > 6);

      startDay = Day(i);

      cout << "How many days are in the month?" << endl;
      do {
          cout >> "Enter 28, 29, 30, or 31: ";
          cin >> numOfDays;
      } while (numOfDays < 28 || numOfDays > 31);

      week = wk1;
      day  = startDay;
      cnt = 1;

      do {
          do {
              cout << "Day #" << cnt << ": ";
              cin >> temperature[week][day];

              day = (day + 1) % 7;
              cnt = cnt + 1;
          } while (day != Sun && cnt < numOfDays);

          week = week + 1;
      } while (cnt < numOfDays);

      endWeek = week - 1;
      endDay  = day - 1;
}

void MonthTemp::PrintResult()
{
      Week week;
      Day  day;

      cout << setiosflags(ios::fixed);
      cout << setprecision(1); //one decimal place

      cout << setw(10) << " "
                       << name << endl << endl;  //month name

      cout      << setw(6) << "Sun"
                << setw(6) << "Mon"
                << setw(6) << "Tue"
                << setw(6) << "Wed"
                << setw(6) << "Thu"
                << setw(6) << "Fri"
                << setw(6) << "Sat"
                << setw(6) << "Avg" << endl;
```

```
    for (week = wk1; week <= endWeek; week = week+1) {
        for (day = Sun; day <= Sat; day = day+1)
            if (temperature[week][day] == EMPTY)
                cout << setw(6) << " ";
            else
                cout << setw(6) << temperature[week][day];

        cout << setw(6) << avg[week] << endl;
    }
}

void MonthTemp::SetName(char *str)
{
    strcpy(name, str);
}
```

With the MonthTemp object defined, our main program can be written as follows:

```
//Program Temperature:  A program to compute the weekly average
//                      temperatures for a given month.

#include "MonthTmp.h"

void main ()
{
    MonthTemp month;

    month.SetName("July");   //for the month of July
    month.GetData();
    month.ComputeAvg();
    month.PrintResult();
}
```

Because we have a MonthTemp object, we can easily extend the program to handle more than one month. For example, to process two months we declare two MonthTemp objects.

```
#include "MonthTmp.h"

void main ()
{
    MonthTemp  month1, month2;

    month1.GetData();
    month2.GetData();
    ...
}
```

The temperature program can be extended even further to accommodate a whole year by declaring an array of MonthTemp objects as

```
enum Month {Jan, Feb, Mar, Apr, May, Jun,
            Jul, Aug, Sep, Oct, Nov, Dec };

MonthTemp year[Dec+1];
```

14.4 Three-dimensional arrays

We visualize a three-dimensional array as a series of two-dimensional arrays placed in layers, as shown in figure 14.8. The index for the layer number may appear anywhere, and it is up to the programmer to decide where to put it. In the following example we will place the layer number as the first index (see figure 14.9).

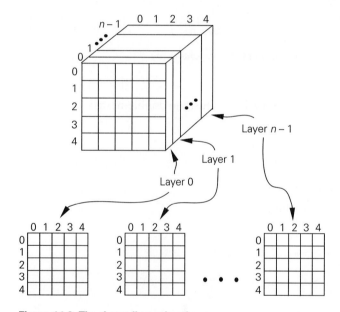

Figure 14.8 The three-dimensional array

Double-nested for loops are used to access the array elements. Assuming the following declaration:

```
int ThreeD[20][5][5]
```

the following code will compute the sum of all elements.

```
int layer, row, col;
int sum = 0;

for (layer = 0; layer < 20; layer = layer+1)
    for (row = 0; row < 5; row = row+1)
        for (col = 0; col < 5; col = col + 1)
            sum = sum + ThreeD[layer][row][col];
```

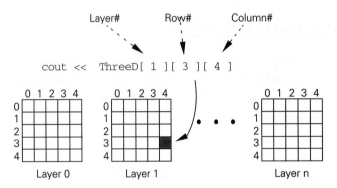

Figure 14.9 How the indexing works for the three-dimensional array

Let's use the 3× 3× 3 array in figure 14.10 to illustrate double-nested for loops.

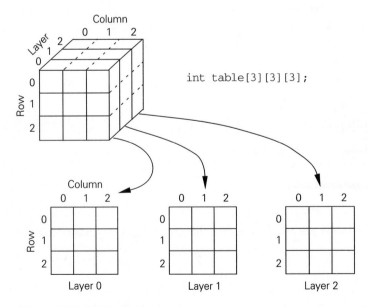

Figure 14.10 3x3x3 array

The following code fragments illustrate the order of visiting array elements. We will identify the order of visiting by displaying the numbers that are assigned to the array elements. We will assign numbers 0, 1, 2, ... to the array elements in the order in which they are visited.

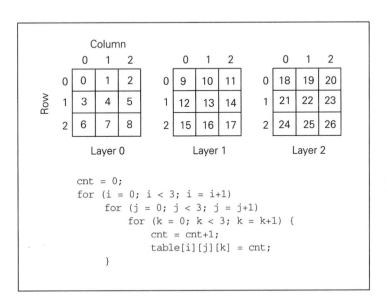

```
cnt = 0;
for (i = 0; i < 3; i = i+1)
    for (j = 0; j < 3; j = j+1)
        for (k = 0; k < 3; k = k+1) {
            cnt = cnt+1;
            table[i][j][k] = cnt;
        }
```

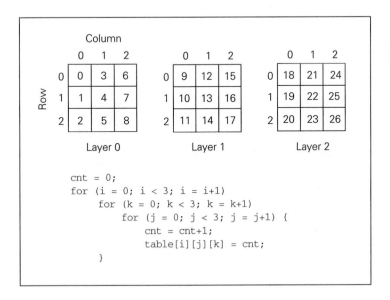

```
cnt = 0;
for (i = 0; i < 3; i = i+1)
    for (k = 0; k < 3; k = k+1)
        for (j = 0; j < 3; j = j+1) {
            cnt = cnt+1;
            table[i][j][k] = cnt;
        }
```

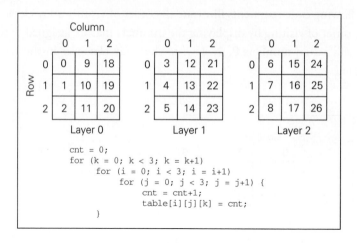

```
cnt = 0;
for (k = 0; k < 3; k = k+1)
    for (i = 0; i < 3; i = i+1)
        for (j = 0; j < 3; j = j+1) {
            cnt = cnt+1;
            table[i][j][k] = cnt;
        }
```

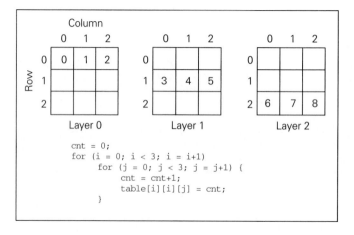

```
cnt = 0;
for (i = 0; i < 3; i = i+1)
    for (j = 0; j < 3; j = j+1) {
        cnt = cnt+1;
        table[i][i][j] = cnt;
    }
```

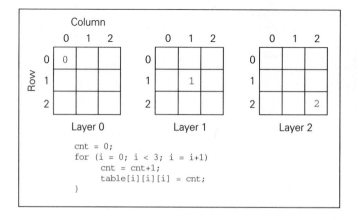

```
cnt = 0;
for (i = 0; i < 3; i = i+1)
    cnt = cnt+1;
    table[i][i][i] = cnt;
}
```

14.5 Passing multidimensional arrays to functions

Passing multidimensional arrays to functions is similar to passing one-dimensional arrays, but with a restriction. We use the pass-by-pointer method to pass multidimensional arrays, but we must specify the size of the indices, except the first index, in the function prototype. Let's look at an example. The following function receives a two-dimensional array and returns its sum.

```
float twoDsum(float num[][10], int rowsize)
{
    float sum = 0.0;
    int i, j;

    for (i = 0; i < rowsize; i = i+1)
        for (j = 0; j < 10; j = j+1)
            sum = sum + num[i][j];

    return sum;
}
```

The size for the second index is declared explicitly as 10. Therefore, we could pass two-dimensional arrays having any number of rows, but the number of columns must be 10. The following calls are all valid:

```
float array1[20][10];
float array2[50][10];
float array3[160][10];
. . .
cout << twoDsum(array1, 20);
cout << twoDsum(array2, 50);
cout << twoDsum(array3, 160);
```

For three-dimensional arrays, the function parameter must indicate the sizes of the second and third indices explicitly. The following function computes the sum of a three-dimensional array.

```
float threeDsum(float num[][10][10], int rowsize)
{
    float sum = 0.0;
    int i, j, k;

    for (i = 0; i < rowsize; i = i+1)
```

```
        for (j = 0; j < 10; j = j+1)
            for (k = 0; k < 10; k = k+1)
            sum = sum + num[i][j][k];

    return sum;
}
```

When we design object-oriented programs, we will most likely make an array part of an object as its data member. Since this object is the one responsible for maintaining the array and contains all necessary functions for maintenance, we do not need to pass the array to another object's function. We will show an example of this design in the next section. We rarely pass multidimensional arrays as arguments to functions in object-oriented programs.

14.6 Sample program: Crypt-Tester

We will use a three-dimensional array to write a simple encryption/decryption program. The idea behind encryption and decryption is to communicate messages without allowing unintended parties to read them. One way to achieve this secrecy is to use a transposition cipher in which the characters of the original message are reordered by the sender using a cipher to create an encrypted message. The receiver of this encrypted message can decrypt it to retrieve the original text by using the same cipher. A three-dimensional array can be used for this purpose. Keep in mind that the algorithm in this program is very primitive, and the code is not that difficult to crack. We need to use a far more advanced technique for practical applications.

We declare a three-dimensional character array as

```
char codeTable[ 3 ][ 4 ][ 4 ]
```

The size of the array is small for the sake of simplicity. The message is placed in the array layer by layer, and within each layer, row by row. For example, the message SARU-MANS FORCES DEFEATED BY HUORNS AT HELMS DEEP is placed in the array as shown in figure 14.11.

Then, for transmission, we extract the characters in the following order:

```
Column 0 of layer 2
Column 0 of layer 1
Column 0 of layer 0

Column 1 of layer 2
Column 1 of layer 1
Column 1 of layer 0
```

```
and so forth.
```

Within each column, we extract characters in ascending order by row number, that is, 0, 1, 2, and 3. The order of extraction will produce the following encrypted message:

```
NTLDDA HSM CS MEETBUAAFE HSEFEYORNOSAE PED RUSR
```

To decrypt the message at the receiving end, we read the characters into the array in the order they were extracted before transmission, as shown above, and extract them in row-by-row order, the way they were originally placed in the array. In other words, we reverse the process of encryption.

	0	1	2	3
0	S	A	R	U
1	M	A	N	S
2		F	O	R
3	C	E	S	

Layer 0

	0	1	2	3
0	D	E	F	E
1	A	T	E	D
2		B	Y	
3	H	U	O	R

Layer 1

	0	1	2	3
0	N	S		A
1	T		H	E
2	L	M	S	
3	D	E	E	P

Layer 2

Figure 14.11 Placement of message in array

Let's write a program that will use this method to encrypt and decrypt a message. We first define an object called `Crypter` to handle the encryption and decryption processes. This object manages the `codeTable` array. Its interface is

"Crypter.h"

```
#include <string.h>

class Crypter {
public:
      char *Encrypt(char *text);
      char *Decrypt(char *text);

private:
      char codeTable[3][4][4];
};
```

The function `Encrypt` receives the original (plain) text and returns the encrypted, or ciphered, text. The other function, `Decrypt`, receives the encrypted text and returns the original text. The implementation of `Crypter` is as follows:

```
#include "Crypter.h"

char *Crypter::Encrypt(char *text)
{
      char *str;
      int i, layer, row, col;
      str = new char[80];

      for (i=0; i< 80; i = i+1) str[i] = ' '; //blank out
      strcpy(str,text); //length of text must be less than 81
      str[strlen(text)] = ' '; //remove the terminator

      //put text into codeTable
      i = 0;
      for (layer = 0; layer < 3; layer = layer+1)
          for (row = 0; row < 4; row = row+1)
              for (col = 0; col < 4; col = col+1) {
                  codeTable[layer][row][col] = str[i];
                  i = i+1;
              }

      //extract text from codeTable in the encrypted format
      i = 0;
      for (col = 0; col < 4; col = col+1)
          for (layer = 2; layer >=0; layer = layer-1)
              for (row = 0; row < 4; row = row+1) {
                  str[i] = codeTable[layer][row][col];
                  i = i+1;
              }

      str[i] = '\0'; //terminate the string
      return str;
}

char *Crypter::Decrypt(char *text)
{
      char *str;
      int i, layer, row, col;

      str = new char[80];
      for (i=0; i< 80; i = i+1) str[i] = ' '; //blank out
      strcpy(str,text); //length of text must be less than 81
      str[strlen(text)] = ' '; //remove the terminator

      //put the (encrypted) text into codeTable
      i = 0;
      for (col = 0; col < 4; col = col+1)
          for (layer = 2; layer >=0; layer = layer-1)
              for (row = 0; row < 4; row = row+1) {
                  codeTable[layer][row][col] = str[i];
                  i = i+1;
              }

      //extract text from codeTable in the original,
      //decrypted format
      i = 0;
      for (layer = 0; layer < 3; layer = layer+1)
          for (row = 0; row < 4; row = row+1)
              for (col = 0; col < 4; col = col+1) {
                  str[i] = codeTable[layer][row][col];
                  i = i+1;
              }

      str[i] = '\0'; //terminate the string
      return str;
}
```

If you look closely at the preceding two functions, you will notice that the ordering of the two `for` loops is reversed, in the `Decrypt` function.

The functions work properly as long as the number of characters in the text is smaller than the size of the `codeTable` array, which is 48 ($3 \times 4 \times 4$). Thus, any text having 48 characters or less can be processed. In case the text has fewer than 48 characters, we must make sure not to insert the NULL terminator `'\0'` of the text into the `codeTable` array. If we do, then the resulting string would be chopped off, since no characters beyond the NULL terminator would be processed by standard string functions such as `strcpy`. Also, when the text size is smaller than the array size, we must fill the remaining array elements with blank spaces (otherwise, the array will have "garbage" characters). For these reasons, we place the following code before the two `for` loops.

```
for (i=0; i< 80; i = i+1) str[i] = ' '; //blank out
strcpy(str,text);
str[strlen(text)] = ' '; //remove the terminator
```

The `Crypter` object can be modified to handle text of any length without necessarily increasing the size of the `codeTable` array. See exercise 10 at the end of this chapter.

A very simple main program to test the `Crypter` object is as follows:

```
//Program Crypt-Tester:  A program to test the
//                       correctness of a Crypter.

#include "Crypter.h"
#include "GUIObj.h"

void main()
{
    OKBox    result;
    Crypter  encoder;
    char     text[80], cipherText[80];

    strcpy(text,
          "SARUMANS FORCES DEFEATED BY HUORNS AT HELMS DEEP");

    strcpy(cipherText, encoder.Encrypt(text));
    result.Display(cipherText);

    strcpy(text, encoder.Decrypt(cipherText));
    result.Display(text);
}
```

The program is purely for testing purposes. We will develop a full-fledged encryption program using a `Crypter` and GUI objects in the next chapter.

14.7 Exercises

1 What is the difference between a one-dimensional array of arrays and a two-dimensional array? Will they be declared differently?

2 The following code fragments assign numbers 0, 1, 2, ... to the elements of the 5 ×5 array shown below. Show the results of executing the code fragments by writing the numbers assigned to each array element.

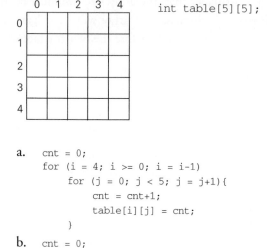

```
int table[5][5];
```

a.
```
cnt = 0;
for (i = 4; i >= 0; i = i-1)
    for (j = 0; j < 5; j = j+1){
        cnt = cnt+1;
        table[i][j] = cnt;
    }
```

b.
```
cnt = 0;
for (i = 4; i >= 0; i = i-1)
    for (j = 4; j >= 0; j = j-1){
        cnt = cnt+1;
        table[i][j] = cnt;
    }
```

c.
```
cnt = 0;
for (j = 4; j >= 0; j = j-1)
    for (i = 0; i < 5; i = i+1){
        cnt = cnt+1;
        table[i][j] = cnt;
    }
```

d.
```
cnt = 0;
for (j = 4; j >= 0; j = j-1)
    for (i = 4; i >= 0; i = i-1){
        cnt = cnt+1;
        table[i][j] = cnt;
    }
```

3 Modify the Temperature program from section 14.3 to use a descendant of Edit-Win for the program interface, instead of cin and cout. Program the OK and

Cancel buttons to input the daily temperatures, and to output the weekly average temperatures.

4 Extend the Temperature program from section 14.3. Instead of keeping a record of only one temperature per day, keep two temperatures per day—the low and high temperatures. Compute the weekly average temperatures for the low and high temperatures. Write the extended program using the same two-dimensional array structure as in the original Temperature program, but define an array element to be a Day object, which contains the low and high temperatures of the day.

5 Repeat the previous exercise using a three-dimensional array having two layers, the first layer for low temperatures and the second layer for high temperatures.

6 Compare the approaches used in exercises 4 and 5. Which approach is more amenable to further extension? Extend both versions of the modified program by including a record of humidity for each day. Which version is easier to extend? Why?

7 The GetData function of the MonthTemp object derives the indices for the last day, endDay, and the last week, endWeek, by adjusting them in the loop. Instead, they can be computed as

```
incr = (numOfDays - 1) / 7;
endDay = (startDay + incr) % 7; //modulo operation
endWeek= (startDay + numOfDays - 1) /7;
```

Explain how these formulas work.

8 A magic square is an arrangement of numbers in the form of an $N \times N$ array in which the sums of every row, every column, and each of the two principal diagonals are equal. For example, the following is a 4×4 magic square.

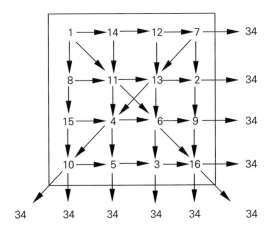

Write a program that accepts a 4 × 4 array and tests it to see if it is a magic square. Extend the program to accept an array of any size up to 10 × 10.

9 The following code fragments assign the numbers 0, 1, 2, ... to the array elements of the 3 × 3 × 3 array shown below. Show the results of executing the following code fragments by writing the numbers assigned to the array elements.

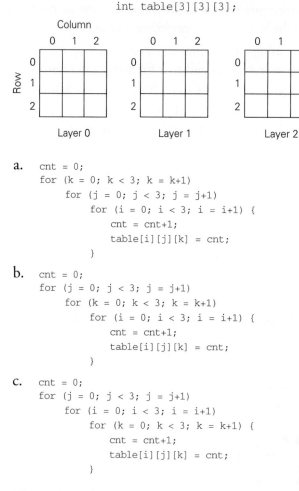

```
int table[3][3][3];
```

a.
```
cnt = 0;
for (k = 0; k < 3; k = k+1)
    for (j = 0; j < 3; j = j+1)
        for (i = 0; i < 3; i = i+1) {
            cnt = cnt+1;
            table[i][j][k] = cnt;
        }
```

b.
```
cnt = 0;
for (j = 0; j < 3; j = j+1)
    for (k = 0; k < 3; k = k+1)
        for (i = 0; i < 3; i = i+1) {
            cnt = cnt+1;
            table[i][j][k] = cnt;
        }
```

c.
```
cnt = 0;
for (j = 0; j < 3; j = j+1)
    for (i = 0; i < 3; i = i+1)
        for (k = 0; k < 3; k = k+1) {
            cnt = cnt+1;
            table[i][j][k] = cnt;
        }
```

10 The Crypter object designed in section 14.6 can handle up to 48 characters. Modify the Crypter so it can handle text of any length. When the text has more than 48 characters, repeat the encryption/decryption algorithm in a series of 48-character blocks. For example, if the text has 150 characters, then repeat the algorithm four times: for the first 48 characters, the second 48 characters, the third 48 characters, and the last 6 characters. Every time the algorithm is repeated, append the output

to the partially built encrypted/decrypted string. Return this string when the repeated execution of the algorithm is completed.

11 You are the undersecretary of secrecy for Mordor. Since your code has been compromised by the fall of Isengard and the loss of the palantir, the dark lord has commanded you to create a simple, new code and a fast procedure for encoding and decoding. You decide to use the following transposition rule:

- Each encoded message will be preceded by four integers:

  N— the number of letters in each rearrangement unit.
  R— the number of rows in the rearrangement array.
  C— the number of columns in the rearrangement array.
  D— a code for indicating the rearrangement order.

- The decoding procedure uses the above numbers as follows:

  1. The message is broken down into units of N letters each.
  2. An array of R rows and C columns is formed.
  3. The units of the message are taken one at a time from the beginning to the end of the message, and placed in the array row-by-row and element-by-element.
  4. The decoded message is formed by extracting the units from the array in the order indicated by D and concatenating them together. If $D = 1$, this order is column-by-column. If $D = 2$, this order is last column to first column and, for each column, reverse row order.

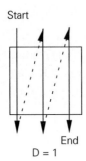

D = 1

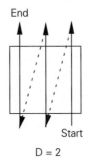

D = 2

Use this decoding procedure to decode the following message:

2 3 5 2 IND CR HNADUSEE ULE ANOSAVZGTH

1. Divide the message into units of two letters each ($N = 2$).

IN|D |CR| H|NA|DU|SE|E |UL|E |AN|OS|AV|ZG|TH

2 and 3. Place the units in a 3 × 5 array ($R = 3$ and $C = 5$)

IN	D	CR	H	NA
DU	SE	E	UL	E
AN	OS	AV	ZG	TH

4. Extract the units from the array in the order shown for *D = 2,* and concatenate them together.

```
THE NAZGUL HAVE CROSSED ANDUIN
```

Write a program to read encoded messages, decode them, and display them. You can implement the table for this program either as a two-dimensional array of strings or as a three-dimensional array of characters.

12 Define a new `Crypter` object that uses the Caesar cipher technique. With this technique, each character of the original text is replaced by the character *P* positions away. For example, if *P* = 2, then we have the following:

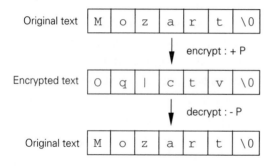

Encryption is done by first converting a character to its ASCII code, adding P to that number, and then converting it back to a character. Logically, the formula is

```
char(int(ch) + P)
```

for encryption and

```
char(int(ch) - P)
```

for decryption. Only the printable characters are processed (ASCII codes 32 to 126). Be sure to wrap around the character correctly. For example:

```
125 + 2
```

should not be `127`, but should wrap around to `32`. Use modulo arithmetic.

chapter 15

Object-oriented program construction

As an illustration of two- and three-dimensional arrays, we designed `Crypter` and `MonthTemp` objects in the previous chapter and wrote very simple test programs. The purpose of the test programs is strictly to show how the functions of `Crypter` and `MonthTemp` are used. In this chapter, we will design a more realistic program using a `Crypter` object. Designing a more practical program that uses a `MonthTemp` object is left as an exercise (exercise 4 at the end of this chapter). Up until now, all of our sample programs have contained a very small number of objects because they were developed mainly for the purpose of illustrating fundamental programming concepts. However, as we move toward developing more useful and practical programs, we will be required to use a large number of different types of objects. With an increase in the number of objects, a guideline for designing objects and composing programs from these objects becomes important. We will describe object-oriented program composition in this chapter.

When constructing a program that utilizes many different types of objects, it is helpful to categorize them into four groups based on the roles they play within the program. Objects are categorized broadly into user interface, control, storage, and application logic.

A *user interface object* manages the interaction between the user and the program. A *control object* assumes the supervisory role of managing other objects in the program. A small program may have only one control object, but a larger program can contain a collection of control objects. A *storage object* handles the storing and retrieving of data. Finally, an *application logic object* captures (or models) the logic of an application. We will present sample objects for the user interface, control, and application logic categories in the next section, and we will describe the storage object in the next chapter.

Keep in mind that these categories are not iron-clad; that is, we do not have to assign every object to one of the four categories. The categories are an informal guideline to aid programmers in constructing an object-oriented program. Deriving an object that does not fall neatly into any one of the categories does not automatically mean that our object design is poor. However, if an object does not fit into any category, the object design probably is faulty. For example, if we have an object that serves the roles of both user interface and application logic, this object is likely to be over-worked, or overloaded. An object with multiple roles is much harder to reuse, and therefore, should be avoided. We will discuss more design considerations in chapter 17. For now, we will show you how to construct a sample encryption/decryption program in which every object serves a single, well-defined role.

15.1 Sample program: Encryption

We begin the design of our sample Encryption program by identifying the objects it uses. An application logic object for the program is the Crypter object designed in the previous chapter. This Crypter object manages the logic of encryption and decryption.

Next, we need a user interface object to handle the input and output of the plain and encrypted messages. We will use a descendant of an EditWin object for this purpose. We shall name this object Interfacer. Since it is a descendant of an EditWin, it will contain the OK and Cancel buttons. For this program the buttons will be labeled Encrypt and Decrypt. The user will type in the text and press the Encrypt button to encode and the Decrypt button to decode. The Interfacer object we define here is used strictly for interacting with users, that is, getting the text for encryption and decryption and displaying the resulting encrypted and decrypted text.

Any object we design should serve a single, well-defined role. Following this rule will enable us to easily reuse existing objects for new programs and to modify existing programs by interchanging objects.

Finally, we need a control object to supervise the Crypter and the Interfacer, a new object called Controller. Controller is one of two control objects in the program. As a design alternative, we could make one of the control objects a supervisor of the other. For example, instead of having a separate control object Controller, we could make the Interfacer control the Crypter. However, this design would overload the Interfacer, since it would be performing the roles of both control and user interface. As stated earlier, such an overloaded object is very hard to manage and use, and therefore should be avoided. The second control object for this program is a MessageHandler. We need a MessageHandler for controlling GUI objects.

Once the participating objects are identified, we must specify how these objects are interrelated in the program, that is, who sends messages to whom in the program. The structure is typical of a program that is designed by the four-category guideline. The main function calls the Controller object's function to start the program. The Controller, in turn, calls the functions of its subordinate objects (Interfacer, Crypter, and MessageHandler) at various points in time. Finally, some of the subordinate objects call the Controller object's functions in response to some events. In this program, Interfacer is the only subordinate object that calls the Controller object's function. The object diagram in figure 15.1 shows the relationships.

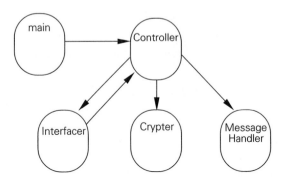

Figure 15.1 Encryption program object diagram

In the remainder of this section, we will describe the participating objects in a top-down fashion, starting with the main function. A Controller serves the role of a supervisor of other objects; therefore, all we have to do inside the main function is to declare and initiate this Controller object, as shown below:

```
//Program Encryption:   A program that encrypts text and
//                      decrypts encoded text.
```

```
#include "Cntlr.h"

void main()
{
    Controller controller;
    controller.Start();
}
```

The Controller object is defined as

```
#include "Crypter.h"
#include "Intfcr.h"

class Controller {
public:
    Controller();

    void Encrypt(char *text);
    void Decrypt(char *text);
    void Start();

private:
    Crypter             crypter;
    Interfacer          interfacer;
    MessageHandler      messageHandler;
};
```

As you can see from the object diagram, the Controller object calls the functions of the three subordinate objects: Crypter, Interfacer, and MessageHandler. The Controller maintains three private data members, crypter, interfacer, and messageHandler, for keeping track of these subordinates.

One constructor function is defined for the Controller:

```
void Controller::Controller()
{
    interfacer.Init(50, 50, 600, 300);
    interfacer.SetOkLabel("Encrypt");
    interfacer.SetCancelLabel("Decrypt");

    interfacer.SetOwner(this);
}
```

The first statement initializes and displays the Interfacer object. The next two statements change the names of its buttons to Encrypt and Decrypt, from the default OK and Cancel. The last statement links the two objects Controller and Interfacer. The Controller object has a data member interfacer that refers to its subordinate Interfacer object. We also need a reference from interfacer back to controller, so that this `Interfacer` object knows which `Controller` object to inform when its buttons are clicked. We will describe the last statement in more detail when we discuss the `Interfacer` object later in this section.

The `Encrypt` function of the `Controller` receives the plain text from the `Interfacer` object, commands the `Crypter` object to encrypt the text, and finally directs the `Interfacer` to display the resulting ciphered text:

```
void Controller::Encrypt(char *text)
{
    char encryptedText[80];
    strcpy(encryptedText, crypter.Encrypt(text));
    interfacer.Display(encrpytedText);
}
```

The `Decrypt` function of the `Controller` is structurally identical to the `Encrypt` function. The only difference is that `Decrypt` calls the `Crypter` object's `Decrypt` function, instead of `Encrypt`:

```
void Controller::Decrypt(char *text)
{
    char originalText[80];
    strcpy(originalText, crypter.Decrpt(text));
    interfacer.Display(originalText);
}
```

Let's move on to the `Interfacer` object. Its definition is

"Intfcr.h"

```
#include "GUIObj.h"

class Controller; //forward reference

class Interfacer: public EditWin {
public:
    void Ok();
    void Cancel();
    void Display(char *text);
    void SetOwner(Controller *c);
private:
    Controller *owner;
};
```

The forward reference is necessary for this declaration. Forward reference is explained in section 15.2.

The `Interfacer` object has a data member, `owner`, which is a pointer to the supervisor `Controller` object. The function `setOwner` receives the `Controller` object and assigns it to the data member `owner` as

```
void Interfacer::SetOwner(Controller *c)
{
    owner = c;
}
```

Using this setup, the `Interfacer` object knows with which `Controller` object to communicate in the event of a button click. Since the `Interfacer` object is a descendant of an `EditWin`, the `Ok` and `Cancel` functions are called when the OK and Cancel buttons are clicked. When the OK button having the label Encrypt is clicked, `interfacer` passes all of the text typed in by the user to its supervisor `Controller` object `owner` for encryption. Thus, the `Ok` function is implemented as

```
void Interfacer::Ok()
{
    owner->Encrypt(ReadAll());
}
```

The `Cancel` function is implemented analogously:

```
void Interfacer::Cancel()
{
    owner->Decrypt(ReadAll());
}
```

As stated earlier, we link the two objects by placing the statement that calls the `Interfacer` object's `SetOwner` function in the `Controller` object's constructor function.

```
void Controller::Controller()
{
    interfacer.Init(50, 50, 600, 300);
    interfacer.SetOkLabel("Encrypt");
    interfacer.SetCancelLabel("Decrypt");

    interfacer.SetOwner(this);     ◄──  This function links two
                                        objects for allowing
                                        mutual reference.

}
```

This design results in a situation where the two objects will have mutual references, as shown in figure 15.2.

The statement

```
interfacer.SetOwner(this);
```

is equivalent to saying

```
My subordinate Interfacer object interfacer, I am your owner
Controller.
```

The *I* in the preceding statement refers to the object that is issuing the statement, that is, the object with a function containing the statement. In C++ we use a reserved word called this in lieu of *I*. The reserved word this is a pointer to an object; it is called a *self-referencing pointer* because it points to itself. The object diagram in figure 15.3 illustrates the effect of executing the preceding C++ statement.

Be aware that we cannot implement the function as

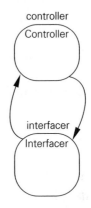

Figure 15.2 Objects have mutual references

```
void Interfacer::Ok()
{
    Controller boss;
    boss.Encrypt(ReadAll());
}
```

This would result in two Controller objects, which does not make sense for this program (see figure 15.4). There should be only one Controller object, not two, in the program.

Finally, the Interfacer object will display the text, plain or ciphered, using its Display function. Its implementation is

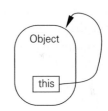

Figure 15.3 The reserved word this refers to itself

```
void Interfacer::Display(char *text)
{
    Clear();
    Insert(0,0, text);
}
```

The Display function is called from the Controller object's Encrypt and Decrypt functions.

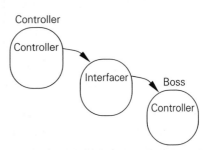

Figure 15.4 Two Controller objects

15.2 Forward reference and include files

As the number of different types of objects used in programs increases, we must pay closer attention to managing various files that contain object definitions (.h files) and implementations (.cpp files). We will use the sample program from the previous section to explain two additional problems involved in compiling and running programs composed of multiple source files.

The first involves the need for a *forward reference declaration* when two objects refer to each other. Consider the relationship between the `Controller` and `Interfacer` objects of our sample program. Each has a data member referring to the other. This is represented in diagram form in figure 15.5.

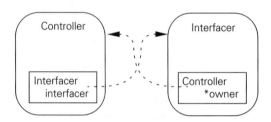

Figure 15.5 Two objects referring to each other

When this type of mutual referencing occurs, the two declarations become cyclic. Remember that when you declare a variable or a data member to be of a certain type (either a primitive data type or an object), the type must already be defined. For example, consider the following two cases, one valid and the other not.

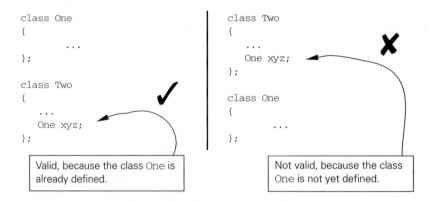

The rule is very simple: the type you declare for a variable or a data member must be defined prior to the declaration. Normally, there is no problem in satisfying this rule, but consider the following cases:

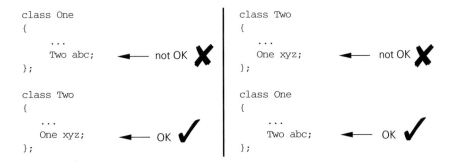

No matter the order in which you declare One and Two, you cannot avoid violating the preceding rule. This type of mutual referencing occurs in object-oriented programming when two objects call each other's functions, as with the Controller and Interfacer. In C++ we use a forward reference declaration to avoid this violation. The forward reference declaration allows us to name the class before actually defining it. For example, to declare mutual referencing One and Two, we can use a forward reference declaration, such as

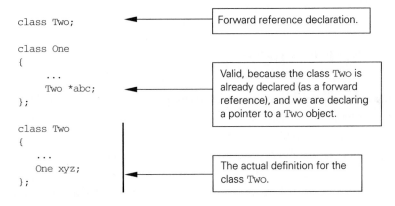

Notice that the declaration

```
Two *abc;
```

inside the class One is a pointer to Two; that is, abc is a pointer to a Two object. The declaration

```
Two abc;
```

would be wrong because, at the point this declaration is made, the class Two is not yet fully defined. Until an object has been fully defined, you can declare only a pointer to it.

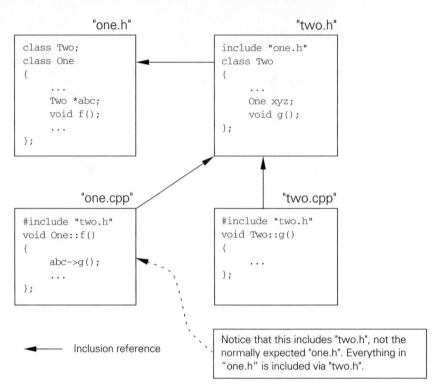

Figure 15.6 Code separated into .h and .cpp files

The preceding code will work just fine if everything is done within a single file. Since we divide class interfaces and implementations into individual files, let's separate the code properly into .h and .cpp files (see figure 15.6).

Notice how the include statements are arranged. The statement in "one.cpp" includes "two.h", not "one.h". Including "one.h" will not work, because then any reference to the Two object, such as abc->g(), cannot be resolved. Just having a forward reference declaration in the "one.h" file is not enough. The forward reference is only a temporary measure to allow the declaration involving the Two object (e.g., Two *abc;) in the "one.h" file. It does not, however, actually define the object. So without including "two.h", the compiler cannot determine, for example, whether or not the function g is defined for the Two object.

The second problem involves the need to avoid including the same header files multiple times. Consider the erroneous situation shown in figure 15.7.

If you do not manage include statements carefully, you could end up trying to define the same thing more than once, which is not allowed. In the example above, because of the two include statements in the "five.h" file, the compiler will try to

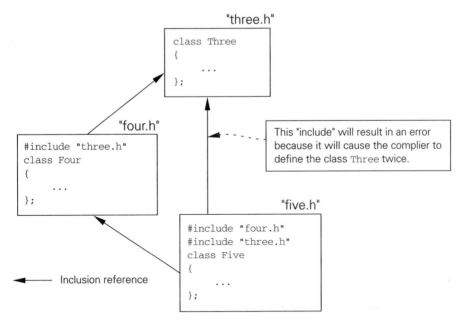

"three.h"

```
class Three
{
    . . .
};
```

"four.h"

```
#include "three.h"
class Four
{
    . . .
};
```

This "include" will result in an error because it will cause the complier to define the class Three twice.

"five.h"

```
#include "four.h"
#include "three.h"
class Five
{
    . . .
};
```

◄——— Inclusion reference

Figure 15.7 Erroneous include statement in "five.h"

include the definition of the class Three twice, which is an error. One obvious way to correct the problem is to remove the offending statement

```
#include "three.h"
```

from the "five.h" file. But such an approach works only for simple cases. If you are dealing with ten, fifteen, or more files, some written by other programmers, it becomes quite difficult to find all of the offending include statements. A better way to avoid multiple inclusion of a file is to use the #ifndef compiler directive (see figure 15.8).

By surrounding an entire file with

```
#ifndef <symbol>
#define <symbol>
. . .
#endif
```

the file will be included only once. After the file is included for the first time, the <symbol> becomes defined, and any subsequent attempt to include the file will fail. By adding this three-statement directive to all .h files, we don't have to worry about the problem of multiple inclusion.

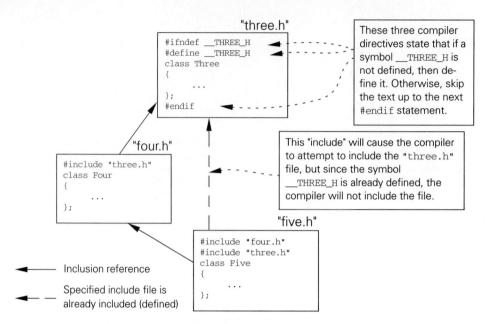

Figure 15.8 The use of #ifndef compiler directive to avoid multiple inclusion of a file

Let's summarize. We can easily avoid potential inclusion problems by adhering to the following rules:

1 Include the following compiler directive in all `.h` files.

```
#ifndef <symbol>
#define <symbol>

...

#endif
```

2 Include the matching `.h file` in all `.cpp` files. In other words, an implementation file XXX.cpp will have the include statement

```
#include "XXX.h"
```

3 Include the `.h` file of the ZZZ object in the YYY.cpp file if the interface file YYY.h contains a forward reference declaration

```
class ZZZ;
```

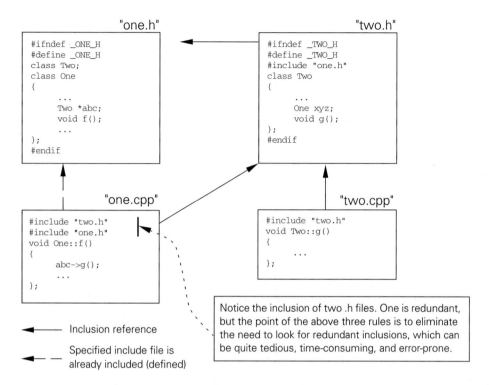

Figure 15.9 Code without inclusion problems

Using these rules, the earlier example now looks like figure 15.9.

We now list the files for the complete Encryption program.

"Cntlr.h"

```
#ifndef __CNTLR_H
#define __CNTLR_H
#include "Crypter.h"
#include "Intfcr.h"

class Controller {
public:
    Controller();

    void Encrypt(char *text);
    void Decrypt(char *text);
    void Start();

private:
    Crypter          crypter;
    Interfacer       interfacer;
    MessageHandler   messageHandler;
};

#endif
```

```
#include "Cntlr.h"

Controller::Controller()
{
      interfacer.Init(50,50,600,300);
      interfacer.SetOkLabel("Encrypt");
      interfacer.SetCancelLabel("Decrypt");
      interfacer.SetOwner(this);
}

void Controller::Start()
{
      messageHandler.Start();
}

void Controller::Encrypt(char *text)
{
      char encryptedText[80];
      strcpy(encryptedText, crypter.Encrypt(text));
      interfacer.Display(encryptedText);
}

void Controller::Decrypt(char *text)
{
      char originalText[80];
      strcpy(originalText, crypter.Decrypt(text));
      interfacer.Display(originalText);
}
```

```
#ifndef __INTFCR_H
#define __INTFCR_H

#include "GUIObj.h"
class Controller; //forward reference

class Interfacer: public EditWin {
public:
      void Ok();
      void Cancel();
      void Display(char *text);
      void SetOwner(Controller *c);

private:
      Controller *owner;
};

#endif
```

```
#include "Cntlr.h"
#include "Intfcr.h"

void Interfacer::SetOwner(Controller *c)
{
      owner = c;
}
```

```
void Interfacer::Ok()
{
     owner->Encrypt(ReadAll());
}

void Interfacer::Cancel()
{
     owner->Decrypt(ReadAll());
}

void Interfacer::Display(char *text)
{
     Clear();
     Insert(0,0,text);
}
```

"Encrypt.cpp"

```
//Program Encryption: Encrypt the text and decrypt
//                          the encoded text.

#include "Cntlr.h"

void main()
{
     Controller controller;
     controller.Start();
}
```

Figure 15.10 shows the inclusion relationships.

15.3 Object reusability and program extensibility

Modular program construction facilitates extension and modification. When a program is constructed from a set of well-defined modules, it can be modified or extended by replacing existing modules with new modules. The new modules may modify or extend the functionality of the replaced modules or better perform the same function (see figure 15.11).

Modules also facilitate faster program development. A new program can be constructed from existing modules, instead of writing the complete program from scratch, as shown in figure 15.12.

Effective modular program construction, of course, hinges upon the availability of well-defined modules. When a desired module is not available or when the available modules are poorly designed, we cannot realize the benefits of modular program construction. How do we make well-designed modules?

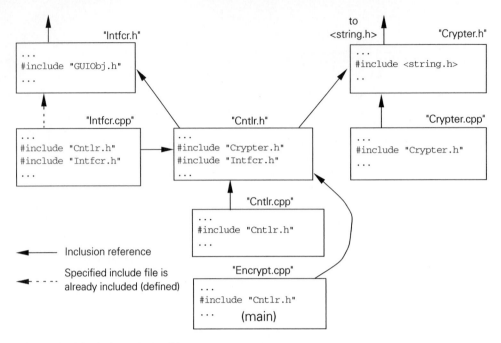

Figure 15.10 Inclusion relationships

In object-oriented programs, an object serves the role of a module. Keep in mind that objects are not the necessary condition for modular program construction. A module can be realized in different ways, and the object-oriented approach is just one way for achieving modular program construction. However, it is a very promising approach since an object fits the role of a module perfectly.

When we equate an object with a module the question, How do we make well-designed modules?" becomes "How do we make well-designed objects?" "While a thorough discussion of object-oriented design is beyond the scope of this book, we can examine some fundamental ideas here.

One key design principle is to design an object so that it has a single, well-defined task. A program task can be categorized into one of the four types: control, application logic, user interface, and storage. We studied these categories earlier. An object in a given category performs the corresponding task of that category. For example, a control object performs the task of controlling and managing other objects in the program. In the Encryption program, a `Controller` is the control object. For a simple program we may need only one control object, but for a more complex program, we may have to use a hierarchy of control objects, similar to using a hierarchy of managers in a corporation. A user interface object performs the task of interacting with users. In the Encryption

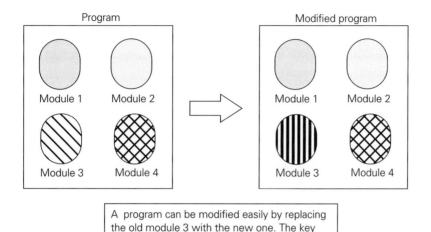

Program

Modified program

Module 1   Module 2

Module 1   Module 2

Module 3   Module 4

Module 3   Module 4

A program can be modified easily by replacing
the old module 3 with the new one. The key
point is that the other modules are unaffected.

Figure 15.11 Modular program construction allows easier modification

program, an `Interfacer` is the user interface object. An application logic object performs the task of modeling the logic of an application. In the Encryption program, a `Crypter` is the application logic object. A storage object performs the task of managing data. We have not seen any storage objects yet, but we will design one in the next chapter.

If an object violates the single-task design principle; that is, if it carries out more than one task, then most likely it is ill formed.[*] For example, the `ScoresWindow` in chapter 12 performs everything from input/output to the computation of averages. In other

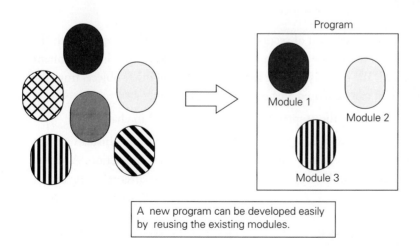

Program

Module 1

Module 2

Module 3

A new program can be developed easily
by reusing the existing modules.

Figure 15.12 Reuse of existing modules

words, it performs the tasks of user interface and application logic. This design may be acceptable for a very small program, but such an all-purpose object is not suitable for a large program. When an object is very specific to a particular program, its chances of being reused are slim. Also, modification of the object becomes more laborious. Even if we need to modify only a very small aspect of an object, we still have to review and understand the whole object before making any changes. Without knowing the totality of the object, we may not be aware that changing change a single line of code will affect other parts of it.

We could have built the encryption program in this chapter by defining a `CodeWindow` object that does all of the tasks, much like the `ScoreWindow` of Chapter 12. Instead, we built the program from a set of objects—one control object, one application logic object, and one user interface object. Because the objects are well-defined, we will be able to modify or extend them. For example, we could modify the program to do the input and output differently by modifying or replacing the user interface object `Interfacer` only, without affecting other objects. We will discuss object-oriented design more in chapter 17.

15.4 Exercises

1 Modify the Encryption program of section 15.1 by replacing the `Crypter` with the new crypter designed in exercise 11 in chapter 14. As long as the public component of the new crypter is the same as the one for the `Crypter`, all other objects from the Encryption program can be reused without any modification.

2 Redo Exercise 1, but using the crypter designed in exercise 12 in chapter 14.

3 Modify the Encryption program by replacing the `Interfacer`. Instead of the `Interfacer`, use the `MenuHandler` and `Menu` objects for user interaction. Add two menu choices: Encrypt and Decrypt. The user enters the text after selecting one of

---

* In principle, an ill-formed object could be performing only a portion of a single task, but the most frequent trait of an ill-formed object is that it performs more than one task.

the two menu choices. Use a `StringTypeIn` object to accept the text from the user. The result of the selected operation is displayed by an `OKBox`. Because the logic of the program is still handled by the `Crypter` and we are changing only the user interface of the program, the `Crypter` object should remain the same.

4 Rewrite the Temperature program of section 14.3 by replacing the `MonthTemp` object. The `MonthTemp` object is ill-formed, because it performs multiple tasks. Replace it with multiple objects that adhere to the single-task design principle presented in this chapter.

5 Write a program that maintains a to-do list. The list consists of entries, and each entry contains an entry number, description, priority, and type. The entry number is an integer ranging from 0 to 999. The priority for an entry designates the urgency of the task, which ranges from zero (not urgent) to five (highly urgent). The type for an entry describes the classification of the task, which can be personal, school work, or club activity. Allow users to enter and delete entries, display the entries by priority or by type, and search for an entry by its entry number.

6 Write a program that allows children to practice arithmetic. The program has four menu choices: Addition, Subtraction, Multiplication, and Division. When one of the choices is selected by the user, the program begins to list ten problems, one at the time.

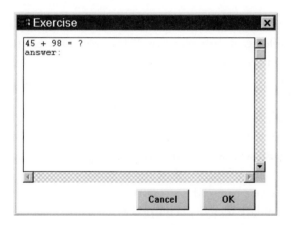

After the user enters the answer and clicks the OK button, the program checks the answer and keeps a tally. When all ten problems are answered, the program displays the number of correct answers. Use the random number generator defined in `util.h` for generating the problems. For the user interface, define a descendant of an `EditWin`.

7 Modify the program created in the previous exercise by using `cin` and `cout` for the user interface. Which objects need to be replaced? Which objects are reusable?

chapter 16

Files

In chapter 1, we briefly explained that a typical computer has two kinds of memory—volatile main memory and nonvolatile secondary memory. When you turn off the power to a computer, the contents of its volatile memory are lost. The contents of its nonvolatile memory, however, are not lost. The most common nonvolatile secondary memory in use today are disks, both hard and floppy types. Secondary memory is also known as *external memory*, and data are stored in secondary memory as *external files*, or more simply, as *files*.

The data manipulated by a program will be lost whenever the program terminates if they are kept in the main memory. Therefore, we must use secondary memory for data storage if we want to save the data we create with a program. Our sample programs so far have not stored any data in secondary memory. This decision may be acceptable for simple programs, but not for more serious, practical programs. Imagine a word processor that does not allow you to save a document. In this chapter we will discuss how to read data from and write data to external files. We will limit our discussion to one of the most basic and versatile types of file, a *text file*, where data are stored in the industry standard ASCII format.

16.1 Writing data to text files

As an example of output to a text file, we will write a program to compute a table showing how $1,000 invested at 5 percent interest grows over ten years when the interest is compounded annually. You can easily extend the program to accept different values for the principal, interest rate, and terms of maturation. We will concentrate on the new topic on hand, that is, how to write data to a text file. The table we output will have a line for each year showing the principal at the beginning of the year, the amount of interest earned during the year, and the principal at the end of the year. Our table will be written to a text file named `"compint.txt"`. Although not required, a common practice is to use the suffix `txt` to denote a file that contains ASCII text data.

> **Note** Appending the suffix `.txt` to the filename is a convention applicable to DOS–based platforms only. For other operating systems, this convention does not apply.

The program is quite short, thanks to the predefined object `fstream`. We can treat an `fstream` object very much like the standard `ostream` (and `istream`) objects `cout` (and `cin`), which means we can use the operators `<<` and `>>` for the `fstream` object. To output the sum of integer variables `x` and `y` to the standard `ostream` object `cout`, for example, we say

```
cout << x + y;
```

To write the same data to the `fstream` object `outFile`, we first execute the code shown in figure 16.1.

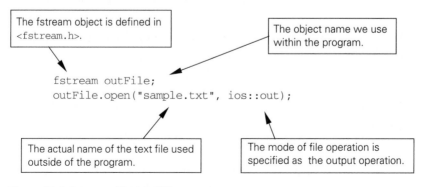

Figure 16.1 fstream object outFile

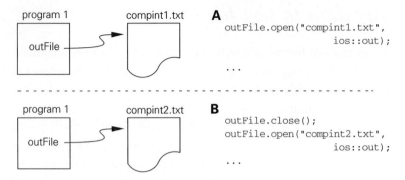

A

```
outFile.open("compint1.txt",
                    ios::out);

...
```

B

```
outFile.close();
outFile.open("compint2.txt",
                    ios::out);

...
```

Figure 16.2 The program accessing two files

to declare outFile as an fstream object and open it (prepare it for use) by calling its open function. Unlike ostream and istream, the fstream object is not predeclared, so we must declare it. In the function call open, we pass two arguments: the name of the

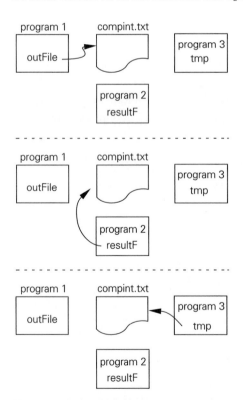

Figure 16.3 Three programs accessing the same file (at different times, not simultaneously)

external file and the mode of access. An external filename is the actual name of an text file, and we must pass it as a string. The access mode specifies the direction of data movement. In this example (figure 16.2) we are writing data to a file, which is an output operation; therefore, the mode of access is ios::out. We will introduce different access modes later in this chapter.

Many beginners are confused about the need for two names—the object name and the external filename—for accessing a single file. This requirement is a matter of necessity and flexibility. We must have two names because the syntax rules for names are different for C++ and the operating system. For example, in one operating system you may include a single dot as a part of the filename (e.g., "compint.txt"), but in C++ you cannot have a dot within a variable name. To compensate for the differences, we create a variable (for the object name) and associate it with the actual filename.

Using two names also allows flexibility. With this arrangement one program can access multiple files (at different times, not simultaneously) using a single `fstream` object. The diagram in figure 16.2 illustrates a program accessing two files, `compint1.txt` and `compint2.txt`. When code A is executed, `outFile` refers to `compint1.txt`, and when code B is executed, `outFile` refers to `compint2.txt`.

Also, this arrangement allows multiple programs to access the same file (again, at different times, not simultaneously).[*] The diagram in figure 16.3 illustrates three programs accessing the same file, `compint.txt`.

Each program is free to choose its own internal object name with which to access the file. Since you can choose whatever name is appropriate for your program, you don't have to worry about a potential naming conflict, for example, using a filename already used as a variable for another purpose.

Once the `fstream` object `outFile` is declared properly, we need only to say

```
outFile << x + y;
```

which has exactly the same syntax as writing to the standard `ostream` object `cout`. After all output is done, we close the file by calling its `close` function:

```
outFile.close();
```

Now we are ready to write the compound interest program:

```
//Program CompoundInterest:   A program to compute the worth of
//                            a principal with rate R
//                            compounded annually for N years.

#include <fstream.h>
#include <iostream.h>

void getInput(float &principal, float &rate, int &numOfyears)
{
    cout << "Interest Computation Program" << endl << endl;
    cout << "This program computes how much your" << endl;
    cout << "principal will worth in N years with" << endl;
    cout << "rate R compounded annually." << endl << endl;

    cout << "Principal (float): " << endl;
```

---

[*] Multiple programs can access the same file simultaneously if they all have read access only. It is also possible to develop a more elaborate file-accessing scheme that allows simultaneous read and write accesses to a single file from multiple programs.

```
    cin  >> principal;

    cout << "Interest Rate - R (float): " << endl;
    cin  >> rate;

    cout << "Number of Years - N (int): " << endl;
    cin  >> numOfyears;

}

void main()
{
    fstream outFile;
    const char tab = '\t';
    const char newline = '\n';
    int i, numOfyears;
    float rate, principal, newPrincipal, currentInterest;

    outFile.open("compint.txt", ios::out);

    getInput(principal, rate, numOfyears);

    for (i = 0; i < numOfyears; i = i+1) {

        currentInterest = rate * principal; //annual interest
        newPrincipal= principal + currentInterest;
                //add it to principal
        outFile << tab << principal << tab << currentInterest
                << tab << newPrincipal << newline;

        principal = newPrincipal;
    }

    outFile.close();
    cout << "Computation is done." << endl;
    cout << "Result is saved in 'compint.txt' " << endl;
}
```

Notice that we are writing numerical values to the text file. Just as it does with other stream objects, C++ automatically performs the conversion: we do not have to worry about it. We can output any primitive data (char, int, float, pointers, etc.) to an fstream object by using the operator <<, which is another very nice feature.

After the program has executed, you can open the file to see the result by using any text editor (including your compiler's) or word processor. When the file is opened, it should resemble the screen in figure 16.4.

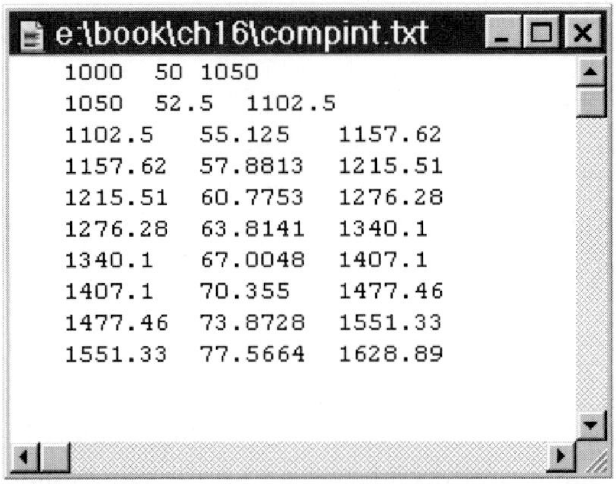

```
e:\book\ch16\compint.txt
1000   50 1050
1050   52.5  1102.5
1102.5    55.125    1157.62
1157.62   57.8813   1215.51
1215.51   60.7753   1276.28
1276.28   63.8141   1340.1
1340.1    67.0048   1407.1
1407.1    70.355    1477.46
1477.46   73.8728   1551.33
1551.33   77.5664   1628.89
```

Input:
principal — 1000.00
rate — 0.05
number of years —
10

Figure 16.4 The content of compint.txt after the program is executed

Although the answer is correct, the numbers are not aligned neatly into three columns. We could use the standard formatting operators available in <iomanip.h>, as we did with the cout and cin. The following modified program formats the output properly.

```cpp
//Program CompoundInterest2:  A program to compute the worth of
//                            a principal with rate R
//                            compounded annually for N years.

#include <fstream.h>
#include <iomanip.h>
#include <iostream.h>

void getInput(float &principal, float &rate, int &numOfyears)
{
    //same as before
}
void main()
{
    fstream outFile;
    int i, numOfyears;
    float rate, principal, newPrincipal, currentInterest;

    outFile.open("compint.txt", ios::out);
    outFile.setf(ios::fixed, ios::floatfield);

    getInput(principal, rate, numOfyears);

    for (i = 0; i < numOfyears; i = i+1) {

        currentInterest = rate * principal; //annual interest
        newPrincipal= principal + currentInterest;
                                //add it to principal
        outFile  << setw(10) << setprecision(2)  << principal
```

```
                 << setw(10) << setprecision(2)  << curInt
                 << setw(10) << setprecision(2)  << newPrin
                 << endl;

            principal = newPrincipal;
        }

        outFile.close();
        cout << "Computation is done." << endl;
        cout << "Result is saved in 'compint.txt' " << endl;
}
```

The function setw determines how many positions (spaces) the value printed following it will occupy. Here, we are allocating 10 positions for each of three values. The function setprecision determines the number of decimal places for the value following it. The output from CompoundInterest2 is shown in figure 16.5.

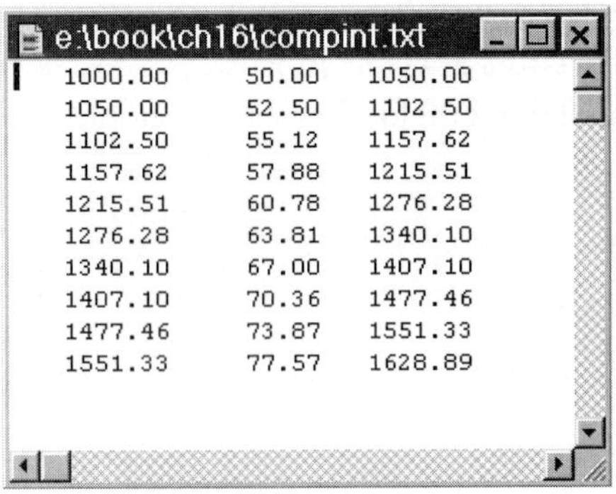


```
1000.00     50.00   1050.00
1050.00     52.50   1102.50
1102.50     55.12   1157.62
1157.62     57.88   1215.51
1215.51     60.78   1276.28
1276.28     63.81   1340.10
1340.10     67.00   1407.10
1407.10     70.36   1477.46
1477.46     73.87   1551.33
1551.33     77.57   1628.89
```

Figure 16.6 Output from CompoundInterest2

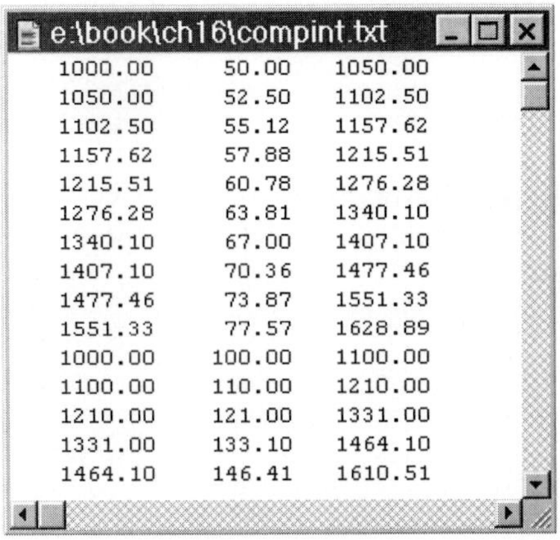


```
1000.00     50.00   1050.00
1050.00     52.50   1102.50
1102.50     55.12   1157.62
1157.62     57.88   1215.51
1215.51     60.78   1276.28
1276.28     63.81   1340.10
1340.10     67.00   1407.10
1407.10     70.36   1477.46
1477.46     73.87   1551.33
1551.33     77.57   1628.89
1000.00    100.00   1100.00
1100.00    110.00   1210.00
1210.00    121.00   1331.00
1331.00    133.10   1464.10
1464.10    146.41   1610.51
```

Figure 16.5 Expected output after running the CompoundInterest2 program again with additional input values

Now let's say we want to append additional values to the table, this time using 10 percent interest for five years. Do you think we will get the result in figure 16.6 by running the `CompoundInterest2` program again, using the input values `1000.00`, `0.10`, and `15`?

The answer is no. We will end up with the output shown in figure 16.7 instead.

```
e:\book\ch16\compint.txt
   1000.00      100.00     1100.00
   1100.00      110.00     1210.00
   1210.00      121.00     1331.00
   1331.00      133.10     1464.10
   1464.10      146.41     1610.51
```

Figure 16.7 Actual output after running the CompoundInterest2 program again with additional input values

The original file `"compint.txt"` is erased and a new text file is created having the same name. In other words, the `ios::out` mode has the effect of erasing the previous contents of the file. To append data to the end of file without erasing the previous data, we open the file using `ios::app` mode. We must change one more statement, as shown below, to get the desired result:

```
outFile.open("compint.txt", ios::app);
```

16.2 Reading data from text files

Reading data from a text file is just as easy as writing data to a text file. Let's read the table from the file `"compint.txt"`. For the following discussion, let's assume that we have a table of 5 percent interest on a $1,000 principal compounded annually for 10 years. Let's say that we wish to read back the table and compute the total interest. We will compute the sum by adding yearly interest, that is, the sum of the second column. We could also compute it by reading the final amount and subtracting the initial principal from it. Here's how we read the numbers back and compute the sum of yearly interest:

```
//Program ReadInterest:  A program to read values from the
//                       second column of a table generated by
//                       the program CompoundInterest and then
```

```
//                          compute the total interest.

#include <fstream.h>
#include <iostream.h>

void main()
{
    fstream inFile;
    int i, numOfyears;
    float rate, principal, newPrincipal,
          currentInterest, totalInterest;

    inFile.open("compint.txt", ios::in);

    numOfyears = 10; //10 lines in the file
    totalInterest = 0.0;

    for (i = 0; i < numOfyears; i = i+1) {

        inFile >> principal
               >> currrentInterest
               >> newPrincipal;

        totalInterest = totalInterest + currentInterest;
    }

    cout << "Total Interest: " << totalInterest;

    inFile.close();
}
```

We open the file in input mode (ios::in) and read data using the stream input operator >>. Because of the automatic conversion of ASCII data to the C++ primitive data type float, we simply specify the number of variables to be read for each line as

```
inFile >> principal >> currectInterest >> newPrincipal;
```

In this program, we assumed there are 10 lines to read, but this approach is not very practical. A more practical programming technique is to include the number of lines to be processed at the beginning of a file. The program can then be modified as follows:

```
...
inFile >> numOfyears;
for (i = 0; i < numOfyears; i = i+1)
...
```

Another approach is to use standard functions for checking file conditions. We can check for several conditions while we process an external file. One of the most frequently used functions is eof, which checks for the end-of-file condition. When we use the eof condition, we do not have to know the number of lines to be processed. We just keep on reading until we reach the end of the file. The ReadInterest program can be rewritten, using the eof function, as

```
//Program ReadInterest2:   A program to read values from the
//                         second column of table generated by
//                         the program CompoundInterest and then
//                         compute the total interest.
//
//                         Read data from the file
//                         until the eof is encountered.

#include <fstream.h>
#include <iostream.h>

void main()
{
    fstream inFile;
    int i;
    float rate, principal, newPrincipal,
            currentInterest, totalInterest;

    inFile.open("compint.txt", ios::in);

    totalInt = 0.0;
    inFile >> principal              //need to read the first
            >> currentInterest       //line before checking eof
            >> newPrincipal;

                                    ┌──────────────────────────────┐
                                    │ eof becomes TRUE when the     │
    while ( !inFile.eof()) {  ◄─────│ end of a file is encountered. │
                                    └──────────────────────────────┘
        totalInterest = totalInterest + currentInterest;
        inFile >> principal
                >> currentInterest
                >> newPrincipal;
    }

    cout << "Total Interest: " << totalInterest;

    inFile.close();
}
```

Here's one more example of reading in data from an external text file and writing data to an external file. This time we read characters from a text file and count the number of times each letter of the alphabet occurs:

```
//Program LetterCount:   Count the number of times each letter
//                       of the alphabet occurs in the file
```

```cpp
#include <fstream.h>
#include <string.h>
#include "GUIObj.h"

void main()
{
    fstream        inFile, outFile;
    StringTypeIn   inpBox;
    OKBox          msgBox;
    char           filename[80];
    char           letter;
    int            i, idx, base, last, count[26];

    //open the input file with read access
    strcpy(filename, inpBox.GetString("Specify Input File", "Name:"));

    inFile.open(filename,ios::in);
    while (inFile.fail()) {
      msgBox.Display("Invalid filename. Please try again.");
      strcpy(filename, inpBox.GetString("Specify Input File", "Name:"));

      inFile.open(filename,ios::in);
    }

    //open the output file with write access
    strcpy(filename, inpBox.GetString("Specify Output File", "Name:"));

    outFile.open(filename,ios::out);
    while (outFile.fail()) {
      msgBox.Display("Invalid filename. Please try again.");
      strcpy(filename,inpBox.GetString("Specify Output File", "Name:"));

      outFile.open(filename,ios::out);
    }

    //read in data and count
    base = int('A');
    while (inFile >> letter)
        if (isalpha(letter)) {
            letter = toupper(letter);
            idx = int(letter) - base;
            count[idx] = count[idx] + 1;
        }

    //save the result
    last = int('Z');
    for (i = base; i<= last; i = i+1)
        outFile << char(i) << '\t' << count[i-base] << endl;

    inFile.close();
    outFile.close();
}
```

The program first opens the input file. It uses a `StringTypeIn` object to get the filename from the user. After it receives the filename, the program attempts to associate the internal `fstream` object `inFile` with the given filename by executing the open function. If it is successful, then the execution of the program continues. The open functions, however, could fail for various reasons. One of the most common reasons is that the filename given by the user is wrong (e.g., misspelled). The first `while` statement checks for this condition with the expression

```
inFile.fail()
```

which returns TRUE (1) to signify a failure. The repetition continues as long as there is a failure. After the input file is opened, the program repeats the same procedure for the output file.

After the input and output files are properly opened, we begin reading characters one at a time from the input file. If the character is a letter in the alphabet, we convert it to its corresponding uppercase letter and increment the corresponding counter (see figure 16.8).

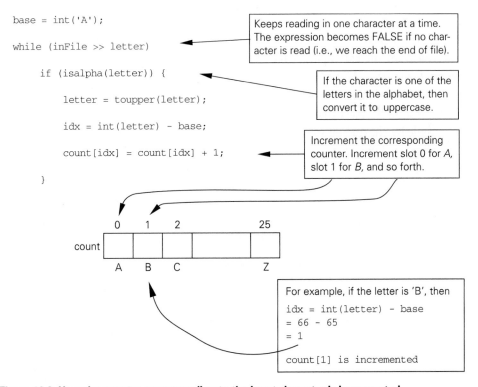

Figure 16.8 How the counter corresponding to the input character is incremented

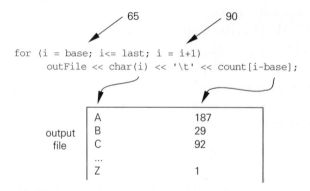

Figure 16.9 The count table written to the output file

After the input file is processed, we write the resulting count table to the output file as shown in figure 16.9.

16.3 The `FileBox` *object*

The file from which the program CompoundInterest reads data is fixed; that is, it always reads data from the external text file `"compint.txt"`. We improved the second sample program `LetterCount` by allowing the user to specify the filename using a `StringTypeIn` object. A further improvement is to let the user specify a text file via a `FileBox` object. A `FileBox` is a GUI object that displays filenames in the selection list so that the user can choose a file by clicking on its name.

To use a FileBox object for selecting an input file, we use the function `GetOpen-FileName` as

```
FileBox fileBox;
...
fileBox.GetOpenFileName();
```

which will display the `FileBox` object shown in figure 16.10.

To use a FileBox object for selecting an output file, we use the function `GetSave-FileName` as

```
FileBox fileBox;
...
fileBox.GetSaveFileName();
```

which will display the `FileBox` object shown in figure 16.11.

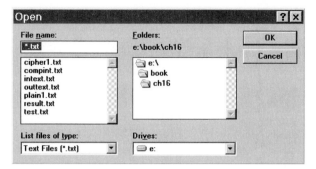

Figure 16.10 Use of GetOpenFileName function

The two functions seem very similar. However, the difference between the two is not only the title (one is Open and the other is Save As) but also how they behave. With the Open FileBox dialog, you are not allowed to specify a nonexistent file. On the other hand, with the Save FileBox dialog, you will be asked whether you wish to overwrite the existing file if you specify an existing file.

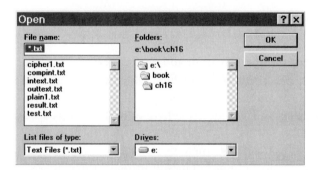

Figure 16.11 Use of GetSaveFileName function

Both functions return the full path name of the selected file. For the MS Windows environment, for example, the functions return a pathname such as `"C:\PRO-GRAMS\CH16\SAMPLE.TXT"`. The functions work similarly for UNIX and Mac environments.

16.4 Sample program: Encryption2

We will now extend the Encryption program in chapter 15 so that the user has the option of saving text in a file and reading text from a file. The modified object diagram is shown in figure 16.12.

The new version of the program has four new objects: a `CryptMnHndler` for processing the menu selection event, a `Menu` for displaying a pull-down menu with

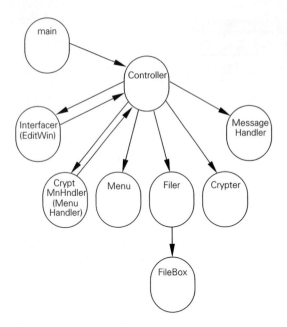

Figure 16.12 Object diagram for Encryption2 program

choices `Open` and `Save`, a `Filer` for reading text from and writing text to a file, and a `FileBox` for allowing the user to select input/output files. Moreover, a `Controller` and an `Interfacer` are modified to accommodate new objects. The `Menu` and `FileBox` objects are the standard GUI objects. We will describe here only the objects specifically designed for this program (a `Filer` and a `CryptMnHndler`) and the objects modified for this program (the `Controller` and the `Interfacer`). The `Filer` is a storage object, and the `CryptMnHndler` is a control object. The full listings of the objects are given at the end of this section.

The `Filer` object has two functions. The function `Open` returns the text from the user-selected file, and the function `Save` writes the text to the user-selected file. Its interface is as follows:

```
class Filer {
public:

    char *Open();
    void Save(char *text);

private:

    fstreamfile;
    FileBoxfileBox;
};
```

The implementation for the functions `Open` and `Save` is straightforward. Both functions use a `FileBox` to allow the user to select a file. The `Save` function is written as

```
void Filer::Save(char *text)
{
    char filename[80];

    strcpy(filename, fileBox.GetSaveFileName());

    if (strcmp(filename,"") != 0 ) {//filename given
        file.open(filename, ios::out);
        file << text;
        file.close();
    }
}
```

> Make sure you allocate enough space to handle the full path name of a file.

We use the standard output operator << to write text to the file.

```
file << text;
```

However, we cannot read in text from the file in the `Open` function using

```
file >> text;
```

because the standard input operator >> will read only until the first blank space. Since we need to read the whole line (we are assuming that text is saved in a file as a single line), including the spaces, we use the standard `getline` function instead.

```
file.getline(text,80);
```

The second argument specifies the maximum number of characters to be read. Here is the `Open` function:

```
char *Filer::Open()
{
    char *filename;
    char *text = new char[80];

    filename = fileBox.GetOpenFileName();

    if (strcmp(filename,"") != 0){ //filename given
        file.open(filename, ios::in);
        file.getline(text,80);
```

```
        file.close();
        return text;
    }
    else  //fileBox is cancelled
        return "";
}
```

The second new object is a `CryptMnHndler`. This object processes the menu selection events by reporting to its owner, which is a `Controller`. The `CryptMnHndler`-`Controller` relationship is analogous to the one between the `Interfacer` and the `Controller`, as the preceding object diagram shows. Similar to the definition for the `Interfacer`, we have a forward reference in the following definition of `CryptMnHndler`. This reference is necessary to set up a two-way communication link between `CryptMnHndler` and `Controller`.

```
class Controller; //forward reference

class CryptMnHndler:public MenuHandler {

public:

    void SetOwner(Controller *boss);

    void MenuFunc1(); //Open...
    void MenuFunc2(); //Save...

private:

    Controller  *owner;

};
```

Implementation of a `CryptMnHndler` is very simple. First, the `SetOwner` function assigns the owner `Controller` object to its data member `owner`.

```
void CryptMnHndler::SetOwner(Controller *boss)
{
    owner = boss;
}
```

The function `MenuFunc1` for handling the menu choice `"Open..."` invokes its owner's `Open` function. This action is equivalent to reporting to its owner that the menu choice `"Open..."` has been selected.

```
void CryptMnHndler::MenuFunc1() //Open...
{
    owner->Open();
}
```

The `Controller` will actually carry out the command. (We will describe the modified `Controller` shortly.) The function `MenuFunc2` does the same thing for the menu choice `"Save..."`.

```
void CryptMnHndler::MenuFunc2()  //Save...
{
    owner->Save();
}
```

Ideally, we should be able to use the `Interfacer` object we created in chapter 15 without any modification in this new program, because the primary task of the `Interfacer` has not changed. Unfortunately, we have to make one modification to the `Interfacer`, namely, adding a function to extract the text typed in by the user so that the `Controller` can save it. This kind of modification is expected when we design new objects. As we increase the frequency of reusing an object (this is the second time we are using an `Interfacer`), its design becomes stabilized, and the chances of reusing it without modification for a new program increase.

The new function `Extract` is actually very simple, so the modification we will make to the Interfacer is very minor. The function uses the inherited function `ReadAll` to read all of the text entered by the user and returns this text:

```
char *Interfacer::Extract()
{
    return ReadAll();
}
```

Unlike the `Interfacer`, which we expect to reuse without any modifications in an ideal situation, we expect to modify the `Controller`. Because the `Controller` is the supervisor of the other objects and because we have new objects, we must modify the `Controller`. However, since all of the dirty work is handled by the subordinate objects, such as `Filer` and `Interfacer`, the extent of the required changes is minimal — new data members corresponding to the subordinate objects and new functions for handling the added responsibilities, in this case, saving text to and reading text from a file. Thus we have three new data members and two new functions:

```
class Controller {
public:

    Controller();  //MODIFIED

    void Encrypt(char *text);
    void Decrypt(char *text);

    void Open();    //NEW: for reading text from a file
    void Save();    //NEW: for saving text to a file
    void Start();

private:

    Crypter             crypter;
    Interfacer          interfacer;
    MessageHandler      msgHandler;

    CryptMnHndler       menuHandler;    //NEW
    Menu                fileMenu;       //NEW
    Filer               filer;          //NEW
};
```

In addition to the two new functions, we must also modify the constructor, so that the menu and the corresponding CryptMnHndler menu handler are properly initialized.

> Calls the data member object's constructor function.

```
Controller::Controller():fileMenu("File")
{
    interfacer.Init(50,50,600,300);                //set up Interfacer
    interfacer.SetOkLabel("Encrypt");
    interfacer.SetCancelLabel("Decrypt");
    interfacer.SetOwner(this);

    //build up the menu and associate it to menuHandler
    fileMenu.AddItem("Open...", menuHandler, 1);
    fileMenu.AddItem("Save...", menuHandler, 2);
    menuHandler.SetOwner(this);
}
```

Notice the function signature. The assignment of the menu text is done only through the Menu object's constructor function. For example, to create a Menu object with the menu text "Special", we declare

```
Menu myMenu("Special");
```

So, logically, we should be able to do the same inside the private component of the `Controller`, as in this example:

```
...
private:
    MenufileMenu("File");
...
```

However, this declaration is not allowed in C++, because the `Menu` is a data member of the `Controller`. Initialization (i.e., using the constructor functions) of an object's data members must be done in the constructor in a very special way, as explained in chapter 10. We place statements for calling the subordinate objects' (i.e., data member objects) respective constructor functions right after the constructor name — `Controller()` in the preceding example. If there are multiple data members, then we use commas to separate the calls to their constructor functions. For example,

```
Controller::Controller()
        : fileMenu("File"), editMenu("Edit"), moveMenu("Movement")
```

An alternative to this approach is to declare a pointer to a `Menu` object as

```
...
private:
    Menu        *fileMenu;
...
```

and define the constructor as

```
ABController::ABController()
{
    fileMenu = new Menu("File");

    ... //the rest is the same as in the above
}
```

Notice that the second approach uses a pointer to a `Menu` object, and therefore, we must use the `new` operator to create the `Menu` object explicitly.

The new functions `Save` and `Open` should be self-explanatory:

```
void Controller::Save()
{
    char text[80];
```

```
        strcpy(text, interfacer.Extract()); //get text and
        filer.Save(text);                    //save it to a file
    }

    void Controller::Open()
    {
        char text[80];
        strcpy(text, filer.Open());      //read text from a file
        interfacer.Display(text);        //and display it
    }
```

As we can see in this example, a program designed in a proper object-oriented manner facilitates modification and extension. When we construct a program from well-defined objects, we can expect to identify an object easily for modification or replacement. By assigning a single, clearly delineated task to an object, we can identify the object responsible for the task when the time comes to change the way it is carried out. For example, if we need to improve the task of encryption and decryption to provide more security, we can immediately identify the object responsible, namely, the Crypter. Everything that has to do with the actual encoding and decoding of the text can be found within the Crypter, and it is the only object with which we have to deal in changing the encryption/decryption algorithm. The same is true of the user interface. Suppose we want to change how the user enters the text. We look for the object responsible for the user interface and find the Interfacer.

The purpose of the four object categories (storage, control, user interface, and application logic) we introduced in chapter 15 is to guide us in deriving well-defined objects. We will discuss object-oriented design further in the next chapter. We close this section with the complete listing of the objects we have designed for the sample program. Figure 16.13 that shows the inclusion references appears at the end of the listing.

"Filer.h"

```
#ifndef __FILER_H
#define __FILER_H

#include <fstream.h>
#include "GUIObj.h"

class Filer {
public:
    char *Open();
    void Save(char *text);

private:
    fstream     file;
    FileBox     fileBox;
};
#endif
```

CHAPTER 16   FILES

```
#include "Filer.h"

char *Filer::Open()
{
     char *filename;
     char *text = new char[80];
     filename = fb.GetOpenFileName();
     if (strcmp(filename,"") != 0){ //filename given
          file.open(filename, ios::in);
          file.getline(text,80);
          file.close();
          return text;
     }
     else  //filebox cancelled
          return "";
}

void Filer::Save(char *text)
{
     char filename[80];
     strcpy(filename, fb.GetSaveFileName());
     if (strcmp(filename,"") != 0 ) {//filename given
          file.open(filename, ios::out);
          file << text;
          file.close();
     }
}
```

```
#ifndef __CMNHD_H
#define __CMNHD_H

#include "GUIObj.h"

class Controller; //forward reference

class CryptMnHndler:public MenuHandler {

public:
     void SetOwner(Controller *boss);

     void MenuFunc1(); //Open...
     void MenuFunc2(); //Save...

private:
     Controller          *owner;

};
#endif
```

```
#include "Cntlr.h"              //We include "Cntlr.h" because of the
                               //forward reference declaration
#include "CMnHd.h"

void CryptMnHndler::SetOwner(Controller *boss)
{
     owner = boss;
}

void CryptMnHndler::MenuFunc1() //Open...
{
```

```
      owner->Open();
}

void CryptMnHndler::MenuFunc2()   //Save...
{
      owner->Save();
}
```

```
#ifndef __INTFCR_H
#define __INTFCR_H

#include "GUIObj.h"

class Controller; //forward reference

class Interfacer: public EditWin {
public:
      void Ok();
      void Cancel();
      void Display(char *text);
      char *Extract();
      void SetOwner(Controller *c);

private:
      Controller *owner;
};
#endif
```

```
#include "Cntlr.h"            //We include "Cntlr.h" because of the
                             //forward reference declaration
#include "Intfcr.h"

void Interfacer::SetOwner(Controller *c)
{
      owner = c;
}

void Interfacer::Ok()
{
      owner->Encrypt(ReadAll());
}

void Interfacer::Cancel()
{
      owner->Decrypt(ReadAll());
}

void Interfacer::Display(char *text)
{
      Clear();
      Insert(0,0,text);
}

char *Interfacer::Extract()
{
      return ReadAll();
}
```

```
#ifndef __CNTLR_H
#define __CNTLR_H

#include "Crypter.h"
#include "Intfcr.h"
#include "CMnHd.h"
#include "Filer.h"

class Controller {
public:

     Controller(); //MODIFIED

     void Encrypt(char *text);
     void Decrypt(char *text);
     void Open();   //NEW: for reading text from a file
     void Save();   //NEW: for saving text to a file
     void Start();

private:

     Crypter                 crypter;
     Interfacer              interfacer;
     MessageHandler          msgHandler;
     CryptMnHndler           menuHandler;    //NEW
     Menu                    fileMenu; //NEW
     Filer                   filer;          //NEW
};
#endif
```

```
#include "Cntlr.h"

Controller::Controller():fileMenu("File")
{
     interfacer.Init(50,50,600,300);       //set up Interfacer
     interfacer.SetOkLabel("Encrypt");
     interfacer.SetCancelLabel("Decrypt");
     interfacer.SetOwner(this);

     //build up the menu and associate it to menuHandler
     fileMenu.AddItem("Open...", menuHandler, 1);
     fileMenu.AddItem("Save...", menuHandler, 2);
     menuHandler.SetOwner(this);   }

void Controller::Save()
{
     char text[80];
     strcpy(text, interfacer.Extract()); //get text and
     filer.Save(text);                                   //save it to a file
}

void Controller::Open()
{
     char text[80];
     strcpy(text, filer.Open());             //read text from a file
     interfacer.Display(text);               //and display it
}

void Controller::Start()
{
     msgHandler.Start();
}
```

```
void Controller::Encrypt(char *text)
{
     char encryptedText[80];
     strcpy(encryptedText, crypter.Encrypt(text));
     interfacer.Display(encryptedText);
}

void Controller::Decrypt(char *text)
{
     char originalText[80];
     strcpy(originalText, crypter.Decrypt(text));
     interfacer.Display(originalText);
}
```

"Encrypt2.cpp"

```
//Program Encryption2: The Encryption program with the
//                          file save and open options.

#include "Cntlr.h"

void main()
{
     Controller controller;
     controller.Start();
}
```

16.5 Exercises

1 Modify the CompoundInterest program by using one or more GUI objects to obtain input values.

2 Interest on savings is usually compounded more often than annually. Modify the CompoundInterest program so that the user can input the number of times per year that the interest is compounded. Remember that if the interest is compounded N times per year, then the interest rate used each time for computation is R/N, where R is the annual interest rate.

3 Modify the CompoundInterest program so that the user can input the name of the file in which the table is written. Use a `FileBox` to get a filename from the user.

4 Modify the Crypter program of chapter 15 so that the program reads in the original text from a user-specified file and writes the ciphered text to another user-specified file. Use a `FileBox` for specifying the input and output files.

5 Modify the LetterCount program to keep separate counts for lower- and uppercase letters.

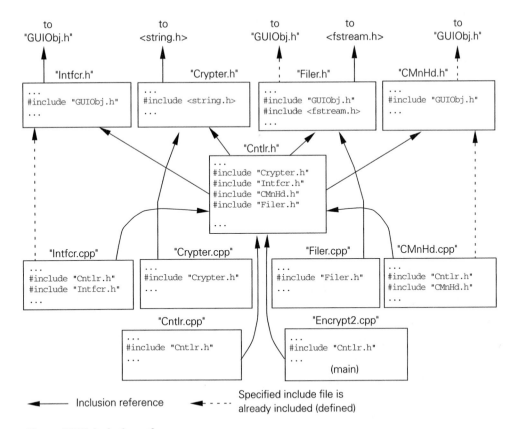

Figure 16.13 Inclusion references

6 You can keep track of the balance in your checking account by accurately subtracting the amount of each check written and adding the amount of each deposit. You also must subtract the monthly service charge, if there is one. Write a program to compute the balance in a checking account. The program will have one input file and one output file. The input file contains the balance at the beginning of the month and information on checks, deposits, and service charges. Each transaction is represented by a code (*C* for a check, *D* for a deposit, and *S* for service charge) and amount. Here's a typical input file:

```
1234.99
C 345.00
C 23.89
D 100.00
C 3.75
S 4.25
```

The program must write the new balance to the output file. Both input and output files are specified by the user using a `FileBox`. They can be the same file, but if they are, the initial content will be lost. An outline of the algorithm for the program follows.

```
open the input file;
read the beginning balance;
while (there are more transactions in the file) {
    read the next transaction;
    if (the transaction is a check or service charge)
        subtract the amount from the balance;
    else
        add the amount to the balance;
}
close the input file;

open the output file;
write the new balance to the output file;
close the output file;
```

7 Write a program to search a text file for a given word. The program will simply report whether or not the word was found in the file. The user will provide the filename using a `FileBox` and the word to be searched using a `StringTypeIn`. Here is an outline of the algorithm for the program:

```
open the file;
get the word to search;
while (there are more words in the file) {
    get the next word;
    if (it is the search word) {
        report success;
        close the file;
        return; //stop the loop & quit
}
report failure;
close the file;
```

For this program, any valid C++ identifier is considered to be a word.

8 The program in the previous exercise will stop when the word is found. Modify the program so it will count the number of times the search word occurs in the file.

9 Modify the `Grading3` program from section 13.5 so that the result is saved to a text file. Make sure all information about each student is saved.

10 Modify the `Temperature` program from section 14.3 so that the daily temperatures are saved to a text file.

11 Modify the program from the previous exercise further so that the user has the option of entering the temperature data from the keyboard (using `cin`) or from a user-specified text file.

12 We want to create an object that not only gets a filename from the user but also opens that file for input. Write an `OpenTextFileBox` object that inherits from a `FileBox`, and define a new method `OpenFile` that opens the selected file.

13 When you run the program `LetterCount` and do not type in the filename of an existing file, the input dialog box will not disappear. Modify the program so it will terminate the program if you type in `Q` instead of an actual filename.

chapter 17

Object-oriented software development

A *program*, as we have seen, is a collection of data items or objects and statements that tell a computer how to accomplish some task, and *programming* is the activity of writing programs. So far, we have seen only relatively small programs. When writing small programs, a programmer can get away with bad practices that would doom a larger program. The examples and exercises in this book provide only the slightest hint about what large software systems might be like. They provide even less information about what the activity of producing those systems might be like. You can appreciate the fact that design and construction methods for a small building such as a doghouse and those used for a skyscraper are quite different. A skyscraper is not just a very large doghouse, and a large software system is not just a very large program. It is a mistake to think that the difference between a program having 50 or 60 lines of code and a software system having 50,000 or 60,000 lines is simply one of scale. Thus we can't provide a complete and realistic example of the development of a large software system, nor can you be expected to participate, as a textbook exercise, in the production of a large system; such systems take teams of programmers months and even years to complete. We can, however, describe the activities of the software development process, and we will illustrate some of those activities in the context of a case study for designing an address book program.

17.1 Software life cycle

The term *software life cycle* refers to a sequence of processes for initiating, developing, and using software systems. The software life cycle can generally be broken down into six major phases: requirements analysis, specification, design, coding, testing and debugging, and operation. A brief description of each phase follows.

1. *Requirements Analysis.* Without having a clear statement of what the final product is supposed to do, we have no goal for which to aim. Thus, the first stage of the software life cycle starts with an analysis of the problem to be solved. The output from this stage is a "requirements document" that lists features or capabilities of a proposed system. For the doghouse example, the requirement analysis may produce a simple one-sentence statement:

    > Build a shelter that comfortably accommodates my dog, Ralph, and
    > that allows Ralph to enter and exit quickly.

    As you can imagine, a requirements document for a more complex system, such as a skyscraper, will have many pages divided into numerous sections and subsections, much like a legal document.

2. *Specification.* In the specification stage, we transform the requirements document produced in the first stage into a list of specific, testable properties. The requirements document only states what is expected of a proposed system in nontechnical terms. In this stage we turn the broadly stated expectation into the concrete specification of a system. For example, what does it mean to "comfortably accommodate" Ralph? We may change this requirement to a concrete specification of the dimension of a doghouse, for example:

    > ... the width of the structure should be at least twice the length of
    > Ralph (so he can easily turn inside the house)...

3. *Design.* After the specification is complete, we can start designing the system. For Ralph's doghouse the design is represented as a set of blueprints and a bill of materials. The design should specify the actual dimensions of the doghouse, the materials to be used, and so forth. The design must be complete and unambiguous, so that any decent do-it-yourselfer could build the doghouse. Given a design, we

must be able to check whether it meets the stated specification. The equivalent of blueprints for software is a collection of object diagrams and object description files. An *object description file* is a language-independent way of describing an object's behavior in terms of functions it supports. It also describes how the functions are implemented.

4 *Coding.* In the coding stage, we translate the design into a real system or product. For Ralph, the product is a real doghouse for him to enjoy. For a software system, the product is a real program written in a particular programming language. If the design is properly done, coding should proceed very smoothly, provided that the programmers are proficient in the chosen programming language.

5 *Testing and Debugging.* During the coding stage, we may introduce coding errors called bugs. A *bug* is a failure of the program to perform as specified. For example, the builder may forget to nail the roof, so it soon starts leaking on poor Ralph, which definitely is not comfortable for him. In software development, a programmer may make a mistake in declaring the size of a character array that causes a peculiar I/O problem. This bug occurred when we were writing the Crypter program for this textbook.

A bug could be (often is) the result of a faulty design. *Debugging* is an activity to eliminate bugs, and *testing* is an activity to find those bugs. Testing involves running the program with different sets of data and scenarios that should include, at the very least, circumstances that cause all parts of the program to execute. It should also include extreme circumstances like very large and very small numbers in the data, data out of the acceptable range, no data at all, and so on.

6 *Operation.* After testing and debugging are done to everybody's satisfaction, the finished product is released for operation. During the operation phase, unforeseen requirements may be introduced, forcing us to upgrade the system. Also, previously undetected bugs could be discovered during the operation phase, forcing us to repair the system. The new system delivered after the newly found bugs are fixed, is called a *maintenance release.* We can expect many maintenance releases over the course of software's expected service lifetime.

We have now identified the stages of the software life cycle, but we have not yet mentioned how one proceeds from one stage to the next. It may be possible to build a doghouse in a rather haphazard way. There may not be a huge functional difference between a poorly constructed doghouse and a professionally constructed doghouse. Ralph may not care. However, we cannot go about building a skyscraper in a casual manner. A single poor implementation could have serious consequences for the overall functionality of the structure and even for the safety of the occupants.

The situation is analogous in software development. When writing small programs, a programmer can get away with bad practices that would doom a larger program. Over the years, as hardware has become faster and as RAM sizes and disk sizes have grown proportionately, the size of programs has increased as well. A program with a few thousand machine language instructions was, in the early days, a large program. Today, software systems with hundreds of thousands of lines of high level language code are common. Such systems, when all their programs are compiled, result in millions of machine language instructions. Today's large software systems cannot be written without very careful adherence to well-established software development methodologies.

Real-world software is produced by teams, and the teams must be managed. Management is always important when groups work together to accomplish a goal. Management techniques for software projects include many traditional, general purpose management practices, as well as some that have been developed specifically for software projects.

It is beyond the scope of this textbook to elaborate on any methodology (including management techniques) in detail. Instead, we will develop a sample application program, going through a development process and emphasizing key points. We will focus mainly on the construction phases (i.e., design and coding), with only cursory references to other phases. We do this because the construction phases are the most fundamental, and also are within the grasp of students having a limited knowledge of programming. Other phases are equally important and crucial, but we do not yet possess all of the necessary skills to fully understand and appreciate their intricacies.

17.2 Developing an address book program

As an illustration of the software life cycle, we will step through the stages and develop a sample application—an address book. Let us begin with the requirements analysis.

17.2.1 Address book requirements analysis

The following paragraph is the output of the requirements analysis. In practice, the requirements document is produced after extensive interviews with the intended users of the program. We will pretend here that the following is the result of our interviews with users:

> We would like to develop a program that maintains an address book. The program must keep track of people, storing the name, age, phone number, and address for each person. The program should

allow us to manipulate multiple address books, for example, one for business contacts, another for personal friends, and so forth. We expect no more than 100 persons to be listed in any address book.

17.2.2 Address book specification

From this requirements document, we must generate a complete, accurate, and consistent list of specifications. The following, in bullet form, is a list of specifications:

- There will be one window to display information on one person.
- The display window will list information along with labels (i.e., Name: John Smith, Age: 13, and so forth).
- The program will allow the user to delete, add, and modify a person's information.
- The program will allow the user to browse through the address book.
- The program will allow the user to create a new address book, open an existing address book, and save changes made to an address book.
- An address book can contain information on at most 100 persons.

17.2.3 Design

In the design stage, we identify the objects. In chapter 15 we mentioned four categories of objects for helping us identify the objects necessary for the program. They are user interface, application logic, control, and storage. In addition to these four categories, we must be aware of another aspect of deriving objects for a program.

One of the key advantages of object-oriented programming (OOP) is code reuse. In other words, instead of always developing new programs from scratch, we attempt to reuse existing code as much as possible. Reusing existing code in OOP implies reusing already defined objects. However, we should be very careful not to push this notion too far. Some objects may be intended to be reused, while other objects may be intended to be used for one particular program. In other words, when we are designing a program, we should be aware of what types of objects we are creating. If an object is intended to be used again, then we should pay special attention so that it is, indeed, programmed for reuse.

Objects can be classified into layers. Objects in different layers are related via inheritance relationships. The lowest layer is the *system layer*. Objects in this layer are independent of any application. The GUI objects used in this book are all System Layer objects for us. The second layer is the *application domain layer*. Objects in this layer are

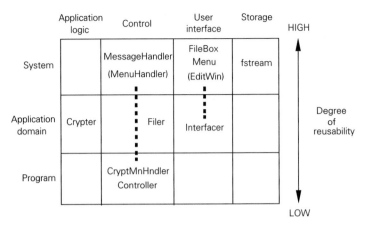

Figure 17.1 Objects classified into three layers

built from system layer objects and are more closely related to particular types of programs. For example, we may have objects defined for business-oriented applications, such as ledger, employee, payroll, and date. These objects are not as generic as those in the system layer; however, they are not tied specifically to any one program. They are useful for particular types of programs. The final layer is the *program layer*. The objects in this layer are custom tailored to a particular program, and they are not intended to be reused in other programs.

For illustration, let's classify objects from the Encryption program in chapter 16 into these three layers. Figure 17.1 shows the objects in appropriate boxes. The dotted lines show inheritance relationships, and the parenthesized classes, such as `MenuHandler` and `EditWin`, signify that no instances, that is, objects, of those classes are created for the program. Parenthesized classes are listed in the diagram to show the heritage of the classes whose instances we create and use. For example, `EditWin` is listed below to show that the `Interfacer` is a descendant of `EditWin`. We create and use an `Interfacer` object, but no `EditWin` object is used in the program.

Notice that the degree of reusability is very high at the system layer and very low (close to 0) as you move toward the program layer. It is possible, though, that you may realize that very similar program layer objects are used in several programs. The main `Controller` is one such object. If you notice this, you should extract the code common among those program layer objects into one application domain object, or even into one system layer object.

Here again, our purpose is not to classify unambiguously all objects into distinct layers. Some objects may seem like system layer objects to us and like application domain layer objects to others. The three-layer approach is mainly a guideline, just as

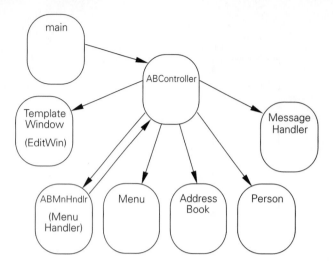

Note: Only the major objects are shown here; for example, standard GUI objects are not shown.

Figure 17.2 Address book program object diagram

the four categories of objects (control, user interface, application logic, and storage) are a guideline. So as long as we are aware of general categories and layers to help us design objects, we are doing fine. We do not have to always classify them rigidly.

Now let us begin designing the sample program at hand. Keep in mind that the following discussion on the design stage will not include all of the design ideas we have considered. In developing the sample program, we have actually gone through a number of minor design changes. To discuss all these design changes would require far too many pages, and they would not be very educational. Instead, to maintain a logical sequence and clarity, we will present our final design in a linear fashion, from the overall design to the design of individual objects. In addition, we will describe our design with some explanation of design alternatives and the reasons certain choices were made.

Our first task is to identify participating objects. Figure 17.2 shows the object diagram for the program. The four-category, three-layer diagram now looks like figure 17.3.

Once the overall design is done, we proceed to design individual objects and specify in detail how to carry out the communication between them. Let's start from the top. The main program, as before, simply creates and initiates the main controller for the program.

```
#include "AdBkCtl.h"
void main()
{
```

```
ABControllercontroller;
controller.Start();
}
```

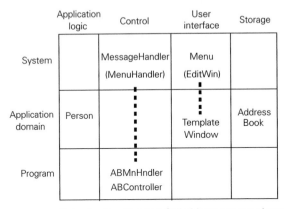

Note: Again, standard GUI objects are not shown.

Figure 17.3 Objects from the AddressBook program classified into four-category, three-layer diagram

ABController manages all the other objects. To design the ABController, we must first assign responsibilities to the subordinate objects so that we know how to let the ABController manage them. Let's begin with the subordinate user interface objects. To allow end users to select all available options, the program will have the menu choices in figure 17.4.

We use three Menu objects—File, Edit, and Movement—for displaying and controlling these menu choices. The menu-selection event is handled by the ABMnHndler, a descendant of MenuHandler. The ABMnHndler will inform the ABController when a menu choice is selected. Processing of menu choices is performed by the ABController,

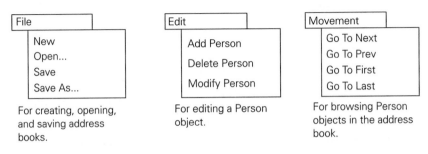

Figure 17.4 The program's menu choices

with the subordinate objects' help. We define an ABController function for each menu choice. The operations for editing and browsing Person objects are performed by the application logic object AddressBook. This object knows how to open and save Person data to an external file, browse through a list of Person objects, and in general, keep track of Person objects. The data for a single Person are displayed using a user interface object, TemplateWindow, a descendant of EditWin. All of these subordinate objects are private data members of the ABController. The following is its interface.

```
class ABController {
public:
    ABController();

    void Start();

    void NewAddrBook(); //processing file menus
    void OpenAddrBook();
    void SaveAddrBook();
    void SaveAsAddrBook();

    void AddPerson(); //processing edit menus
    void DeletePerson();
    void ModifyPerson();

    void GotoNext();   //processing movement menus
    void GotoPrev();
    void GotoFirst();
    void GotoLast();

private:
    Menu fileMenu;
    Menu editMenu;
    Menu moveMenu;

    ABMnHndlr         menuHandler;
    MessageHandler    msgHandler;
    TemplateWindow    onePersonDisplay;
    AddressBook       addrBook;

    void SetupMenu();

};
```

Let's look at the implementation of a few functions. (The complete listing is provided at the end of the chapter.) One constructor function is defined for the ABController. The purpose of this constructor is to initialize the three Menu objects properly by

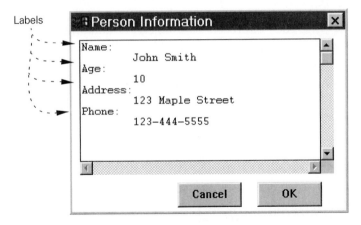

Figure 17.5 Display for a single Person object

assigning the text for each. As explained in the previous chapter, the calls to the data members' constructor functions are made within the function's signature, as shown in the following contsructor function for the `ABController` class.

```
ABController::ABController()
    : fileMenu("File"), editMenu("Edit"), moveMenu("Movement")
{
}
```

The function calls the data members' contructor functions within its signature, not within its function body.

We want the display of a single Person object to look something like the screen in figure 17.5. The window will display not only the data but also the labels Name, Age, and so forth. We could easily create some private data members inside the `Tem-plateWindow` to store the values for the labels, but should we? No, because the values of those labels should be determined by the object to be displayed; in this program the object to be displayed is `Person`. Remember that the `TemplateWindow` is a general purpose object responsible just for displaying data. It should not have any knowledge about the data it displays. If we tie the labels for the `Person` directly into the `TemplateWindow`, then it works only with a `Person` object. We should then call the object `PersonWindow`, since it only works for a `Person` object. We want it to be more general. In other words, we want our window to be at the application domain layer, not at the program layer. Our approach is to ask the `Person` object for a list of labels to be printed and pass this information to the `TemplateWindow`. We use an array of pointers to characters for passing along this information. (See Section 14.1 for a discussion on an array of pointers to characters.)

The setup of subordinate `Menu` and `TemplateWindow` objects is done inside the `Start` function.

```
void ABController::Start()
{
    Person oneEntry;
    char*attributes[AB_MAXENTRY]= {0};

    SetupMenu();

    //initialize the display window and set its list of prompts
    oneEntry.GetAttr(attributes);
    onePersonDisplay.Init(100,75,350,250);
    onePersonDisplay.setLabel(attributes);
    onePersonDisplay.SetTitle("Person Information");

    msgHandler.Start();
}
```

AB_MAXENTRY is a global constant
defined in the file "AdBkCtl.h"

The private function `SetupMenu` sets up the menu choices and associates the corresponding menu handler.

```
void ABController::SetupMenu()
{
    //set itself as an owner of menuHandler
    menuHandler.SetOwner(this);

    //add individual menu choices
    fileMenu.AddItem("New",           menuHandler, 1);
    fileMenu.AddItem("Open...",        menuHandler, 2);
    fileMenu.AddItem("Save",           menuHandler, 3);
    fileMenu.AddItem("Save as...",     menuHandler, 4);

    editMenu.AddItem("Add Person",     menuHandler, 5);
    editMenu.AddItem("Delete Person",  menuHandler, 6);
    editMenu.AddItem("Modify Person",  menuHandler, 7);

    moveMenu.AddItem("Go To Next",     menuHandler, 8);
    moveMenu.AddItem("Go To Prev",     menuHandler, 9);
    moveMenu.AddItem("Go To First",    menuHandler,10);
    moveMenu.AddItem("Go To Last",     menuHandler,11);
}
```

The ABController coordinates all processing of menu choices. The program has three groups of choices (three menus): File, Edit, and Movement. We will describe how one menu item from each menu is processed. Processing other menu items within the same menu is very similar, as you can see in the complete listing at the end of the chapter. Let's start with the File menu and explain the function OpenAddrBook, which is representative of other file-related functions. This function is executed in response to the selection of the menu choice "Open..." The MenuHandler intercepts the menu selection event and notifies its owner ABController by calling the function OpenAddr-Book. The basic logic of the function is

```
if (there are any changes made to the current address book
    and the changes are not saved) {
    ask user to save or discard changes;
    if (user wants to save) {
    save the current address book;
    }
}
get the name of a file to open;
if (name is okay) {
    open the file;
}
```

First, let's see which subordinate objects will collaborate and provide the necessary services to the ABController for realizing the OpenAddrBook function. In addition to the obvious GUI object collaborators, we have an AddressBook object. Remember that this object is the main workhorse of our program and handles the actual management of Person objects. It is our Storage object. Since this object manages the data, it will be responsible for determining whether there are any unsaved changes to the current address book. Coding the above logic in C++ becomes:

```
void ABController::OpenAddrBook()
{
    YesNoBox prompt;
    char    filename[50];
    FileBox fileBox;

    if (addrBook.DataChanged()) {
        //save any unsaved modified data if the user wants to
        if (prompt.Ask(
            "Data has changed, but not saved. Save now?"))
            //the user says YES, so save the current addrbook
            addrBook.Save();
    }
```

```
    //get the name of file to open
        strcpy(filename,fileBox.GetOpenFileName());

    if (strcmp(filename,"") != 0) //name is given
        addrBook.Open(filename); //so open it
    //else
    //cancelled, so do nothing
}
```

Notice that we are proceeding in the design phase in a top-down manner. We may also call our design approach responsibility driven. Here, while designing an ABController, we delegate some tasks, or responsibilities, to the Storage object AddressBook. In other words, we are defining the interface of AddressBook from the client's perspective. We are starting from the topmost object and giving responsibilities to the subordinate objects. Then we will gradually implement these subordinate objects. At this point some subordinate objects may already exist; if so, we look at their definitions and identify the functions we can use. GUI objects such as YesNoBox and FileBox are subordinate objects that already exist, so we simply look up their definitions and use them accordingly.

For the Edit menu, we will describe the function for adding a new Person object. We will explain the other two functions, for deleting and modifying a Person object, in the next chapter because these functions require a search. For all three functions, we assume that the operations are applied to the currently displayed Person object. For example, while browsing data, the user may type in data for a new Person and select the menu choice "Add Person". This causes the function AddPerson to be executed. This function requests the TemplateWindow to return the data entered in the window. The function then assigns the returned data to the Person object and requests the Address-Book to add this new Person object. The basic logic is

```
request data from Template window;
data are returned;
assign data to Person object;
ask AddrBook to add this Person to its list;
```

Translating the preceding logic to C++ yields:

```
void ABController::AddPerson()
{
    char        *attributes[AB_MAXENTRY];
    Person      *oneEntry = new Person;
```

```
onePersonDisplay.GetData(attributes)
oneEntry->SetValue(attributes);
addrBook.Add(oneEntry);
}
```

Notice that a pointer to the Person object is passed to the AddressBook's Add function. Although other means of communication are possible, we chose to use a pointer because it provides the most flexible approach. One specific advantage of this approach is that the memory allocated when using a pointer is not erased after the function is terminated. Had we used a straightforward object declaration, as in

```
Person oneEntry;
```

the memory allocated for this locally declared object would be erased when the function terminated. Notice also that the local variable oneEntry is a pointer to a Person object, not a Person object itself, so we need to explicitly create a Person object. This is done with the statement

```
Person *oneEntry = new Person;
```

which is a shorthand for

```
Person*oneEntry;
...
oneEntry = new Person;
```

For the Movement menu, we will explain the function that displays the next Person object. In our implementation, positions such as next, previous, and so forth are relative to the current Person object being displayed. Since the data are not stored in any particular order, *previous,* for example, simply means the person stored prior to the currently displayed Person. The basic logic for displaying the previous Person object is:

```
ask AddrBook to return the previous object;
if (there is a previous Person) {
    get values from this Person;
    tell TemplateWindow to display the values;
}
else {
    display error message;
}
```

We use a pointer to a `Person` object to communicate with the `AddressBook`. The function `Prev` will return NULL (0) if there is no previous `Person` and a pointer to a `Person` object if there is one. The function `SetData` of `TemplateWindow` will display the passed data along with the already assigned set of prompts. So we have

```
void ABController::GotoPrev()
{
    Person *oneEntry;
    char*values[AB_MAXENTRY];

    if (oneEntry = addrBook.Prev())  {
    oneEntry->GetValue(values);
    onePersonDisplay.SetData(values);
    }
    else {//no previous data
    OKBox message;
    message.Display("No More Data");
    }
}
```

Now let's look at the `TemplateWindow` object for handling the user interface. This User Interface object is at the application domain layer. It is intended to be part of a database application domain. It can be used to display, for example, `Person`, `Equipment`, `Department`, and so forth. It is not at the program layer because it is not tied specifically to displaying a `Person` object. To achieve this flexibility, being able to display templates for different types of objects, we pass an array of pointers to characters. The basic functionality of setting and getting data is inherited from the `EditWin`. Its interface is

```
#include <string.h>
#include "guiobj.h"
const int MAXENTRY = 5;

class TemplateWindow : public EditWin {
public:
    void GetData(char *value[]);
    //get a list of entry data

    void SetData(char *value[]);
    //displays the data with correct labels

    void SetLabel(char *tmpl[]);
    //set the list of labels for attribute entries

private:
    char *label[10];
```

```
        int labelSize;

    };
```

The function setLabel receives an array of pointers to characters and assigns them to the data member label. The values are displayed along with the data. Notice that to achieve generality, the function is set to accept an array (of pointers to characters) of an arbitrary size.

```
    void TemplateWindow::setLabel(char *tmpl[])
    {
        int i=0;
        while (tmpl[i] != 0) {  //not NULL
        label[i] = new char[20];
        strcpy(label[i],tmpl[i]); //tmpl[i] shorter than 20
        i = i+1;
        }
        labelSize = i;
    }
```

The function SetData receives an array of character pointers and displays the data with the already assigned prompts. (See the Person Information window earlier in the chapter.)

```
    void TemplateWindow::SetData(char *value[])
    {
        char str[40];
        Clear();
        for (int i=0; i<labelSize; i = i+1) {
        InsertLine(2*i,label[i]);
        strcpy(str,"      ");
        strcat(str,value[i]);
        InsertLine(2*i+1,str);
        }
    }
```

The function GetData returns the data as an array of character pointers. We assume that the data will be added to the database on individual lines (line 0, 1, 2, and 3) with no leading spaces. Therefore, the user must first erase everything and then type in the four values before choosing the menu selection AddPerson. Another possibility is to use a StringTypeIn object for getting the four values. (See exercise 6 at the end of this chapter.)

```
void TemplateWindow::GetData(char *value[])
{
    int i;
    for (i=0; i<labelSize; i = i+1)
    strcpy(value[i],ReadLine(i));
}
```

The Person object is used for each person's information. It keeps track of his or her name, age, address, and phone number. The functions SetValue and GetValue assign and retrieve the person data. The function GetAttr returns a set of attribute names. This function is used by the main controller to determine the labels to be displayed. These two functions are rather straightforward, so we will show only the header interface file here. The implementation file is listed at the end of the chapter.

```
#include <stdlib.h>

class Person  {
public:
    void SetValue(char *value[]);
    //assigns data to each attributes

    void GetAttr(char *attr[]);
    //returns a set of attribute names

    void GetValue(char *value[]);
    //returns a set of attribute values;

    int NumAttr();
    //returns the number of attributes
private:
    char name[20];
    intage;
    charaddress[40];
    charphone[14];
};
```

Finally, we are ready for the AddressBook object, the main workhorse of this program. The AddressBook object manages the address book. It is capable of adding, deleting, and modifying the data. Also, it is capable of browsing the list. It is capable of storing the address book in a file and reading data stored in a file into an address book. In addition to these operations, it supports a number of queries about its status. The functions DataChanged, HasData, and so forth allow client objects to ask AddressBook whether the data have changed, if any new data have been added, and so forth. Its interface is as follows:

```
const int AB_MAXSIZE = 100;
class AddressBook {
public:
    AddressBook();

    void Clear();

    int HasData();
    //return TRUE if AddressBook contains any data

    int DataChanged();
    //return TRUE if any data are modified

    int HasFile();
    //return TRUE if AddressBook has an associated file

    void Open(char *filename);
    //open the file filename and load the data

    void Save();
    //save the data to the currently associated file

    void Save(char *filename);
    //save the data into filename

    void Add(Person *person);
    //add a person to the address book

    Person *Next();
    //returns the next person in the list

    Person *Prev();
    //returns the previous person in the list

    Person *First();
    //returns the first person in the list

    Person *Last();
    //returns the last person in the list

private:

    fstream     addrBookFile;
    char        adBkFilename[50];
    Person      *entry[AB_MAXSIZE];
    int         entryCount;
    int         current;
    int         dataChanged;
};
```

```
<M — # of entries>                           3
<N — # of attributes for each>               4
<attr 1 data for entry #1>                   john ape
<attr 2 data for entry #1>                   10
...                                          123 Maple St.
<attr N data for entry #1>                   123-444-5555
...                                          jack bee
<attr 1 data for entry #M>                   12
<attr 2 data for entry #M>                   333 Maple St.
...                                          123-444-6656
<attr N data for entry #M>                   jill cat
                                             20
                                             34 Front Ave.
                                             123-444-0099
```

| Generic format. | A sample file with info on three persons, with four attributes per person. |

Figure 17.6 Format for storing data in the file

Many of the supported functions are straightforward, so they will not be explained any further here. Let's look at the Open function, which opens a new address book file. When the specified file is opened successfully, the AddressBook starts reading the data in the file and loads up the array of Person pointers. The format for storing data in the file is shown in figure 17.6.

The Open function is implemented as follows. The File object addrBookFile is a subordinate of the AddressBook, handling file input and output:

```
void AddressBook::Open(char *filename)
{
    addrBookFile.open(filename,ios::in);
    strcpy(adBkFilename,filename);

    char *value[10], tmpStr[255];
    int entrySize, attrSize, i, j;

    addrBookFile >> entrySize; //read control
    addrBookFile >> attrSize;   //information
    addrBookFile.getline(tmpStr,255); //read pass
                                    //the second line
    entryCount = entrySize;      //read in data
    for (i=0; i<entrySize; i =i+1) {

        //read one person info
        for (j=0; j<=attrSize-1; j =j+1) {
```

```
                      addrBookFile.getline(tmpStr,255);
                      value[j] = new char[strlen(tmpStr)+1];
                      strcpy(value[j],tmpStr);
              }

              entry[i] = new Person;
              entry[i]->SetValue(value);
      }

      addrBookFile.close();
}
```

The other functions for file input and output are similar to the Open function and will not be explained here. Please refer to the code listing at the end of the chapter.

Next, we will discuss the operation of adding a new person. To add a new person, the AddressBook finds the next open slot and inserts the data. The array of Person pointers—entry—is used by the AddressBook for manipulating data.

```
void AddressBook::Add(Person *person)
{
    if (entryCount < AB_MAXSIZE) { //still has space to add
    entry[entryCount] = person;
    entryCount = entryCount + 1;
    changed = 1;
}
```

To add a new person, we find the next available slot in the entry array and set it to point to the passed Person object.

The movement operations are straightforward. We will show the Next function. The other functions have very similar logic. Basically the Next function first checks whether or not there is a next Person object, relative to the currently selected Person object. If there is a next Person, then we adjust the variable current and return the pointer to the next Person. The function is written as:

```
Person *AddressBook::Next()
{
    if (entryCount <= 0 || current == entryCount-1)
    return 0; //error, no entry or no prev
    else {
    current = current + 1;
    return entry[current];
    }
}
```

This concludes our design. When the design is completed, it is beneficial to perform a *design review*, or *design walkthrough*, to catch any errors. In a design review, designers explain their design to another group of programmers. Explaining your thinking to others often helps you catch any oversights.

As we explained earlier, we have presented the design in a linear fashion, from the design of overall program structure to the individual objects, but in reality we have gone through a number of redesigns. Frequently, if not always, the way we structure the objects turns out to be inconsistent or inefficient. In such cases we must backtrack and redesign some portions of the code to eliminate the inconsistency or inefficiency. In fact, we may even backtrack to the specification or requirements analysis phase. Backtracking to an earlier step in the software life ccycle is an expected aspect of software development, so we should always allocate time for backtracking in the overall software development schedule.

17.2.4 Coding

Since we have already presented the complete program listing, it may seem that all we have to do now is to type the program. Well, not quite. Because this is a textbook, we have made a couple of simplifying assumptions. First, the result of our design is presented in C++ code. In actual practice, it is more likely that a design will be expressed in terms of a PDL (program design language) which is not tied to any particular programming language. A PDL allows us to express high level design concepts without being tied to the peculiarities of a particular language. Using a PDL allows us to implement the design in different programming languages. If we use the syntax and semantics of one particular programming language to express our design, then it would be very difficult to implement our thinking in another language. To leave our options open, we normally describe the design in a PDL.

Second, the program listing we have provided in this chapter is already tested (but we won't claim that the program will work under all circumstances). So, as long as we don't make any typing errors and arrange the source code files correctly, following the rules of the compiler used, we can just type in the code and run it. In reality, what we derive in the design stage almost always contains some design errors. It is, therefore, unreasonable to expect to run the whole program correctly on the first try. Rather, we must plan our implementation. We will code and debug a portion of it before adding other portions, instead of coding the complete program first and trying to debug the whole thing at once. We can call such intermixing of coding and debugging *incremental implementation* because we test in a piecemeal manner. Incremental implementation is useful, because it enables us to locate a bug much more quickly than when we test the whole program. When a bug occurs while running the whole program, we must search the whole program for it. On the other hand, when a bug occurs while running a portion of the program, we have to search a much smaller area. This method allows us to pinpoint the source of a problem faster.

Since we are mixing the coding and debugging, we might view the process as performing the coding and testing phases concurrently. However, the testing phase entails a more formal and complete approach to testing than what we include with the debugging during the incremental implementation described here. In incremental implementation we want to verify that two elements are working correctly:

1 That the connections between objects are set up correctly. We check, for example, whether the client invokes the server's function correctly (i.e., matching the types and the number of parameters).

2 That the server's function is working correctly. Assuming that the data are passed correctly to the function, we must make sure that the function does the computation and returns the correct result.

The goal in incremental implementation is to make sure that the portion of the program we want to add will fit in correctly with the existing portion.

The first step in coding our sample program incrementally is to create the main program and run it.

```
#include "AdBkCtl.h"
void main()
{
    ABControllercontroller;
    controller.Start();
}
```

To run and test this main program, we need the ABController defined in the header "AdBkCtl.h". Instead of putting the real code in the file, we start with a dummy ABController. For example, we could define a temporary ABController as

```
class ABController {
public:
    Start();
};

ABController::Start()
{
    OKBoxmsg;
    msg.Display("inside ABController Start");
}
```

What do we get by doing this test? Although it may seem trivial, you may be amazed that even a simple "dummy" program like the one above may not compile and link correctly the first time around. For example, we may make a mistake declaring the directory for our program. In any case, we should divide our program into small, manageable pieces. Compiling the preceding code is analogous to testing the foundation of a new house.

The function Start, as it now stands, is called a *function stub*, or *stub*. A function stub is a placeholder, temporary function to test the program structure, that is, to verify that the function is called correctly. A common technique is to place simple output statements inside a stub to verify this process, which is what we did for the Start function. If we pass arguments to a function, then we include output statements to display the values of these arguments. In this way we can verify that the values are passed correctly to the function. After the stub is verified, we replace the output statements with the real code.

Once the main program runs as expected, we can gradually fill in the details for the ABController and include additional objects as appropriate. The next step is incorporating an additional object. Let's say we choose to add a TemplateWindow object. We code and test functions which set the labels and display one Person. We could test the TemplateWindow by executing the following code:

Dummy ABController

```
#include "tmplwndw.h"
class ABController {
public:
    Start();
private:
    TemplateWindowonePersonDisplay;
};

ABController::Start()
{
    char*attributes[4];
    attributes[0] = "Name:";
    attributes[1] = "Age:";
    attributes[2] = "Address";
    attributes[3] = "Phone:";
    onePersonDisplay.setLabel(attributes);

    char    *values[4];
    values[0] = "Fredric Chopin";
    values[1] = "36";
    values[2] = "123 les Champs Elysees";
    values[3] = "111-222-3333";
```

```
    onePersonDisplay.setLabel(values);

}
```

TemplateWindow Interface

```
#include <string.h>
#include "GUIObj.h"

class TemplateWindow : public EditWin {
public:
    void SetData(char *value[]);
    //displays the data with correct prompts

    void setLabel(char *tmpl[]);
    //set the list of prompts for attribute entries

private:
    char *label[10];
    int labelSize;
};
```

TemplateWindow Implementation

```
#include "tplwndw.h"
void TemplateWindow::setLabel(char *tmpl[])
{
    int i=0;
    while (tmpl[i] != 0) {   //not NULL
        label[i] = new char[20];
        strcpy(label[i],tmpl[i]);
        i++;
    }
    labelSize = i;
}

void TemplateWindow::SetData(char *value[])
{
    char str[40];
    Clear();
    for (int i=0; i<labelSize; i = i+1) {
        InsertLine(2*i,label[i]);
        strcpy(str,"      ");
        strcat(str,value[i]);
        InsertLine(2*i+1,str);
    }
}
```

We continue in this manner, adding one object after another, until all the objects are incorporated into the program. When a design error occurs, most likely we will detect it by seeing incompatibility while trying to incorporate an additional object. For example, we may notice that adding object *C* to already integrated objects *A* and *B* will cause a problem, because the data passed back by *B* to *A* are not in a form compatible with the way we want to pass the same data from *A* to *C*.

17.2.5 Testing

The fact that we are able to integrate all objects into the program using incremental implementation is no guarantee that the program will run correctly under all circumstances. Incremental implementation only enables us to detect any glaring design errors. Testing involves a more systematic approach to running the program with many different test data sets. There are basically three approaches to testing. These approaches are not mutually exclusive; in fact, it is preferable to use all three.

The first is an external approach. With this approach, we care only about external interactions. In other words, we just want to make sure that the program produces the expected results. For our address book program, we will try every menu choice. For each menu choice, we prepare varying sets of data to verify that the program behaves as expected. For data, we may try typical values, extreme values, and invalid values. For all the input values we try, we should know what the result will be. We should never use an arbitrary value and notice that the result seems to be OK.

The second is an internal approach. With this approach, we care only about the internal workings. With the external approach, we do not care whether any part of the program never gets executed. We are concerned only with the program producing expected results. In contrast, with the internal approach, we make sure that every part of the program is executed. We must prepare a set of test data to ensure that every function of every object is executed.

The third is a beta test approach. With this approach, we ask other people to use the program for a certain period of time. People who use the prerelease program are called beta testers. We just let them use the program and wait for error reports. The larger the number of beta testers, the more reliable the testing will be. For example, if 10,000 beta testers cannot find any error, it is unlikely that another 1,000 people will find an error.

17.2.6 Operation

After the program is thoroughly tested to everyone's satisfaction, we release the program for actual use. Unfortunately, not everybody will live happily ever after. Three things are sure to occur. First, some users will want new features not included in the original specification. Second, some users will complain that the program is not fast enough. And third, some users will find unknown bugs. Unless we choose to ignore all these problems and pretend to live happily ever after, we must do something about them. All three things require modifications to the existing program. One of the major selling points of object-oriented programming is its support of easier program modification. For example, if users require a better interface, we could produce one by changing the `TemplateWindow` only, without touching other parts of the program.

17.3 Program listing for the address book

This section contains the complete descriptions (interface and implementation files) for the major objects of the Address Book program. Figure 17.7, showing the inclusion references, appears at the end of the listings.

"ABMain.cpp"

```
//Program Address Book: A program that maintains an
//                              address book.

#include "AdBkCtl.h"

void main()
{
    ABController controller;
    controller.Start();
}
```

"AdBkCtl.h"

```
#ifndef _ADBKCTL_H
#define _ADBKCTL_H

#include "ABMnHd.h"
#include "Person.h"
#include "AddrBook.h"
#include "TplWndw.h"
const int AB_MAXENTRY = 10;

class ABController {
public:
    ABController();

    void Start();

    void NewAddrBook(); //for processing file menus
    void OpenAddrBook();
    void SaveAddrBook();
```

```
      void SaveAsAddrBook();

      void AddPerson(); //for processing edit menus
      void DeletePerson();
      void ModifyPerson();

      void GotoNext();   //for processing movement menus
      void GotoPrev();
      void GotoFirst();
      void GotoLast();

private:
      Menu fileMenu;
      Menu editMenu;
      Menu moveMenu;

      ABMnHndlr                   menuHandler;
      MessageHandler              msgHandler;
      TemplateWindow              onePersonDisplay;
      AddressBook                 addrBook;

      void SetupMenu();

};
#endif
```

```
#include "AdBkCtl.h"

ABController::ABController()
      : fileMenu("File"), editMenu("Edit"), moveMenu("Movement")
{
}

void ABController::Start()
{
      Person oneEntry;
      char *attributes[AB_MAXENTRY];

      SetupMenu();

      //initialize the display window and its list of labels
      oneEntry.GetAttr(attributes);
      onePersonDisplay.Init(100,75,350,250);
      onePersonDisplay.setLabel(attributes);
      onePersonDisplay.SetTitle("Person Information");

      msgHandler.Start();
}

void ABController::SetupMenu()
{
      //set itself as an owner of menuHandler
      menuHandler.SetOwner(this);

      //add individual menu choices
      fileMenu.AddItem("New",                    menuHandler, 1);
      fileMenu.AddItem("Open...",                menuHandler, 2);
      fileMenu.AddItem("Save",                    menuHandler, 3);
      fileMenu.AddItem("Save as...",             menuHandler, 4);

      editMenu.AddItem("Add Person",             menuHandler, 5);
      editMenu.AddItem("Delete Person",          menuHandler, 6);
      editMenu.AddItem("Modify Person",          menuHandler, 7);
```

```
      moveMenu.AddItem("Go To Next",                          menuHandler, 8);
      moveMenu.AddItem("Go To Prev",                          menuHandler, 9);
      moveMenu.AddItem("Go To First",                         menuHandler,10);
      moveMenu.AddItem("Go To Last",                          menuHandler,11);
}

void ABController::NewAddrBook()
{
      YesNoBox prompt;

      //if data exists, prompt the user
      if (addrBook.DataChanged()) {
          //save current data if the user wants to
          if (prompt.Ask(
              "Data have been changed, but not yet saved. Save now?"))
              //user say YES, so save the address book
              addrBook.Save();
          }
      else
          addrBook.Clear();
}

void ABController::OpenAddrBook()
{
      YesNoBox prompt;
      char filename[50];
      FileBox fileBox;

      if (addrBook.DataChanged()) {
          //save any unsaved modified data if the user wants to
          if (prompt.Ask(
              "Data have been changed, but not saved yet. Save now?"))
              //user say YES, so save it
              addrBook.Save();
          }

      //get the name of file to open
      strcpy(filename,fileBox.GetOpenFileName());

      if (strcmp(filename,"") != 0) //name is given
          addrBook.Open(filename); //so open it
      //else
      //cancelled, so do nothing
}
void ABController::SaveAddrBook()
{
      char filename[50];
      FileBox fileBox;

      //is there changed data to save?
      if (addrBook.DataChanged())
          if (addrBook.HasFile()) //already has associated file
              addrBook.Save();
          else  {
              strcpy(filename,fileBox.GetSaveFileName());
              if (strcmp(filename,"") != 0) //name is given
                  addrBook.Save(filename);//so save it
              //else
              //cancelled, so do nothing
          }
}

void ABController::SaveAsAddrBook()
```

```
{
     char filename[50];
     FileBox fileBox;
     OKBox msg;

     //is there any data to save?
     if (addrBook.HasData()) { //get the name of file to save
         strcpy(filename,fileBox.GetSaveFileName());
         if (strcmp(filename,"") != 0) //name is given
             addrBook.Save(filename);//so save it
         //else
         //cancelled, so do nothing
     }
     else
         msg.Display("No data to save");
}
void ABController::DeletePerson()
{
}
void ABController::ModifyPerson()
{
}
void ABController::AddPerson()
{
     char *attributes[AB_MAXENTRY];
     Person        *oneEntry;

     onePersonDisplay.GetData(attributes)
     oneEntry->SetData(attributes);
     addrBook.Add(oneEntry);
     onePersonDisplay.Clear();
}

void ABController::GotoNext()
{
     Person *oneEntry;
     char     *values[AB_MAXENTRY];

     if (oneEntry = addrBook.Next())  {
         oneEntry->GetValue(values);
         onePersonDisplay.SetData(values);
     }
     else {//no next data
         OKBox msg;
         msg.Display("No More Data");
     }
}

void ABController::GotoPrev()
{
     Person *oneEntry;
     char     *values[MAXENTRY];

     if (oneEntry = addrBook.Prev())  {
         oneEntry->GetValue(values);
         onePersonDisplay.SetData(values);
     }
     else {//no previous data
         OKBox msg;
         msg.Display("No More Data");
     }
}
void ABController::GotoFirst()
```

```
{
     Person *oneEntry;
     char     *values[MAXENTRY];

     if (oneEntry = addrBook.First())  {
          oneEntry->GetValue(values);
          onePersonDisplay.SetData(values);
     }
     else {//no data
          OKBox msg;
          msg.Display("No Data");
     }
}

void ABController::GotoLast()
{
     Person *oneEntry;
     char     *values[MAXENTRY];

     if (oneEntry = addrBook.Last())  {
          oneEntry->GetValue(values);
          onePersonDisplay.SetData(values);
     }
     else {//no data
          OKBox msg;
          msg.Display("No Data");
     }
}
```

```
#ifndef __ADBKMNHD_H
#define __ADBKMNHD_H

#include "GUIobj.h"

class ABController;  //forward reference

class ABMnHndlr:public MenuHandler {

public:
     void SetOwner(ABController *boss);

     void MenuFunc1(); //New
     void MenuFunc2(); //Open...
     void MenuFunc3(); //Save
     void MenuFunc4(); //Save as...
     void MenuFunc5(); //Add Person
     void MenuFunc6(); //Delete Person
     void MenuFunc7(); //Modify Person
     void MenuFunc8(); //Go To Next
     void MenuFunc9(); //Go To Prev
     void MenuFunc10();//Go To First
     void MenuFunc11();//Go To Last

private:
     ABController          *owner;
};
#endif
```

```
#include "AdBkCtl.h"

#include "ABMnHd.h"

void ABMnHndlr::SetOwner(ABController *boss)
{
    owner = boss;
}

void ABMnHndlr::MenuFunc1() //New
{
    owner->NewAddrBook();
}
void ABMnHndlr::MenuFunc2()  //Open..
{
    owner->OpenAddrBook();
}

void ABMnHndlr::MenuFunc3()//Save
{
    owner->SaveAddrBook();
}

void ABMnHndlr::MenuFunc4()//Save As...
{
    owner->SaveAsAddrBook();
}

void ABMnHndlr::MenuFunc5()//Add Person
{
    owner->AddPerson();
}

void ABMnHndlr::MenuFunc6()//Delete Person
{
    owner->DeletePerson();
}

void ABMnHndlr::MenuFunc7()//Modify Person
{
    owner->ModifyPerson();
}
void ABMnHndlr::MenuFunc8()//Go To Next
{
    owner->GotoNext();
}
void ABMnHndlr::MenuFunc9()//Go To Prev
{
    owner->GotoPrev();
}
void ABMnHndlr::MenuFunc10()//Go To First
{
    owner->GotoFirst();
}

void ABMnHndlr::MenuFunc11()//Go To Last
{
    owner->GotoLast();
}
```

```
#ifndef _TPLWNDW_H
#define _TPLWNDW_H

#include <string.h>
#include "GUIobj.h"

class TemplateWindow : public EditWin {
public:
     void GetData(char *value[]);
     //get a list of entry data

     void SetData(char *value[]);
     //display the data with correct prompts

     void setLabel(char *tmpl[]);
     //set the list of prompts for attribute entries

private:
     char *label[10];
     int labelSize;
};
#endif
```

```
#include "TplWndw.h"

void TemplateWindow::setLabel(char *tmpl[])
{
     int i=0;
     while (tmpl[i] != 0) {  //not NULL
          label[i] = new char[20];
          strcpy(label[i],tmpl[i]);
          i = i+1;
     }
     labelSize = i;
}

void TemplateWindow::SetData(char *value[])
{
     char str[40];
     Clear();
     for (int i=0; i<labelSize; i=i+1) {
          InsertLine(2*i,label[i]); //display labels
          strcpy(str,"        ");
          strcat(str,value[i]);
          InsertLine(2*i+1,str);     //display values
     }
}

void TemplateWindow::GetData(char *value[])
{
     for (int i=0; i<labelSize; i=i+1) {
          value[i] = new char[40];
          strcpy(value[i],ReadLine(i));
     }
}
```

```
#ifndef __PERSON_H
#define __PERSON_H

#include <stdlib.h>
#include <string.h>

class Person  {
public:
      void SetValue(char *value[]);
      //assigns data to each attributes

      void GetAttr(char *attr[]);
      //returns a set of attribute names

      void GetValue(char *value[]);
      //returns a set of attribute values;

      int NumAttr();
      //returns the number of attributes
private:
      char        name[20];
      int         age;
      char        address[40];
      char        phone[14];
};
#endif
```

```
#include "Person.h"

void Person::GetValue(char *value[])
{
      value[0] = new char[strlen(name)+1];
      strcpy(value[0],name);

      value[1] = new char[3];
      itoa(age,value[1],10);

      value[2] = new char[strlen(address)+1];
      strcpy(value[2],address);

      value[3] = new char[strlen(phone)+1];
      strcpy(value[3],phone);
}

void Person::GetAttr(char *attr[])
{
      attr[0] = "Name:";
      attr[1] = "Age:";
      attr[2] = "Address:";
      attr[3] = "Phone:";
}

void Person::SetValue(char *value[])
{
      strcpy(name,value[0]);
      age = atoi(value[1]);
      strcpy(address,value[2]);
      strcpy(phone,value[3]);
}

int Person::NumAttr()
{
      return 4;
}
```

```
#ifndef _ADDRBOOK_H
#define _ADDRBOOK_H

#include <fstream.h>
#include "Person.h"
#include "GUIObj.h"
const int AB_MAXSIZE = 100;

class AddressBook {
public:
     AddressBook();

     void Clear();

     int HasData();             //return TRUE if it contains any data

     int DataChanged();         //return TRUE if any data is modified

     int HasFile();             //return TRUE if it has an associated file

     void Open(char *filename);
     //open the file filename and load the data

     void Save();       //save the data to the currently associated file

     void Save(char *filename);          //save the data  into filename

     void Add(Person *person);
     //add a person to the address book

     Person *Next();
     //returns the next person in the list

     Person *Prev();
     //returns the previous person in the list

     Person *First();
     //returns the first person in the list

     Person *Last();
     //returns the last person in the list
private:
     fstream        addrBookFile;
     char           adBkFilename[50];
     Person         *entry[AB_MAXSIZE];
     int            entryCount;
     int            current;
     int            changed;
};
#endif
```

```
#include "AddrBook.h"
#include "Person.h"

AddressBook::AddressBook()
{
     Clear();
}

void AddressBook::Clear()
{
     entryCount     = 0;
     current        = -1;
```

```
        changed         = 0;
        strcpy(adBkFilename,"");
}

int AddressBook::HasData()
{
        if (entryCount > 0)
            return 1;
        else
            return 0;
}

int AddressBook::DataChanged()
{
        return changed;
}

int AddressBook::HasFile()
{
        if (strcmp(adBkFilename,"") != 0)
            return 1;
        else
            return 0;
}

void AddressBook::Open(char *filename)
{
        char *value[10], tmpStr[255];
        int entrySize, attrSize, i, j;

        addrBookFile.open(filename,ios::in);
        strcpy(adBkFilename,filename);

        addrBookFile >> entrySize; //read control
        addrBookFile >> attrSize;  //information
        entryCount = entrySize;

        addrBookFile.getline(tmpStr,255); //read past
                                                    //the second line
        //read in data
        for (i=0; i<entrySize; i = i+1) {

            //read one person info
            for (j=0; j<attrSize; j =j+1) {
                addrBookFile.getline(tmpStr,255);
                value[j] = new char[strlen(tmpStr)+1];
                strcpy(value[j],tmpStr);
            }

            entry[i] = new Person;
            entry[i]->SetValue(value);
        }

        addrBookFile.close();
}

void AddressBook::Add(Person *person)
{
        if (entryCount < AB_MAXSIZE) { //still has space to add
            entry[entryCount] = person;
            entryCount = entryCount + 1;
            changed = 1;
        }
}
```

```
void AddressBook::Save()
{
    int attrSize, i, j; char *value[10];

    if (HasFile()) {//save if there's file
        addrBookFile.open(adBkFilename,ios::out);
        attrSize = entry[0]->NumAttr();

        addrBookFile << entryCount << "\n"; //save control
        addrBookFile << attrSize   << "\n";  //information

        for (i=0; i<entryCount; i = i+1) {
            entry[i]->GetValue(value);
            //read one person info
            for (j=0; j<attrSize; j = j+1)
                addrBookFile << value[j] << "\n";
            delete entry[i];
        }

        addrBookFile.close();
        changed = 0;
    }
}

void  AddressBook::Save(char *filename)
{
    int attrSize, i, j; char *value[10];

    addrBookFile.open(filename,ios::out);
    attrSize = entry[0]->NumAttr();

    addrBookFile << entryCount << "\n"; //save control
    addrBookFile << attrSize   << "\n";  //information

    for (i=0; i<entryCount; i = i+1) {
        entry[i]->GetValue(value);
        //read one person info
        for (j=0; j<attrSize; j = j+1)
            addrBookFile << value[j] << "\n";
        delete entry[i];
    }

    addrBookFile.close();
    changed = 0;
}

Person *AddressBook::Next()
{
    if (entryCount <= 0 || current == entryCount-1)
        return 0; //error, no entry or no prev
    else {
        current = current + 1;
        return entry[current];
    }
}

Person *AddressBook::Prev()
{
    if (entryCount <= 0 || current == 0)
        return 0; //error, no entry or no prev
    else {
        current = current - 1;
        return entry[current];
    }
}
```

```
Person *AddressBook::First()
{
    if (entryCount <= 0)
        return 0; //error, no entry
    else {
        current = 0;
        return entry[current];
    }
}

Person *AddressBook::Last()
{
    if (entryCount <=0)
        return 0; //error, no entry
    else {
        current = entryCount-1;
        return entry[current];
    }
}
```

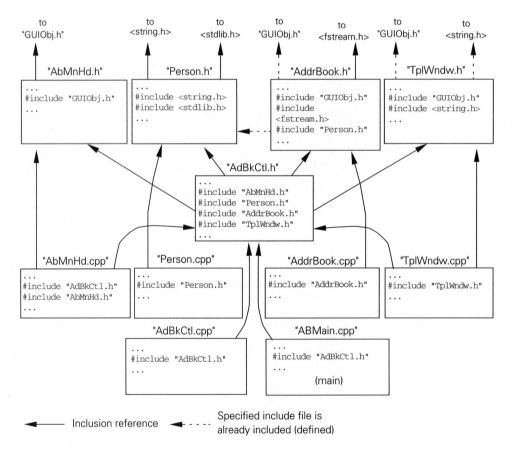

Figure 17.7 Inclusion references

CHAPTER 17   OBJECT-ORIENTED DEVELOPMENT

17.4 Exercises

1 Define a `ListWindow` object (descendant of an `EditWin`) that displays a list of strings. Define a function called `Display` that accepts an array of pointers to `char` and displays the strings. For example, executing the following code

```
ListWindow listWindow;
char *value[4] = {"one", "two", "three", "four"};
listWindow.Display(value);
```

will display

```
one
two
three
four
```

2 Incorporate the `ListWindow` defined in the previous exercise into the Address Book program to display the names of all `Person` objects in the address book.

3 Write a program that will accept a month (1–12) and year (1593 to the present) from the user and display a calendar for that month. For example, with an input of 9 and 1993, the program will display the figure on the left below: To display a specified month, you must first print the outline of the month (below right).

September 1993						
S	M	T	W	T	F	S
			1	2	3	4
5	6	7	8	9	10	11
12	13	14	15	16	17	18
19	20	21	22	23	24	25
26	27	28	29	30		

September 1993						
S	M	T	W	T	F	S

Then determine the day for the first of the month (for September 1993 it is Wednesday) to start printing the dates. After day 1 is placed, continue printing successive dates (2, 3, 4, ...) moving left to right, row by row. Stop when the last day of the month (28, 29, 30, or 31) is printed.

Here are some of the calendar facts you need to know for writing this program:

- January 1, 1593, was a Saturday.

- A year divisible by four is a leap year. However, years ending in 00 are not leap years unless they are divisible by 400, for example, 1800 and 1900 are not leap years, but 1600 and 2000 are.

- April, June, September, and November have 30 days. February has 28 days in nonleap years and 29 days in leap years. All other months have 31 days.

- Any given month may have either four, five, or six weeks. For example, February 1998 has four weeks, September 1993 has five weeks, and January 1994 has six weeks.

- The weekday (Monday, Tuesday, etc.) of any date can be determined by counting the number of days since Saturday, January 1, 1593. We can do this calculation because we know the number of days in each month (watch out for Februaries). Once the total number of days is determined, we divide that number by seven (number of days in a week). The remainder of the division is between 0 and 6. Since we are counting from Saturday, the remainder 0 means Saturday, 1 means Sunday, 2 means Monday, and so forth.

You can use a descendant of a `Turtle` to print out both the outline and the days of a month.

4 Define an `Appointment` object that allows you to set the date, time, and a brief description of an appointment. You need to decide how to represent the date and time (e.g., do you use three integers or one string for a date?).

5 Incorporate the `Appointment` object defined in the previous exercise into the Address Book program. Add a new Appointment menu with choices New Appointment, Search Appointment, and Delete Appointment. For each menu choice, you must carry out an appropriate operation. You need to define a new object that keeps track of all appointments.

6 With the present Address Book program, when the end user selects the menu choice `Add Person`, the data values for a new `Person` must already be entered in the window on line 0, line 1, line 2, and line 3 with no leading spaces on all lines. This method is somewhat restrictive and not very robust (e.g., selecting the menu choice without entering any data values will result in an error). Modify the input procedure for adding new person information. With the new procedure, the program asks the user for each value using a `StringTypeIn` object.

7 Modify the Address Book program so that the modified program handles information on automobiles, instead of persons.

8 Write an airline seat reservation system. The system can accommodate up to five airplanes. Every airplane has the same seating arrangement:

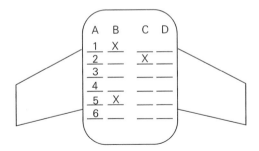

When a seat is reserved, an *X* is placed in its position. In the above diagram, seats 1A, 2C, and 5B are reserved. The Seating menu has choices Assign and Cancel. A reservation is made by first selecting the menu choice Assign and then specifying the seat position and the name of a passenger (use `StringTypeIn` objects). A reservation is canceled by selecting the menu choice Cancel. Make a second menu Airplane whose menu items are the names of the airplanes (e.g., Plane 1, Plane 2, and so forth). Selecting any of the Airplane menu choices will display its current seat assignments. The display window is a descendant of an `EditWin`. (Note: The outline of an airplane shown above is for illustration purpose only; you don't have to draw the wings and the body of the airplane.)

9 Modify the airline reservation system in the previous exercise to allow a ticket agent to enter the *X*s directly on the displayed seating arrangement. When the clerk clicks the OK button, the program prompts the ticket agent for the customer names for the newly entered *X*s.

10 Modify the airline reservation system again to save the seating arrangements of all airplanes in files. Use a separate file for each airplane. Add appropriate menu choices to open and save seating arrangement files.

11 Modify the original airline reservation system to handle an arbitrary number of airplanes. You may limit the maximum number of airplanes (e.g., 30) the program can handle. You do not have to set a fixed maximum if you save the airplane seating arrangements (see exercise 10). If you save all airplane information to files, you only need to open one file at any one time.

12 Incorporate all three modifications of the airline reservation system into one program.

chapter 18

Fundamental algorithms— searching and sorting

The Address Book program we wrote in chapter 17 is very limited in its functionality. For example, it would be much better if it allowed the user to search for a desired person or displayed the names in alphabetical order. These two operations—searching and sorting—are very common in many different types of computer programs. Knowledge of basic techniques for searching and sorting is considered fundamental to the study of computer science. In this chapter, we will explain some classic algorithms for searching and sorting. Keep in mind the methods we show in this chapter are very basic, and they represent only a very small percentage of known algorithms.

To make our discussion lucid and simple, we will use an array of integers to explain searching and sorting algorithms. All the techniques we present here are adaptable to an array of any object or primitive data type. At the end of the chapter, we will show you how the deletion and modification functions of the `AddressBook` object are implemented using one of the search algorithms introduced in this chapter.

18.1 Searching

We will start our discussion of fundamental algorithms with searching. The first step is to formalize the searching problem for an integer array:

> Given a search value X, return the position (index) in the array where the search value X is located, if such X exists. Otherwise, return EMPTY (-1). We assume there are no duplicate values in the array.

For example, given the array shown in figure 18.1, the search algorithm will return 5 for the search value 987.

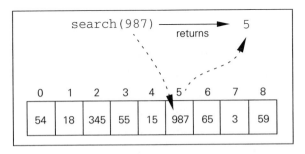

Figure 18.1 Search algorithm returns 5

For the purpose of writing a complete function for each of the algorithms we present in this chapter, we will define an object called Collection, which has the following interface:

```
const int NOT_FOUND  = -1;
const int EMPTY       = -1;
const int TABLE_FULL  = -1;
const int MAXSIZE     = 97;

class Collection {
public:
    int LSearch(int searchValue);
    int BSearch(int searchValue);
    int HInsert(int value);
    int HSearch(int searchValue);
    void SSort();
    void BSort();
    void MSort(int low, int high);
    int RLSearch(int low, int high, int searchValue);
    int RBSearch(int low, int high, int searchValue);
```

```
        void SetData(int *list, int lsize);
        void GetData(int *list, int lsize);
        void Clear();

    private:
        void Merge(int low, int i, int high);
        int size = 0;
        int element[MAXSIZE];
};
```

How the private data members are used will become clear as we start explaining various algorithms. Notice that you cannot mix and match the functions. For example, you cannot call LSearch and then call HSearch. Doing so will have an unpredictable result. The Collection object is defined here solely for pedagogic purposes.

18.1.1 Linear search

One obvious way to search for a value is to start from the first position of the array and repeatedly look at successive positions until the value is found or until there are no more values left in the array to search. This technique is called a *linear search* because we search sequentially from the first to the last position in a linear (i.e., straight) progression. Another name for a linear search is a *sequential search*. The linear (sequential) search is frequently used as a benchmark for comparing other search methods. The function LSearch is defined as

```
int Collection::LSearch ( int searchValue)
{
    int i;
                              ┌─────────────────────────────────────┐
                              │ size must have a correct value before│
                              │ this function is called.             │
                              └─────────────────────────────────────┘
    for (i = 0; i <= size-1; i = i+1)
        if (element[i] == searchValue) //found, so return
            return i;//the position

    //searched all entries, but no match was found
    return NOT_FOUND;
}
```

If the number of entries in the array is N, then there will be N comparisons for any unsuccessful case (i.e., when a value is not found). In the case of a successful search, there will be a minimum of one comparison and a maximum of N comparisons. On the average, if we assume we search for every entry with equal frequency, then there will be approximately $N/2$ comparisons.

Is this result good? Can we hope for another algorithm that yields better performance? These are the kinds of questions computer scientists ask. Computer scientists strive to find a better solution and mathematically prove that a known solution is the best solution. Is the linear search the best search algorithm? Yes and no. Yes if the following three conditions are assumed:

1 Data are stored in a one-dimensional array.

2 There is no ordering of data.

3 The basic operation for searching is the comparison of two values.

If we relax any one of these three conditions, we can develop an algorithm yielding much better performance. In the next two sections, we will show you how performance can be improved by not assuming the second and the third conditions. Relaxing the first condition and designing a more intricate structure for organizing data is the subject of more advanced computer science study.

18.1.2 Binary search

If we remove the second condition and assume that there is some ordering of the data, then we can improve the performance of the linear search. Imposing an ordering means that the entries in the array are arranged in ascending or descending order by values. We call such an array a *sorted array.* Here we will assume that the values are arranged in ascending order. Figure 18.2 is a sorted array.

If a given array is sorted, then we can improve search performance dramatically by using a *binary search*. Notice that with a linear search, we can eliminate only one value from further consideration when a comparison results in no match. If we can devise a scheme that can eliminate more than one value after each negative comparison (i.e., a comparison that results in no match), we can improve performance. Since we eliminate more than one value for each negative comparison, the binary search eliminates a larger number of values for the same number of comparisons than the linear search eliminates. By eliminating more values for the same number of comparisons, the whole binary search algorithm will terminate sooner than the linear search. If the array is sorted, a linear search can also be improved by making a slight change in the algorithm, although the improvement is not as dramatic as the improvement of a binary search. (See exercise 1 at the end of this chapter.)

0	1	2	3	4	5	6	7	8
3	15	18	54	55	59	65	345	987

Figure 18.2 Sorted array

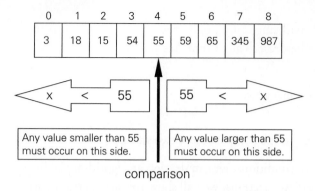

Figure 18.3 **By making one comparison at the middle position, we can determine whether a given number is located in the first half or the second half of the array.**

Let's start with an example, using the above sorted array. Suppose we search for 65, and we make the first comparison with the value in the fifth, or the middle, position, that is, element[4]. After this comparison, which results in no match, we can conclude that if the value 65 is indeed in the array, then it must occur somewhere between element[5] and element[8]. Why? Because the array is sorted and since 65 is greater than 55, the value must be in a position after the position of 55 (see figure 18.3).

The effect of one comparison is to eliminate half of the array from further comparisons. A comparison has three possible outcomes, and figure 18.4 shows a generalized situation.

Using the preceding rules, a typical search pattern may look like figure 18.5. Comparisons will continue until either the value is found or there are no more entries in the array to search. In the case of a successful search, we will eventually find a match in one of the

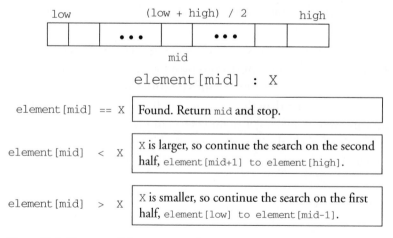

Figure 18.4 **Three possible outcomes of a comparison**

CHAPTER 18 FUNDAMENTAL ALGORITHMS

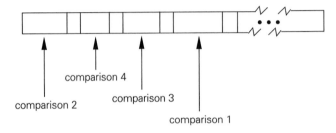

Figure 18.5 A typical search pattern

comparisons, and then we can stop. However, in the case of an unsuccessful search, how can we tell when to stop? How do we know when there are no more values to search? With the linear search, it was easy. We stopped when we finished looking at the last position in the array. Since we are not doing such a sequential sweep of the array with the binary search, we need some other criteria to detect when there are no more values to search. We do this by keeping track of the beginning and ending positions of the portion of the array that is still being searched. We will call the variables for keeping track of the beginning and ending positions low and high, respectively. Figure 18.6 shows how the values for low and high change for a sample unsuccessful search. We assume the original array is of size 20, and we search for the value 55, which is not in the array.

Notice that the value of low only increases, starting from 0, and the value of high only decreases, starting from the size of the array. The difference (high - low) shows the number of entries still left to be searched. If the search value is not located in the array, then eventually the condition

```
low > high
```

becomes TRUE and we terminate the unsuccessful search. Here is the function BSearch:

```
int Collection::BSearch ( int searchValue )
{
    int low = 0, high = size-1, mid;
    while (low <= high) {
        mid = (low + high) / 2 ; //the result is truncated
        if (element[mid] == searchValue) //FOUND
            return mid;
        else if (element[mid] < searchValue)
            low = mid + 1;
        else // element[mid] > searchValue
            high = mid - 1;
    }
    return NOT_FOUND;
}
```

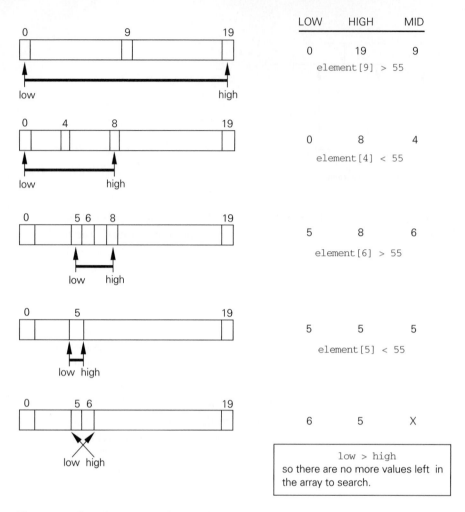

LOW	HIGH	MID
0	19	9

element[9] > 55

0	8	4

element[4] < 55

5	8	6

element[6] > 55

5	5	5

element[5] < 55

6	5	X

low > high
so there are no more values left in
the array to search.

Figure 18.6 Sample unsuccessful search

How good is a binary search? Let's look at an unsuccessful search. With a linear search, we know there are always N comparisons for any unsuccessful search (assuming the array is not sorted). Will the binary search reduce the number of comparisons for an unsuccessful search? Let's see. After each comparison, the size of the remaining portion is always cut into half (roughly, it differs slightly depending on whether the current portion has an odd or even number of entries). We know that an unsuccessful search will terminate if we cannot divide the remaining portion into half anymore (i.e., low > high). We can derive the total number of comparisons by computing how many times we can divide the original array. Table 18.1 shows how many times the original array can be divided into halves. We assume that the size of the original array is a power of 2 (2, 4, 8, 16, 32, ...) to make the explanation simple. With a little more detailed mathematics, you can show the same result for an array of any size.

We can find the maximum number of comparisons by solving the value for K in the above table. That is, we solve the following equation for K:

$$\frac{N}{2^K} = 1$$

Thus we have

$$N = 2^K$$

$$\log_2 N = K$$

Table 18.1 Number of times original array can be divided into halves

Comparison #j	Size of a remaining portion after jth comparison
0	N
1	$\frac{N}{2} = \frac{N}{2^1}$
2	$\frac{N}{4} = \frac{N}{2^2}$
...	...
K	$\frac{N}{2^K} = 1$

For example, when the size of original array is 1,024, then there will be at most $\log_2 1024 = 10$ comparisons using a binary search, compared to 1,024 comparisons using a linear search. The difference between the two algorithms gets larger as the size of an array gets larger.

18.1.3 Hashing

If we remove the third condition—using only the comparison as the basic operation—then we can also improve performance. We are not going to eliminate the comparison operation all together. We are going to incorporate a mathematical function to reduce the number of comparisons drastically. With a hashing method, the values are stored in assigned places. We use a mathematical function to assign the place to store a value. The mathematical function used for this purpose is called a *hashing function*. There are many different types of hashing functions, and we choose the one most appropriate for a given application. We will use the most common type, the *division method*, here. We define the division hashing function as follows:

```
H( k ) = k % tableSize
```

where `tablesize` is the size of an array and the `%` operator is the modulus operator (it returns the remainder of a division operation). Figure 18.7 shows how four values are assigned to an array of size 9. We use `EMPTY` `(-1)` to denote an empty position.

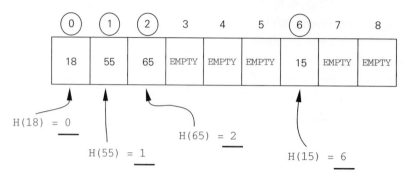

Figure 18.7 Four values assigned to an array of size 9

Let's first study how a new value is added to the hash table. A new value `X` is placed at the position `H(X)` in the table. For example, to insert the value 22, we compute its address, which is `H(22)` `= 4`, and place the value at the designated location (see figure 18.8).

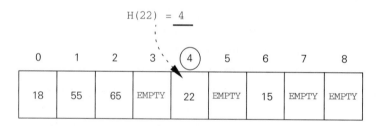

Figure 18.8 New value added to the hash table

In the ideal situation, this step is all we need to do, that is, simply place a new value into the location computed by applying the hash function to the value. In some cases we can maintain this ideal situation by carefully selecting the hash function and the size of the table relative to the number of values to be stored in the table. However, in almost all cases, either we cannot find such an optimal solution or an optimal solution requires unacceptably heavy space usage. A correct insertion algorithm, therefore, must handle the less than ideal situation.

The less than ideal situation occurs when we cannot place a new value at the location computed by the hash function. How is this possible? Consider adding the value 64 to the above array. Since

```
H( 64 ) = 1
```

we would place it in position 1. But that position is already occupied by another value, 55. This situation is called a *collision*. As long as we use a hashing function, we cannot avoid the problem of collisions.[*] This is why we still need to carry out a certain number of tests (comparison operations) with the hashing method; that is, we need to check whether there is a collision. A technique to resolve the collision problem is known as a *collision resolution technique*. The study of hashing search methods amounts to a study of hashing functions and collision resolution techniques.

We will describe here the simplest collision resolution technique, *linear probing*. With the linear probing technique, we look at the next position when

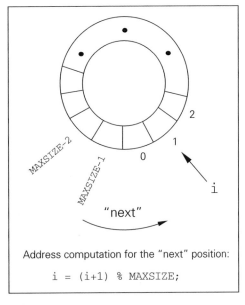

Address computation for the "next" position:

```
i = (i+1) % MAXSIZE;
```

Figure 18.9 "Next" positions determined in a cyclic manner

there is a collision. If this position is open, the value is placed there. If this position is also already occupied, then we move on to the next position. We continue this process until an open position is found. We know a position is open if it is marked EMPTY (i.e., the value stored in the position is –1).

The "next" position is determined in a cyclic manner. Normally, the next position of address i is simply i+1. However, the next position of the last position (address MAXSIZE-1) is the first position in the array (location 0), as illustrated in figure 18.9.

We apply the modulo function to compute the correct next position. The following is the insertion function.

```
int Collection::HInsert( int value)
{
```

---

[*] If we know all the values up front, then we can devise a tailor-made, collision–free hash function for the given values. However, we very rarely know all values beforehand.

```
    int i;

    if (size == MAXSIZE)

        return TABLE_FULL; //fully occupied; cannot add it

    else {

        i = value % MAXSIZE;

        while (element[i] != EMPTY) //collision! move to
            i = (i+1) % MAXSIZE;//the next position

        element[i] = value;//insert the value
        size = size + 1;

        return i; //signal success
    }
}
```

We use the data member `size` to keep track of the number of values in the array. The array is 100 percent occupied if `size` is equal to `MAXSIZE`. We test this condition first. If `size` is not equal to `MAXSIZE`, then there is an open position in which to insert the given value, so we apply the hash function and carry out the linear probing scheme to insert the value. When the value is inserted, the `size` is incremented by one, and the address of the position where this new value is inserted is returned.

To search for a given value, we essentially repeat the insertion algorithm. We first compute the address of the value to be searched for by using the same hashing function. Then, if necessary, we carry out the linear probing scheme until either the value is located in the table or we can determine that the value is not in the table. We determine that the value is not in the table when an empty position is encountered or all positions have been searched. If the table is not full, then an empty position will always be encountered. Only in the case when the table is full or the search value is not in the table, do we have to search every position of the table. The following is the search function with linear probing.

```
int Collection::HSearch( int searchValue)
{
    int i = searchValue % MAXSIZE;

    int cnt = 0;

    while (cnt != MAXSIZE) { //still more positions to search

        if (element[i] == searchValue)  //found

            return i;

        else if (element[i] == EMPTY)    //not found
```

```
            return NOT_FOUND;

        cnt = cnt + 1;

        i = (i+1) % MAXSIZE;
    }

    //searched all positions but no match was found
    return NOT_FOUND;
}
```

On the average, we expect to insert or search a value without having any collisions which means that a hashing algorithm basically requires one comparison.[*] However, we cannot eliminate the possibility of doing up to N (the size of the array) comparisons, which is the same as the linear search. With a binary search, the number of comparisons is always $\log_2 N$. Table 18.2 summarizes the performance of the three search techniques.

Table 18.2 Search performances of linear, binary, and hashing methods for an array of size N.

	Average case	Worst case
Linear search	$N/2$	N
Binary search	$\log_2 N$	$\log_2 N$
Hashing	1	N

18.2 Sorting

One of the requirements of the binary search technique is that the values in the array are sorted. There are also many other situations where we need to have data sorted in some specified order. Arranging values in a collection into ascending or descending order is called *sorting*. In this section we discuss two basic sorting techniques. We will describe a more advanced sorting technique in the next section.

---

[*] Here we are not literally counting every logical test inside the if and while statements. We are actually counting the number of times the loop body is executed, because this value directly corresponds to the number of times a collision occurs. In other words, in the case of N collisions, the loop body is executed N times. The number of actual tests done inside the loop is proportional to the number of times the loop body is executed, so by counting the number of times the loop body is executed, we can get a good estimate of the algorithm's performance.

We assume here that the values are already placed in the array, and we will sort them into ascending order. We do not consider the maintenance of a sorted array, that is, adding a new value or removing an existing value and maintaining the sorted order. We also apply the condition that no extra array is used in the sorting process. We call such a sorting technique *in situ sorting*. *In situ* means *in place*. In this section we will study some of the well-known in situ sorting algorithms. Let's formalize the sorting problem as follows:

> Given an array with N values in it, arrange the N values in the array into ascending order without using any additional array.

18.2.1 Selection sort

Consider the array in figure 18.10.

Which value should be in the first position? The value 3, of course. It is the smallest value in the array, and therefore it should occupy the first position in the sorted array. We can easily write code for finding the smallest value as

```
minLoc = 0;
for (i = 1; i <= 8; i = i+1)
    if (element[i] < element[minLoc]) minLoc = i;
```

The variable minLoc keeps track of the position of the current minimum value. It is initialized to 0 and adjusted in the for loop whenever a value smaller than the current minimum is found. When the loop terminates, minLoc is the index of the smallest value in the array. In the preceding example, minLoc would be equal to 7, the position occupied by 3.

Once the smallest value is located, we move it to the first position, where it belongs. So we say

```
element[0] = element[minLoc]
```

which results in the array shown in figure 18.11.

0	1	2	3	4	5	6	7	8
54	18	345	55	15	987	65	3	59

Figure 18.10 Sample array

CHAPTER 18   FUNDAMENTAL ALGORITHMS

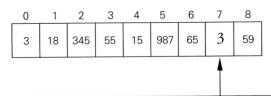

0	1	2	3	4	5	6	7	8
3	18	345	55	15	987	65	*3*	59

This place should be blank, but the assignment operator is really only a copying operation, so the original value is still here. We write it in a different style to signify its special nature.

Figure 18.11 The state after the minimum value is copied to the first position

The value 3 went to the right place, but we've lost the value 54. Since the value 3 has vacated position 7, we can move the value 54 there. We interchange the two by executing

```
temp= element[0];
element[0] = element[minLoc];
element[minLoc] = temp;
```

which correctly results in figure 18.12.

Now that the smallest value is in the correct position (without losing any values), we proceed to find the next smallest element and move it to the correct position, which is the second. The same method works by applying the routine from positions 1 to 8, instead of from positions 0 to 8. This logic makes sense because position 0 has the correct minimum value and should not be considered any further. If we execute

```
minLoc = 1;
for (i = 2; i <= 8; i = i+1)
    if (element[i] < element[minLoc]) minLoc = i;

temp           = element[1];
element[1]     = element[minLoc];
element[minLoc] = temp;
```

the array now looks like figure 18.13.

Sorted	Unsorted							
0	1	2	3	4	5	6	7	8
3	18	345	55	15	987	65	54	59

Figure 18.12 The state after the values 3 and 54 are interchanged

Sorted		Unsorted						
0	1	2	3	4	5	6	7	8
3	15	345	55	18	987	65	54	59

Figure 18.13 The state after the second interchange is made

We repeat the process of finding the minimum in the remaining unsorted portion, from positions 2 to 8. Every time the minimum is located for a unsorted portion, we increase the size of the sorted portion by one and decrease the size of the unsorted portion

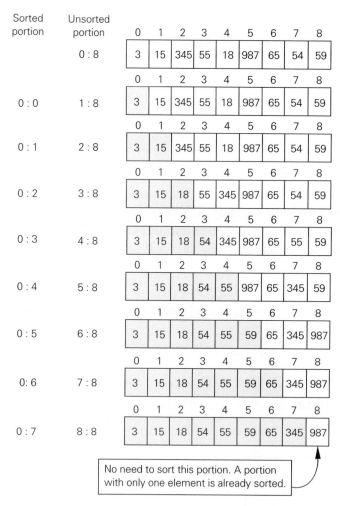

Figure 18.14 Sequence of shrinking unsorted portions

CHAPTER 18   FUNDAMENTAL ALGORITHMS

by 1. We continue repeating the process of finding the minimum in the shrinking unsorted portions until there's only one element left in the unsorted portion. Figure 18.14 illustrates the sequence of shrinking unsorted portions.

The complete algorithm is

```
void Collection::SSort()
{
    int temp, top, i, minLoc;

    for (top = 0; top <= size-2; top = top+1) {

        minLoc = top;

        for (i = top+1; i <= size-1; i = i+1)

            if (element[i] < element[minLoc]) minLoc = i;

        temp= element[top];
        element[top] = element[minLoc];
        element[minLoc] = temp;
    }
}
```

Is the selection sort a good sorting algorithm? Well, the answer depends on what we mean by *good*, of course. In comparing different sorting algorithms, we can count two things: the number of comparisons and the number of data movements. We will show you how to count the number of comparisons, and use this number as a criteria for evaluating the sorting algorithms discussed in this chapter. We will consider only the comparisons here for two reasons: a comparison is a more costly operation than a data movement; and considering only one criteria simplifies the analysis. In general, we want an algorithm that minimizes the number of times the most costly operation is executed. If two algorithms have the same performance in terms of the number of times they execute the comparison operation, then we may want to compare the two further by counting the number of data movements each requires. A detailed analysis is beyond the scope of this book, so we will limit our discussion to evaluating sorting algorithms using only the comparison operation as an evaluation criteria.

The selection sort has one comparison (the `if` statement inside the nested `for` loops), so we can easily count the total number of comparisons by counting the number of times the inner loop is executed. For each execution of the outer loop, the inner loop is executed `size - top` times. Variable `size` is fixed (i.e., will have the same value), but the variable `top` ranges from `0` to `size-2`. So the total number of comparisons is computed by finding the sum of the right column in table 18.3.

With a little bit of mathematics, we can show that

$$size + (size - 1) + (size - 2) + \ldots + 2$$

$$= \sum_{t=2}^{size} (i) = \sum_{i=1}^{size} i - 1 = \frac{size(size + 1)}{2} - 1$$

$$= \frac{size^2 + size - 2}{2} \cong size^2$$

Table 18.3 Values in right column show the number of comparisons made to find the smallest number

Top	Size – top
0	size
1	size – 1
2	size – 2
...	...
size – 2	2

This results shows that the total number of comparisons is roughly the square of the size of the array. Since this is a quadratic function, the total number of comparisons grows quite dramatically as the size of an array gets larger. Is there a better sorting algorithm?

18.2.2 Bubble sort

Let's call an execution of the inner loop of the selection sort a *pass*. If the size of an array is N, then there will be N passes, because the inner loop is executed N times. The net effect of one pass of the selection sort is the migration of the smallest (in the current range of positions) to its correct position. Since an array gets sorted only by moving around values, the whole routine will finish sooner if we increase the number of data movements for the same number of comparisons. In other words, instead of making one move after each pass, as the selection sort does, we should try to make as many data movements as possible in any given pass, thereby reducing the total number of passes made to sort the whole array.

The bubble sort is one such algorithm. With the bubble sort we will make the same number of passes as the selection sort only in the worst case. For the average case, the bubble sort will be able to sort the whole array before performing the N passes. The key to the bubble sort is its pairwise comparison and exchanges during a pass. Consider figure 18.15, which illustrates the effect of one bubble sort pass.

The bubble sort performs a total of eight pairwise comparisons, the same number of comparisons made by the selection sort during its one pass. The only difference is whether we are comparing a value with the current minimum value (selection sort) or comparing the next two values (bubble sort). The net effect of bubble sort's one pass is that the largest value is moved to the last position of an array. From this fact, we know that the bubble sort has at least the equivalent performance of the selection sort.[*]

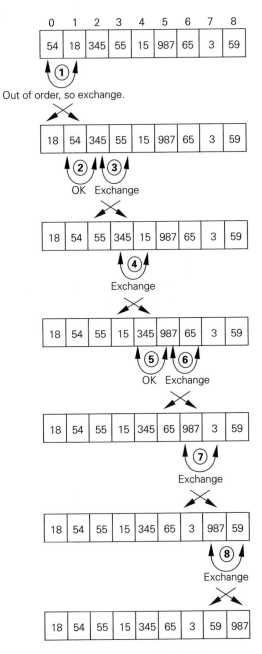

Figure 18.15 Effect of one pass of bubble sort

---

* Keep in mind that we are considering only the number of comparisons here. The bubble sort, in fact, requires a larger number of data movements than the selection sort.

In addition to the guaranteed effect, we can normally expect something more from the bubble sort. Unlike the selection sort, more than one exchange could occur during one bubble sort pass. Since we are sorting into ascending order, if a pairwise comparison tells us that the value in the lower position (the left in the diagram) is larger than the value in the higher position, then we switch them because they are out of order. The diagram shows the values 54 and 345, among others, moved toward their correct places. The reason we call this sorting technique a *bubble* sort is because if you flip the array vertically, with the right side up, then the effect of one pass is that values move toward the top just like air bubbles move toward the surface of water. Since we are moving more values with the same number of comparisons, we can expect the bubble sort to perform better than the selection sort under most situations. That is, it will sort the array with fewer comparisons than the selection sort requires. Later in this section, we will refer to the situations in which the bubble sort does not perform any better than the selection sort.

After one pass, we know for sure that the largest value is in the last position. So, for the next pass, we eliminate this last position from further consideration. The last pass will have only two values (in the first and second positions) for consideration. Let's put this idea into more concrete form:

```
void Collection::BSort()
{
    int temp, bottom, i;

    for (bottom = size-1; bottom >= 1; bottom = bottom-1)

        for (i = 0; i <= bottom-1; i++)

            if (element[i] > element[i+1]) {

            temp= element[i];
            element[i] = element[i+1];
            element[i+1] = temp;
            }
}
```

The preceding function will work, but not as well as advertised. In fact, the function will carry out the same number of comparisons as the function for the selection sort. The whole benefit of the bubble sort is the possibility that the array gets sorted before doing all of the passes because of the effect of moving multiple values during one pass. However, there is no logic in the preceding function to test for this condition. As we proceed from one pass to the next pass, we need to check whether the array gets sorted. How do we check for this? If the array is sorted and we carry out a pass, then what will happen? Since the array is sorted, no pair will be out of order for all the comparisons we make. We can conclude that the array is sorted if no exchanges occur during a pass. In other words, we know the array was not sorted if we end up doing an exchange after one of the pairwise comparisons.

To test whether the array is sorted, therefore, requires a simple checking of whether any exchange is made during a pass. If there are no exchanges, then the array is sorted, so we stop. Otherwise, the array is still not sorted, so we continue. With this idea incorporated, the function becomes

```
void Collection::BSort()
{
    int temp, bottom, i, noSwitch;

    for (bottom = size-1; bottom >= 1; bottom = bottom-1) {

        noSwitch = 1; //TRUE

        for (i = 0; i <= bottom-1; i = i+1)

            if (element[i] > element[i+1]) {

                temp= element[i];
                element[i] = element[i+1];
                element[i+1] = temp;

                noSwitch = 0; //switch made, so FALSE
            }

        if (noSwitch) //sorted, so stop
            return;
    }
}
```

Under most situations, the function terminates before performing all of the possible passes, and therefore, the bubble sort will sort the array with fewer comparisons than the selection sort. Is there a situation where the bubble sort does not perform better than the selection sort? When the original array is in descending order (i.e., the exact reverse of how we are trying to arrange the values), despite the many exchanges, only the largest value moves into the correct place and no other values move closer to their final destinations. Because of this, all passes will be performed, and therefore, the total number of comparisons will be the same as the total for the selection sort.

Although the bubble sort generally performs better than the selection sort, these two sorts are grouped into the same category, because both algorithms have a performance proportional to N^2, where N is the size of the array. Another group of techniques has a performance proportional to $N \log_2 N$, an order of magnitude better than those in the N^2 performance group. We will present one of the $N \log_2 N$ sorting algorithms, called *mergesort*, in the next section.

18.3 Recursive algorithms

Mergesort and other high-performance sorting algorithms can be expressed most naturally and intuitively as recursive functions. A *recursive function* is a function having statements that makes a function call to itself. So far, we have seen only function calls to other functions. Let's say we have two functions func1 and func2. The organization we have seen so far resembles the following:

```
func1(...)
{
  ...
}

func2(...)
{
  ...
 func1(...); //calls func1
  ...
}
```

With a recursive function, we have this situation:

```
func1(...)
{
  ...
 func1(...);
  ...
}
```

A keen observer may be wondering how the recursive calling shown here will ever stop. Since the calls are made to the same function, the function seems to keep on calling itself in an infinite cycle. This concern is valid, because if you are not careful, you could indeed create an infinite cycle of never-ending recursive calls. We will explain how to write a recursive function correctly in the following section.

18.3.1 A sample recursive function

Let's start with a very simple mathematical function. Suppose we want to compute the sum of the first N positive integers. We can define a (nonrecursive) function to do the task.

```
int GetSum(int N);
{
    int sum = 0, i;

    for (i = 1; i <= N; i = i+1)
    sum = sum + i;

    return sum;
}
```

Let's see how the same function can be implemented recursively.

Recursive functions are actually nothing new to mathematicians. Mathematicians strive to express ideas in the most concise manner. For example, we can define the summation of the first N integers mathematically in recursive form as shown here:

$$
sum(N) = \begin{cases} 1 & \text{if } N = 1 \\ N + sum(N-1) & \text{otherwise} \end{cases}
$$

The definition states that if N is 1, then the function sum(N) has the value 1. Otherwise, it states the function sum(N) has the value that is the sum of N and the result of sum(N-1). For example, the function sum(4) is evaluated as shown in figure 18.16.

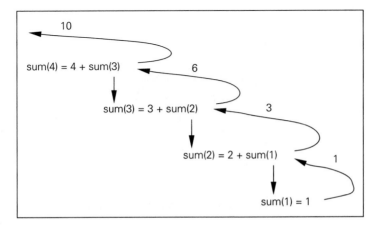

Figure 18.16 Sequence of recursive calls to evaluate sum(4)

Let's write a recursive sum function. The function parallels the preceding mathematical definition for the summation function very closely.

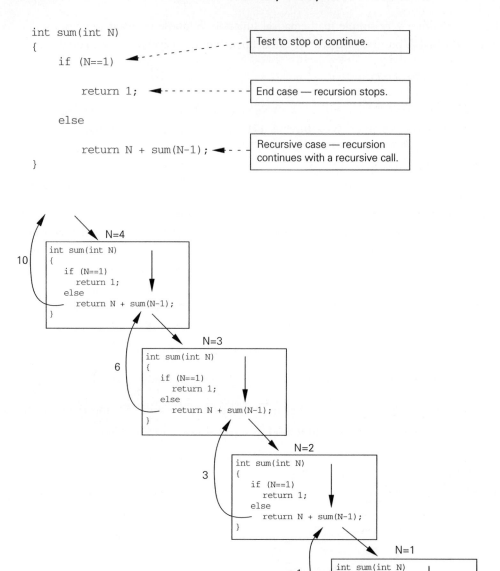

```
int sum(int N)
{
    if (N==1)                        ◄ - - - - - - -  Test to stop or continue.

        return 1;                    ◄ - - - - - - -  End case — recursion stops.

    else

        return N + sum(N-1);         ◄ - - -  Recursive case — recursion
}                                             continues with a recursive call.
```

Figure 18.17 Control flow of the recursive sum function

Figure 18.17 illustrates the control flow of the recursive sum function. The three major ingredients in any recursive function are

- A test to stop (or continue) the recursion
- A recursive call (to continue the recursion)
- An end case (to terminate the recursion)

When a recursive call is made, we should pass arguments different from the incoming parameters. In the preceding diagram, the incoming parameter is N, while the argument passed in the recursive call is N-1. This difference eventually leads to a condition that stops the recursion. The key point is to make sure that the recursive calls are eventually terminated. For the recursive sum function, the difference of 1 in the incoming parameter eventually makes N become 1 and causes the recursion to stop.

18.3.2 Recursive search algorithms

To explore recursive functions a little further, let's express the linear and binary search routines as recursive functions. The first step in writing a recursive function is to express the basic idea recursively, analogous to what we did for the mathematical definition of the sum function. The most important part of this definition is to set up the arguments and parameters correctly.

What should be the incoming parameters for the recursive linear search function? Incoming parameters must specify the scope of the problem at that point in recursion. For example, with the recursive sum function, the input parameter N specifies the number of first positive integers to add. With the recursive linear search, we pass the portion of the array that still needs to be searched. We will pass three values: the low index, the high index, and the search value. The low index specifies the starting position, and the high index the ending position. Using these parameters, we can define a recursive linear search routine in this mathematical notation:

```
RLSearch(low, high, searchValue)
```

$$
= \begin{cases}
\text{return -1} & \text{if low > high} \\
\text{return low} & \text{if element[low] ==} \\
& \text{searchValue} \\
\text{return RLSearch(low+1, high, searchValue)} & \text{if element[low] !=} \\
& \text{searchValue}
\end{cases}
$$

In this recursive definition, we have two end cases—one for an unsuccessful search (if `low > high`) and another for a successful search (if `element[low] == search-Value`). If neither end case occurs, then a recursive call is made. Notice the difference in the incoming parameters and the arguments passed in the recursive call. In actual code, the function is written as

```
int Collection::RLSearch ( int low, int high, int searchValue)
{
    if (low > high)//not found

        return NOT_FOUND;

    else if (element[low] == searchValue) //found

        return low;

    else    //continue the search

        return RLSearch(low+1, high, searchValue);
}
```

The recursive binary search is very similar in structure to the recursive linear search except that the recursive binary search has two recursive calls. In mathematical notation, we have

```
RBSearch(low, high, searchValue)
```

$$
= \begin{cases}
\text{return NOT\_FOUND} & \text{if low > high} \\
\text{return mid} & \text{if element[mid] ==} \\
& \qquad \text{searchValue} \\
\text{return RBSearch(mid+1, high, searchValue)} & \text{if element[mid] <} \\
& \qquad \text{searchValue} \\
\text{return RBSearch(low, mid-1, searchValue)} & \text{if element[mid] >} \\
& \qquad \text{searchValue}
\end{cases}
$$

where `mid` is the midpoint between `low` and `high`. Expressing this mathematical notation as a C++ function, we obtain

```
int Collection::RBSearch ( int low, int high, int searchValue)
{
    int i;
```

```
            if (low > high)//not found

                return NOT_FOUND;

        else {

            i = (low + high) / 2;

            if (element[i] == searchValue) //found

                return i;

            else if (element[i] < searchValue)

                return RBSearch(i+1, high, searchValue);

            else
                return RLSearch(low, i-1, searchValue);
        }
    }
```

18.3.3 Recursive mergesort

The recursive functions we have written so far are purely for instructional purposes. In other words, the sum, linear search, and binary search functions are not normally written recursively in practice. One major benefit of a recursive function is its conciseness and clarity in expressing an algorithm. The price we pay for this advantage is the added cost of running the recursive routine. Because the execution of a recursive function requires the system to keep track of function calls, executing a recursive function incurs a lot more overhead than executing nonrecursive, or iterative, functions. Consequently if we can express a recursive routine just as clearly and concisely in a nonrecursive format, then we should express the routine non-recursively. The three functions mentioned above meet this criteria, and therefore, should be written nonrecursively.

In this section, we will describe a sorting method called *mergesort* that is normally written in a recursive format because expressing the method in an iterative format loses clarity. The mergesort sorting technique runs in time proportional to $N\log_2 N$.

The basic idea for a mergesort is simple. To sort an array, we divide it in half, sort the two halves, and then merge them into one. Figure 18.18 illustrates this idea.

What we have just described is a recursive definition because we are trying to define a sort in terms of two smaller sorts. At the second level of recursion, we divide the two halves into four quarters. At the third level of recursion, we divide the four quarters into eight eighths, and so forth, until no more division is possible, that is, until a subarray has only one entry. Figure 18.19 shows the sequence of operations for the first half of the array.

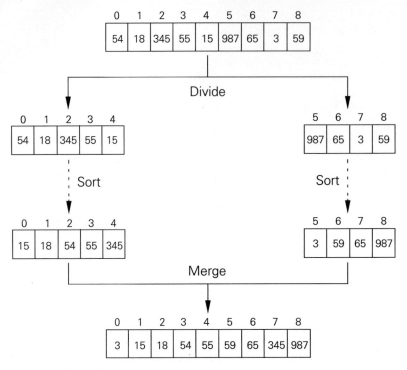

Figure 18.18 Divide and merge phases of mergesort

As you can see from the illustration, when the sublist has only one entry, then no more division is possible or necessary because an array of one entry is trivially sorted, so this case will end the recursion. There will be two recursive calls—one for the left half and another for the right half. We can specify the left and right halves by passing the appropriate indices for them. When control is returned from a recursive call, we have two sorted subarrays. We will call a nonrecursive function to merge these two sorted subarrays. A mergesort is defined as

```
void Collection::MSort( int low, int high)
{
    int mid;
    if (low == high) //no more division possible
        return;
    else {
        mid = (low + high) / 2;
        MSort(low, mid);   //sort the left half
```

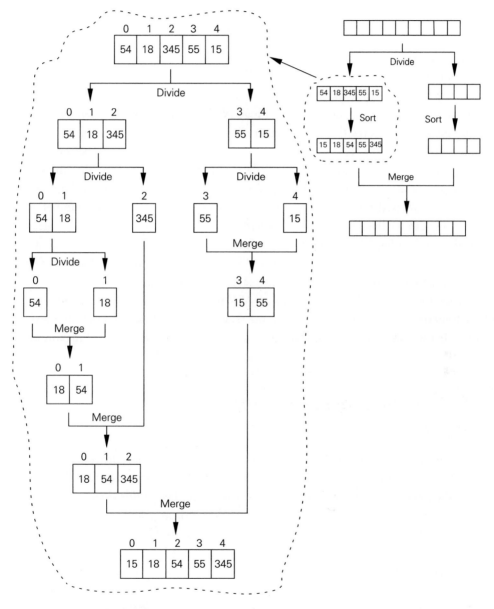

Figure 18.19 Sequence of operations for first half of array

```
        MSort(mid+1,high); //sort the right half

        //at this point, we have two sorted sub-arrays:
        //element[low]...element[mid] and
        //element[mid+1]...element[high]
        //We merge them to get the final result

        Merge(low, mid, high);
    }
}
```

The function `Merge` is a nonrecursive function that merges two sorted subarrays. We need an additional array for the merging operation, so the mergesort algorithm is not an *in situ* sort. We define the `Merge` function in Exercise 5 at the end of this chapter.

The performance of the mergesort is $N \log_2 N$. We will give you an overall idea of how the mergesort achieves this performance. The real workhorse of mergesort is its merging routine. To merge two sorted arrays of size K, the maximum number of comparisons is approximately $2K$. Now, to simplify the argument, let's assume that the size of an array is a positive power of 2, that is, $N = 2^i$, for some positive integer i. Applying the same logic we used for the binary search, we know that the maximum number of times an array can be divided is i, which is $\log_2 N$. Let's call the number of times an array is divided a *level*. At level 1, the original array is divided into two halves. At level 2, two halves are divided into four quarters. At level j, 2^{j-1} subarrays of size $N/2^{j-1}$ are divided into 2^j subarrays, each having $N/2^j$ elements. At level j, the maximum total number of comparisons for merging 2^j subarrays of size $N/2^j$ is N, because there are 2^{j-1} merges, with each merge taking at most $N/2^{j-1}$ comparisons. Therefore, at any level the maximum number of comparisons is N. Since the mergesort has $\log_2 N$ levels, the maximum total number of comparisons for the whole mergesort is $N \log_2 N$.

18.4 Sample program: completing the address book

We have not yet implemented all the functions of the Address Book program. Two of the unimplemented functions, `Delete` and `Modify`, require a search function. We can complete the job by using the binary search algorithm described in this chapter. The `Add` function of an `AddressBook` given in chapter 17 does not assume any ordering and, therefore, inserts the pointer to the newly added `Person` into the next available slot, as shown in figure 18.20.

For a binary search to work correctly, the `entry` array must be sorted. The `Add` function needs to be changed so that the pointer to a newly added `Person` will be inserted into the proper position in the array. We assume for this program that the `Person`

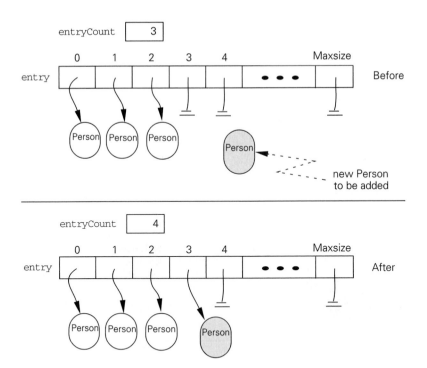

Figure 18.20 Person goes into next available slot

objects are sorted in ascending order by name. With this order, the modified `Add` function must first determine where to insert the pointer to the newly added `Person`. Let's say this position is `I`. The function must then move all pointers from `I` to `entryCount` one position down (to the right direction in our diagrams) to make room to insert the pointer to the newly added `Person`. Figure 18.21 illustrates the steps.

A pseudocode for the modified `Add` function is

```
if (there is still space to add a Person) {

    set loc to the last entry;

    while (person to be added is alphabetically "smaller"
            than the one pointed to by the pointer in the loc
            position of the entry table) {

        move the pointer at loc in the entry one slot to right;
        decrement loc;
    }

    insert the pointer to the Person at the loc position;
    increment entryCount and set variable "changed" to TRUE;
}
```

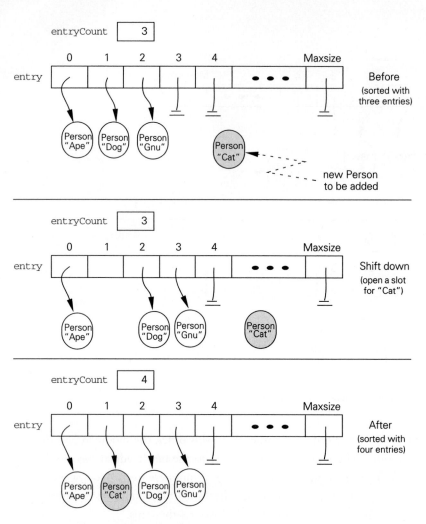

Figure 18.21 Sorting of the entry array

The actual code for the modified Add function is

```
void AddressBook::Add(Person *person)
{
    int loc;

    if (entryCount < AB_MAXSIZE) {

        loc = entryCount-1;

        while (person < entry[loc]) { //shift down
```

```
            entry[loc+1] = entry[loc];
            loc = loc-1;
        }

        entry[loc+1] = person;

        entryCount = entryCount+1;
        changed = 1; //changed is TRUE
    }
}
```

For the expression

```
    while (person < entry[loc])
```

to work, we must define (overload) the operator < for the Person object. Since we are comparing Person objects based on their names, we can implement the function as

```
    int Person::operator< (Person *person)
    {
        if (strcmp(name, person->name) < 0)

        return 1; //TRUE

        else

        return 0; //FALSE
    }
```

Before we implement the Delete and Modify functions, let us first implement the Search function used by both. The Search function will use the binary search algorithm. Given the name of a Person, the Search function will return the corresponding position in the entry array if this Person is found. Otherwise, the function returns NOT_FOUND (–1). The following is the Search function.

```
    int AddressBook::Search(char *key)
    {
        int mid, result, low = 0, high = entryCount-1;
        char *entryName;

        while (low <= high) {

            mid =  (low + high) / 2);

            entryName = entry[mid]->GetKey(); //get the name

            result = strcmp(entryName,key);
```

```
        if (result == 0)        //found

            return mid;

        else if (result < 0) //element[mid] < searchValue

            low = mid + 1;

        else                    // element[mid] > searchValue

            high = mid - 1;

    }

    return NOT_FOUND;

}
```

The function GetKey is a newly defined function for the Person object that returns the name of the person. Its implementation is

```
char *Person::GetKey()
{
    char *result = new char[50];
    strcpy(result, name);
    return result;
}
```

We are now ready to implement the Delete and Modify functions. Let's start with the Delete function. The function will first use the Search function to locate the Person to be deleted. If the Person is found, then Delete removes the pointer to the Person to be deleted from the entry array. The removal of one pointer will leave a hole in the array, and we need to fill this hole (otherwise, the binary search won't work), which we will achieve by shifting up (moving left in our diagrams) the entries below the hole. Figure 18.22 illustrates the operation.

Thus the Delete function is implemented as

```
    void AddressBook::Delete(char *key)
    {
        int loc = Search(key);

        if ( loc >= 0 ) { //found

            delete entry[loc];

            while (loc < entryCount) {

                entry[loc] = entry[loc+1];
                loc = loc+1;
            }
        }
    }
```

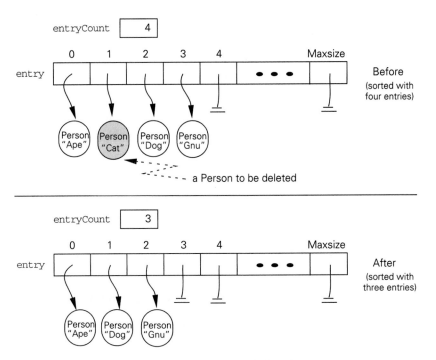

Figure 18.22 Implementing the Delete and Modify functions

Notice that the function does nothing when the searched-for person is not found. We could rewrite the function so it returns the result of the operation, such as 1 for successful deletion and 0 otherwise.

The Modify function will first search for the Person with the given name. If it finds the Person, then the Person's other data (age, address, etc.) are replaced with those passed to the function. We use the Person object's SetValue function to perform this task. The input parameter to the Modify function is an array of char pointers for name, age, and so forth. The function is implemented as follows:

```
void AddressBook::Modify(char *value[])
{
    int loc = Search(value[0]);

    if (loc >= 0)
    entry[loc]->SetValue(value);
}
```

Finally, the DeletePerson and ModifyPerson functions of the ABController need to be implemented. Implementing these functions is left as exercise 9.

18.5 Exercises

1. The linear search algorithm presented in this chapter has the same performance whether an array is sorted or not. For a sorted array, we showed that a binary search dramatically improves performance over a linear search. However, the performance of a linear search can be improved from N to N/2 if the array is sorted by adding a testing condition to stop before comparing all elements. Write a modified linear search algorithm for a sorted array. Notice that the modified linear search algorithm works only for a sorted array, so it is not a true improvement. A truly improved algorithm should work on both sorted and unsorted arrays.

2. The bubble sort's best-case performance executes only the first pass, with $N{-}1$ comparisons. What is the best-case performance for the other two sorting methods?

3. We assume the value of -1 to denote an empty slot in an array. What should we do if -1 is one of the possible values? *Hint:* Use two one-dimensional arrays or an array of pairs (data, status).

4. In chapter 10 we defined a function gcd for finding the greatest common divisor of two integers. Rewrite the function gcd using recursion.

5. Write the Merge function for the mergesort algorithm. The following diagram illustrates the basic idea behind the merging of two sorted arrays into one sorted array.

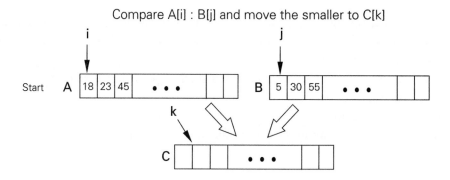

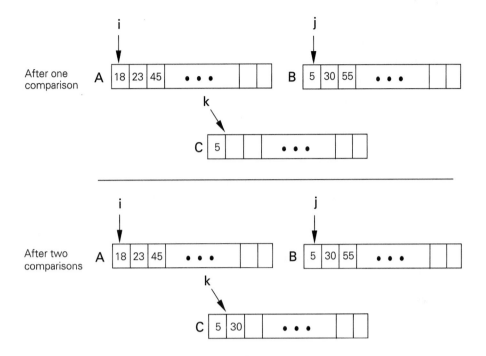

When all elements of either array are moved to the C array, then move the remaining elements from the other array to the C array.

6   At most, how many comparisons will the Merge function make in merging two sorted arrays of size *N*?

7   Write a nonrecursive Mergesort function. This exercise is not easy, because you have to devise a mechanism for keeping track of the portions of an array that need to be merged and divided further.

8   In this chapter we considered only the number of comparisons for evaluating the performance of sorting algorithms. Determine the number of data movements for the selection sort and the bubble sort. Which is the better algorithm if we consider the number of data movements?

9   Complete the Address Book program by implementing the ABController object's DeletePerson and ModifyPerson functions. For the DeletePerson function, use a StringTypeIn to get a person's name. For the ModifyPerson function also, use a StringTypeIn to get values for the name, age, address, and phone.

10 Implement an alternative style of deleting a Person object in the Address Book program. Delete the Person currently displayed in the Person Information window.

When the currently displayed Person is deleted, the Person following the deleted Person will be displayed in the window.

11 Add a new menu choice, Find, to the Address Book program. The Find function, which is executed when the user selects this menu choice, searches for a person by his/her name or age. Use a StringTypeIn and other GUI objects for entering name or age and specifying which value is used for the search.

12 Add a new menu choice Sort to the Address Book program. The Sort function, which is executed when the user selects this menu choice, displays a list of people's names in descending order by age.

13 Modify the AddressBook object so that Person objects are stored in the entry table by using the hashing technique. Apply the hashing function to the sum of a name's first three characters' ASCII values.

14 Modify the Address Book program so that no duplicate Person object is added to the list. A Person object is a duplicate of another Person object in the list if the objects have the same name.

appendix A

GUI objects

All GUI objects are described in this appendix. For the portions that are platform dependent, please refer to the readme file that comes with the source code. If the constructors do not require any parameters, then they are not listed explicitly.

Objects and the functions within these objects are listed in alphabetical order. Sample uses of each function are listed below each description.

Library Name	GUIObj

Description	This library contains various objects for handling the user interface of a program.

Object	*Description*
EditWin	An EditWin is a general purpose editor. Although you can use this object as is, you are expected to define a descendant of EditWin to override the functions Ok and Cancel with your own code for application-specific processing.
FileBox	A FileBox is used to retrieve the name of a file that is to be opened (i.e., to read data from) or saved (i.e., to write data to).
FloatTypeIn	A FloatTypeIn is used for getting a float value from the user.
InputBox	An InputBox serves the roles of IntTypeIn, FloatType, and StringTypeIn. This object is provided for convenience: you need only one object to input integers, floats, and strings.

531

IntTypeIn	An IntTypeIn is used for getting an integer value from the user.
Menu	A Menu is used for each pull-down menu that appears in the program's menu bar.
MenuHandler	A MenuHandler processes a menu event.
OKBox	An OKBox is used for displaying simple data including string (array of char), int, float, and char (a single character).
StringTypeIn	A StringTypeIn is used for getting a string value from the user.
YesNoBox	A YesNoBox is used for getting a Yes or No answer from the user.

Class Name	EditWin

Description	An EditWin is a general purpose editor. Although you can use this object as is, you are expected to define a descendant of EditWin to override the functions Ok and Cancel with your own code for application-specific processing.

Function	*Description*

virtual void Cancel();	This function is called automatically when the Cancel button is clicked. The function does nothing, so override this function in the descendant of EditWin with an appropriate function body. You may also call this function from your code.
	
	`EditWin ew;`
	`...`
	`ew.Cancel();`
	
	(*Note:* You normally do not call this function from your program as shown above.)

void Clear();	This function clears (erases) the current contents of the EditWin.
	
	`EditWin ew;`
	`...`
	`ew.Clear();`

```
void
Delete( int lineNo,
        int charPos,
        int length);
```

This function deletes a string of `length` characters, beginning at the position `charPos` in line number `lineNo`. The first line is line number 0, and the first character position of any line is 0. The function does nothing when an invalid `lineNo` or `charPos` is given. When a string has fewer characters than the designated `length`, this function deletes the string to the end of the text.

```
EditWin ew;
...
ew.Delete(4, 3, 12);
```

```
void
DeleteLine(
        int lineNo);
```

This function deletes the line number `lineNo`. The function does nothing for an invalid `lineNo`.

```
EditWin ew;
...
ew.DeleteLine(4);
```

```
void
Done();
```

This function must be called at the end of all other function calls to an `EditWin`. The call is necessary to activate the event loop (see chapter 12). Note: if you use a `MessageHandler` and call its `Start` function, then the call to the `Done` function is not required.

```
EditWin ew;
...
ew.Done();
```

```
int
GetNumLines();
```

This function returns the number of lines in the edit field.

```
EditWin ew;
int lineCnt;
...
lineCnt =
    ew.GetNumLines();
```

```
void
Init(   int x,
        int y,
        int w,
        int h );
```

This function opens the `EditWin` with its left, topmost corner at the screen position (x,y), with width w pixels, and height h pixels. This function must be called before calling other `EditWin` functions.

```
EditWin ew;
...
ew.Init(10,10,300,200);
```

```
void
Insert( int lineNo,
        int charPos,
        char *str);
```

This function inserts a string `str` into the line number `lineNo` at position `charPos`.

```
EditWin ew;
...
ew.Insert(2,4,"Hello");
```

```
void
InsertLine (
        int lineNo,
        char *str);
```

This function inserts a string str as a new line at the line number lineNo. The text at the line number lineNo prior to the insertion will be shifted down (i.e., it becomes lineNo+1 after the insertion).

```
EditWin ew;
...
ew.InsertLine(2,"Hi");
```

```
virtual void
Ok();
```

This function is called automatically when the OK button is clicked. The function does nothing, so you are required to override this function in a descendant of EditWin to add your processing. You may also call this function from your code.

```
EditWin ew;
...
ew.Ok();
```

(*Note:* You normally do not call this function from your program as shown above.)

```
char
*Read(  int lineNo,
        int charPos,
        int length);
```

This function returns the string of length characters beginning at the character position charPos of the line number lineNo. When a string has fewer characters than the designated length, this function reads the string to the end of the text.

```
EditWin ew;
...
ew.Read(4, 3, 12);
```

```
char
*ReadAll();
```

This functions returns the whole content of the EditWin.

```
EditWin ew;
char *str[2048];
...
strcpy(str,
    ew.ReadAll();
```

```
char
ReadLine(
        int lineNo);
```

This function returns the string at line lineNo. This function returns a null string when an invalid lineNo is given.

```
EditWin ew;
...
ew.ReadLine(4);
```

```
void
SetCancelLabel(
        char *label);
```

This function changes the label of the Cancel button to label.

```
EditWin ew;
...
ew.SetCancelLabel("Clear");
```

`void`
`SetOkLabel(`
`    char *label);`
	This function changes the label of the OK button to `label`. The button can hold up to 15 characters. When the label contains more than 15 characters, the string is truncated.
	
	```EditWin ew;```
	```...```
	```ew.SetOkLable("Done");```

`void`
`SetTitle(`
`    char *title);`
	This function sets the title of `EditWin` to `title`. The default title is `Editor`.
	
	```EditWin ew;```
	```...```
	```ew.SetTitle("Students");```

`void`
`Write(char *str)`
	This function writes the string `str` at the end of the current text.
	
	```EditWin ew;```
	```...```
	```ew.Write("Hi There");```

`void`
`WriteLine(`
`    char *str);`
	This function writes the string `str` as a separate line at the end of the current text.
	
	```EditWin ew;```
	```...```
	```ew.WriteLine("TOTAL");```

Class Name   FileBox

Description A `FileBox` is used to retrieve the name of a file that is to be opened (i.e., to read data from) or saved (i.e., to write data to).

Function	*Description*

`char`
`*GetOpenFileName();`
	This function returns the name of a file to be opened. The function displays a standard file dialog box where the user can specify the file to open. The function returns a null string when either an invalid filename (a nonexistent file or an invalid character string) is entered or the Cancel button is clicked.
	
	```char filename[13];```
	```FileBox fb;```
	```strcpy(filename,```
	``` fb.GetOpenFileName());```

```
if (strcmp(filename,"")==0){
    //filename not valid
}
else {
    //filename is okay
}
```

char
*GetSaveFileName();

This is the same as the above, except the specified file is for saving data. A warning dialog box is displayed when an existing file is specified. The user can choose to overwrite the file (i.e., replace the old content with the new data, which is a normal save operation) or to cancel the operation.

```
char filename[13];
FileBox fb;
strcpy(filename,
    fb.GetSaveFileName());
if (strcmp(filename,"")==0){
    //filename not valid
}
else {
    //filename is okay
}
```

Class Name	FloatTypeIn

Description	A FloatTypeIn is used for getting a float value from the user.

Function	*Description*

float
GetFloat(
    char *title,
    char *msg);
	This function displays a dialog box with a title and a msg. The dialog box can accept only real numbers. An appropriate error message is displayed for invalid input. The dialog box cannot be terminated unless a valid float is entered.

```
float temperature;
FloatTypeIn infloatBox;
...
temperature =
    infloatBox.GetFloat(
    "Daily Temperature",
    "Type in the value:");
```

Class Name	InputBox

Description	An `InputBox` serves the roles of `IntTypeIn`, `FloatType`, and `StringTypeIn`. This object is provided for convenience: you only need one object to input integers, floats, and strings.

Function	*Description*

`int`
`GetInt(`
`    char *title,`
`    char *msg );`
	This function displays a dialog box with a `title` and a `msg`. The dialog box can accept only integers. An appropriate error message is displayed for invalid input. The dialog box cannot be terminated unless a valid integer is entered. The maximum characters allowed for both `title` and `msg` is 15.
	
	```int size;\nfloat temperature;\nchar name[30];\nInputBox inpBox;\nsize =\n inpBox.GetInt(\n "Rectangle Size",\n "Type in the value:");\ntemperature =\n inpBox.GetFloat(\n "Daily Temperature",\n "Type in the value:");\nstrcpy(name,\n inpBox.GetString(\n "Name",\n "Type in your name:"));```

`float`
`GetFloat(`
`    char *title,`
`    char *msg );`
	This function displays a dialog box with a `title` and a `msg`. The dialog box can accept only real numbers. An appropriate error message is displayed for invalid input. The dialog box cannot be terminated unless a valid `float` is entered. The maximum characters allowed for both `title` and `msg` is *XX.*
	
	(Sample use same as above.)

`char`
`*GetString(`
`    char *title,`
`    char *msg );`
	Same as `StringTypeIn`.

IntTypeIn

Description   An IntTypeIn is used for getting an integer value from the user.

Function	*Description*
| ```
int
GetInt(
      char *title,
      char *msg );
``` | This function displays a dialog box with a `title` and a `msg`. The dialog box can accept only integers. An appropriate error message is displayed for invalid input. The dialog box cannot be terminated unless a valid integer is entered. The maximum characters allowed for both `title` and `msg` is 15.

```
int size;
IntTypeIn intBox;
size =
    intBox.GetInt(
        "Rectangle Size",
        "Type in the value:");
``` |

Class Name   Menu

Description   A Menu is used for each pull-down menu that appears in the program's menu bar.

Function	*Description*
| ```
Menu(char *name);
``` | This is a constructor function to define a new `Menu` object with `name` (i.e., label).

```
Menu editMenu("Edit");
``` |
| ```
void
AddItem(
   char *itemName,
   MenuHandler &mh,
   short funcNum);
``` | This function adds a new menu item `itemName` to this `Menu` and sets a `MenuHandler` (actually, a descendant of `MenuHandler`) as the object for processing a menu selection event. The third parameter `funcNum` determines which function of `MenuHandler` is called when this menu item choice is selected. For example, when `funcNum` is 3, then the function `MenuFunc3` is called. For every menu item you add, you must supply corresponding `MenuFuncX` functions in your descendant `MenuHandler` class. |
```

```
Menu editMenu("Edit");
MyMenuHandler mh;
...
editMenu.AddItem("Add",
    mh,
    3);
```

Class Name	MenuHandler

Description

A descendant of the MenuHandler object is required to process menu item choices. You can have only one descendant of MenuHandler object, and the descendant object can handle up to twenty distinct functions. Functions are named MenuFunc1, MenuFunc2, ..., and MenuFunc20. You cannot change these names of the functions. You associate the menu items and the functions to be executed in response to the selection of the menu items by calling the function AddItem.

Function	*Description*
void MenuFunc1();	This function is executed in response to the selection of the associated menu item.

```
Menu editMenu("Edit");
MyMenuHandler mh;
...
editMenu.AddItem("Add",
    mh,
    3);
```

. . . .

void MenuFunc20();	This function is executed in response to the selection of the associated menu item.

```
Menu myMenu("Special");
MyMenuHandler mh;
...
myMenu.AddItem("Execute",
    mh,
    20);
```

Class Name	OKBox

Description
An `OKBox` is used for displaying simple data including string (array of char), `int`, `float`, and `char` (a single character).

Function	*Description*

`void`
`Display(char *s);`
	This function displays a string `s` in a simple dialog box with an OK button. The dialog box is closed when you click the OK button.
	
	```OKbox msg;```
	```...```
	```msg.Display("I Love C++");```

`void`
`Display(int i);`
	Same as above, except this function displays an integer.
	
	```OKbox msg;```
	```...```
	```msg.Display(345);```

`void`
`Display(float x);`
	Same as above, except this function displays a real number.
	
	```OKbox msg;```
	```...```
	```msg.Display(23.98);```

`void`
`Display(char ch);`
	Same as above, except this function displays a single character.
	
	```OKbox msg;```
	```...```
	```msg.Display('A');```

Class Name	StringTypeIn

Description
A `StringTypeIn` is used for getting a string value from the user.

Function	*Description*

`char`
`*GetString(`
`    char *title,`
`    char *msg );`
	This function displays a dialog box with a `title` and a `msg`. The dialog box can accept only strings. An appropriate error message is displayed for invalid input. The dialog box cannot be

terminated unless you input a string data. The maximum characters allowed for both `title` and `msg` is 15. The maximum length of the returned string is 2048 characters.

```
char name[30];
StringTypeIn inpBox;
strcpy(name,
    inpBox.GetString(
        "Name",
        "Type in your name:"));
```

Class Name	YesNoBox

Description	A YesNoBox is used for getting a Yes or No answer from the user.

Function

Description

```
Boolean
Ask(char *prompt);
```

This displays a dialog box with two buttons: Yes and No. The dialog box also includes a string `prompt`. The function returns TRUE (1) if the Yes button is clicked. Otherwise, it returns FALSE(0).

```
int result;
YesNoBox question;
int =
    question.Ask("Continue?");
```

appendix B

Turtle

The Turtle object is described in this appendix. For the portions that are platform dependent, please refer to the readme files that come with your source code.

If constructors do not require any parameters, then they are not listed here.

Functions are listed in alphabetical order. Sample uses of each function are listed below each description. For all sample code in the table, we assume the variable t is declared as a Turtle.

The Color data type is an enumerated data type defined for use with the Turtle. It is defined as

```
enum Color    BLACK, WHITE, BLUE, DARKBLUE, CYAN, DUSTYBLUE, GREEN, DARK-
              GREEN, YELLOW, DARKYELLOW, RED, DARKRED, MAGENTA, PURPLE,
              LIGHTGRAY, DARKGRAY
```

Library Name	Turtles

Description	This library contains a Turtle object to be used for drawing simple figures and illustrating various programming concepts.

Object	*Description*
Turtle	A Turtle object is used for drawing simple figures.

Class Name   Turtle

Description   A `Turtle` object is used for simple drawing.

Function	Description
`void ChangePenColor( Color c);`	This function changes the `Turtle`'s pen color to c. `t.ChangePenColor(BLUE);`
`void ChangePenSize(int s);`	Change the `Turtle`'s pen size to s. `t.ChangePenSize(5);`
`void Done();`	This function must be called at the end of all other function calls to a `Turtle`. The call activates the event loop (see chapter 12). If the `MessageHandler` is used, then a call to this function is not necessary. `t.Done();`

`void GetXY( int &x, int &y);`	This function returns the current position of the `Turtle`. The variables x and y store the `Turtle`'s coordinates, that is, horizontal and vertical positions, on the drawing board.
	
	`int h,v;`
	`t.GetXY(h,v);`

`void GoToPos( int x, int y);`	This function moves the `Turtle` to the position (x,y). The line is drawn if the pen is down. `t.GoToPos(200, 340);`
`void Init(int x, int y);`	This function initializes the `Turtle` with its heading 0 degrees; current position at (x,y); pen down, and pen color BLACK. If this function is not called, then the `Turtle` will initially be at (0,0); its pen color BLACK; and pen down. `t.Init(150, 300);`
`void Init(int x, int y, int angle, int penDown, Color c);`	This function is the second form of `Init` with which you can initialize other characteristics of the `Turtle`. The `Turtle` is set at position (x,y); facing angle degree; pen color c; and pen up (0) or down (1). `t.Init(100,200,90,0,GREEN);`

`virtual void`
`LeftButtonClicked`
`        (int x, int`
`y);`
	This function is executed in response to the left button click of a mouse with more than one button or to the button click of a mouse with one button. The `Turtle`'s `LeftButtonClicked` does nothing. You must define a descendant of `Turtle` and override this function to add application-specific processing in response to the left button click.

```
class MyTurtle:public Turtle
{
...
void LeftButtonClicked
    int x, int y)
{
    t.Star(x,y);
};
...
};
```

`void` `Move(int distance);`	This function moves the `Turtle` distance pixels from the current postion in the direction of the current heading.

```
t.Move(50);
```

`void` `PenDown();`	This function puts down the `Turtle`'s pen. The pen must be down in order to draw a picture.

```
t.PenDown();
```

`void` `PenUp();`	This function picks up the `Turtle`'s pen. When the pen is up, no drawing can take place.

```
t.PenUp();
```

`virtual void`
`RightButton-`
`Clicked(int x, int`
`y);`
	This function is executed in response to the right button click of a mouse with more than one button or to the Command-click of a mouse with one button. The `Turtle`'s `RightButtonClicked` does nothing. You must define a descendant of `Turtle` and override this function to add your application-specific processing in response to the right button click.

```
class MyTurtle:public Turtle
    {
    ...
    void RightButtonClicked
        int x, int y)
    {
        t.Star(x,y);
    };
    ...
    };
```

void SlowDown();	This function puts the `Turtle` into slow mode. It is useful if you want to see the drawing of a picture as it takes place. If the `Turtle` is not in this mode, the picture will appear almost instantaneously as the window appears on the screen. If the `Turtle` is already in a slow mode, calling this function has no effect. `t.SlowDown();`
void SpeedUp();	This function puts the `Turtle` into normal mode; that is, line drawing is not shown. Calling this function when the `Turtle` is already in normal mode has no effect. `t.SpeedUp();`
void Turn(double angle);	This function makes the `Turtle` turn `angle` degrees from the current heading. `t.Turn(140);`

void
TurnTo(double
      angle);
	This function changes the `Turtle`'s heading to `angle`. The current heading is irrelevant.
	
	    `t.TurnTo(90);`

appendix C

Utility

Utility objects and functions are described in this appendix.

Library Name	Utility

Description

This library contains a random number generator object and a nonobject function `ftoa` for converting `float` to string.

Object	*Description*
`RandomNumGenerator`	This object is used to generate random numbers.

Function	*Description*
`char *ftoa(float num)`	This nonobject function is used to convert a float data value to a string (array of characters).

Class Name	RandNumGenerator

Description   A `RandNumGenerator` object is used for generating pseudo random numbers.

Function	*Description*

`int`
`GetRN(int max)`
	This function generates a random number between 0 and max–1.
	
	`RandNumGenerator rgen`
	`rgen.GetRN(100);`

NonObject Function	*Description*
`char` `*ftoa(float num)`	This function converts a `float` to a string. `cout << ftoa(34.55);`

appendix D

Syntax rules

Simplified syntax (production) rules for C++ are given here. Syntax rules provided here are not complete for the full C++ language. The rules are limited to the language constructs described in this textbook. Some syntax categories are explained in prose style instead of using production rules.

identifier
  letter character-list$_{opt}$

character-list
  character
  character character-list

character
  digit
  letter

  _

digit
  0 | 1 | ... | 9

letter
      `a | b | ... | z | A | B | ... | Z`

type-declaration
      type-specifier id-list
      `const` *type-specifier id-initializer-list*
      `enum` *identifier* { *enumerator-list* }

type-specifier
      `int | short | long | short int | long int |`
      `float | double | double long`

id-list
      id-declarator
      id-declarator , *id-list*

id-declarator
      modifier$_{opt}$ *identifier initializer*$_{opt}$
      modifier$_{opt}$ *identifier size-declarator array-initializer*$_{opt}$

modifier

size-declarator
      [*constant-expression*]
      [*constant-expression*] *size-declarator*

      id-initializer-list
      id-initializer
      id-initializer , *id-initializer-list*

id-initializer
  identifier   *initializer*

initializer
  = *constant*

array-initializer
  = {   *constant-expression-list*   }

enumerator-list
  enumerator
  enumerator   *enumerator-list*

enumerator
  identifier
  identifier = *constant-expression*

constant-expression-list
  constant-expression
  constant-expression   *constant-expression-list*

  expression
  expression binary-operator expression
  identifier = *expression*
  term
  function-call

term
  factor
  – *expression*

factor
>(*expression*)
>*constant*

binary-operator
>+ | - | * | / | %

logical-expression
>*expression*
>*expression* *relational-operator* *expression*
>(*logical-expression*)
>! *logical-expression*
>*logical-expression* *logical-operator* *logical-expression*

logical-operator
>&&
>||

relational-operator
>< | <= | != | == | >= | >

for-statement
>for (*initialization*$_{opt}$; *testing*$_{opt}$; *counting*$_{opt}$) *statement*

initialization
>*expression*

testing
>*expression*

counting
    expression

statement
    expression-statement
    compound-statement
    while-statement
    do-while-statement
    for-statement
    switch-statement
    labeled-statement
    return-statement
    `break`

switch-statement
    `switch` **(** *expression* **)** *statement*

labeled-statement
    `case` *constant-expression* **:** *statement-list*
    `default` **:** *statement-list*

    constant-expression
    identifier
    constant

expression-statement
    expression $_{opt}$ **;**

compound-statement
    { *statement-list* $_{opt}$ **}**

statement-list
    statement
    statement-list statement

while-statement
    while   (*logical-expression*) *statement*

do-while-statement
    do *statement* **while** (*logical-expression*) *;*

return-statement
    return *expression ;*

function-call
    identifier (*expression-list* $_{opt}$)

expression-list
    expression
    espression , *expression-list*

class-definition
    class-heading { *member-list* $_{opt}$ } *;*

class-heading
    class *identifier base-specifier* $_{opt}$

base-specifier
    : *access-specifier* $_{opt}$*identifier*

access-specifier
>   **public**
>   **private**

member-list
>   *member-definition*   *member-list*

member-definition
>   *constructor-definition*
>   *function-definition*
>   *data-member-declaration*
>   **public**   :
>   **private**   :

constructor-function
>   *function-definition*
>   *function-prototype* : *member-initializer-list function-body*

member-initializer-list
>   *member-initializer*
>   *member-initializer* , *member-initializer-list*

member-initializer
>   *identifier*   (*expression*   )

data-member-declaration
>   *type-specifier*   *data-member-list;*
>   **const**   *type-specifier*   *data-member-list;*

data-member-list
>   *identifier*
>   *identifier*   ,   *data-member-list*

function-definition
      function-prototype   *function-body*

function-prototype
      function-type-specifier *function-name* (*parameter-list*$_{opt}$)

function-type-specifier
    void
    type-specifier

function-name
    identifier
    identifer **::** *identifier*
    operator*operator*
    identifier **::** **operator** *operator*

parameter-list
    type-specifier *identifier*
    type-specifier *identifier* **,** *parameter-list*

function-body
    { *statement* **}**

The syntax category *constant* is any valid constant of numerical data types: short, int, float, etc.

The syntax category *operator* is any one of the operators listed in table 10.1 in chapter 10.

index

A

Address Book 479
address operator 232
algorithm 2
alias 242
argument 26
array of characters 180
arrays 344
    multidimensional 379
    sorted 497
    three-dimensional 393
    two-dimensional 379
arrays of characters, one-dimensional 381
arrays of objects 352
arrays of pointers to objects 354
ASCII 167, 168
assembly language 13, 14
assembly program 14
assignment operator 56

B

Backus Naur Form 29
base object type 286
batch processing 149
binary number system 7
BNF 29
break 157
bug 456

C

C 15
C++
    arithmetic operators 55
    reserved words 32
    shorthand operators 59
case-insensitive languages 31
central processing unit 6
chalkboard algorithm 1
char 167
character functions 176
character-based input 83
character-based user interface 74
characteristic 11
cin 73
class
    base 286
    child 287
    derived 286
    parent 286
class inheritance hierarchy 287
COBOL 14
code reuse 297
coding 456, 474
collision 503
collision resolution technique 503
commands 24
comment 22
comparison operators 104
compiler 15

compiler error 17
compilers 14
compound-statement 96
constants 47
    named 47
    symbolic 47
constructor 254
control character 77
cout 73
cout window 75
CPU 6

D

dangling else 144
data
    representation of 9
data members 254
data members, initialization of 254
debugging 456
declarations 24
declare an object 250
define an object 250
dereference operator 233
derived object type 286
design 455
    review 474
    walkthrough 474
Display 23
dot notation 26
double 65
do-while 111
do-while statement 111
    syntax of 112
dynamic allocation 354

E

EBCDIC 167
echo printing 83
EditWin 310
    functions defined for 312
encapsulated 298
endl 77, 175
ENIAC 46
enumerated types 370

eof 435
error
    execution 17
    linker 17
    logical 17
escape character 170
escape sequences 169, 170
event 308
event loop 309
event queue 309
event-driven program 308
event-driven programming 308
executable file 16
executing computer programs 16
external files 426
external functions 16
external memory 426

F

FileBox 438
files 426
first program 21
float 65
FloatTypeIn 69
for 92
for loop 93
for loops and arrays 384
for statement 93
    control expression of a 94
formatted output 81
FORTRAN 14
forward reference declaration 414
fraction 267
function 199
    argument 203
    body 201
    calling a 26
    calls 201
    definition 200
    format for calling a 26
    hashing 501
    mechanism of passing values to the 204
    parameter 201
    prototype 201

return statement in the 202
self-contained 220
function body 201
function call control flow 202
functional decomposition 215
functions
nonobject 199
object 199

G

gcd 272
GetInt 50
global variables 217
grading program 320
grading program with menus 331
GUIObj.h 22

H

header 22
header file 22
hertz 6

I

I/O devices 7
identifiers 24
if 130
if statement 132, 154
syntax of the 134
include 76
incremental implementation 474
indexed expression 182
indirect addressing 235
inheritance 283
input errors, handling 147
input operator >> 84
input/output devices 7
int 49
integer division 55
integers 52
data type 53
integrated development environments 17
interactive I/O 147
interface and implementation files 265

IntTypeIn 49
ios, fixed 82
istream 73

L

layer
application domain 458
program 459
system 458
LeftButtonClicked 338
line delimiter 314
linear probing 503
literal constant 47
loaders 14
local 219
logical expressions 103, 106
long 52
long double 65
long int 52

M

machine language 13
main 23
main function 23
main program 23
maintenance release 456
manipulator 78
mantissa 11
megahertz 6
member functions 254
Menu 326
MenuHandler 326
message 25
MessageHandler 326
mixed-mode expression 66
mnemonic 14
modular construction 200
multifile program organization 207
multiple selections 140
multi-word palindromes 192

N

naming-conflict problem 223

nested loops 113
noninteractive I/O 149
nonnumerical data types 167
nonprinting control characters 169
nonterminal 32
nonvolatile memory 7
numeric data 9
    integer 9
    real 9

O

object
    application logic 408
    control 408
    storage 408
    user interface 408
object behavior 41
object definition, syntax of an 253
object description file 456
object diagrams 26
object file 16
object instance 250
object method 254
object reusability 421
object type 250
object-oriented program composition 407
OKBox 20
operation 456
operator precedence 58
ostream 73
output format manipulators 84
output operator 77
overloaded C++ operators 276
overloaded operators 275
owner object 271

P

palindrome 190
parameter 201
pass-by-pointer 231, 238
pass-by-reference 231, 242
pass-by-value 205, 231
Person 260
pixels 37

pointer 232
portable 174
porting 174
primitive data types 267
private 253
private inheritance 288
processor 6
production rules 32
Program
    AnySquare 49
    AnySquare2 53
    ASCII 178
    Average2 208
    Circle 119
    Circle2 123
    Click 339
    CompoundInterest 429
    CompoundInterest2 431
    Count 177
    CountChar 317
    Crypt-Tester 401
    Dissect 183
    Encryption 409
    Galaxy 286
    Grade 141
    Grading 325
    Grading2 332
    Grading3 369
    Graph 294
    Hello 75
    Hello2 77
    House 40
    LetterCount 435
    ManySquares 115
    ManySquares2 146
    ManySquares3 162
    MoveAndTurn 98
    One 21
    Palindrome 191
    Palindrome2 194
    Parallelogram 60
    Pinwheel 92
    PlusSign 62
    Puffball 93
    Quad 69

Quad2 132
Quad3 135
Quad4 136
Quad5 138
Quad6 245
ReadInterest 433
ReadInterest2 435
ShootingStars 290
Sonnet 311
Square 34
Square2 39
Square3 39
Square4 48
Statistic 87
Statistic2 110
Statistic3 150
String 188
Temperature 392
TestMenu 328
ThreeLines 314
ThreeLines2 315
Tunnel 114
Two 27
Volume 80
Volume2 81
Volume3a 100
Volume4 101
Volume5 102
Volume6 112
Volumes 152
Volumes2 158
Volumes3 171
Volumes4 215
Volumes5 223
Volumes6 252
Volumes7 254
Volumes8 257
program decomposition 209
program design language 474
program extensibility 421
program portability 174
pseudocode 100
public 253
public inheritance 287

Q

quadratic equations 68

R

random access memory 6
real numbers 65
    data types for 65
recursive mergesort 519
recursive search algorithms 517
relational operators 104, 106, 107
repetition control flow 92
requirements analysis 455
reserved words 31
return value 23
reusable 199
RightButtonClicked 338
round-off error 117, 120

S

scientific notation 11
scope resolution operator 265
search
    binary 497
    linear 496
    sequential 496
search performances
    binary 505
    hashing 505
    linear 505
searching 494
Secondary storage 7
selection control flow 130
self-contained 298
self-referencing pointer 413
sequential control flow 92
sequential execution 27
setiosflags 82
setprecision 82
setw 81
short 53
side effects 57
signed integers 10
single-task principle 424

software life cycle 455
sorting 494
    bubble 510
    in situ 506
source program 15
specification 455
strcat 185, 186
strcmp 185
strcpy 185
strdup 185, 187
string 180
string functions, standard 184, 185
string variable 180
StringTypeIn 189
strlen 185
subscripts 344
switch 151
switch statement
    execution of the 155
symbolic programming 14
syntax rules 29

T

TemplateWindow 468
terminals 32
testing 456
testing and debugging 456
text file 426
    output to a 427
    reading data from a 433
this 413
turtle object 33
TwoDGraph 292
twos-complement representation 10
type casting 118, 178
type mismatch 118

V

variable 49
variables 47
void function 23
volatile memory 7

W

while 100
while loop 102
while statement 102
    syntax of 106

Y

YesNoBox 115